NELSON'S COMPLETE BOOK OF BIBLE MAPS & CHARTS

OLD AND NEW TESTAMENTS

Revised and Updated Edition

Thomas Nelson Publishers

Nashville • Atlanta • London • Vancouver

Library of Congress Cataloging-in-Publication Data

Nelson's complete book of Bible maps & charts. Old and New Testaments.—Expanded comfort print ed.
    p. cm.
   Includes indexes.
   ISBN 0-7852-1154-3
   1. Bible—Handbooks, manuals, etc. 2. Bible—Geography— Maps. I. Thomas Nelson Publishers.
[BS417.N448 1996]
220.9'022'3—dc20   95–50465
                                        CIP

Printed in the United States of America.

Contents

The New Testament

Introduction

Welcome to *Nelson's Complete Book of Bible Maps and Charts—Revised and Updated Edition*. We hope that by compiling into one book the maps and study charts used in many of Nelson's Bibles and reference books, we will be providing every Christian with an essential tool which can enhance the study of God's Word. Designed to be easy to use and quickly referenced, *Nelson's Complete Book of Bible Maps and Charts—Revised and Updated Edition* offers a visual overview of the geography, politics, and thematic issues of Scripture.

The maps and charts follow the order of the books of the Bible and are placed in conjunction with short passages of text that give pertinent historical or thematic background explanations. The charts are often a summary of events or themes in the Bible, allowing the reader to get a quick grasp of a subject before or after reading the Bible passage, while the maps can add to an understanding of the politics and geography of the Bible. The "At A Glance" charts, for instance, present a summary of each book, showing the focus and topics discussed, the location and time of the events, and gives the text references for each division. The maps detailing Paul's missionary journeys (pp. 370–371) show the incredible distances this remarkable man traveled in order to spread the Gospel and minister to the faithful.

Charts can also help the reader understand themes that extend over several books, link seemingly unrelated elements of the text, or summarize extrabiblical ideas about the text. "Temptation: The Two Adams Contrasted" (p. 10), for instance, shows the different ways that Adam and Jesus Christ handled temptation, while "New Testament Women" (p. 337) gives references for the actions of some of the most outstanding characters of the New Testament. "Three Synoptic Gospel Source Theories" (p. 298) visually demonstrates three of the theories which explain the literary similarities of Matthew, Mark, and Luke.

Biblical maps and charts can be helpful not only to the reader but to the teacher as well. Anyone who has struggled with conveying the meaning or history behind a biblical passage knows how useful a visual aid can be. For this reason, many of the charts and maps in this book are on individual pages for easy copying. You are invited to copy those pages as visual aids for your personal use or for use by study groups. Intended for use in the classroom or seminar, such copies make excellent handouts or can be easily projected onto a screen.

Nelson's Complete Book of Bible Maps and Charts—Revised and Updated Edition is not intended as a reference book just for the shelf. It is intended to be a supplement to other curriculum material for the classroom, seminar, or sermon. We hope it will prove to be so beneficial that it will become a standard resource for your personal or group Bible study.

THE OLD TESTAMENT

Old Testament Overview

Persons	Periods and Events	Contemporary Cultures	Old Testament Books Written
Adam	BEFORE THE PATRIARCHS Creation Flood	Prehistorical Era	
Abraham, Isaac, Jacob, Joseph	PATRIARCHS Abraham enters the land c. 2090 B.C. Joseph Prime Minister c. 1885–1805	Patriarchal Narratives reflect culture of Mesopotamia and Egypt	Job?
	EGYPTIAN SOJOURN c. 1875–1445	Egypt enslaves the Israelites	
Moses	WILDERNESS WANDERING c. 1445–1405		Genesis, Exodus, Leviticus, Numbers, Deuteronomy
Joshua, Deborah, Gideon, Jephthah, Samson	CONQUEST AND JUDGES c. 1405–1050	Palestine occupied, various nations oppress Israel	Joshua, Judges
Samuel, Saul, David, Solomon	UNITED MONARCHY Established 1050	Surrounding nations defeated by Israel	Ruth, Samuel, Psalms, Song of Solomon, Proverbs, Ecclesiastes
DIVIDED MONARCHY 931–722 Divided 931 SOUTH: Rehoboam	NORTH: Jeroboam I	Aramean Kingdom 931–732	
Jehoshaphat Uzziah	Ahab Jeroboam II		Obadiah, Joel Jonah, Amos, Hosea, Isaiah, Micah
Hezekiah		Fall of Aram c. 732 Assyrian domination of Palestine 745–650	Nahum, Zephaniah
	Fall of Samaria c. 722		
Josiah	JUDAH ALONE 722–586		Jeremiah, Lamentations, Habakkuk, Kings, Daniel, Ezekiel
	Daniel's Captivity		
	Ezekiel's Captivity		
Jeremiah	Fall of Jerusalem c. 586	Babylonian Supremacy 625–539	
Zerubbabel Haggai Zechariah	RESTORATION 538–c. 400 Second Temple	Medo-Persian Rule 539–331	Haggai, Zechariah
	Ezra's Return c. 458		Chronicles, Ezra, Esther
Malachi	Nehemiah's Return c. 444		Nehemiah, Malachi

THE PENTATEUCH

The first five books of the Bible—Genesis, Exodus, Leviticus, Numbers, and Deuteronomy—are called by the Jews the Torah, a Hebrew term meaning "law" or "teaching." The translators of the Septuagint (Greek Old Testament) called this grouping the Pentateuch, that is, "the fivefold book" (from the Greek *penta*, "five," and *teuchos*, "volume").

Traditionally, conservative Jews and Christians have held that Moses was in large measure responsible for the Pentateuch. Both the Old and New Testaments ascribe to Moses the authorship of this body of literature (Josh. 1:7; Dan. 9:11–13; Luke 16:29; John 7:19; Acts 26:22; Rom. 10:19), and there was general agreement regarding Moses' role until the eighteenth century.

In the modern period, however, it has often been asserted that behind the Pentateuch as we now have it are four separate documents (referred to as J, E, D, and P) which stem from a variety of periods in Israel's history and which were pieced together late in the Old Testament era. This theory (known as the "Documentary Hypothesis") arose in part to explain a number of questions about the text of the Pentateuch which are particularly apparent in Genesis. These include stories that seem to be virtual duplicates of each other, the use of particular divine names in certain portions of the text, sudden changes in style from one incident to another, and so forth.

It is doubtless the case that the Documentary Hypothesis owed much to naturalistic and evolutionary presuppositions regarding the development of ancient human society. Furthermore, little lasting agreement among scholars has emerged regarding the precise character and extent of the documents and sources which are alleged to lie behind the Pentateuch as we have it. It can now also be shown that many of the features which formerly seemed so strange are typical of other literatures from the ancient period. While not every problem has been fully explained, there are no compelling reasons to abandon Mosaic authorship.

While each book of the Pentateuch is concerned with God's covenantal relationship with His people, each book is, nevertheless, distinct and has its own particular subject matter.

The Pentateuch constitutes the first part of a major sequential biblical narrative extending from Genesis through 2 Kings. In this first section the accounts of creation and humankind's early history (Gen. 1—11) are linked to events in the lives of the patriarchs Abraham, Isaac, Jacob, and Joseph (Gen. 12—50). Those stories, in turn, are linked with accounts of Israel's greatest prophet, Moses. They include conflict with Egypt's pharaoh (Ex. 1—11), the rescue of Israel by God from Egypt (Ex. 12—15), Israel's rebellion and forty years of wandering in the wilderness (Ex. 16—Num. 21), and their arrival at the entrance to Canaan, the Land of Promise (Num. 22—Deut. 34).

The first book of the Pentateuch, Genesis, covers the vast period of time from creation to the journey into Egypt. The remaining four books, Exodus—Deuteronomy, cover a period of only about forty years.

The Pentateuch

Book	Key Idea	The Nation	The People	God's Character	God's Role	God's Command
Genesis	Beginnings	Chosen	Prepared	Powerful Sovereign	Creator	"Let there be!"
Exodus	Redemption	Delivered	Redeemed	Merciful	Deliverer	"Let my people go!"
Leviticus	Worship	Set Apart	Taught	Holy	Sanctifier	"Be holy!"
Numbers	Wandering	Directed	Tested	Just	Sustainer	"Go in!"
Deuteronomy	Renewed Covenant	Made Ready	Retaught	Loving Lord	Rewarder	"Obey!"

Chronology of Israel in the Pentateuch

Date	Event	Reference
Fifteenth day, first month, first year	Exodus	Exodus 12
Fifteenth day, second month, first year	Arrival in Wilderness of Sin	Exodus 16:1
Third month, first year	Arrival in Wilderness of Sinai	Exodus 19:1
First day, first month, second year	Erection of Tabernacle	Exodus 40:1, 17
	Dedication of Altar	Numbers 7:1
	Consecration of Levites	Numbers 8:1–26
Fourteenth day, first month, second year	Passover	Numbers 9:5
First day, second month, second year	Census	Numbers 1:1, 18
Fourteenth day, second month, second year	Supplemental Passover	Numbers 9:11
Twentieth day, second month, second year	Departure from Sinai	Numbers 10:11
First month, fortieth year	In Wilderness of Zin	Numbers 20:1, 22–29; 33:38
First day, fifth month, fortieth year	Death of Aaron	Numbers 20:22–29; 33:38
First day, eleventh month, fortieth year	Moses' Address	Deuteronomy 1:3

Nelson's Complete Book of Bible Maps and Charts © 1993 by Thomas Nelson, Inc.

GENESIS

As the title indicates, Genesis is a book of beginnings (the word "Genesis" comes from the Greek term meaning origin, source, birth, or beginning). In its description of God's creation of the world, the fall of man, the origins of the peoples of the earth, and the beginnings of God's covenant relationship with His chosen people Israel, the book of Genesis provides the context and sets the stage for the rest of Scripture.

Author

Although the book of Genesis does not name its author, Scripture and much of church history ascribe the book to Moses. Both the Old and New Testaments repeatedly testify to the Mosaic authorship of the Pentateuch (e.g., Josh. 1:7; Dan. 9:11–13; Luke 16:29; John 7:19; Acts 26:22; Rom. 10:19), and Mosaic authorship was not seriously questioned until the eighteenth century. Conservative Christians and Jews continue to acknowledge Moses as the author on the basis of the testimony of Scripture and the absence of plausible alternatives.

Date

In writing the book of Genesis, Moses doubtless utilized older written sources and oral traditions, as well as material directly revealed to him by God (Num. 12:8). Trained in the "wisdom of the Egyptians" (Acts 7:22), Moses had been providentially prepared to understand and integrate, under the inspiration of God, all the available records, manuscripts, and oral narratives. The composition of the book was probably undertaken during the wilderness exile of Israel (c. 1446–1406 B.C.).

Themes and Literary Structure

The literary structure of Genesis is built around eleven separate units, each headed with the word *generations* in the phrase *These are the generations* or *The book of the generations:* (1) Introduction to the Generations (1:1—2:3); (2) Heaven and Earth (2:4—4:26); (3) Adam (5:1—6:8); (4) Noah (6:9—9:29); (5) Sons of Noah (10:1—11:9); (6) Shem

Genesis at a Glance

FOCUS	FOUR EVENTS				FOUR PEOPLE			
REFERENCE	1:1 ——— 3:1 ———		6:1 ——— 10:1 ———		12:1 ——— 25:19 ———		27:19 ——— 37:1 — 50:26	
DIVISION	CREATION	FALL	FLOOD	NATIONS	ABRAHAM	ISAAC	JACOB	JOSEPH
TOPIC	HUMAN RACE				HEBREW RACE			
	HISTORICAL				BIOGRAPHICAL			
LOCATION	FERTILE CRESCENT (Eden-Haran)				CANAAN (Haran-Canaan)			EGYPT (Canaan-Egypt)
TIME	c. 2000 YEARS c. 4000+ – c. 2166 B.C.				281 YEARS c. 2166–1885 B.C.			81 YEARS (1885–1804 B.C.)

Nelson's Complete Book of Bible Maps and Charts © 1993 by Thomas Nelson, Inc.

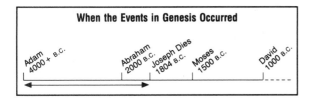

When the Events in Genesis Occurred

Adam 4000+ B.C.　Abraham 2000 B.C.　Joseph Dies 1804 B.C.　Moses 1500 B.C.　David 1000 B.C.

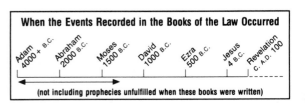

When the Events Recorded in the Books of the Law Occurred

Adam 4000+ B.C.　Abraham 2000 B.C.　Moses 1500 B.C.　David 1000 B.C.　Ezra 500 B.C.　Jesus 4 B.C.　Revelation c. A.D. 100

(not including prophecies unfulfilled when these books were written)

(11:10–26); (7) Terah (11:27—25:11); (8) Ishmael (25:12–18); (9) Isaac (25:19—35:29); (10) Esau (36:1—37:1); (11) Jacob (37:2—50:26).

Genesis is the first chapter in the history of the *redemption* of man. In this work, four great events and four great people are emphasized.

Chapters 1—11 are dominated by four momentous events which form a basis for all subsequent biblical history.

(1) **Creation:** God is the sovereign creator of matter and energy, space and time. Human beings are the pinnacle of this creation.

(2) **Fall:** Though originally good, this creation became subjected to corruption through the sin of Adam. In spite of the devastating curse of the Fall, God promises hope of redemption through the seed of the woman (3:15).

(3) **Flood:** As humanity multiplies, sin also multiplies until God is compelled to destroy the human race with the exception of Noah and his family.

(4) **Nations:** Though we are all children of Adam through Noah, God fragments the single culture and language of the post-flood world and scatters the peoples over the face of the earth.

Chapters 12—50 deal with four great people (Abraham and his descendants Isaac, Jacob, and Joseph), through whom God will bless the nations. The calling of Abraham (ch. 12) is the pivotal point in the book. The covenant promises God makes to Abraham are foundational to God's program of bringing salvation to all peoples.

OUTLINE OF GENESIS

Part One: Primeval History (1:1—11:9)

The Six Days of Creation

According to the book of Genesis, God created the world and all that is in it in six days. Then He declared it all to be "very good" (1:31). The Creator rested on the seventh day (2:1–3).

While there were other "creation stories" among the pagan nations of the ancient world, the biblical account is unique in that God existed before creation and called the physical world into being from nothing (1:1, 2; John 1:2, 3). These pagan nations, particularly the Babylonians, believed the material universe was eternal and that it brought their gods into being. But Genesis describes a God who is clearly superior to the physical world.

God began organizing a shapeless and barren earth (1:2), providing light (1:3–5), and separating land from water (1:6–10). The creation of plant and animal life followed, including creatures of the sea, air, and land (1:11–25). Man and woman were created on the sixth day (1:26–28), before the Creator's Sabbath rest (2:1–3).

Scholars disagree about the length and character of the creation "days." Some believe these were actual twenty-four-hour days, some believe they were periods of undetermined length, while others see the six-day creation sequence as a literary framework. Regardless of the length of these days, the biblical writer declares that God created the world in orderly fashion as part of a master plan. The world did not just evolve on its own or by accident.

The "gap" theory, advanced to reconcile the biblical account of creation with geology, holds that creation in Genesis 1:1 was followed by catastrophe (1:2), then succeeded by God's re-creation or reshaping of the physical world (1:3–31). But this theory reduces God to a weak being with little control over His own creation. The powerful God who created the world also presides over its destiny.

Man and woman are the crowning achievements of God's creative work (Ps. 8:5). As free moral beings who bear the image of God, they were assigned dominion over the natural world (1:27, 28). They alone among the living creatures of the world are equipped for fellowship with their Creator.

God's Creative Work

Though some scholars interpret the creation narratives of Genesis 1:1—2:3 and 2:4–25 as evidence for the presence of two different and inconsistent creation accounts, 2:4 does not introduce a new creation account but is rather an expansion of 1:26–27. The second chapter presupposes the first, and the differences are complementary and supplementary, not contradictory.

	Genesis 1	Genesis 2
Creation Accounts	God the Creator Elohim God as powerful Creation of the universe Climaxes with man The six days of creation	God the covenant-keeper YAHWEH God as personal Creation of man Climaxes with marriage The sixth day of creation

The Garden of Eden

The Garden of Eden was the first home of Adam and Eve, the first man and woman (2:4—3:24). Eden is a translation of a Hebrew word which means "Delight," suggesting a "Garden of Delight." The garden contained many beautiful and fruitbearing trees, including the "tree of life" and "the tree of the knowledge of good and evil" (2:9).

Pinpointing the exact location of the Garden of Eden is difficult, although the best theory places it near the source of the Tigris and Euphrates rivers in the Armenian highlands (see map). A major catastrophe, perhaps the Flood of Noah's time, may have wiped out all traces of the other two rivers mentioned—the Pishon and the Havilah (2:11). But modern space photography has produced evidence that two rivers, now dry beds, could have flowed through the area centuries ago.

God commanded Adam and Eve not to eat of the tree of the knowledge of good and evil (2:17). They fell from their original state of innocence when Satan approached Eve through the serpent and tempted her to eat of the forbidden fruit (3:1–5). She ate the fruit and also gave it to her husband to eat (3:6, 7). Their disobedience plunged them and all of the human race into a state of sin and corruption.

Because of their unbelief and rebellion, they were driven from the garden. Other consequences of their sin were loss of their innocence (3:7), pain in childbearing and submission of the wife to her husband (3:16), the cursing of the ground and the resultant hard labor for man (3:17–19), and separation from God (3:23, 24).

The apostle Paul thought of Christ as the Second Adam who would save the old sinful Adam through His plan of redemption and salvation. "For as in Adam all die, even so in Christ all shall be made alive" (1 Cor. 15:22).

The Garden of Eden may have been located near the Tigris River, which the Bible calls Hiddekel (2:14).

Nelson's Complete Book of Bible Maps and Charts © 1993 by Thomas Nelson, Inc.

The Two Adams Contrasted

Genesis 3:15 contains the promise of redemption, a promise fulfilled with the coming of Christ. The New Testament portrays Christ as the "Second Adam" whose obedience and sacrificial death on the cross undo Adam's disobedience (Rom. 5:12–21; 1 Cor. 15:45). As the "Second Adam," Jesus triumphed over the same sort of temptation to which the first Adam succumbed.

Temptation: The Two Adams Contrasted

1 John 2:16	Genesis 3:6 First Adam	Luke 4:1–13 Second Adam—Christ
"the lust of the flesh"	"the tree was good for food"	"command this stone to become bread"
"the lust of the eyes"	"it was pleasant to the eyes"	"the devil ... showed Him all the kingdoms"
"the pride of life"	"a tree desirable to make one wise"	"throw Yourself down from here"

Ages of the Patriarchs

The curse brought about by the Fall of Adam resulted in death for Adam and his posterity. Though lifespans were initially quite long (averaging over nine hundred years), they rapidly declined after the Flood.

Biblical genealogies (e.g., in Genesis, 1 Chronicles, etc.) are not necessarily sequential in the precise sense. In keeping with ancient genealogical practices, names are sometimes omitted within the list. The Hebrew term translated "begot" may also be translated "became the ancestor of."

How Old Were the Patriarchs?

ADAM 930 years (Gen. 5:5)

SETH 912 years (Gen. 5:8)

ENOSH 905 years (Gen. 5:11)

ENOCH 365 years (Gen. 5:23)

METHUSELAH 969 years (Gen. 5:27)

LAMECH 777 years (Gen. 5:31)

NOAH 950 years (Gen. 9:29)

The Flood  The Flood

SHEM 600 years (Gen. 11:10, 11)

EBER 464 years (Gen. 11:16, 17)

TERAH 205 years (Gen. 11:32)

ABRAHAM 175 years (Gen. 25:7)

ISAAC 180 years (Gen. 35:28)

JACOB 147 years (Gen. 47:28)

JOSEPH 110 years (Gen. 50:26)

The patriarchs who lived before the Flood had an average lifespan of about 900 years (Gen. 5). The ages of post-Flood patriarchs dropped rapidly and gradually leveled off (Gen. 11). Some suggest that this is due to major environmental changes brought about by the Flood.

Spiritual Decline in the Patriarchal Age

First Generation	Second Generation	Third Generation	Fourth Generation
Abraham	Ishmael and Isaac	Esau and Jacob	Joseph and his eleven brothers

Abraham:
  man of faith
  believed God
	Ishmael:
	  not son of
	  promise
	Isaac:
	  called on God
	  believed God
		Esau:
		  unspiritual
		  little faith
		Jacob:
		  at first compro-
		  mised, later
		  turned to the Lord
			Joseph:
			  man of God
			  showed faith
			Brothers:
			  treachery, immo-
			  rality, lack of sep-
			  aration from
			  Canaanites

Abraham:
  built altars to God
  (Gen. 12:7, 8;
  13:4, 18; 22:9)
	Isaac:
	  built an altar to
	  God (Gen. 26:25)
		Jacob:
		  built altars to God
		  (Gen. 33:20;
		  35:1, 3, 7)
			No altars were built
			to God in the fourth
			generation

Noah's Ark

The ark was a vessel built by Noah to save himself, his family, and animals from the flood sent by God (6:14—9:19). The ark was about 450 feet long, 75 feet wide, and 45 feet high, with three decks. Scholars have calculated that a vessel of this size would hold more than 43,000 tons.

After almost a year on the water, the ark came to rest on Mount Ararat in what is now Turkey. Numerous attempts across the centuries to find the remains of the vessel have been futile. Shifting glaciers, avalanches, hidden crevices, and sudden storms make mountain climbing in the area extremely dangerous.

The ark reveals both the judgment and mercy of God. His righteous judgment is seen in the destruction of the wicked, but His mercy and care are demonstrated in His preservation of Noah, and, through him, of the human race. The ark is a striking illustration of Christ, who preserves us from the flood of divine judgment through His grace.

From the ancient world there are several other flood stories that are remarkably similar to the biblical account in many details. In the most famous of these, Utnapishti, the Babylonian "Noah," constructed a boat, which was about 180 feet long, 180 feet wide, and 180 feet high—hardly a seaworthy design. In stark contrast to these stories, the book of Genesis presents a holy and righteous God who sends the flood in judgment against sin and yet mercifully saves Noah and his family because of their righteousness.

In the New Testament, Jesus spoke of the Flood and of Noah and the ark, comparing "the days of Noah" with the time of "the coming of the Son of Man" (Matt. 24:37, 38; Luke 17:26, 27). Other references to the Flood include Hebrews 11:7; 1 Peter 3:20; and 2 Peter 2:5.

Does the Bible Really Say That?

Common Sayings from Genesis—Many popular sayings have their roots in the Bible. Yet people often use these phrases without recognizing their biblical origins. Here are several common sayings or phrases that can be traced to the book of Genesis.

Saying or Phrase	Meaning Today	Original Context or Meaning
A Garden of Eden.	A paradise of unspoiled beauty and unlimited resources.	The place where God originally put Adam and Eve, before their sin (Gen. 2:8, 15).
Forbidden fruit.	A pleasure or delight that we ought not to enjoy, but which is also more attractive because it is off-limits; often refers to sexual gratification.	The fruit of the tree of the knowledge of good and evil, which Adam and Eve were told not to eat (Gen. 2:17; 3:3).
Adam's apple.	The hard lump of cartilage that is often prominent in a man's throat.	The tradition that a piece of the forbidden fruit (popularly thought of as an apple) became stuck in Adam's throat (Gen. 3:6).
Fig leaf.	In art, a small covering for the genitalia; figuratively, any means of protecting oneself from embarrassment.	The coverings that Adam and Eve made after they sinned and became aware of their nakedness (Gen. 3:7).
Am I my brother's keeper?	A rhetorical question often posed to evade responsibility in regard to someone else.	The question with which Cain replied when the Lord asked him where Abel was, whom Cain had murdered (Gen. 4:9).
Forty days and forty nights.	A long passage of time.	The duration of the downpour that caused the flood of Noah's time (Gen. 7:12).
Babel, or a Tower of Babel.	A symbol of confusion and chaos.	The place where God confused the languages of the nations in order to disperse them throughout the earth (Gen. 11:1–9).
The Promised Land.	An image of ultimate freedom, happiness, and self-determination.	The phrase used to describe the land that God promised to give Abraham's descendants, the land of Canaan, said to be flowing with milk and honey (Gen. 12:7; 15:18–21).
A mess of pottage.	An allusion to being cheated or shortchanged.	The bargain by which Jacob gained the family birthright from his elder brother Esau in exchange for a bowl of red stew called "pottage" in some translations (Gen. 25:27–34).

The Tower of Babel

The Tower of Babel was built on the plain of Shinar, a site probably in ancient Babylonia in southern Mesopotamia, some time after the great flood of Noah's time. A symbol of man's sinful pride and rebellion, the structure was built to satisfy the people's vanity: "Let us make a name for ourselves" (Gen. 11:4).

The pyramid-like tower was expected to reach heaven. These people were trying to approach God on their own self-serving terms, but they learned that the gates of heaven cannot be stormed. Men and women must approach the holy God in reverence and humility.

This tower was built of bricks and mortar, since no stones were available on the flat plains of southern Mesopotamia. The Babel Tower appears to be similar to the ziggurats the ancient inhabitants of southern Mesopotamia built as places for the worship of their gods. Both Assyrian and Babylonian kings prided themselves on the height of these pagan temples, boasting of building them as high as heaven.

One such tower, built in Ur, Abraham's ancestral city in southern Mesopotamia, about 2100 B.C., was a pyramid consisting of three terraces of diminishing size. The temple was climbed by converging stairways. The uppermost part of the tower was an altar devoted to pagan worship.

God intervened to prevent the builders of Babel from partaking of the power and glory that belongs only to Him. The language of the builders was confused so they could no longer communicate with one another. In their frustration, they abandoned the project. Then the prideful builders were scattered abroad (11:7, 8). How small and weak this tower was in comparison to God's power! Humankind's misguided efforts at self-glorification brought on confusion and frustration and their dispersion throughout the world.

Abraham's Family

The genealogy of Shem (11:10–26) serves to introduce the figure of Abraham, a native of the Mesopotamian city of Ur. God's redemptive plan now focuses on the family and descendants of one individual. Abraham's role in Scripture is foundational to the rest of Scripture: all of God's subsequent redemptive dealings with humanity are related to the covenant God made with Abraham.

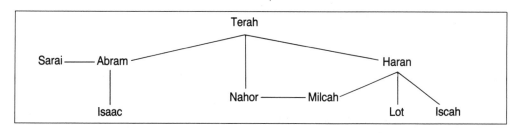

The Abrahamic Covenant

The Abrahamic Covenant is unconditional, depending solely upon God who obligates Himself in grace to bring about what He has promised. The covenant was first given in broad outline and was later confirmed to Abraham in greater detail (13:14–17; 15:1–7, 18–21; 17:1–8).

See chart, "The Abrahamic Covenant," on page 18.

Abraham's Journey of Faith

Abraham's 1,500-mile journey was fueled by faith. "And he went out, not knowing where he was going. By faith he dwelt in the land of promise as in a foreign country, . . . for he waited for the city which has foundations, whose builder and maker is God" (Heb. 11:8–10).

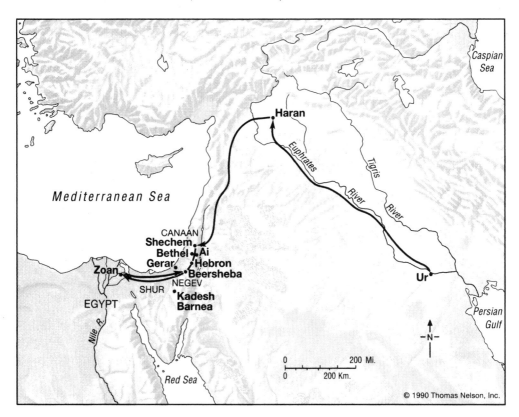

Isaac and Jacob

God's faithfulness to His covenant promise is beautifully illustrated in the birth of Isaac to Abraham's aged and barren wife Sarah (21:1–3). Rather than finding a wife for Isaac from among the peoples of Canaan, Abraham sent his servant to Mesopotamia to find a wife from his own people (ch. 24).

To Isaac and Rebekah were born the twins Jacob and Esau, but God indicated that the line of covenant promise would pass through Jacob (25:23). Dispute over the birthright and fatherly blessing caused Jacob to flee from his brother Esau to Mesopotamia where Jacob married Leah and Rachel (chs. 27—29) and where he stayed for twenty years. Jacob fathered twelve sons (35:22–26), who became the fathers of the twelve tribes of Israel. Judah, the fourth son of Jacob, was the one through whose line of descent the promised Messiah would come (49:10).

See map on page 16.

Jacob Returns to Canaan

After twenty years in northern Mesopotamia, Jacob returned to Canaan. On the way he encountered God face-to-face at Penuel (32:30, 31).

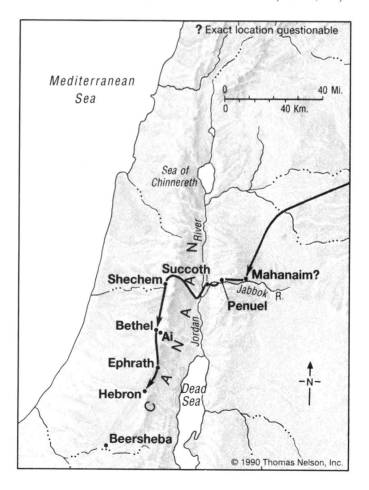

The Life of Jacob

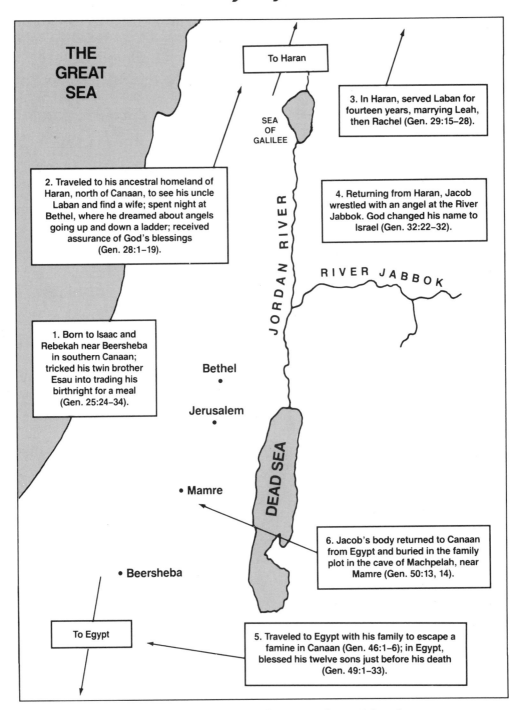

THE GREAT SEA

To Haran

SEA OF GALILEE

3. In Haran, served Laban for fourteen years, marrying Leah, then Rachel (Gen. 29:15–28).

2. Traveled to his ancestral homeland of Haran, north of Canaan, to see his uncle Laban and find a wife; spent night at Bethel, where he dreamed about angels going up and down a ladder; received assurance of God's blessings (Gen. 28:1–19).

4. Returning from Haran, Jacob wrestled with an angel at the River Jabbok. God changed his name to Israel (Gen. 32:22–32).

JORDAN RIVER

RIVER JABBOK

1. Born to Isaac and Rebekah near Beersheba in southern Canaan; tricked his twin brother Esau into trading his birthright for a meal (Gen. 25:24–34).

Bethel
•

Jerusalem
•

• Mamre

DEAD SEA

6. Jacob's body returned to Canaan from Egypt and buried in the family plot in the cave of Machpelah, near Mamre (Gen. 50:13, 14).

• Beersheba

To Egypt

5. Traveled to Egypt with his family to escape a famine in Canaan (Gen. 46:1–6); in Egypt, blessed his twelve sons just before his death (Gen. 49:1–33).

Nelson's Complete Book of Bible Maps and Charts © 1993 by Thomas Nelson, Inc.

Joseph

Resented by the ten sons of Leah and her concubine, Joseph, a son of Jacob through Rachel, was sold by his brothers into slavery in Egypt (ch. 37). There he was imprisoned but later rose to be second in command to the Egyptian Pharaoh. Joseph was the instrument used by God to preserve the family of Jacob during time of famine (chs. 41—46) and so to preserve the line of covenant promise from destruction.

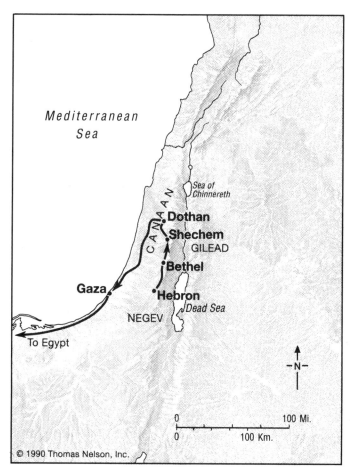

The Nations of Genesis 10

Genesis 10 is called the "Table of Nations" and is structured in terms of the descendants of the three sons of Noah: Japheth (vv. 2–5), Ham (vv. 6–20), and Shem (vv. 21–31). Many names mentioned in chapter 10 are identifiable with nations of ancient times, some of which have continued down to the present.

See the following pages for additional reproducibles on the book of Genesis.

The Nations of Genesis 10

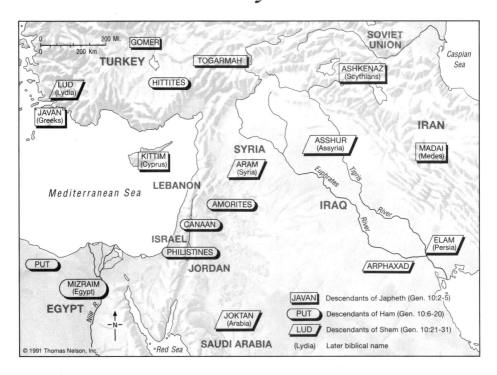

The Abrahamic Covenant

Genesis 12:1–3	God initiated His covenant with Abram when he was living in Ur of the Chaldeans, promising a land, descendants, and blessing.
Genesis 12:4, 5	Abram went with his family to Haran, lived there for a time, and left at the age of 75.
Genesis 13:14–17	After Lot separated from Abram, God again promised the land to him and his descendants.
Genesis 15:1–21	This covenant was ratified when God passed between the sacrificial animals Abram laid before God.
Genesis 17:1–27	When Abram was 99 God renewed His covenant, changing Abram's name to Abraham ("Father of a Multitude"). Sign of the covenant: circumcision.
Genesis 22:15–18	Confirmation of the covenant because of Abraham's obedience.

The Abrahamic covenant was foundational to other covenants:
- The promise of land in the Palestinian Covenant (Deut. 30:1–10)
- The promise of kingly descendants in the Davidic Covenant (2 Sam. 7:12–16)
- The promise of blessing in the "Old" and "New" Covenants (Ex. 19:3–6; Jer. 31:31–40)

Travels of the Patriarchs

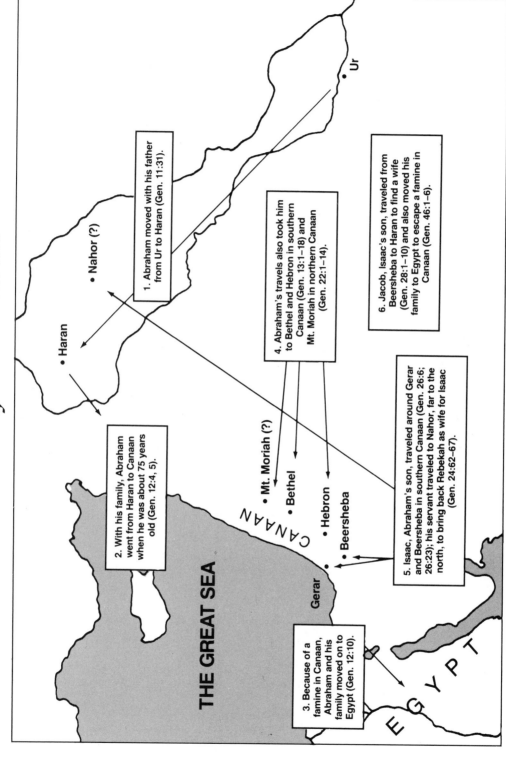

• Ur

1. Abraham moved with his father from Ur to Haran (Gen. 11:31).

• Nahor (?)

• Haran

4. Abraham's travels also took him to Bethel and Hebron in southern Canaan (Gen. 13:1–18) and Mt. Moriah in northern Canaan (Gen. 22:1–14).

6. Jacob, Isaac's son, traveled from Beersheba to Haran to find a wife (Gen. 28:1–10) and also moved his family to Egypt to escape a famine in Canaan (Gen. 46:1–6).

2. With his family, Abraham went from Haran to Canaan when he was about 75 years old (Gen. 12:4, 5).

• Mt. Moriah (?)

• Bethel

• Hebron

• Beersheba

CANAAN

5. Isaac, Abraham's son, traveled around Gerar and Beersheba in southern Canaan (Gen. 26:6; 26:23); his servant traveled to Nahor, far to the north, to bring back Rebekah as wife for Isaac (Gen. 24:62–67).

Gerar •

THE GREAT SEA

3. Because of a famine in Canaan, Abraham and his family moved on to Egypt (Gen. 12:10).

E G Y P T

Nelson's Complete Book of Bible Maps and Charts © 1993 by Thomas Nelson, Inc.

Mentioned First in Genesis

Altar	8:20	Forgiveness	50:17	Preacher to become	
Angel	16:7	Friend	38:12	drunk	9:20, 21
Archer	21:20			Prophecy	3:15
		Game	25:28	Purchase of land	23:3–20
Bird	1:21	Gardener	2:15		
		Gift	9:3	**Question**	3:1
Camp	32:2	God	1:1		
Cave dweller	19:30	Gold	2:11	**Rain**	7:1–12
Chariot	41:43	Grave	23:6	Rainbow	9:13
Child	11:30	Guilt	26:10		
Child named before				**Saddle**	22:3
birth	16:11	**Harlot**	34:31	Shipbuilder	6:14, 22
City builder	4:17	Hate	24:60	Sin	3:1–24
Coffin	50:26	Heart	6:5	Snake	49:17
Command	1:3	Heavens	1:1	Sword	3:24
		Heir	15:2		
Darkness	1:2	Hunter	10:8, 9	**Temptation**	3:1–6
Death	24:67	Husband	3:6	Tower	11:4, 5
Dew	27:28				
Disaster	19:19	**Idols**	31:19	**Veil**	24:65
Dream	20:3			Violence	6:11
Drunk	9:21	**Jail**	39:20		
Dungeon	40:15	Joy	31:27	**Wage contract**	29:15–20
				War	14:2
Earth	1:1	**Kill**	4:8	Wealth	31:1
Embalming	50:2	King	14:1	Well	16:14
Execution	40:20–22	Kiss	27:26	Wife	2:24
				Wind	8:1
Family	8:19	**Man to interpret**	41:15	Wine	9:21
Farmer	4:2	Man to wear a ring	41:42	Wish	23:8
Father	2:24	Murderer	4:8	Witness	21:30
Fear	9:2			Woman thief	31:19
Food	1:29	**Oath**	21:23, 24	Words spoken to man	1:28
Food control	41:25–36	**Pilgrim**	12:1–8	Worship	4:3–5
		Prayer	4:26		

EXODUS

The book of Exodus records the redemption of the people of Israel from slavery in Egypt and their establishment as a nation governed by terms of God's covenant and the laws of God. During the roughly four hundred years in Egypt, the family of Jacob grew from seventy people to between two and three million.

Hebrew-speaking Jews have always used the initial Hebrew words of the book of Exodus as its title, calling it *ve'elleh shemot*, which means "Now these are the names." The Greek title is *Exodus*, a word meaning "exit," "departure," or "going out."

Author

Together with the rest of the Pentateuch (Genesis—Deuteronomy), Exodus is ascribed by Scripture to Moses. Portions of Exodus specifically name Moses as the author (17:14; 24:3, 4; 34:27), and writers throughout the Old and New Testaments unite in recognizing Mosaic authorship (Mal. 4:4; John 1:45; Rom. 10:5). Furthermore, Jesus himself recognizes the Mosaic origin of the book (Mark 7:10; 12:26; Luke 20:37; John 5:46, 47; 7:19–23).

Since the eighteenth century, some scholars have challenged the Mosaic authorship of Exodus in favor of a series of oral and written sources that were woven together by editors late in Israel's history. Such arguments are far from conclusive, particularly since little lasting agreement has emerged as to the precise character and extent of the documents which are alleged to lie behind the text of Exodus as we now have it.

Date

Like the remainder of the Pentateuch, Exodus was written during the wilderness wandering of Israel between the time of the Exodus and the death of Moses. Moses probably kept a record of God's work, which he then edited in the Plains of Moab shortly before his death (c. 1406 B.C.).

Continued on page 23

Exodus at a Glance

FOCUS	REDEMPTION FROM EGYPT				REVELATION FROM GOD	
REFERENCE	1:1 ——— 2:1 ———		5:1 ———	15:22 ———	19:1 ——— 32:1 ——— 40:38	
DIVISION	THE NEED FOR REDEMPTION	THE PREPARATION FOR REDEMPTION	THE REDEMPTION OF ISRAEL	THE PRESERVATION OF ISRAEL	THE REVELATION OF THE COVENANT	THE RESPONSE OF ISRAEL TO THE COVENANT
TOPIC	NARRATION				LEGISLATION	
	SUBJECTION		REDEMPTION		INSTRUCTION	
LOCATION	EGYPT			WILDERNESS	MOUNT SINAI	
TIME	430 YEARS			2 MONTHS	10 MONTHS	

Nelson's Complete Book of Bible Maps and Charts © 1993 by Thomas Nelson, Inc.

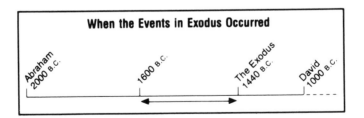

When the Events in Exodus Occurred

Abraham 2000 B.C. — 1600 B.C. — The Exodus 1440 B.C. — David 1000 B.C.

Continued from page 21

The question of the date of the book of Exodus is related to the date of the Exodus event. First Kings 6:1 states that the Exodus occurred 480 years before the founding of the temple (966 B.C.), which implies a 1446 B.C. date for the Exodus from Egypt. Some scholars argue that archaeological evidence points to a date of about 1275 B.C., and they contend that the 480 years of 1 Kings 6:1 should be seen as a symbolic number (one forty-year generation times the twelve tribes equals 480). The archaeological evidence is ambiguous, however, and the 1446 B.C. date is adopted here.

Themes and Literary Structure

 The book of Exodus is easily divided into two main sections: the redemption from slavery in Egypt (chs. 1—18) and the revelation from God at Mt. Sinai (chs. 19—40).

Central to the book of Exodus is the concept of redemption. Because of his faithfulness to the covenant promises made to Abraham, Isaac, and Jacob, God delivers His people from slavery, preserves them during the wilderness wandering, and prepares them to enter the Land of Promise.

Israel was redeemed from bondage in Egypt into a covenant relationship with God. Now that the people had experienced God's deliverance, guidance, and protection, they were ready to be taught what God expected of them. On Mt. Sinai, Moses received God's moral, civil, and ceremonial laws, as well as the pattern for the tabernacle to be built in the wilderness.

OUTLINE OF EXODUS

Part One: Redemption from Egypt (1:1—18:27)

Egypt

Bordered by the Mediterranean Sea on the north, the Sinai Peninsula and the Gulf of Suez on the east, and the Lybian desert on the west, Egypt is a land with a rich and well-recorded ancient history. Some of our knowledge of Egypt's ancient history stems from the work of the Egyptian priest Manetho (c. 270 B.C.), who records events of 31 dynasties, beginning c. 3200 B.C. The chart which follows begins with Ahmosis I, the founder of the eighteenth dynasty. According to the "early date" theory of the Exodus (adopted here), the Pharaoh of the Exodus was probably Amenhotep II; according to the "late date" theory, the Pharaoh was probably Rameses II.

Egyptian Pharaohs

Ahmosis I	1570–46 B.C.	Amenhotep IV	1379–62 B.C.
Amenhotep I	1546–26 B.C.	Smenkhkare	1364–61 B.C.
Thutmose I	1526–12 B.C.	Tutankhamon	1361–52 B.C.
Thutmose II	1512–04 B.C.	Ay	1352–48 B.C.
Thutmose III	1504–1450 B.C.	Horemheb	1348–20 B.C.
Hatshepsut	1504–1483 B.C.	Rameses I	1320–18 B.C.
Amenhotep II	1450–25 B.C.	Seti I	1318–04 B.C.
Thutmose IV	1425–17 B.C.	Rameses II	1304–1236 B.C.
Amenhotep III	1417–1379 B.C.	Merneptah	1236–1223 B.C.

Pagan Egyptian Gods

Religion in ancient Egypt was characterized by a complex polytheism, as a wide variety of local deities and nature gods were worshiped by the people. Many gods were associated with fertility and agriculture, and the protection of virtually every aspect of life was ascribed to some deity. The ten plagues were direct challenges to the worship of Egyptian deities who were thought to protect Egyptian life and property. In this way the supremacy of Yahweh, the God of Israel, was vividly demonstrated.

See chart, "Pagan Gods of Egypt," on page 26.

The Ten Plagues of Egypt

Pharaoh, the ruler of Egypt, refused to release the Hebrew people from slavery and allow them to leave his country. So the Lord sent ten plagues upon the Egyptians to break Pharaoh's stubborn will and to demonstrate His power and superiority over the pagan gods of the Egyptians.

These plagues occurred within a period of about nine months, in the following order:

1. The water of the Nile River turned into blood (7:14–25).

Continued on page 27

Pagan Gods of Egypt

Name	Responsibility	Form or Sacred Animal
Aker	Earth-god • Helper of the dead	Two lion heads
Amon	Wind-god • God of Thebes • Helper of the pious	Human (ram and goose sacred)
Anubis	Glorifier of the dead	Jackal-headed, black-skinned
Apis	Ensures fertility	Bull
Aton	Sun-god	
Atum	Primordial creature-god	Serpent-human
Bes	Protection at birth • Dispenser of virility	Group of demons
Edjo	Goddess of Delta/Lower Egypt	Uraeus serpent
Geb	Earth-god • Consort of Nut • Begetter of Osiris	Human
Hathor	Sky-goddess • Goddess of love, dance, alcohol	Cow
Heket	Primordial goddess	Frog
Horus	Sky-god	Falcon
Isis	Goddess of life, healing • Daughter of Geb Consort/sister of Osiris • Mother of Horus	Human
Khepri	Primordial god • Rising sun	Scarabaeus
Khnum	Giver of the Nile • Creator of mankind	Human with ram's head
Khons	Moon-god	Human
Maat	Justice • Daughter of Ra	Human
Meskhenet	Goddess protector of newborns and of destiny	
Min	God of virility and reproduction	
Mut	"Eye of the sun," consort of Amon	Vulture or human
Nekhbet	Goddess of Upper Egypt	
Nut	Sky-goddess • Consort of Geb Mother of Osiris and Seth • Mother of heavenly bodies	
Osiris	Dead pharoahs • Ruler of dead, life, vegetation	
Ptah	Creator-god • Lord of artisans	
Ra	God of sun, earth and sky • Father of Maat • National god	Human with falcon head
Sekhmet	Goddess of war and sickness	Human with lion head
Selket	Guardian of life • Protector of dead	Scorpion
Seshat	Goddess of writing and books	
Seth	God of chaos, desert and storm, crops • Brother of Osiris	
Shu	God of air, bearer of heaven	
Sobek	Creator-god	Crocodile
Sothis	God of Nile floodwaters	
Thermuthis	Goddess of fertility and harvest; fate	Serpent
Thoth	God of wisdom, moon, chronology • Messenger of gods	Ibis or baboon
Thoueris	Goddess of fertility and women in labor	Hippopotamus

Nelson's Complete Book of Bible Maps and Charts © 1993 by Thomas Nelson, Inc.

Continued from page 25

2. Frogs overran the countryside (8:1–15).
3. People and animals were infested with lice (8:16–19).
4. Swarms of flies covered the land (8:20–32).
5. Disease killed the livestock of Egypt (9:1–7).
6. Boils and sores infected the Egyptians and their animals (9:8–12).
7. Hail destroyed crops and vegetation (9:13–35).
8. Swarms of locusts covered the land (10:1–20).
9. Thick darkness covered Egypt for three days (10:21–29).
10. The Egyptian firstborn, both of the people and their animals, were destroyed by God's death angel (11:1—12:30).

In all of these plagues, the Israelites were protected, while the Egyptians and their property were destroyed. The Hebrews were delivered from the final plague when they marked their houses, at God's command, by sprinkling the blood of a lamb on their doorposts. The death angel "passed over" the Hebrew houses.

At this final demonstration of God's power, the Pharaoh gave in and allowed Moses and the Israelites to leave Egypt. This deliverance became one of the most memorable occasions in Hebrew history. The Passover is celebrated annually even today to commemorate God's deliverance of the Hebrew people from slavery.

The Ten Plagues on Egypt

The Plague	The Effect
1. Blood (7:20)	Pharaoh hardened (7:22)
2. Frogs (8:6)	Pharaoh begs relief, promises freedom (8:8), but is hardened (8:15)
3. Lice (8:17)	Pharaoh hardened (8:19)
4. Flies (8:24)	Pharaoh bargains (8:28), but is hardened (8:32)
5. Livestock diseased (9:6)	Pharaoh hardened (9:7)
6. Boils (9:10)	Pharaoh hardened (9:12)
7. Hail (9:23)	Pharaoh begs relief (9:27), promises freedom (9:28), but is hardened (9:35)
8. Locusts (10:13)	Pharaoh bargains (10:11), begs relief (10:17), but is hardened (10:20)
9. Darkness (10:22)	Pharaoh bargains (10:24), but is hardened (10:27)
10. Death of firstborn (12:29)	Pharaoh and Egyptians beg Israel to leave Egypt (12:31–33)
God multiplied His signs and wonders in the land of Egypt that the Egyptians might know that He is the Lord.	

Nelson's Complete Book of Bible Maps and Charts © 1993 by Thomas Nelson, Inc.

Moses' Flight & Return to Egypt

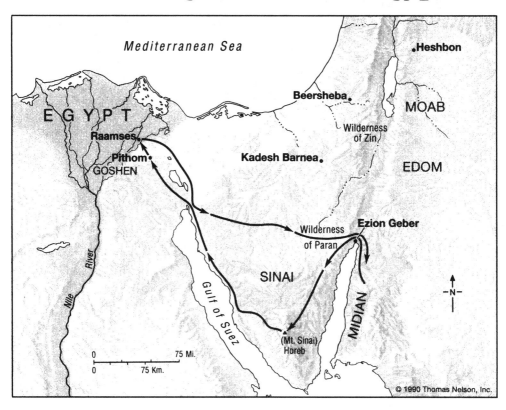

Moses

Born to Hebrew slave parents during dangerous times, Moses was miraculously protected and prepared by God to be the instrument of liberation for His people. To this end, Moses was raised in the Egyptian court and educated "in all the wisdom of the Egyptians" (Acts 7:22). At age forty, after attempting to protect a fellow Israelite and killing an Egyptian, Moses fled to the wilderness of Midian. There he remained another forty years, married, and fathered two sons. Upon receiving the call of God from out of the burning bush (3:2— 4:17), Moses returned to Egypt to lead the people of Israel out of Egypt.

The figure of Moses is central to the religion of the Old Testament. As the instrument of the Mosaic Covenant and the divinely appointed recipient of the Law, Moses helped to establish the form which the Old Testament worship and life of God's chosen people was to take for the remainder of the Old Testament period.

Though the circumstances are very different, it is an interesting parallel that Moses and Christ both faced the threat of death as infants, and that both were saved to accomplish a great redemption and to establish a blood covenant between God and His people.

See map, "The Life of Moses," on page 30.

Revelation at Sinai

On Mt. Sinai, Moses receives God's moral, civil, and ceremonial laws, as well as the pattern for the tabernacle to be built in the wilderness. After God judges the people for their worship of the golden calf, the tabernacle is constructed and consecrated. It is a building of beauty in a barren land and reveals much about the person of God and the way of redemption.

The Mosaic Covenant given at Sinai was given to the nation of Israel so that those who believed God's promise to Abraham would know how they should conduct themselves. The Mosaic Covenant in its entirety governed three areas of their lives: (1) the commandments governed their personal lives, particularly as they related to God (20:1–26); (2) the judgments governed their social lives, particularly as they related to one another (21:1—24:11); and (3) the ordinances governed their religious lives so that the people would know how to approach God on the terms that He dictates (24:12—31:18).

The Mosaic Covenant did not replace or set aside the Abrahamic Covenant. Rather, it was added alongside the Abrahamic Covenant so the people of Israel would know how to conduct their lives until Jesus Christ, the Messiah, would come and make a complete and perfect sacrifice for sin, a sacrifice toward which the Mosaic sacrifices only point. The Mosaic law was not given as a way

Continued on page 32

The Life of Moses

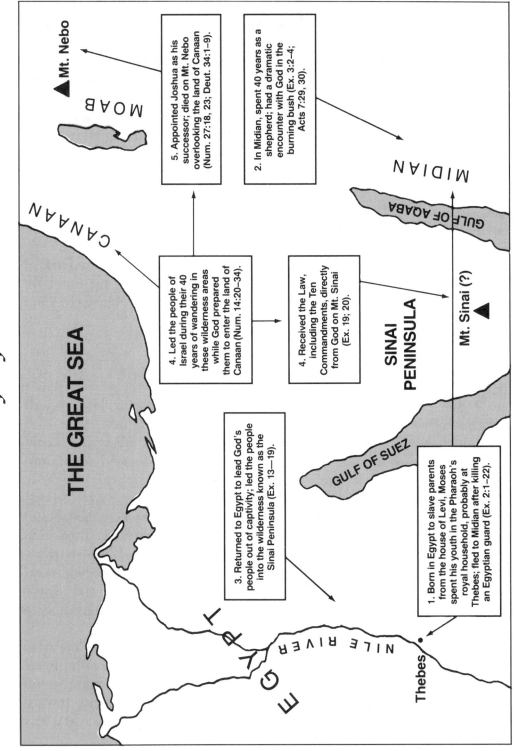

Mt. Nebo

MOAB

5. Appointed Joshua as his successor; died on Mt. Nebo overlooking the land of Canaan (Num. 27:18, 23; Deut. 34:1–9).

2. In Midian, spent 40 years as a shepherd; had a dramatic encounter with God in the burning bush (Ex. 3:2–4; Acts 7:29, 30).

MIDIAN

GULF OF AQABA

CANAAN

4. Led the people of Israel during their 40 years of wandering in these wilderness areas while God prepared them to enter the land of Canaan (Num. 14:20–34).

4. Received the Law, including the Ten Commandments, directly from God on Mt. Sinai (Ex. 19; 20).

THE GREAT SEA

SINAI PENINSULA

Mt. Sinai (?)

3. Returned to Egypt to lead God's people out of captivity; led the people into the wilderness known as the Sinai Peninsula (Ex. 13—19).

GULF OF SUEZ

EGYPT

NILE RIVER

Thebes

1. Born in Egypt to slave parents from the house of Levi, Moses spent his youth in the Pharaoh's royal household, probably at Thebes; fled to Midian after killing an Egyptian guard (Ex. 2:1–22).

Nelson's Complete Book of Bible Maps and Charts © 1993 by Thomas Nelson, Inc.

The Exodus from Egypt

The precise route taken by the Israelites to Mt. Sinai after their departure from Egypt is uncertain. As the map indicates, scholars have proposed both northern and southern routes, with the southern path the most likely. It took approximately two months to reach Sinai, where the Israelites encamped for roughly ten months during the period of divine revelation.

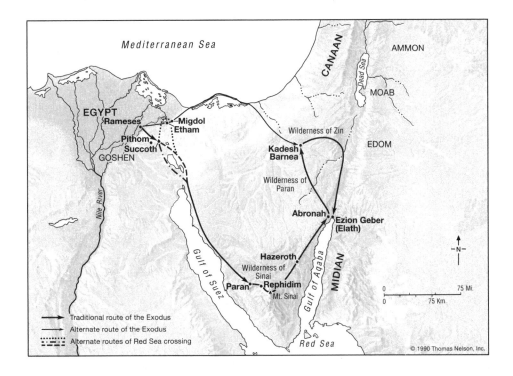

Continued from page 29

of meriting salvation, but that human beings might realize that they are helpless and hopeless apart from the saving grace of Christ (Gal. 3:19–24).

The Ten Commandments

The Ten Commandments (see Ex. 20:1–17) were laws given by God as guidelines for daily living. Although God gave the commandments to His people through Moses at Mount Sinai more than three thousand years ago, they are still relevant today. These laws are also known as the Decalogue, from the Greek word meaning "ten words."

The Ten Commandments are divided into two sections. The first four commandments govern our relationship to God, while commandments five through ten speak of our relationship to other people. The meaning of the Ten Commandments may be stated briefly as follows:

1. Trust God only (20:3, 4).
2. Worship God only (20:5, 6).
3. Use God's name in ways that honor Him (20:7).
4. Rest on the Sabbath day and think about God (20:8–11).
5. Respect and obey your parents (20:12).
6. Protect and respect human life (20:13).
7. Be true to your husband or wife (20:14).
8. Do not take what belongs to others (20:15).
9. Do not lie about others (20:16).
10. Be satisfied with what you have (20:17).

About 1,300 years after God gave these commandments, Jesus upheld them. He actually placed these laws on a higher plane, demanding that the spirit, as well as the legal aspects, of the laws be observed. He placed His stamp

At Mount Sinai Moses received God's commandments to His people.

of approval on the commandments by declaring, "Do not think that I came to destroy the Law or the Prophets. I did not come to destroy but to fulfill" (Matt. 5:17).

The Code of Hammurabi, an ancient law code named after an early king of Babylonia, bears many similarities to the Ten Commandments. However, the Law given at Mount Sinai reflects a high view of the nature of God and His holiness and His requirements of His people.

Ark of the Testimony

Also known as the ark of the covenant, the ark of the Lord, and the ark of God, the ark of the Testimony was the object most sacred to the Israelites during their time in the wilderness.

Do we know what the ark of the Testimony looked like? We cannot be positive, but there is a clear and detailed description in the Old Testament (Ex. 25:10–22). Archaeologists have discovered depictions of the ark (for example, a stone carving of the ark was found at the excavation of a synagogue in Capernaum).

Artist's conception of the ark of the Testimony.

From the biblical account, we can determine these facts about its physical appearance: It was a box about 45 inches long, 27 inches wide, and 27 inches high, made from acacia wood. Four poles were inserted into rings on the side of the ark so it could be carried by four men.

The lid on the ark, called the mercy seat, was made of gold. The Hebrew word traditionally translated "mercy seat" could be rendered "place of atonement," because this was where the high priest sprinkled blood once each year on the Day of Atonement as the atonement for sin (Lev. 16:15). Mounted on this lid were two winged creatures (cherubim), which faced each other with outstretched wings. Inside the ark were the two stone tablets containing the Ten Commandments, which Moses had received from God at Mount Sinai (Ex. 20). It also contained a golden pot of manna and Aaron's rod that budded (Heb. 9:4), reminders of God's provision for the needs of the Israelites in the wilderness.

The Israelites believed that God lived among them in the tabernacle between the wings of the cherubim on the mercy seat. God spoke to Moses from this place (Num. 7:89) during their years of wandering in the wilderness as they were being prepared to enter the Promised Land.

The ark was carried ahead of the Israelites when they left Mount Sinai (Num. 10:33); when they crossed the Jordan River to enter Canaan (Josh. 4:9–11); and when they circled the walls of Jericho before that city fell (Josh. 6:1–20). After many other travels, it was finally placed in Solomon's temple in Jerusalem (1 Kin. 8:1–9), only to disappear after the destruction of Jerusalem by the Babylonians in 586 B.C.

The ark served as a visible reminder of God's presence with the Hebrew people. The mercy seat, covered with gold, symbolized God's throne and His rule in the hearts of those who acknowledge Him as their sovereign Lord.

Aaron as High Priest

When the priesthood was instituted in the wilderness, Moses consecrated his brother Aaron as the first high priest of Israel (Ex. 28; 29; Lev. 8; 9). The priesthood was set within the tribe of Levi, from which Aaron was descended, and Aaron's sons inherited the position of high priest from their father.

The high priest's dress represented his function as mediator between God and people. Over his regular priestly garments the high priest wore an ephod, a two-piece apron. He also wore a breastplate of judgment with twelve precious stones. These were engraved with the names of the twelve tribes of Israel (Ex. 28:15–30). In the pocket of the breastplate, directly over the high priest's heart, were the Urim and Thummim (28:30), the medium through which God communicated His will to the people.

The high priest's dress represented his function as mediator between God and people.

The high priest was responsible for seeing that the duties of all the priests were carried out (2 Chron. 19:11). His most important responsibility occurred annually on the Day of Atonement. On this day he entered the Holy of Holies, or the Most Holy Place, in the tabernacle and made sacrifice first for his own sins, then for the sins committed by all the people during the year just ended (Ex. 30:10).

David organized twenty-four groups of priests to serve at the tabernacle during his reign as king of Judah. Kings Hezekiah and Josiah assisted the high priest in reform and restoration of the temple. In the New Testament, the high priest was referred to as ruler of the people (Acts 23:4, 5) and was the presider over the Sanhedrin, the highest ruling body of the Jews (Matt. 26:57–59).

The New Testament speaks of Jesus in figurative terms as a "High Priest." He was not of the order of Aaron but of Melchizedek, an eternal priesthood (Heb. 5:10). He had no need to offer sacrifice for His own sin, for He had no sin (Heb. 7:27, 28). He offered His own blood, once for all (Heb. 9:12, 26; 10:10, 12). Therefore, we may come boldly into the presence of God through the "one Mediator between God and men, *the* Man Christ Jesus" (1 Tim. 2:5).

The Tabernacle

The tabernacle was a portable tent or sanctuary used by the Israelites as a place for worship during their early history. In the Old Testament, it is frequently called "the tent of meeting," indicating that it was the primary place of encounter between God and His people. The structure was built in accordance with God's instructions to Moses on Mount Sinai during the people's years of wandering in the wilderness (Ex. 26; 35). With the people contributing materials and labor, the tabernacle was completed to God's specifications. God blessed their handiwork by covering the tent with a cloud and filling the sanctuary with His glory (40:34).

The outer courtyard of the tabernacle was a fenced rectangle about 150 feet long by 75 feet wide (27:9–19). The courtyard contained a bronze altar for animal sacrifices (27:1–8) and a laver where the priests washed before entering the tent (30:17–21).

The tabernacle itself, measuring 15 by 45 feet, had two main sections: the outer room known as the holy place, and the inner room called the Holy of Holies, or Most Holy Place (26:33).

The outer room contained an altar where an incense offering was burned (30:1–10); the seven-branched gold candlestick (25:31–40); and a table for showbread, signifying God's presence (25:23–30).

The inner room, or Holy of Holies, was separated from the outer area by a veil, or curtain (26:31–37). This sacred part of the tabernacle was entered only once a year by the high priest on the Day of Atonement. In a special ceremony on this day, he made atonement for his own sins and then offered sacrifice to atone for the sins of the people. This most sacred enclosure had only one item of furniture, the ark of the covenant.

The lid of the ark was called the mercy seat. Upon it were two gold cherubim that faced each other. The ark contained the stone tablets with the Ten Commandments (Deut. 10:4, 5), a gold pot filled with manna (Ex. 16:33, 34), and Aaron's rod that budded (Num. 17:10).

During the years when the people of Israel were wandering in the wilderness, the tabernacle was moved with them from place to place (Ex. 40:36–38). When the Israelites pitched camp in the wilderness, the tabernacle was to be placed in the center, with the Levites, who were charged with its care (Num. 4), camping next to it (Num. 1:53). Then the tribes were to be arrayed in specific order on the four sides of the tabernacle (Num. 2). This shows what an important role the tabernacle played in the religious life of God's people.

After the conquest of Canaan, the tabernacle was moved to Shiloh where it remained through the period of the judges (Josh. 18:1). Later the tabernacle was also stationed at Nob (1 Sam. 21:1–6) and Gibeon (1 Kin. 3:4). When the temple was completed, Solomon had the tabernacle moved to Jerusalem (1 Kin. 8:4). Apparently there was no further need for the tabernacle after the completion of the temple, which became the permanent place of worship for the nation and the center of its religious life.

The many references to the tabernacle in the New Testament should be understood in light of the incarnation, when God's Son became a human being. Because the tabernacle was the place where God and His people met, John declared that the Word had become flesh and "tabernacled" among us (John 1:14; the Greek word is translated "dwelt" in the New King James Version). Paul spoke of Christ as the "propitiation" for sin in Romans 3:25. He used the same Greek word that referred to the mercy seat of the ark where the high priest made annual atonement. The laver where priests washed before serving in the tabernacle may be reflected in Titus 3:5.

Revelation 8:3–5 speaks of the golden incense altar. Practically every feature of the tabernacle is found in the epistle to the Hebrews, a book that describes Jesus as the great High Priest and the ultimate and eternal sacrifice for our sins.

The Plan of the Tabernacle

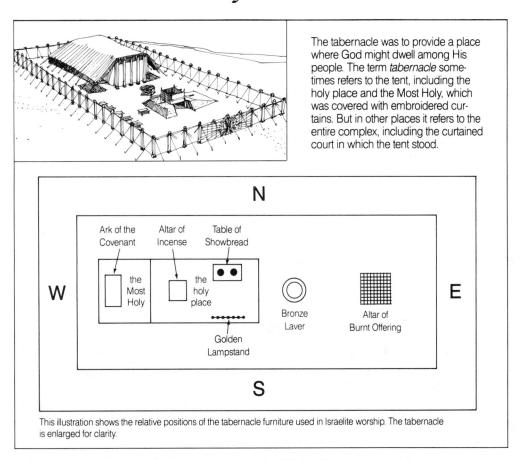

The tabernacle was to provide a place where God might dwell among His people. The term *tabernacle* sometimes refers to the tent, including the holy place and the Most Holy, which was covered with embroidered curtains. But in other places it refers to the entire complex, including the curtained court in which the tent stood.

N

W

Ark of the Covenant

Altar of Incense

Table of Showbread

the Most Holy

the holy place

Bronze Laver

Altar of Burnt Offering

E

Golden Lampstand

S

This illustration shows the relative positions of the tabernacle furniture used in Israelite worship. The tabernacle is enlarged for clarity.

Nelson's Complete Book of Bible Maps and Charts © 1993 by Thomas Nelson, Inc.

The Furniture of the Tabernacle

Ark of the Covenant
(Ex. 25:10–22)
The ark was most sacred of all the furniture in the tabernacle. Here the Hebrews kept a copy of the Ten Commandments, which summarized the whole covenant.

Bronze Laver
(Ex. 30:17–21)
It was to the laver of bronze that the priests would come for cleansing. They must be pure to enter the presence of God.

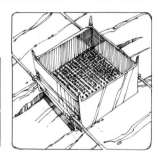

Altar of Burnt Offering
(Ex. 27:1–8)
Animal sacrifices were offered on this altar, located in the court in front of the tabernacle. The blood of the sacrifice was sprinkled on the four horns of the altar.

Golden Lampstand
(Ex. 25:31–40)
The gold lampstand stood in the holy place, opposite the table of showbread. It held seven lamps, flat bowls in which a wick lay with one end in the oil of the bowl and the lighted end hanging out.

Table of Showbread
(Ex. 25:23–30)
The table of showbread was a stand on which the offerings were placed. Always in God's presence on the table were the 12 loaves of bread representing the 12 tribes.

Altar of Incense
(Ex. 30:1–10)
The altar of incense inside the tabernacle was much smaller than the altar of burnt offering outside. The incense burned on the altar was a perfume of a sweet-smelling aroma.

Nelson's Complete Book of Bible Maps and Charts © 1993 by Thomas Nelson, Inc.

LEVITICUS

It has been said that it took God only one night to get Israel out of Egypt, but it took forty years to get Egypt out of Israel. In Exodus, Israel is redeemed and established as a kingdom of priests and a holy nation; and in Leviticus Israel is taught how to fulfill their priestly call. They have been led out from the land of bondage in Exodus and into the sanctuary of God in Leviticus. They move from redemption to service, from deliverance to dedication.

The Hebrew title of the book is *wayyiqra*, the first word of the text meaning "And He called." The Greek title appearing in the Septuagint is *Leutikon* (meaning "that which pertains to the priests"), from which the Latin Vulgate version derived the title *Leviticus*. The title is somewhat misleading, for although the book deals extensively with the priests and their various tasks, it must be remembered that all Israelites were to know and keep the Law.

Author

The kind of arguments used to confirm the Mosaic authorship of Genesis and Exodus also apply to Leviticus because the Pentateuch is a literary unit. The content of the book itself also points strongly to Moses as the human author. Fifty-six times in the twenty-seven chapters of Leviticus it is stated that God imparted these laws to Moses (see, e.g., 1:1; 4:1; 6:1, 24; 8:1).

Date

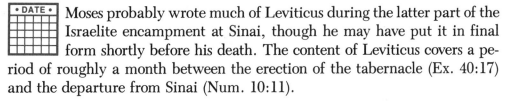

Moses probably wrote much of Leviticus during the latter part of the Israelite encampment at Sinai, though he may have put it in final form shortly before his death. The content of Leviticus covers a period of roughly a month between the erection of the tabernacle (Ex. 40:17) and the departure from Sinai (Num. 10:11).

Leviticus at a Glance

FOCUS	SACRIFICE				SANCTIFICATION				
REFERENCE	1:1 —— 8:1 —————— 11:1 ———— 16:1 —— 18:1 — 21:1 — 23:1 ———— 25:1 ———— 27:1 — 27:34								
DIVISION	THE LAWS OF				THE LAWS OF SANCTIFICATION				
	THE OFFERINGS	CONSECRATION OF THE PRIESTS	CONSECRATION OF THE PEOPLE	NATIONAL ATONEMENT	FOR THE PEOPLE	FOR THE PRIESTS	IN WORSHIP	IN THE LAND OF CANAAN	THROUGH VOWS
TOPIC	THE WAY TO GOD				THE WALK WITH GOD				
	THE LAWS OF ACCEPTABLE APPROACH TO GOD				THE LAWS OF CONTINUED FELLOWSHIP WITH GOD				
LOCATION	MOUNT SINAI								
TIME	c. 1 MONTH								

Nelson's Complete Book of Bible Maps and Charts © 1993 by Thomas Nelson, Inc.

Themes and Literary Structure

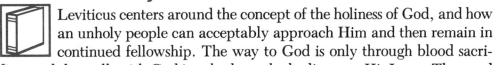

Leviticus centers around the concept of the holiness of God, and how an unholy people can acceptably approach Him and then remain in continued fellowship. The way to God is only through blood sacrifice, and the walk with God is only through obedience to His Laws. The word "holy" occurs ninety times in Leviticus, and the word "sanctify," seventeen times. The Hebrew root *q-d-sh*, "holy" (in adjective, noun, and verb forms) appears 152 times in Leviticus.

Leviticus falls into two major sections: the first dealing predominantly with the sacrificial system of worship (chs. 1—17), and the second dealing primarily with the sanctification of the people of Israel as a whole through ceremonial and moral holiness (chs. 18—27).

OUTLINE OF LEVITICUS

The Levitical Offerings

Prominent in the book of Leviticus is the sacrificial system. The burnt offering was the only sacrifice entirely consumed upon the altar, and therefore it is sometimes called the whole offering. The grain offering was a tribute offering made in order to secure or maintain the divine favor, indicating that the fruits of a person's labor should be dedicated to God. The peace offering was designed to provide expiation and permits the one who makes the offering to eat the meat of the sacrifice. It was often given on a joyous occasion. The sin offering was employed to remove impurity from the sanctuary. The trespass offering, also referred to as the guilt offering or the offering of reparation, was given for violation of the sanctity of the property of God or of another person, usually by use of a false oath.

See chart, "The Levitical Offerings," on pages 44, 45.

Festivals or Feasts

The liturgical calendar also holds a significant place in the book of Leviticus. In ancient Israel there were seven annual religious festivals especially ordained by God:

1. **Passover** (*pesah*, Heb.).
   Ex. 12:1–28, 43–49; Lev. 23:5; Num. 28:16; Deut. 16:1–8

Time: The evening of the fourteenth day of Nisan (Abib), the first month of the biblical year (March/April).

Purpose: (1) To commemorate Israel's deliverance from Egyptian bondage. (2) To remind the children of Israel that God "passed over" their houses, i.e., spared the firstborn of the Israelites (Ex. 12:27).

Prophetic Significance: (1) Christ is our Passover (cf. John 1:29; 19:36; 1 Cor. 5:7; 1 Pet. 1:18, 19). (2) The Passover is the foundation for the Lord's Supper (cf. Matt. 26:17–30; Mark 14:12–25; Luke 22:1–20). (3) The Passover foreshadows the marriage supper of the Lamb (cf. Matt. 26:29; Mark 14:25; Luke 22:16–18).

2. **Feast of Unleavened Bread** (*matsot*, Heb.).
   Ex. 12:15–20; 13:3–10; Lev. 23:6–8; Num. 28:17–25; Deut. 16:3–8

Time: It began on the fifteenth day of Nisan (Abib) and continued for one week (March/April).

Purpose: To commemorate the hardships of Israel's hurried flight from Egypt (Ex. 12:39). The absence of leaven symbolized complete consecration and devotion to God.

Prophetic Significance: (1) Unleavened bread is a type of Christ (cf. John 6:30–59; 1 Cor. 11:24). (2) Unleavened bread is a type of the true church (cf. 1 Cor. 5:7, 8).

3. **Day of Firstfruits** (*bikkurim*, Heb.).
   Lev. 23:9–14

Time: On the day after the Sabbath of Passover week (March/April).

Continued on page 46

The Levitical Offerings

Name	Scripture References	Purpose	Consisted of	God's Portion	Priests' Portion	Offerer's Portion	Prophetic Significance
(1) Burnt Offering (olah, Heb.): a. Sweet aroma; b. Voluntary.	Lev. 1:3–17; 6:8–13.	(1) To propitiate for sin in general (1:4). (2) To signify complete dedication and consecration to God; hence it is called the "whole burnt offering."	According to wealth: (1) Bull without blemish (1:3–9); (2) Male sheep or goat without blemish (1:10–13); (3) Turtledoves or young pigeons (1:14–17).	Entirety burned on the altar of burnt offering (1:9); except the skin (7:8).	Skin only (7:8).	None.	Signifies complete dedication of life to God: (1) On the part of Christ (Matt. 26:39–44; Mark 14:36; Luke 22:42; Phil. 2:5–11). (2) On the part of the believer (Rom. 12:1, 2; Heb. 13:15).
(2) Grain Offering (minhah, Heb.): a. Sweet aroma; b. Voluntary.	Lev. 2:1–16; 6:14–18; 7:12, 13.	The grain offering accompanied all the burnt offerings; it signified one's homage and thanksgiving to God.	Three types: (1) Fine flour mixed with oil and frankincense (2:1–3); (2) Cakes made of fine flour mixed with oil and baked in an oven (2:4), in a pan (2:5), or in a covered pan (2:7); (3) Green heads of roasted grain mixed with oil and frankincense (2:14, 15).	Memorial portion burned on the altar of burnt offering (2:2, 9, 16).	Remainder to be eaten in the court of the tabernacle (2:3, 10; 6:16–18; 7:14, 15).	None.	Signifies the perfect humanity of Christ: (1) The absence of leaven typifies the sinlessness of Christ (Heb. 4:15; 1 John 3:5). (2) The presence of oil is emblematic of the Holy Spirit (Luke 4:18; 1 John 2:20, 27).
(3) Peace Offering (shelem, Heb.): a. Sweet aroma; b. Voluntary.	Lev. 3:1–17; 7:11–21, 28–34.	The peace offering generally expressed peace and fellowship between the offerer and God; hence it culminated in a communal meal. There were three types: (1) Thank Offering: to express gratitude for an unexpected blessing or deliverance. (2) Votive Offering: to express gratitude for a blessing or deliverance granted when a vow had accompanied the petition. (3) Freewill Offering: to express gratitude to God without regard to any specific blessing or deliverance.	According to wealth: (1) From the herd, a male or female without blemish (3:1–5); (2) From the flock, a male or female without blemish (3:6–11); (3) From the goats (3:12–17). Note: Minor imperfections were permitted when the peace offering was a freewill offering of a bull or a lamb (22:23).	Fatty portions burned on the altar of burnt offering (3:3–5).	Breast (wave offering) and right thigh (heave offering; 7:30–34).	Remainder to be eaten in the court by the offerer and his family: a. Thank offering —to be eaten the same day (7:15). b. Votive and freewill offerings—to be eaten the first and second day (7:16–18). Note: this is the only offering in which the offerer shared.	Foreshadows the peace which the believer has with God through Jesus Christ (Rom. 5:1; Col. 1:20).

Name	Scripture References	Purpose	Consisted of	God's Portion	Priests' Portion	Offerer's Portion	Prophetic Significance
(4) Sin Offering (*hattat*, Heb.): a. Non-sweet aroma; b. Compulsory.	Lev. 4:1—5:13; 6:24–30.	To atone for sins committed unknowingly, especially where no restitution was possible. Note Num. 15:30, 31: The sin offering was of no avail in cases of defiant rebellion against God.	(1) For the high priest, a bull without blemish (4:3–12). (2) For the congregation, a bull without blemish (4:13–21). (3) For a ruler, a male goat without blemish (4:22–26). (4) For a commoner, a female goat or female lamb without blemish (4:27–35). (5) In cases of poverty, two turtledoves or two young pigeons (one for a sin offering, the other for a burnt offering) could be substituted (5:7–10). (6) In cases of extreme poverty, fine flour could be substituted (5:11–13; cf. Heb. 9:22).	(1) Fatty portions to be burned on the altar of burnt offering (4:8–10, 19, 26, 31, 35). (2) When the sin offering was for the high priest or congregation, the remainder of the bull was to be burned outside the camp (4:11, 12, 20, 21).	When the sin offering was for a ruler or commoner, the remainder of the goat or lamb was to be eaten in the tabernacle court (6:26).	None.	Prefigures the fact that in His death: (1) Christ was made sin for us (2 Cor. 5:21); (2) Christ suffered outside the gates of Jerusalem (Heb. 13:11–13).
(5) Trespass Offering (*asham*, Heb.): a. Non-sweet aroma; b. Compulsory.	Lev. 5:14—6:7; 7:1–7.	To atone for sins committed unknowingly, especially where restitution was possible.	(1) If the offense were against the Lord (tithes, offerings, etc.), a ram without blemish was to be brought; restitution was reckoned according to the priest's estimate of the value of the trespass, plus one-fifth (5:15, 16). (2) If the offense were against man, a ram without blemish was to be brought; restitution was reckoned according to the value plus one-fifth (6:4–6).	Fatty portions to be burned on the altar of burnt offering (7:3–5).	Remainder to be eaten in a holy place (7:6, 7).	None.	Foreshadows the fact that Christ is also our trespass offering (Col. 2:13).

Nelson's Complete Book of Bible Maps and Charts © 1993 by Thomas Nelson, Inc.

Continued from page 43

Purpose: To dedicate and consecrate the firstfruits of the barley harvest.

Prophetic Significance: (1) Firstfruits is a type of the bodily resurrection of Christ (cf. 1 Cor. 15:20–23). (2) Firstfruits is a guarantee of the bodily resurrection of all believers (cf. 1 Cor. 15:20–23; 1 Thess. 4:13–18). (3) Firstfruits is a type of the consecration of the church.

4. Feast of Pentecost (or Weeks: *shabuot*, Heb.).
   Lev. 23:15–22; Num. 28:26–31; Deut. 16:9–12

Time: The day after the seventh Sabbath after the Day of Firstfruits (May/June).

Purpose: To dedicate and consecrate the firstfruits of the wheat harvest.

Prophetic Significance: The outpouring of the Holy Spirit upon the church occurred on the Day of Pentecost (Acts 2). The two loaves, representative of the Jew and Gentile, contained leaven because sin is found within the church.

5. Day of Trumpets (*rosh hashanah*, Heb.).
   Lev. 23:23–25; Num. 10:10; 29:1–6

Time: The first day of the seventh month (Tishri), the sabbatical month (September/October).

Purpose: To usher in and consecrate the seventh month as the sabbatical month.

Prophetic Significance: In the N.T. the blowing of the trumpet is associated with the return of our Lord (cf. Matt. 24:31; 1 Cor. 15:52; 1 Thess. 4:16).

6. Day of Atonement (*yom kippur*, Heb.).
   Lev. 16; 23:26–32; Num. 29:7–11

Time: The tenth day of the seventh month (Tishri—September/October).

Purpose: To make annual atonement for the sins of the priests and the people, and for the tabernacle (temple).

Prophetic Significance: The Day of Atonement finds its ultimate fulfillment in the crucifixion of Christ (cf. Heb. 9). It represents the redeeming work of Christ more adequately than any other O.T. type.

7. Feast of Tabernacles (Booths or Ingathering; *sukkot*, Heb.).
   Lev. 23:33–43; Num. 29:12–38; Deut. 16:13–17

Time: The fifteenth through twenty-first of the seventh month (Tishri), with an eighth day added as a climax to all the feasts (September/October).

Purpose: (1) To commemorate God's deliverance and protection during the wilderness wanderings (23:43). (2) To rejoice in the completion of all the harvest (23:39).

Prophetic Significance: The Feast of Tabernacles foreshadows the peace and prosperity of the millennial reign of Christ (Zech. 14:16).

Israel's Other Sacred Times

Besides the Annual Feasts, Israel's time was marked by these other sacred events.

Sabbath Every seventh day was a solemn rest from all work (Ex. 20:8–11; 31:12–17; Lev. 23:3; Deut. 5:12–15).

Sabbath Year Every seventh year was designated a "year of release" to allow the land to lie fallow (Ex. 23:10, 11; Lev. 25:1–7).

Year of Jubilee The 50th year, which followed seven Sabbath years, was to proclaim liberty to those who were servants because of debt, and to return lands to their former owners (Lev. 25:8–55; 27:17–24; Ezek. 46:17).

The New Moon The first day of the Hebrew 29- or 30-day month was a day of rest, special sacrifices, and the blowing of trumpets (Num. 28:11–15; Ps. 81:3).

Dedication (Lights or *Hanukkah*) An eight-day feast in the ninth month (Chislev) commemorating the cleansing of the temple from defilement by Syria, and its rededication (John 10:22).

Purim (Lots) A feast on the 14th and 15th of the 12th month (Adar). The name comes from Babylonian *Pur*, meaning "Lot" (Esth. 9:18–32).

The Jewish Calendar

The Jews used two kinds of calendars:
  Civil Calendar—official calendar of kings, childbirth, and contracts.
  Sacred Calendar—from which festivals were computed.

NAMES OF MONTHS	CORRESPONDS WITH	NO. OF DAYS	MONTH OF CIVIL YEAR	MONTH OF SACRED YEAR
TISHRI	Sept.–Oct.	30 days	1st	7th
HESHVAN	Oct.–Nov.	29 or 30	2nd	8th
CHISLEV	Nov.–Dec.	29 or 30	3rd	9th
TEBETH	Dec.–Jan.	29	4th	10th
SHEBAT	Jan.–Feb.	30	5th	11th
ADAR	Feb.–Mar.	29 or 30	6th	12th
NISAN	Mar.–Apr.	30	7th	1st
IYAR	Apr.–May	29	8th	2nd
SIVAN	May–June	30	9th	3rd
TAMMUZ	June–July	29	10th	4th
AB	July–Aug.	30	11th	5th
***ELUL**	Aug.–Sept.	29	12th	6th

The Jewish day was from sunset to sunset, in 8 equal parts:

FIRST WATCH . . . . .SUNSET TO 9 P.M.
SECOND WATCH . . . . .9 P.M. TO MIDNIGHT
THIRD WATCH . . . . .MIDNIGHT TO 3 A.M.
FOURTH WATCH . . . . .3 A.M. TO SUNRISE

FIRST HOUR . . . . .SUNRISE TO 9 A.M.
THIRD HOUR . . . . .9 A.M. TO NOON
SIXTH HOUR . . . . .NOON TO 3 P.M.
NINTH HOUR . . . . .3 P.M. TO SUNSET

*Hebrew months were alternately 30 and 29 days long. Their year, shorter than ours, had 354 days. Therefore, about every three years (7 times in 19 years) an extra 29-day month, VEADAR, was added between ADAR and NISAN.

NUMBERS

Numbers is the book of wanderings. Most of the book describes Israel's experiences in the wilderness. Israel as a nation is in its infancy at the outset of this book, only thirteen months after the Exodus from Egypt. In Numbers, the nation goes through a painful process of testing and maturation in which God teaches His people the consequences of rebellion and irresponsible decisions. The forty years of wilderness experience transform them from a rabble of ex-slaves into a nation ready to take possession of the Promised Land.

The book of Numbers takes its name from the two numberings of the Israelites—the first at Mt. Sinai (ch. 1) and the second on the plains of Moab (26:1–51). Jewish writings usually refer to the book by the fifth Hebrew word in 1:1, *bemidbar*, meaning "in the wilderness." The Greek title in the Septuagint is *Arithmoi*, meaning "numbers," a term taken over into the Latin Vulgate where the title is translated *Liber Numeri*, "Book of Numbers."

Author

The evidence that points to Moses as the author of Numbers is similar to that for the previous books of the Pentateuch. There are in Numbers more than eighty claims that "the LORD spoke to Moses." It is apparent (33:2) that Moses kept detailed records as an eyewitness of the events in this book. As the central character in Exodus through Deuteronomy, he was better qualified than any other person to write these books.

Some scholars have claimed that the third-person references to Moses (e.g., 8:23; 14:36; 15:1, 22) point to an author different from Moses. Such use of the third person may seem unusual to the Western mind, but it was commonly employed by ancient writers and is used consistently in each book in which the name of Moses appears (e.g., Ex. 24:1; Lev. 6:1; Deut. 5:1).

Date

Leviticus covers only one month, but Numbers stretches over almost thirty-nine years (c. 1444–1405 B.C.). It records Israel's movement from the last twenty days at Mt. Sinai, the wanderings round Kadesh Barnea, and finally the arrival in the plains of Moab in the fortieth year.

Continued on page 51

Numbers at a Glance

FOCUS	THE OLD GENERATION		THE TRAGIC TRANSITION				THE NEW GENERATION		
REFERENCE	1:1 —————— 5:1 ——————		10:11 — 13:1 — 15:1 —————— 20:1 — 26:1 ——————				28:1 —————— 31:1 — 36:13		
DIVISION	ORGANIZATION OF ISRAEL	SANCTIFICATION OF ISRAEL	TO KADESH	AT KADESH	IN WILDERNESS	TO MOAB	REORGANIZA-TION OF ISRAEL	REGULATIONS OF OFFERINGS AND VOWS	CONQUEST AND DIVISION OF ISRAEL
TOPIC	ORDER		DISORDER				REORDER		
	PREPARATION		POSTPONEMENT				PREPARATION		
LOCATION	MOUNT SINAI		WILDERNESS				PLAINS OF MOAB		
TIME	20 DAYS		38 YEARS 3 MONTHS AND 10 DAYS				c. 5 MONTHS		

Nelson's Complete Book of Bible Maps and Charts © 1993 by Thomas Nelson, Inc.

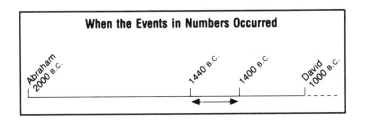

Continued from page 49

Moses no doubt kept this record of events in the course of the wilderness wanderings.

Themes and Literary Structure

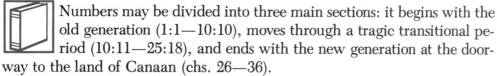 Numbers may be divided into three main sections: it begins with the old generation (1:1—10:10), moves through a tragic transitional period (10:11—25:18), and ends with the new generation at the doorway to the land of Canaan (chs. 26—36).

Numbers records two generations (chs. 1—14 and 21—36), two numberings (chs. 1 and 26), two journeys (chs. 10—14 and 21—27), and two sets of instructions (chs. 5—9 and 28—36). It illustrates both the kindness and the severity of God (Rom. 11:22) and teaches that God's people can move forward only as they trust and depend on Him.

The theme of divine judgment on unbelief is prominent in Numbers, which records the failure of Israel to believe in the promise of God and the resulting judgment of wandering in the wilderness for forty years. The critical turning point in the book may be seen in chapter 14, when Israel heeded the warnings of the fearful spies and rejected God by refusing to go up and conquer the Promised Land. God judges Israel "according to the number of the days in which you spied out the land, forty days, for each day you shall bear your guilt one year, *namely* forty years, and you shall know My rejection" (14:34).

The book of Numbers is more than a warning against unbelief and disobedience, however. Throughout it testifies to the grace and mercy of God and points forward to the divine grace to be displayed in Jesus Christ. The divine presence and guidance is evident in the pillar of fire and cloud (10:11). God's care for His people is seen in the daily provision of manna for food and in the rock which provided water for the people to drink, gifts which prefigure the coming of Christ (John 6:31–33; 1 Cor. 10:4). A vivid illustration of divine mercy is seen in the provision of the bronze serpent as the means of healing those who had been bitten by poisonous snakes, a picture of the crucifixion (21:4–9; cf. John 3:14).

OUTLINE OF NUMBERS

Part One: The Preparation of the Old Generation to Inherit the Promised Land (1:1—10:10)

**Part Two: The Failure of the Old Generation
to Inherit the Promised Land (10:11—25:18)**

Encampment of the Tribes

With the military census completed in chapter 1, instructions for the organization of the tribes and their armies are given. The camp is organized with three tribes on each side of the tabernacle with Yahweh's dwelling place in the midst of the camp. Further, when they break camp and march, the six tribes on the east and south set out, followed by the Levites with the tabernacle traveling in the center (2:17), followed by the six tribes on the west and north, respectively. Whether encamped or on the march, the tabernacle is central. One tribe is given priority among the three on each side of the tabernacle, Judah on the east (2:9), Reuben on the south (2:16), Ephraim on the west (2:24), and Dan on the north (2:31).

See chart, "Placement of Tribes in the Israelite Encampment," page 54.

From the Wilderness to Canaan

The book of Numbers, which takes Israel from Sinai to Kadesh Barnea, and then to the plains of Moab, reports almost nothing about the forty years of wandering which intervened between their first departure from Kadesh Bar-

Placement of Tribes
in the Israelite Encampment

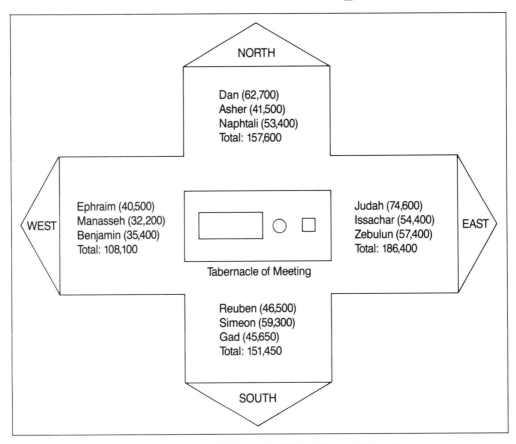

NORTH

Dan (62,700)
Asher (41,500)
Naphtali (53,400)
Total: 157,600

WEST

Ephraim (40,500)
Manasseh (32,200)
Benjamin (35,400)
Total: 108,100

Tabernacle of Meeting

Judah (74,600)
Issachar (54,400)
Zebulun (57,400)
Total: 186,400

EAST

Reuben (46,500)
Simeon (59,300)
Gad (45,650)
Total: 151,450

SOUTH

Nelson's Complete Book of Bible Maps and Charts © 1993 by Thomas Nelson, Inc.

nea (14:25) and their second (20:22). Neither itinerary nor chronology are given. Events occurring just before and just after the forty years are mentioned: The defeat in their abortive attempt to enter the land on their own strength (14:45), and their request for permission to travel through Edom (20:14). Between these two events are recorded certain laws as well as narratives relating the failures of Israel's leaders.

Wanderings of the Israelites

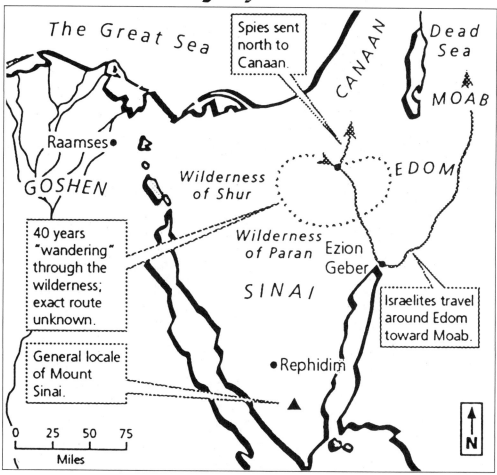

The Great Sea

Spies sent north to Canaan.

CANAAN

Dead Sea

MOAB

Raamses•

Wilderness of Shur

EDOM

GOSHEN

40 years "wandering" through the wilderness; exact route unknown.

Wilderness of Paran

Ezion Geber

SINAI

Israelites travel around Edom toward Moab.

General locale of Mount Sinai.

•Rephidim

0   25   50   75
Miles

N

The Cycle of Good and Bad in Scripture

A GREAT GOOD . . .	. . . FOLLOWED BY A GREAT EVIL
The world is created (Gen. 1–2).	Adam and Eve rebel and fall into sin, resulting in shame, fear, pain, toil and death (Gen. 3).
Noah is obedient in preparing for the flood and his survival in the ark (Gen. 6:13–22; 7:23).	Noah falls into a drunken stupor and nakedness which embarrasses his sons and leads to Canaan's curse (Gen. 9:20–25).
God delivers the people from the Egyptians by parting the Red Sea (Ex. 14:21–31).	The people complain about a lack of water (Ex. 15:22–25).
God gives the Ten Commandments to Moses (Ex. 20:1–17).	The people worship a golden calf (Ex. 32:1–6).
Aaron and his sons begin their spiritual leadership (Lev. 9:1–24).	Aaron's two oldest sons offer "profane fire" before the Lord and are killed as a result (Lev. 10:1–3).
David affirms God's covenant with him (2 Sam. 6).	David commits adultery with Bathsheba and arranges for the murder of her husband Uriah (2 Sam. 11:1–27).
Elijah triumphs over the prophets of Baal on Mount Carmel (1 Kin. 18:20–46).	Elijah flees in fear from the wrath of Jezebel and complains that God does not take care of him (1 Kin. 19:1–18).
Jonah successfully proclaims repentance to pagan Nineveh (Jon. 3).	Jonah expresses disappointment in Nineveh's repentance and complains about a lack of personal comfort (Jon. 4).
Peter affirms that Jesus is the Messiah of God (Matt. 16:16).	Peter is rebuked by Jesus for attempting to subvert God's purposes (Matt. 16:22–23).
Jesus enters Jerusalem to cheering crowds (Luke 19:28–40).	Jesus is crucified after angry mobs demand His death (Luke 23:13–49).
Barnabas makes a generous gift to the church of the proceeds from a land sale (Acts 4:36–37).	Ananias and Sapphira attempt to deceive Peter about a similar act of "charity" and are slain by God as a result (Acts 5:1–11).

DEUTERONOMY

euteronomy consists of a series of farewell messages by Israel's 120-year-old leader, Moses. It is addressed to the new generation destined to possess the Land of Promise. Like Leviticus, Deuteronomy contains a vast amount of legal detail, but its emphasis is on laypersons rather than the priests. Moses reminds the new generation of the importance of obedience if they are to learn from the sad example of their parents.

The name of the book comes from the Greek word *Deuteronomion*, meaning "second law," which was incorrectly used in the Septuagint to translate Deut. 17:18 (the NKJV correctly renders it "a copy of this law"). Deuteronomy, however, is not a second law but an adaptation and expansion of much of the original law given on Mt. Sinai.

Author

The Mosaic authorship of Deuteronomy has been vigorously attacked by critics who claim that Moses is only the originator of the traditions upon which these laws are based. The usual argument is that the book was anonymously written not long before 621 B.C. and used by King Josiah to bring about his religious reform.

Both the internal and external evidence for Mosaic authorship is strong, however. Deuteronomy itself includes about forty claims that Moses wrote it. The book appears to fit the time of Moses, not that of Josiah, and geographical and historical details indicate a firsthand knowledge of the period between the Exodus and the Conquest. Furthermore, the remainder of the Old Testament attributes Deuteronomy and the rest of the Pentateuch to Moses (Josh. 1:7; Judg. 3:4; 1 Kin. 2:3; Ezra 3:2; Ps. 103:7; Mal. 4:4). Christ himself directly attributes it to Moses (Matt. 19:7–9; John 5:45–47). Finally, recent studies have shown that Deuteronomy appears to follow the treaty form used in the fifteenth and fourteenth centuries B.C., a form appropriate for this covenant renewal document.

Deuteronomy at a Glance

FOCUS	FIRST SERMON	SECOND SERMON				THIRD SERMON		
REFERENCE	1:1 ——— 4:44	——— 12:1 ——— 16:18 —		21:1 —	27:1 ———	29:1 ———	31:1 — 34:12	
DIVISION	REVIEW OF GOD'S ACTS FOR ISRAEL	EXPOSITION OF THE DECALOGUE	CEREMONIAL LAWS	CIVIL LAWS	SOCIAL LAWS	RATIFICATION OF COVENANT	PALESTINIAN COVENANT	TRANSITION OF COVENANT MEDIATOR
TOPIC	WHAT GOD HAS DONE	WHAT GOD EXPECTED OF ISRAEL				WHAT GOD WILL DO		
	HISTORICAL	LEGAL				PROPHETICAL		
LOCATION	PLAINS OF MOAB							
TIME	c. 1 MONTH							

Nelson's Complete Book of Bible Maps and Charts © 1993 by Thomas Nelson, Inc.

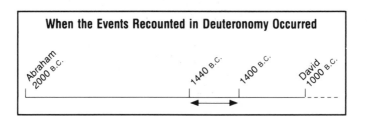

When the Events Recounted in Deuteronomy Occurred

Abraham 2000 B.C. ———— 1440 B.C. ———— 1400 B.C. ———— David 1000 B.C.

Date

Like Leviticus, Deuteronomy does not progress historically. It takes place entirely on the plains of Moab due east of Jericho and the Jordan River and covers about one month. The book was written at the end of the forty-year period in the wilderness (c. 1405 B.C.) when the new generation was on the verge of entering Canaan.

Themes and Literary Structure

Deuteronomy, in its broadest outline, is the record of the renewal of the covenant given at Mt. Sinai. This covenant is reviewed, expanded, enlarged, and finally ratified in the plains of Moab. Moses accomplishes this primarily through three sermons that move from a retrospective, to an introspective, and finally to a prospective look at God's dealings with Israel.

Moses first sermon (1:1—4:43) provides the background of the covenant by stressing what God has done for Israel since the Exodus from Egypt. The theme of God's provision for and protection of His people is highlighted, together with the divine punishment which follows disobedience.

The second discourse covers the specific requirements of the covenant, adapting the laws of Exodus to the new situation which would prevail after they had entered the Promised Land. Thus special attention is given to prohibitions of idolatry and other pagan practices, the establishment of a central sanctuary, and preparation for a kingdom.

In the third discourse Moses writes history in advance. He predicts what will befall Israel in the near future (blessings and cursings) and in the distant future (dispersion among the nations and eventual return). Moses lists the terms of the covenant soon to be ratified by the people. Finally, because Moses will not be allowed to enter the land, he appoints Joshua as his successor and delivers a farewell address to the nation. Chapter 34 contains an obituary for Moses, perhaps written by his successor Joshua.

OUTLINE OF DEUTERONOMY

Part One: Moses' First Sermon: "What God Has Done for Israel" (1:1—4:43)

Capital Punishment

As part of the covenant curses for disobedience, the Law of Moses prescribes the death penalty for a variety of serious offenses. These offenses constituted particularly gross violations of God's covenant with His people. While such penalties may seem severe to modern men and women, they serve to underscore the high standard of conduct to which God's people are called. Israel had received many rich blessings from God, and "to whom much is given, from him much will be required" (Luke 12:48).

Crimes Allowing the Death Penalty

Crime	Scripture Reference
1. Premeditated Murder—Death Penalty Required	Exodus 21:12–14, 22, 23
2. Kidnapping	Exodus 21:16; Deuteronomy 24:7
3. Striking or Cursing Parents	Exodus 21:15; Leviticus 20:9; Proverbs 20:20; Matthew 15:4; Mark 7:10
4. Magic and Divination	Exodus 22:18
5. Bestiality	Exodus 22:19; Leviticus 20:15, 16
6. Sacrificing to False Gods	Exodus 22:20
7. Profaning the Sabbath	Exodus 35:2; Numbers 15:32–36
8. Offering Human Sacrifice	Leviticus 20:2
9. Adultery	Leviticus 20:10–21; Deuteronomy 22:22
10. Incest	Leviticus 20:11, 12, 14
11. Homosexuality	Leviticus 20:13
12. Blasphemy	Leviticus 24:11–14, 16, 23
13. False Prophecy	Deuteronomy 13:1–10
14. Incorrigible Rebelliousness	Deuteronomy 17:12; 21:18–21
15. Fornication	Deuteronomy 22:20, 21
16. Rape of Betrothed Virgin	Deuteronomy 22:23–27

Nelson's Complete Book of Bible Maps and Charts © 1993 by Thomas Nelson, Inc.

Mountains of the Bible

Mountains are a location where God has met with His people throughout the Scripture. God gave Moses the Law atop Mt. Sinai, and Moses commanded that an altar be built atop Mt. Ebal when the Israelites entered the Promised Land. Although God did not permit Moses to enter that long-awaited land, He did allow him to view it from Mt. Pisgah. God buried Moses there on the mountain with His own hands. Following are several significant mountains of the Scriptures:

Mt. Ararat: Ararat (in modern Turkey), where Noah's ark came to rest (Gen. 8:4).

Mt. Carmel: Carmel, where Elijah was victorious over the prophets of Baal (1 Kin. 18:9–42).

Mt. Ebal: Ebal (opposite Mt. Gerizim), where Moses commanded that an altar be built after the Hebrews entered the Promised Land.

Mt. Gerizim: Gerizim, where Jesus talked with the Samaritan woman at the well (John 4:20).

Mt. Gilboa: Gilboa, where King Saul and his sons were killed in a battle with the Philistines (1 Chr. 10:1, 8).

Mt. Hermon: Hermon, a mountain range that marked the northern limit of the conquest of Canaan (Josh. 11:3, 17).

Mt. Lebanon: Lebanon, source of cedar wood for Solomon's temple in Jerusalem (1 Kin. 5:14, 18).

Mt. Olivet: Olivet, or Mt. of Olives, where Jesus gave the discourse on His Second Coming (Matt. 24:3).

Mt. Pisgah: Pisgah, or Nebo, where Moses viewed the Promised Land.

Mt. Sinai: Sinai, or Horeb (near Egypt), where the Law was given to Moses (Ex. 19:2–25).

Hymns and Songs

The earliest recorded song in the Bible is referred to as the Song of Moses (see Ex. 15). This hymn was sung by the people to celebrate God's miraculous deliverance of the Hebrews from the Egyptian army at the Red Sea (Ex. 14:3–30), and Moses sang again just before his death. Other significant hymns and songs in the Old Testament include the following:

Personality	Description	Biblical Reference
Israelites	Sung by the people as they dug life-saving wells in the wilderness	Num. 21:14–18
Moses	A song of praise to God by Moses just before his death	Deut. 32:1–44
Deborah and Barak	A victory song after Israel's defeat of the Canaanites	Judg. 5:1–31
Israelite Women	A song to celebrate David's defeat of Goliath	1 Sam. 18:6, 7
Levite Singers	A song of praise at the dedication of the temple in Jerusalem	2 Chr. 5:12–14
Levite Singers	A song of praise, presented as a marching song as the army of Israel prepared for battle	2 Chr. 20:20–23
Levite Singers	A song at the temple restoration ceremony during Hezekiah's reign	2 Chr. 29:25–30

THE HISTORICAL BOOKS

The books from Joshua through Esther in the Old Testament are known as the historical books. They cover about seven hundred years in the history of God's chosen people, the nation of Israel.

Major events covered by these books include (1) the settlement of the people in the Promised Land after their escape from Egypt and their years of wandering in the wilderness; (2) the transition from rule by judges to rule by kings; (3) David's anointing as king of the united kingdom; (4) the division of the nation into northern and southern factions; (5) the destruction of the northern kingdom; and (6) the captivity and return of the southern kingdom.

Here are brief summaries of the themes of the twelve books in this significant section of the Old Testament:

Joshua: The capture and settlement of the Promised Land.

Judges: The nation of Israel is rescued by a series of judges, or military leaders. Three of the best-known deliverers were Deborah, Gideon, and Samson.

Ruth: A beautiful story of God's love and care.

Samuel anoints David as king.

1 and 2 Samuel: The early history of Israel, including the reigns of Saul and David.

1 and 2 Kings: A political history of Israel focusing on the reigns of selected kings from the time of Solomon to the captivity of the Jewish people by the Babylonians.

1 and 2 Chronicles: A religious history of Israel, covering the same period as 2 Samuel and 1 and 2 Kings.

Ezra: The return of the Jewish people from captivity in Babylon to Jerusalem.

Nehemiah: The rebuilding of the walls of Jerusalem after the Jewish exiles returned from Babylon.

Esther: God's care for His people under gentile rule.

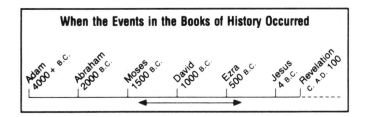

When the Events in the Books of History Occurred

Adam 4000+ B.C. · Abraham 2000 B.C. · Moses 1500 B.C. · David 1000 B.C. · Ezra 500 B.C. · Jesus 4 B.C. · Revelation c. A.D. 100

JOSHUA

oshua, the first of the twelve historical books (Joshua—Esther), forges a link between the Pentateuch and the remainder of Israel's history. Through three major military campaigns, the people of Israel learn a crucial lesson under Joshua's capable leadership: victory comes through faith in God and obedience to His word, rather than through numerical or military superiority.

This theme is underscored by the name of the book itself. Joshua's name, which means "Yahweh is Salvation," is symbolic of the fact that although he is the leader of Israel during the conquest, the Lord is the Conqueror.

Author

Jewish tradition assigns authorship of this book to Joshua himself, and there is little doubt that portions of the book are to be ascribed to him (24:26). Some narratives were added later, however, such as Othniel's capture of Kirjath Sepher (15:13–19), Dan's migration to the north (19:47), and the account of Joshua's death and burial (24:29–33). In addition, the recurring phrase "to this day" (5:9; 13:13; 15:63) indicates a time of writing later than the events themselves. Thus, the final composition of the book was completed after the lifetime of Joshua, perhaps as late as the early kingdom period under Saul.

Date

While a precise date for the composition of Joshua is uncertain, the events described take place between the beginning of the Conquest (1405 B.C.) and the death of Joshua (c. 1390 B.C.). If the later date of the Exodus is accepted (see Exodus), however, the beginning of the Conquest would date to c. 1250–1200 B.C.

Themes and Literary Structure

The book of Joshua divides neatly into two principal sections: chapters 1—12 record the Conquest; chapters 13—24 describe the assignment of tribal territories and the dispersal of the tribes throughout the Land of Promise.

Continued on page 68

Joshua at a Glance

FOCUS	CONQUEST OF CANAAN		SETTLEMENT IN CANAAN			
REFERENCE	1:1 ——— 6:1 ———		13:8 ——— 14:1 ———		20:1 ——— 22:1 ———	24:33
DIVISION	PREPARATION OF ISRAEL	CONQUEST OF CANAAN	SETTLEMENT OF EAST JORDAN	SETTLEMENT OF WEST JORDAN	SETTLEMENT OF RELIGIOUS COMMUNITY	CONDITIONS FOR CONTINUED SETTLEMENT
TOPIC	ENTERING CANAAN	CONQUERING CANAAN	DIVIDING CANAAN			
	PREPARATION	SUBJECTION	POSSESSION			
LOCATION	JORDAN RIVER	CANAAN	TWO AND A HALF TRIBES—EAST JORDAN NINE AND A HALF TRIBES—WEST JORDAN			
TIME	c. 1 MONTH	c. 7 YEARS	c. 8 YEARS			

Nelson's Complete Book of Bible Maps and Charts © 1993 by Thomas Nelson, Inc.

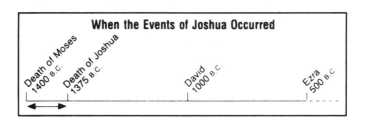

When the Events of Joshua Occurred

Death of Moses 1400 B.C.
Death of Joshua 1375 B.C.
David 1000 B.C.
Ezra 500 B.C.

Continued from page 66

The theme of conquest and occupation pervades the book of Joshua. The setting of the first five chapters begins east of the Jordan River as Joshua replaces Moses, and Israel crosses the Jordan on dry land and prepares for war. Like a wise general, Joshua utilizes a divide-and-conquer strategy. His campaign begins in central Canaan (chs. 6—8), thus preventing a massive Canaanite alliance against Israel. Then Joshua moves to southern Canaan (chs. 9, 10), and finally to northern Canaan (chs. 11, 12).

Though there are no direct messianic prophecies in the book, Joshua is clearly a type of Christ. His name *Yeshua* ("Yahweh is Salvation") is the Hebrew equivalent of the name "Jesus." In his role of triumphantly leading the people into their possessions, he foreshadows the One who will bring "many sons to glory" (Heb. 2:10).

The scarlet cord, which provided safety for Rahab and her house (Josh. 2:17–21), portrays safety through the blood of Jesus (Heb. 9:19–22). Amazingly, this gentile woman is found in the genealogy of Jesus Christ (Matt. 1:5).

OUTLINE OF JOSHUA

Joshua's Victories

Under Joshua's leadership, the people of Israel entered Canaan about 1405 B.C. to drive out the Canaanites and claim the Land of Promise. A careful study of the military campaigns described in the book of Joshua shows that Joshua had a carefully planned strategy of conquest. He first established the Israelites in the central part of Canaan, then conducted campaigns into the southern and northern parts of the land to complete the takeover. While these campaigns are described briefly in Joshua 1—11, they probably covered a period of about seven years, from 1405 to 1398 B.C. By the time Joshua died (24:29), the Israelites had driven most of the Canaanites out of Palestine and divided the land among the twelve tribes of Israel.

    See maps, "The Conquest of Cannan," page 70.

Settlement of Tribes

After the conquest of the Promised Land under Joshua, the land formerly occupied by the Canaanites was assigned to the descendants of the sons of Jacob (13—21). In a restricted sense, the land stretched from the Jordan River on the east to the Great Sea (Mediterranean) on the west. Reuben, Gad, and Manasseh eventually inhabited land east of the Jordan. From north to south, it covered the territory between the Sinai peninsula and the ancient coastal nation of Phoenicia. Land was allotted to the descendants of all Jacob's sons except Levi (13:33). Levi's portion went to the two sons of Joseph—Manasseh and Ephraim (14:3, 4). The Levites were set apart for priestly service; their portion was to be God Himself (Num. 18:20). However, God provided 48 cities

Continued on page 71

The Conquest of Canaan

Central and Southern Campaigns

From the military camp at Gilgal Joshua launched two campaigns, thus conquering central and southern Canaan.

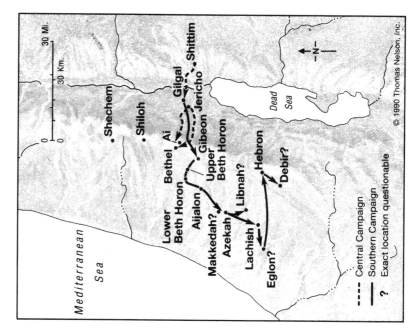

Northern Campaign

After conquering central and southern Canaan, Joshua took his forces northward to Hazor.

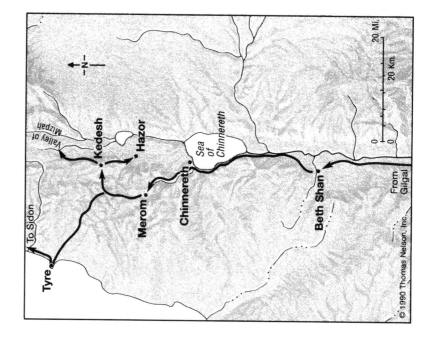

Continued from page 69

throughout Palestine for use by the Levites (Josh. 21:1–42). This map shows the approximate locations of the tribal settlements, based on the boundaries mentioned in the book of Joshua.

See map, "Settlement of the Tribes," page 72.

Cities of Refuge

Six cities of refuge were designated throughout Israel in Old Testament times to provide a haven for people who killed other persons by accident. Protection like this was necessary because of the "avenger of blood," the relative who considered it his duty to slay the killer. Eligibility for refuge was determined by a judge. For convenience, three of the cities were located on either side of the Jordan River.

See map, "Cities of Refuge," page 73.

Joshua's Charges to Israel

Joshua's farewell addresses in chapters 23 and 24 provide a fitting conclusion to the book as a whole. A comparison of chapters 23 and 24 suggests that chapter 23 was spoken specifically to the leaders of Israel (23:2), whereas chapter 24 was to the whole assembly (24:1).

In chapter 23, Joshua rehearses the mighty acts of God on Israel's behalf in giving them the Land of Promise, and he exhorts the leaders to continued faithfulness in the future. Chapter 24 constitutes a covenant renewal ceremony in which Israel commits herself to serve the Lord and to reject the worship of all false gods. The form of the covenant here, as well as in Deuteronomy, has been recognized as based upon a common ancient treaty formula. The formula contains a preamble ("Thus says the LORD God of Israel"); a historical prologue (vv. 2–13); covenant stipulation and requirements (vv. 14, 15); warnings against covenant disobedience (vv. 19, 20); witnesses (v. 22); and a depositing of the covenant document (v. 26).

Tribal Identities

The twelve tribes of Israel were the tribes of: (1) Reuben; (2) Simeon; (3) Levi; (4) Judah; (5) Dan; (6) Naphtali; (7) Gad; (8) Asher; (9) Issachar; (10) Zebulun; (11) Joseph (Ephraim and Manasseh); (12) Benjamin.

Famous descendants from these tribes were: Levi—Aaron, Moses, Eli, Ezra, John the Baptist; Judah—Caleb, David, Solomon, Isaiah (?), Jesus Christ; Dan—Samson; Naphtali—Barak, Elijah (?); Asher—Anna; Joseph (Ephraim and Manasseh)—Joshua, Gideon, Samuel; Benjamin—Saul, Esther, Saul of Tarsus (Paul).

Settlement of the Tribes

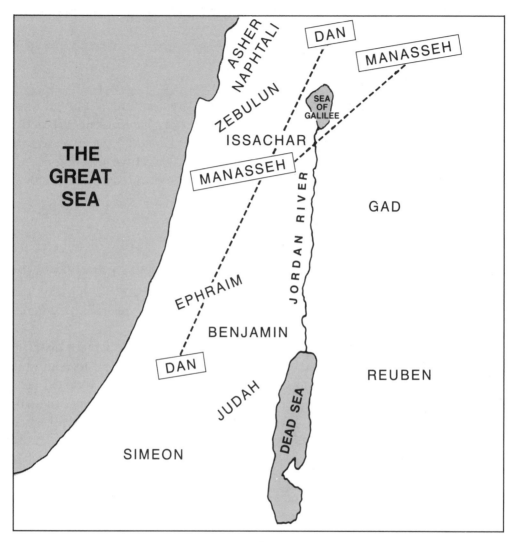

THE GREAT SEA

ASHER
NAPHTALI
ZEBULUN
ISSACHAR

SEA OF GALILEE

DAN

MANASSEH

MANASSEH

JORDAN RIVER

GAD

EPHRAIM

BENJAMIN

DAN

REUBEN

JUDAH

DEAD SEA

SIMEON

Nelson's Complete Book of Bible Maps and Charts © 1993 by Thomas Nelson, Inc.

Cities of Refuge

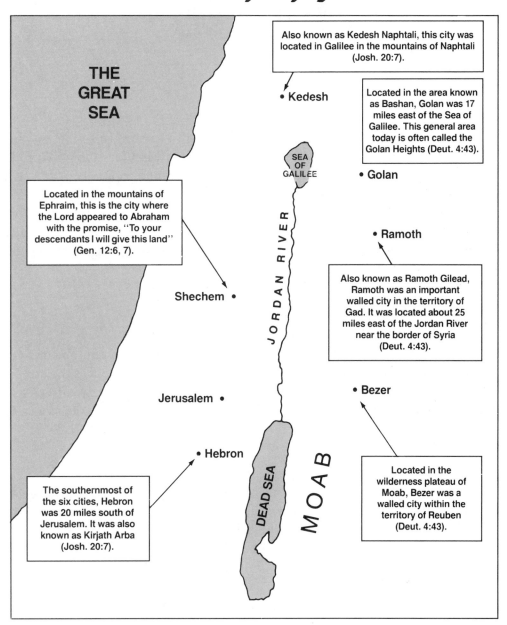

Also known as Kedesh Naphtali, this city was located in Galilee in the mountains of Naphtali (Josh. 20:7).

Located in the area known as Bashan, Golan was 17 miles east of the Sea of Galilee. This general area today is often called the Golan Heights (Deut. 4:43).

Located in the mountains of Ephraim, this is the city where the Lord appeared to Abraham with the promise, "To your descendants I will give this land" (Gen. 12:6, 7).

Also known as Ramoth Gilead, Ramoth was an important walled city in the territory of Gad. It was located about 25 miles east of the Jordan River near the border of Syria (Deut. 4:43).

The southernmost of the six cities, Hebron was 20 miles south of Jerusalem. It was also known as Kirjath Arba (Josh. 20:7).

Located in the wilderness plateau of Moab, Bezer was a walled city within the territory of Reuben (Deut. 4:43).

THE GREAT SEA

SEA OF GALILEE

• Kedesh

• Golan

• Ramoth

JORDAN RIVER

Shechem •

• Bezer

Jerusalem •

• Hebron

DEAD SEA

MOAB

JUDGES

The book of Judges stands in stark contrast to Joshua. In Joshua an obedient people conquered the land through trust in the power of God. In Judges, however, a disobedient and idolatrous people are repeatedly oppressed by their enemies.

The Hebrew title of the book is *Shophetim*, meaning "judges." The word not only carries the idea of maintaining justice and settling disputes but can also have the meaning "liberate" and "deliver." First the judges deliver the people, then they rule and administer justice.

Author

The author of Judges is anonymous, but Samuel or one of his prophetic students may have written it. Jewish tradition contained in the Talmud attributes Judges to Samuel, and certainly he was the crucial link between the period of the judges and the period of the kings. It is likely that Samuel or one of his contemporaries compiled the book from oral and written sources.

Date

The approximate date of composition may be fixed by a number of statements in the book itself. The passages 18:31 and 20:27 show that Judges was written after the ark of the covenant was removed from Shiloh (cf. 1 Sam. 4:3–11). The repeated phrase "In those days there was no king in Israel" (17:6; 18:1; 19:1; 21:25) indicates that Judges was written after the commencement of the monarchy. The fact that the Jebusites were dwelling in Jerusalem "to this day" (1:21) means that it was written before 1004 B.C. when David took control of the city (2 Sam. 5:5–9).

The events covered in Judges range from c. 1380 B.C. to 1045 B.C. Evidently, the rulerships of some of the judges overlap because not all of them ruled over the entire land. Judges describes cycles of apostasy, oppression, and deliverance in the southern region (3:7–31), the central region (6:1—10:5), the eastern region (10:6—12:15), and the western region (13:1—16:31).

Judges at a Glance

FOCUS	DETERIORATION		DELIVERANCE						DEPRAVITY		
REFERENCE	1:1 ——— 2:1 — 3:5 ——— 4:1 ——— 6:1 ——— 10:6 ——— 12:8 ——— 13:1 ——— 17:1 ——— 19:1 ——— 20:1 — 21:25										
DIVISION	ISRAEL FAILS TO COMPLETE THE CONQUEST	GOD JUDGES ISRAEL	SOUTHERN CAMPAIGN	NORTHERN CAMPAIGN (1st)	CENTRAL CAMPAIGN	EASTERN CAMPAIGN	NORTHERN CAMPAIGN (2nd)	WESTERN CAMPAIGN	SIN OF IDOLATRY	SIN OF IM-MORALITY	SIN OF CIVIL WAR
TOPIC	CAUSES OF THE CYCLES		CURSE OF THE CYCLES						CONDITIONS DURING THE CYCLES		
	LIVING WITH THE CANAANITES		WAR WITH THE CANAANITES						LIVING LIKE THE CANAANITES		
LOCATION	CANAAN										
TIME	c. 350 YEARS										

Nelson's Complete Book of Bible Maps and Charts © 1993 by Thomas Nelson, Inc.

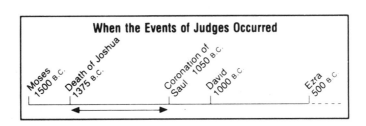

When the Events of Judges Occurred

Moses 1500 B.C. — Death of Joshua 1375 B.C. — Coronation of Saul 1050 B.C. — David 1000 B.C. — Ezra 500 B.C.

Themes and Literary Structure

The book of Judges is organized primarily along thematic rather than chronological lines. The book opens with a description of Israel's deterioration, continues with seven cycles of oppression and deliverance, and concludes with two vivid examples of Israel's depravity.

The theme of deterioration is highlighted as Judges begins with short-lived military successes after the death of Joshua but quickly turns to the repeated failure of the people to drive out their enemies. The primary reasons for their failure are a lack of faith and a lack of obedience to God (2:1–3).

Repeated deliverances by God are described in the middle section of the book (3:5—16:31) which presents seven cycles of apostasy, oppression, cry for deliverance, salvation, and rest. Israel vacillates between obedience and apostasy as the people continually fail to learn from their mistakes. Nevertheless, the times of rest and peace are longer than the times of bondage, and the monotony of Israel's sins can be contrasted with the creativity of God's methods of deliverance.

See chart, "The Period of the Judges," page 81.

The depravity characteristic of the time of the judges is illustrated in chapters 17—21 with vivid examples of personal and tribal idolatry and immorality. The book as a whole illustrates the sad results of Israel's disobedience as summarized in 21:25: "In those days *there was* no king in Israel; everyone did *what was* right in his own eyes."

OUTLINE OF JUDGES

Part One: The Deterioration of Israel and Failure to Complete the Conquest (1:1—3:4)

Israel's Judges

After the death of Joshua, the nation of Israel was ruled by judges, or heroic military deliverers, for about 300 years until the united monarchy was established under King Saul. The era of the judges was a time of instability and moral depravity, a dark period when "everyone did *what was* right in his own eyes" (17:6). The judges tried to rally the people against their enemies, but many of the judges were morally weak and the people often turned to idolatry. Along with the well-known judges, there were several minor judges whose battles are not recorded in the Bible: Abimelech, Tola, Jair, Ibzan, Elon, and Abdon.

See map, "Israel's Judges," page 80.

Gideon

In his campaign against Midian, Gideon's small force of three hundred men surprised the Midianites encamped in the Valley of Jezreel. Following the initial night attack, the confused Midianites fled and Gideon and his men pursued their kings, Zebah and Zalmunna, across the Jordan River to Karkor where they were captured (8:10–21).

The fifth of the judges described in the book (6:11—8:35), Gideon's example is typical. Called by the angel of the Lord to deliver Israel from the oppression of the Midianites, Gideon acted to stamp out idolatrous practices, and his miraculous victory over the Midianite horde was a vivid illustration to Israel of God's power to save His people. Nevertheless, even after his great victory, Gideon himself became a snare and a cause of idolatry to his own family and to Israel by making a sacred ephod (8:22–28).

The Battles of Gideon

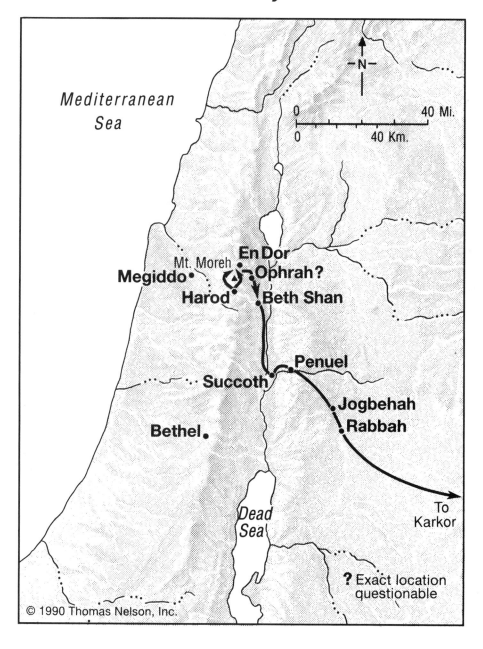

Israel's Judges

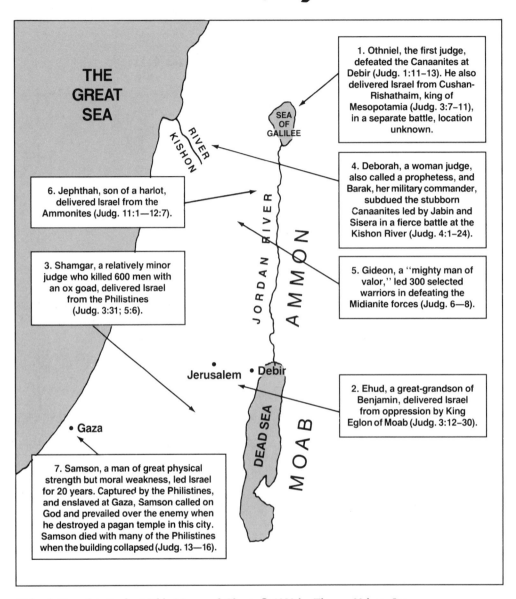

THE GREAT SEA

SEA OF GALILEE

RIVER KISHON

JORDAN RIVER

AMMON

MOAB

DEAD SEA

Jerusalem • Debir

• Gaza

1. Othniel, the first judge, defeated the Canaanites at Debir (Judg. 1:11–13). He also delivered Israel from Cushan-Rishathaim, king of Mesopotamia (Judg. 3:7–11), in a separate battle, location unknown.

4. Deborah, a woman judge, also called a prophetess, and Barak, her military commander, subdued the stubborn Canaanites led by Jabin and Sisera in a fierce battle at the Kishon River (Judg. 4:1–24).

6. Jephthah, son of a harlot, delivered Israel from the Ammonites (Judg. 11:1—12:7).

5. Gideon, a "mighty man of valor," led 300 selected warriors in defeating the Midianite forces (Judg. 6—8).

3. Shamgar, a relatively minor judge who killed 600 men with an ox goad, delivered Israel from the Philistines (Judg. 3:31; 5:6).

2. Ehud, a great-grandson of Benjamin, delivered Israel from oppression by King Eglon of Moab (Judg. 3:12–30).

7. Samson, a man of great physical strength but moral weakness, led Israel for 20 years. Captured by the Philistines, and enslaved at Gaza, Samson called on God and prevailed over the enemy when he destroyed a pagan temple in this city. Samson died with many of the Philistines when the building collapsed (Judg. 13—16).

Nelson's Complete Book of Bible Maps and Charts © 1993 by Thomas Nelson, Inc.

The Period of the Judges

Events and Judges	Years
Israel serves Cushan-Rishathaim (3:7, 8)	8
Peace following Othniel's deliverance (3:7–11)	40
Israel serves Moab (3:12)	18
Peace follows Ehud's deliverance (3:12–30)	80
Shamgar delivers Israel from Philistines (3:31)	1
Israel serves Canaan (4:1–3)	20
Peace following deliverance by Deborah and Barak (4:1—5:31)	40
Israel serves Midian (6:1–6)	7
Peace following Gideon's deliverance (6:1—8:35)	40
Abimelech, king of Israel (9:1–57)	3
Tola's career (10:1, 2)	23
Jair's career (10:3–5)	22
Israel serves Ammon and Philistia (10:6–10)	18
Jephthah's career (10:6—12:7)	6
Ibzan's career (12:8–10)	7
Elon's career (12:11, 12)	10
Abdon's career (12:13–15)	8
Israel serves Philistia (13:1)	40
Samson's career (12:1—16:31)	20

Nelson's Complete Book of Bible Maps and Charts © 1993 by Thomas Nelson, Inc.

The Period of the Judges (1375–1050 B.C.)

Judge and Tribe	Scripture References	Major Events	Oppressors	Period of Oppression	Period of Rest
(1) **Othniel** (Judah) Son of Kenaz, the younger brother of Caleb	Judg. 1:11–15; 3:1–11 Josh. 15:16–19 1 Chr. 4:13	(1) Othniel was the nephew of Caleb (3:11) and became his son-in-law after the capture of Kirjath Sepher (1:12, 13). (2) Defeated Cushan-Rishathaim, king of Mesopotamia (3:10).	Cushan-Rishathaim, king of Mesopotamia (3:8)	8 years (3:8)	40 years (3:11)
(2) **Ehud** (Benjamin) Son of Gera	Judg. 3:12—4:1	(1) Ehud, the left-handed Benjamite, personally slew Eglon, the fat king of Moab (3:21, 22). (2) Led in the slaying of 10,000 Moabites (3:29).	Eglon, king of Moab (3:12) Ammonites (3:13) Amalekites (3:13)	18 years (3:14)	80 years (3:30)
(3) **Shamgar** (Perhaps foreign) Son of Anath	Judg. 3:31; 5:6	(1) Shamgar slew 600 Philistines with an oxgoad (3:31).	Philistines (3:31)	Not given	Not given
(4) **Deborah** (Ephraim) and **Barak** (Naphtali) Son of Abinoam	Judg. 4:1—5:31 Heb. 11:32	(1) Deborah, a prophetess and judge, was the wife of Lapidoth (4:4; 5:7). (2) Deborah and Barak defeated Sisera (with his 900 iron chariots) at the Battle of Kishon (4:13–16). (3) Sisera killed by Jael, the wife of Heber, with a tent peg (4:21). (4) The Song of Deborah (ch. 5) recounts the victory of Deborah and Barak over Sisera. (5) Barak is listed among the "Heroes of the Faith" in Heb. 11:32.	Jabin, king of Canaan (4:2); Sisera was the commander of his army (4:2)	20 years (4:3)	40 years (5:31)
(5) **Gideon** (Manasseh) Son of Joash the Abiezrite Also called: Jerubbaal (6:32; 7:1); Jerubbesheth (2 Sam. 11:21)	Judg. 6:1—8:32 Heb. 11:32	(1) The Angel of the Lord appeared to Gideon at Ophrah as he was beating out wheat in the winepress (6:11–18). (2) Gideon's offering consumed by fire (6:19–24). (3) Gideon destroyed the altar of Baal by night (6:25–27). (4) Gideon "put out the fleece" twice for a "sign" (6:36–40). (5) Gideon reduced his army from 32,000 to 10,000 to 300 (7:2–8); he routed the Midianites with trumpets, pitchers, and torches (7:16–22). (6) Oreb and Zeeb killed by the Ephraimites (7:24—8:3). (7) Gideon took revenge on the men of Succoth and Penuel for not giving his army bread (8:5–9, 14–17). (8) Gideon killed Zebah and Zalmunna (Midianite kings) in revenge for the death of his brothers at Tabor (8:18–21). (9) Gideon made a gold ephod which led the people into idolatry (8:24–27).	Midianites (6:1, 3, 33; 7:12) Amalekites (6:3, 33; 7:12) "People of the East" (6:3, 33; 7:12)	7 years (6:1)	40 years (8:28)
(6) **Abimelech** (Manasseh) Son of Gideon by a concubine	Judg. 8:33—9:57 2 Sam. 11:21	(1) Abimelech slew all his half brothers (70) except Jotham, the youngest (9:5). (2) Abimelech defeated Gaal, who conspired against him (9:26–41). (3) Abimelech captured Shechem and razed the city (9:42–49). (4) At Thebez a woman threw a millstone which hit Abimelech on the head; Abimelech then had his armorbearer kill him with a sword (9:50–54).	Civil war		Abimelech ruled over Israel 3 years (9:22)

Judge and Tribe	Scripture References	Major Events	Oppressors	Period of Oppression	Period of Rest
(7) **Tola** (Issachar) Son of Puah	Judg. 10:1, 2	(1) Tola was probably from one of the leading families of Issachar (cf. Gen. 46:13; Num. 26:23).			Judged Israel 23 years (10:2)
(8) **Jair** (Gilead-Manasseh)	Judg. 10:3–5	(1) Jair was probably a descendant of the Jair who distinguished himself during the days of Moses and Joshua (Num. 32:41; Deut. 3:14; Josh. 13:30; 1 Kin. 4:13; 1 Chr. 2:21). (2) Jair had 30 sons who were itinerant judges (10:4).			Judged Israel 22 years (10:3)
(9) **Jephthah** (Gilead-Manasseh) Son of Gilead by a harlot (11:1)	Judg. 10:6—12:7 Heb. 11:32	(1) Jephthah was the son of Gilead by a harlot (11:1); he was driven off by his vengeful half brothers and fled to the land of Tob (11:2, 3). (2) Elders of Gilead brought Jephthah back and made him their chief at Mizpah (11:4–11). (3) Jephthah sent a message to the King of Ammon saying that the Israelites had been in possession of Gilead for 300 years—too long for the Ammonites to challenge their right to it (11:26). (4) Jephthah subdued the Ammonites, conquering some 20 cities (11:32, 33). (5) Jephthah devoted his daughter to the service of the Lord for the rest of her life, in fulfillment of his foolish vow (11:31–40). (6) Jephthah defeated the Ephraimites, who were offended because they had not been asked to join in the battle against the Ammonites (12:1–6).	Philistines (10:7) Ammonites (10:7) Civil war with the Ephraimites (12:4)	18 years (10:8)	Judged Israel 6 years (12:7)
(10) **Ibzan** (Judah or Zebulun)ˈ (Bethlehem-Zebulun; cf. Josh. 19:15)	Judg. 12:8–10	(1) Ibzan had 30 sons and 30 daughters, for whom he arranged marriages; this indicates his wealth and social prominence (12:9). (2) A Jewish tradition identifies Ibzan with Boaz of Bethlehem-Judah.			Judged Israel 7 years (12:9)
(11) **Elon** (Zebulun)	Judg. 12:11, 12	(1) The only information given concerning Elon is that he was buried at the Aijalon in Zebulun, distinguishing it from the better-known Aijalon in Danite territory (12:12).			Judged Israel 10 years (12:11)
(12) **Abdon** (Ephraim, 12:15) Son of Hillel	Judg. 12:13–15	(1) The wealth and prominence of Abdon is revealed by the fact that he had 40 sons and 30 grandsons, who all rode on mounts (12:14). (2) Abdon was a native of Pirathon and was later buried there (12:13, 15).			Judged Israel 8 years (12:14)
(13) **Samson** (Dan, 13:2) Son of Manoah	Judg. 13:1— 16:31 Heb. 11:32	(1) Samson's birth was announced by the Angel of the Lord; he was consecrated a Nazirite from birth (ch. 13). (2) Samson slew a lion barehanded (14:5, 6). (3) Samson slew 30 Philistines at Ashkelon (14:19). (4) Samson caught 300 foxes, tied them in pairs with a torch between their tails, and turned them into the grain fields of the Philistines (15:1–8). (5) Samson slew a thousand Philistines with the jawbone of an ass (15:14–19). (6) Samson carried off the gate of Gaza (16:1–3). (7) Samson was conquered by Delilah, blinded, and imprisoned at Gaza (16:4–22). (8) Samson pulled down the Temple of Dagon, killing himself and about 3,000 Philistines (16:23–31).	Philistines (13:1)	40 years (13:1)	Judged Israel 20 years (15:20; 16:31)

Nelson's Complete Book of Bible Maps and Charts © 1993 by Thomas Nelson, Inc.

RUTH

R uth is a story of love, devotion, and redemption set in the distressing context of the period of the judges. It presents a Moabite woman who forsakes her pagan heritage in order to cling to the people of Israel and to the God of Israel. Because of her faithfulness in a time of national faithlessness, God rewards her by giving her a new husband, a son, and a privileged position in the ancestral line of David and Christ.

Author

The author of Ruth is not identified by the text. Jewish tradition attributes the work to Samuel, but this is unlikely since David appears in Ruth 4:17, 22, and Samuel died prior to David's coronation as king. The composition of the book probably dates to the early kingdom period. That David's son Solomon is not mentioned in the genealogy may indicate that Ruth was written during David's reign as king. The anonymity of the work should not, however, detract from its profound spiritual value and literary beauty.

Date

Though the date of composition is uncertain, the story of Ruth itself takes place in the latter part of the period of the judges (c. 1100 B.C.) and covers a time span of about twelve years. This period of Israel's history was generally a desert of rebellion and immorality, but the story of Ruth stands in contrast as an oasis of integrity and righteousness.

Themes and Literary Structure

The brief yet beautiful story of Ruth is crafted with care by its unknown author. As the chart "Ruth at a Glance" demonstrates, the narrative is symmetrical with a structure of parallel elements that meet in the middle of the book (the end of ch. 2).

This literary structure serves to highlight several important themes. Most prominent is the theme of redemption. The Hebrew word for kinsman *(goel)*

Continued on page 86

Ruth at a Glance

FOCUS	RUTH'S LOVE DEMONSTRATED		RUTH'S LOVE REWARDED	
REFERENCE	1:1 ——————— 1:19 —————————		3:1 ——————— 4:1 ——————— 4:22	
DIVISION	RUTH'S DECISION TO STAY WITH NAOMI	RUTH'S DEVOTION TO CARE FOR NAOMI	RUTH'S REQUEST FOR REDEMPTION BY BOAZ	RUTH'S REWARD OF REDEMPTION BY BOAZ
TOPIC	RUTH AND NAOMI		RUTH AND BOAZ	
	DEATH OF FAMILY	RUTH CARES FOR NAOMI	BOAZ CARES FOR RUTH	BIRTH OF FAMILY
LOCATION	MOAB	FIELDS OF BETHLEHEM	THRESHING FLOOR OF BETHLEHEM	BETHLEHEM
TIME	c. 12 YEARS			

Nelson's Complete Book of Bible Maps and Charts © 1993 by Thomas Nelson, Inc.

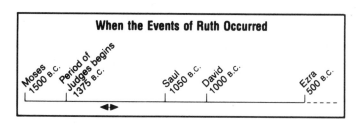

When the Events of Ruth Occurred

Moses 1500 B.C. — Period of Judges begins 1375 B.C. — Saul 1050 B.C. — David 1000 B.C. — Ezra 500 B.C.

Continued from page 84

appears thirteen times in Ruth and basically means "one who redeems." By buying back the land of Naomi, as well as marrying Ruth and fathering a son to keep the family line alive, Boaz acts as a redeemer. This temporal redemption by Boaz points to God's redeeming work, which reaches its climax in Christ's giving Himself "that He might redeem us from every lawless deed" (Titus 2:14).

Another key term in the story is "kindness," meaning covenant loyalty (1:8; 2:20; 3:10). Ruth and Boaz illustrate what covenant righteousness and loyalty are in an era when "everyone did *what was* right in his own eyes" (Judg. 21:25). This loyalty is expressed in the same terms as those describing God's covenant relationship with His people.

The providence of God is also highlighted. Although the book describes common people in common settings, they were being guided by the mysterious hand of God, who was using their uncommon faith to prepare the way for Israel's greatest king, David (4:22). The name of God occurs twenty-three times in the eighty-five verses of Ruth. No event in the life of God's people is insignificant, because He is constantly involved.

OUTLINE OF RUTH

Part One: Ruth's Love Is Demonstrated (1:1—2:23)

Part Two: Ruth's Love Is Rewarded (3:1—4:22)

From Outsider to Royal Ancestress

The book of Ruth begins in the land of Moab, a region east of the Dead Sea, where the family of Elimelech had moved to escape famine in their native Judah. The Moabites, descendants of Abraham's nephew Lot, worshiped Chemosh and other pagan gods. Scripture records a number of times when they fought against Israel (Judg. 3:12–30; 1 Sam. 14:47; 2 Sam. 8:11, 12; 2 Kin. 3:4–27). Ruth takes place about two centuries after the first war and about eighty years before the second.

With the death of Elimelech and his two sons, his widow Naomi and Ruth, the Moabite widow of one of the sons, returned to Judah to the ancestral home, Bethlehem. There they hoped to reclaim the family property.

See map, "The Story of Ruth," page 88.

Ruth—A Foreshadow of Redemption

Elimelech and Naomi were of the tribe of Judah and from the city of Bethlehem, where they had rights to ancestral property. But when Naomi's husband and sons died, she was unable to regain the property apart from two legal customs: "leviratic marriage" and "the redemption of the land." The "redemption of land" custom obligated the next of kin to buy back the property which had been sold due to foreclosure or poverty so as to keep it in the family (Lev. 25:25–28). The "leviratic marriage" custom required the nearest relative of a deceased man to marry his widow (Deut. 25:5–10). Any offspring from this union carried the name and inheritance of the former husband. Since Naomi was beyond childbearing years, her daughter-in-law Ruth became her substitute in marriage and bore a son to perpetuate the family name. Boaz accepted the obligations of both customs: as the redeemer (goel) he legally cleared the land of all further claims and as a responsible male relative he married Ruth and fathered a son to continue the family name.

The concept of the kinsman-redeemer or goel is an important portrayal of the work of Christ. The goel must (1) be related by blood to those he redeems (Deut. 25:5, 7–10; John 1:14; Rom. 1:3; Phil. 2:5–8; Heb. 2:14, 15); (2) must be able to pay the price of redemption (Ruth 2:1; 1 Pet. 1:18, 19); and (3) must be willing to redeem (Ruth 3:11; Matt. 20:28; John 10:15, 18; Heb. 10:7).

The Story of Ruth

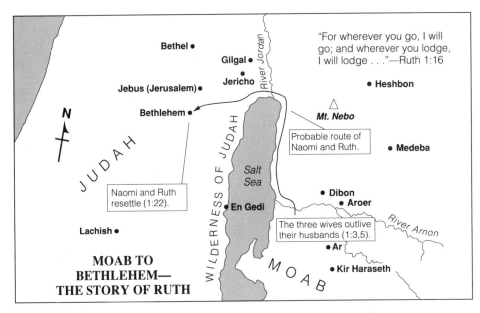

"For wherever you go, I will go; and wherever you lodge, I will lodge . . ."—Ruth 1:16

Bethel •

Gilgal •

Jericho •

Jebus (Jerusalem) •

Bethlehem •

• Heshbon

△ *Mt. Nebo*

Probable route of Naomi and Ruth.

• Medeba

River Jordan

N

J U D A H

W I L D E R N E S S   O F   J U D A H

Salt Sea

Naomi and Ruth resettle (1:22).

• En Gedi

• Dibon
• Aroer

River Arnon

The three wives outlive their husbands (1:3,5).

Lachish •

MOAB TO BETHLEHEM— THE STORY OF RUTH

M O A B

• Ar

• Kir Haraseth

Nelson's Complete Book of Bible Maps and Charts © 1993 by Thomas Nelson, Inc.

A Distinguished Descendant

The book of Ruth concludes with a ten-name genealogy (4:18–22), which presents the royal ancestry of David. Thus, the book ends with a reminder of redemption by focusing on this vital link in which Jew and Gentile unite to share in the ancestry of King David, through whom came Jesus the Christ (1 Chron. 2:5–15; Matt. 1:1; Luke 3:31–33). Indeed, the setting of the book of Ruth in Bethlehem of Judah brings to mind the birth of Ruth's descendant, Jesus Christ, in that same city of Bethlehem (Luke 2:7).

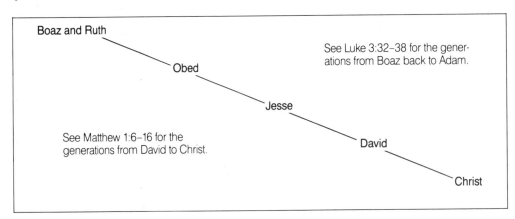

Boaz and Ruth

Obed

See Luke 3:32–38 for the generations from Boaz back to Adam.

Jesse

See Matthew 1:6–16 for the generations from David to Christ.

David

Christ

Kinsman-Redeemer

O.T. Qualification	Christ's Fulfillment
1. Blood Relationship	Gal. 4:4, 5; Heb. 2:16, 17
2. Necessary Resources	1 Cor. 6:20; 1 Pet. 1:18, 19
3. Willingness to Buy	John 10:15–18; 1 John 3:16

The Family Tree of Ruth

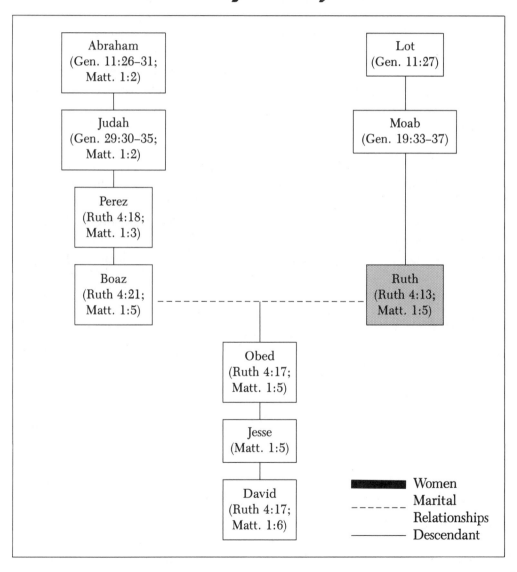

1 SAMUEL

The book of 1 Samuel describes the transition of leadership in Israel from judges to kings. Three characters are prominent in the book: Samuel, the prophet and last judge; Saul, the first king of Israel; and David, anointed as king but not yet recognized as Saul's successor.

The two books of Samuel were originally one in the Hebrew text, but were divided when they were translated into Greek. Thus the Septuagint (Greek Old Testament) and English translations divide Samuel into two books, even though this introduces an artificial division into what is actually one continuous account.

Author

The book of 1 Samuel is anonymous. Jewish tradition claims that the prophet Samuel wrote the books that bear his name, while the prophets Gad and Nathan supplied supplementary information concerning the years following Samuel's death (25:1). Nevertheless, there is no reference to an author in the book. The biblical text does indicate that Samuel made some written records (10:25) and that prophetic figures (Samuel, Nathan, and Gad) chronicled many of the acts of King David (1 Chron. 29:29). Because Old Testament prophets generally served as historians of their times, it is not unlikely that the books of Samuel were compiled by an unnamed prophet from the writings of Samuel, Gad, and Nathan, as well as from other unnamed sources.

Date

Because of references (e.g., 27:6) which presuppose the division of Israel into northern and southern kingdoms and because there is no reference to the fall of Samaria, the final composition of the books of Samuel probably took place between the division of the kingdoms in 931 B.C. and the fall of Samaria in 722 B.C. It is likely that Samuel was composed early in the divided kingdom, perhaps around 900 B.C.

First Samuel covers the ninety-four-year period from the birth of Samuel to

Continued on page 92

1 Samuel at a Glance

FOCUS	SAMUEL		SAUL		
REFERENCE	1:1 ———— 4:1 ————		8:1 ———— 13:1 ————		15:10 ——— 31:13
DIVISION	FIRST TRANSITION OF LEADERSHIP: ELI-SAMUEL	JUDGESHIP OF SAMUEL	SECOND TRANSITION OF LEADERSHIP: SAMUEL-SAUL	REIGN OF SAUL	THIRD TRANSITION OF LEADERSHIP: SAUL-DAVID
TOPIC	DECLINE OF JUDGES		RISE OF KINGS		
	ELI	SAMUEL	SAUL		DAVID
LOCATION	CANAAN				
TIME	c. 94 YEARS				

Nelson's Complete Book of Bible Maps and Charts © 1993 by Thomas Nelson, Inc.

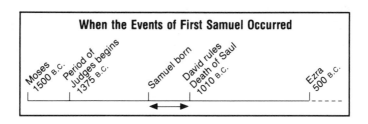

When the Events of First Samuel Occurred

Moses 1500 B.C. — Period of Judges begins 1375 B.C. — Samuel born — David rules — Death of Saul 1010 B.C. — Ezra 500 B.C.

Continued from page 90

the death of Saul (c. 1105–1011 B.C.). Much of it deals with conflicts with the Philistines, against whom Saul and David repeatedly fought.

Themes and Literary Structure

 First Samuel records the crucial transition from the theocracy under the judges to the monarchy under the kings. The book is built around three key figures: Samuel (chs. 1—7), Saul (chs. 8—31), and David (chs. 16—31).

The book describes the growing desire on the part of the people of Israel for a king, and the roles that various individuals played in the beginning and continuation of the Hebrew kingship. Kingship is depicted as ultimately a theological rather than a political matter. The God of Israel continues to be the true King of Israel. The earthly king would represent the nation before God and would be ultimately responsible to Him. Indeed, the book clearly reveals that the success or failure of the anointed king would be determined by his obedience or disobedience to the Law and his commitment to the will of God.

In introducing the kingship, 1 Samuel also introduces Israel's greatest king, David, who is chosen by God to replace Saul. Though by no means perfect, David proves to be a man after God's "own heart" (13:14), and 2 Samuel 7:4–17 records the institution of the Davidic Covenant, in which God promises David that the throne of his kingdom will be established forever, a promise fulfilled in the eternal reign of David's descendant Jesus.

David is one of the primary Old Testament types of the person of Christ. He was born in Bethlehem, works as a shepherd, and rules as king of Israel. He becomes the forerunner of the messianic King; the New Testament specifically calls Christ the "seed of David according to the flesh" (Rom. 1:3) and "the Root and the Offspring of David" (Rev. 22:16).

Samuel also highlights the consequences of sin. First Samuel 15 records the tragic transition of kingship from Saul to David. As in all three leadership changes recorded in 1 Samuel, God removes His blessing from one and gives it to another because of sin. "Because you have rejected the word of the LORD, He also has rejected you from *being* king" (15:23).

Part One: Samuel, the Last Judge (1:1—7:17)

Part Two: Saul, the First King (8:1—31:13)

Samuel

Samuel's story begins late in the turbulent time of the judges when Eli is the judge-priest of Israel. The birth of Samuel and his early call by God are found in chapters 1—3. Because of his responsiveness to God (3:19), he was confirmed as a prophet at a time when the "word of the Lord was rare" (3:1).

Corruption at the Shiloh tabernacle site by Eli's notoriously wicked sons led to Israel's defeat in the crucial battle with the Philistines (4:1–11). The sacred ark of the covenant was lost to the enemy; the priesthood was disrupted by the deaths of Eli and his sons; and the glory of God departed from the tabernacle (4:21). Samuel began to function as the last of the judges and the first in the order of the prophets (Acts 3:24). His prophetic ministry (7:3–17) led to a revival in Israel, the return of the ark, and the defeat of the Philistines.

When Samuel was old and his sons had proved to be unjust judges, the people requested a king "like all the nations" (8:5). Samuel warned the people of the dangers of a monarchy but he followed God's command and anointed Saul as king (10:1). When God rejected Saul because of his disobedience, God commissioned Samuel to anoint David as Israel's next king (16:1–13). After this, the elderly Samuel returned to his home in Ramah where he died during the latter portion of Saul's reign (25:1).

Samuel is a type of Christ in that he was a prophet, priest, and judge. Highly revered by the people, he was the instrument used by God to usher in a new period in the history of Israel.

See maps, "The Life and Ministry of Samuel," on page 95, and "Capture of the Ark," on page 96.

The Philistines

During most of this period, the warlike Philistines along the Mediterranean seacoast dominated the scene. These people, from whose name comes the term "Palestine," were invaders who originated from Greece and the island of Crete to the west. The Philistines of Canaan tended to adopt the culture and religion of the native Canaanites whom they ruled. Thus, the Philistine deities described in the Old Testament (e.g., 5:2–5) are actually Canaanite gods.

The Philistines lived in the coastal plain areas, and the hill country in which many of the Israelites lived protected them from total conquest by the warlike Philistines. The Philistines' pioneering use of iron in the Middle East is cited as explanation for their early dominance of the area (13:19–22), and the threat posed by the Philistines was a major factor in Israel's desire for a king to lead them. Because of Saul's disobedience, he had only limited military success against the Philistines, and he died in battle at Mt. Gilboa. Later, when David was finally able to subdue them, the way was open for him to begin to establish his empire.

See map, "The Philistine Threat," on page 97.

The Life and Ministry of Samuel

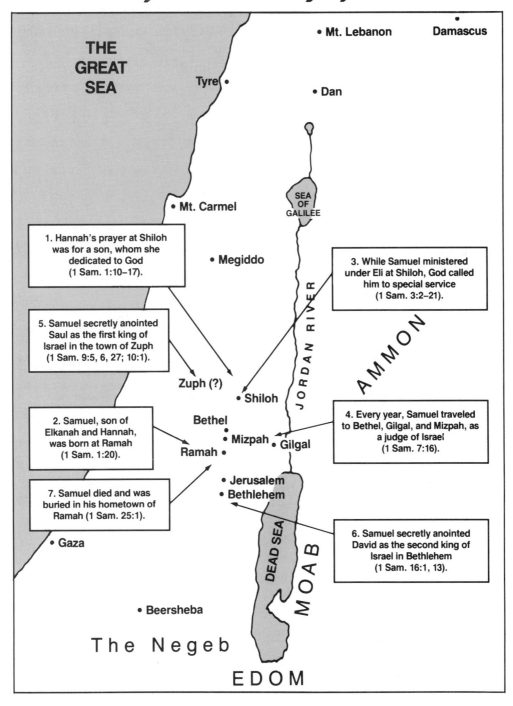

THE GREAT SEA

Mt. Lebanon

• Damascus

• Tyre

• Dan

SEA OF GALILEE

• Mt. Carmel

1. Hannah's prayer at Shiloh was for a son, whom she dedicated to God (1 Sam. 1:10–17).

• Megiddo

3. While Samuel ministered under Eli at Shiloh, God called him to special service (1 Sam. 3:2–21).

JORDAN RIVER

AMMON

5. Samuel secretly anointed Saul as the first king of Israel in the town of Zuph (1 Sam. 9:5, 6, 27; 10:1).

Zuph (?)

• Shiloh

2. Samuel, son of Elkanah and Hannah, was born at Ramah (1 Sam. 1:20).

Bethel
• Mizpah
Ramah • • Gilgal

4. Every year, Samuel traveled to Bethel, Gilgal, and Mizpah, as a judge of Israel (1 Sam. 7:16).

• Jerusalem
• Bethlehem

7. Samuel died and was buried in his hometown of Ramah (1 Sam. 25:1).

6. Samuel secretly anointed David as the second king of Israel in Bethlehem (1 Sam. 16:1, 13).

• Gaza

DEAD SEA

MOAB

• Beersheba

The Negeb

EDOM

Capture of the Ark

The ark of the covenant, a sacred portable chest, was the most sacred object in the tabernacle and the temple. It symbolized God's presence and His covenant with Israel. Believing the ark would protect them in battle, the army of Israel carried the sacred chest into conflict with the Philistines. The Philistines captured the ark but were eager to return it when they were visited by a series of plagues.

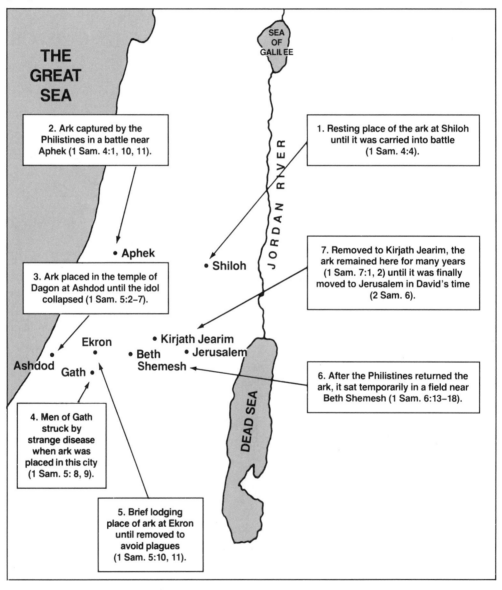

THE GREAT SEA

SEA OF GALILEE

JORDAN RIVER

DEAD SEA

2. Ark captured by the Philistines in a battle near Aphek (1 Sam. 4:1, 10, 11).

1. Resting place of the ark at Shiloh until it was carried into battle (1 Sam. 4:4).

• Aphek

• Shiloh

3. Ark placed in the temple of Dagon at Ashdod until the idol collapsed (1 Sam. 5:2–7).

7. Removed to Kirjath Jearim, the ark remained here for many years (1 Sam. 7:1, 2) until it was finally moved to Jerusalem in David's time (2 Sam. 6).

Ekron •

Ashdod • Gath •

• Kirjath Jearim
• Beth   • Jerusalem
Shemesh

6. After the Philistines returned the ark, it sat temporarily in a field near Beth Shemesh (1 Sam. 6:13–18).

4. Men of Gath struck by strange disease when ark was placed in this city (1 Sam. 5: 8, 9).

5. Brief lodging place of ark at Ekron until removed to avoid plagues (1 Sam. 5:10, 11).

Nelson's Complete Book of Bible Maps and Charts © 1993 by Thomas Nelson, Inc.

The Philistine Threat

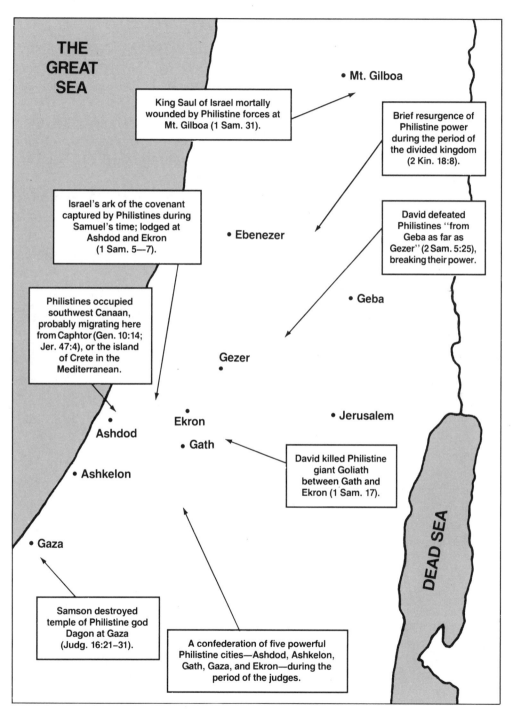

THE GREAT SEA

• Mt. Gilboa

King Saul of Israel mortally wounded by Philistine forces at Mt. Gilboa (1 Sam. 31).

Brief resurgence of Philistine power during the period of the divided kingdom (2 Kin. 18:8).

Israel's ark of the covenant captured by Philistines during Samuel's time; lodged at Ashdod and Ekron (1 Sam. 5—7).

• Ebenezer

David defeated Philistines "from Geba as far as Gezer" (2 Sam. 5:25), breaking their power.

• Geba

Philistines occupied southwest Canaan, probably migrating here from Caphtor (Gen. 10:14; Jer. 47:4), or the island of Crete in the Mediterranean.

Gezer •

• Ekron

• Jerusalem

• Ashdod

• Gath

David killed Philistine giant Goliath between Gath and Ekron (1 Sam. 17).

• Ashkelon

DEAD SEA

• Gaza

Samson destroyed temple of Philistine god Dagon at Gaza (Judg. 16:21–31).

A confederation of five powerful Philistine cities—Ashdod, Ashkelon, Gath, Gaza, and Ekron—during the period of the judges.

Nelson's Complete Book of Bible Maps and Charts © 1993 by Thomas Nelson, Inc.

Saul

The story of Saul, one of the saddest in the Old Testament, is one of good beginnings but concludes in abject failure. Anointed by the prophet Samuel as God's response to Israel's request for a king (10:1), Saul enjoyed initial success in his military efforts (11:1–11) but a victory over the Philistines was darkened by his presuming to offer a sacrifice to God in Samuel's absence (13:8–14). For this transgression, Samuel warned Saul that his kingdom would not continue. Saul's failure to destroy all of Amalek (15:9), in direct disobedience of God's command, resulted in God sending Samuel to anoint the shepherd boy David as Saul's successor (16:1–13).

Rejected by God, tormented by evil spirits, and frightened by the success of David, Saul slowly descended into madness as he repeatedly sought to kill David. Saul's military situation worsened, and in desperation Saul even sought to consult the spirit of Samuel through a medium (28:7–25). The next day Saul went out to do battle with the Philistines and, having been severely wounded, took his own life (31:1–6).

See chart, "King Saul's Decline and Fall," below; the map, "Saul's Military Campaigns," on page 100; and the map, "Before David Became King," on page 101.

King Saul's Decline and Fall

Causes	Results
A presumptuous sacrifice	Loss of kingdom foretold (13:14)
A foolish curse	Curse falls on Jonathan (14:24, 44)
Spared Agag and flocks	Loss of kingdom (15:28)
Lost fellowship with God	Unanswered prayer (28:6)
Visits a medium	Doom predicted (28:19)
Takes his own life	End of dynasty (31:4, 6)

The Family Tree of Saul

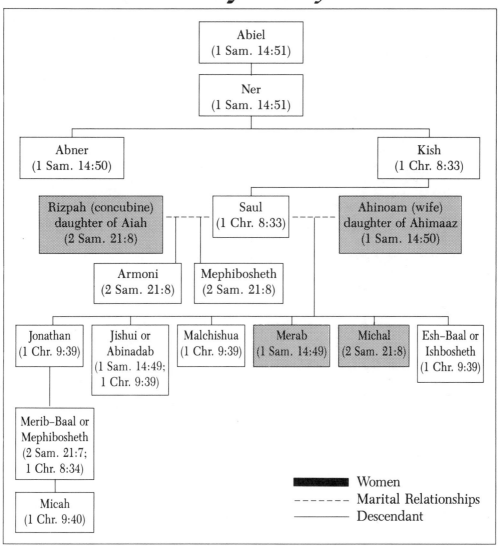

Abiel
(1 Sam. 14:51)

Ner
(1 Sam. 14:51)

Abner
(1 Sam. 14:50)

Kish
(1 Chr. 8:33)

Rizpah (concubine)
daughter of Aiah
(2 Sam. 21:8)

Saul
(1 Chr. 8:33)

Ahinoam (wife)
daughter of Ahimaaz
(1 Sam. 14:50)

Armoni
(2 Sam. 21:8)

Mephibosheth
(2 Sam. 21:8)

Jonathan
(1 Chr. 9:39)

Jishui or
Abinadab
(1 Sam. 14:49;
1 Chr. 9:39)

Malchishua
(1 Chr. 9:39)

Merab
(1 Sam. 14:49)

Michal
(2 Sam. 21:8)

Esh–Baal or
Ishbosheth
(1 Chr. 9:39)

Merib–Baal or
Mephibosheth
(2 Sam. 21:7;
1 Chr. 8:34)

Micah
(1 Chr. 9:40)

▬▬▬ Women
------- Marital Relationships
——— Descendant

Saul's Military Campaigns

As the first king of the united kingdom of Israel, Saul's major task was to subdue the nation's enemies. At first, he won several decisive battles. But his campaigns bogged down when he turned his attention to David, attempting to wipe out what he perceived as a threat to his power. Saul and his sons were eventually killed by the Philistines.

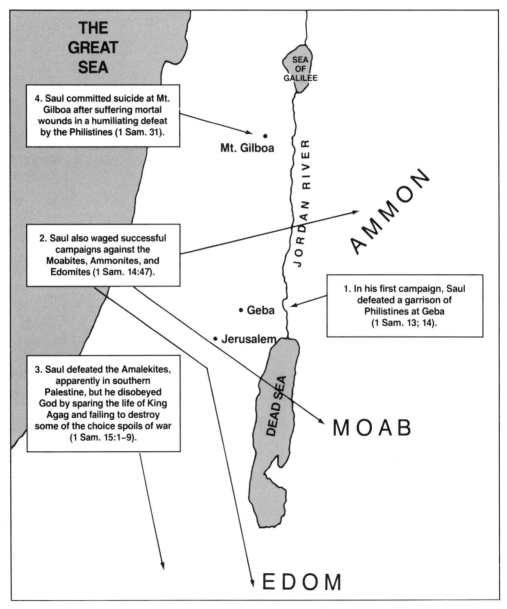

THE GREAT SEA

SEA OF GALILEE

4. Saul committed suicide at Mt. Gilboa after suffering mortal wounds in a humiliating defeat by the Philistines (1 Sam. 31).

• Mt. Gilboa

JORDAN RIVER

AMMON

2. Saul also waged successful campaigns against the Moabites, Ammonites, and Edomites (1 Sam. 14:47).

1. In his first campaign, Saul defeated a garrison of Philistines at Geba (1 Sam. 13; 14).

• Geba

• Jerusalem

3. Saul defeated the Amalekites, apparently in southern Palestine, but he disobeyed God by sparing the life of King Agag and failing to destroy some of the choice spoils of war (1 Sam. 15:1–9).

DEAD SEA

MOAB

EDOM

Nelson's Complete Book of Bible Maps and Charts © 1993 by Thomas Nelson, Inc.

Before David Became King

Near Sochoh David defeated the giant Goliath (ch. 17). Once Saul's wrath was kindled against the shepherd soldier, David fled Saul's presence and journeyed to Adullam. Taking his family to the safety of Moab, he established camp at the stronghold (22:4), now known as Masada. From there his activity took him north to Aphek and south to Amalek.

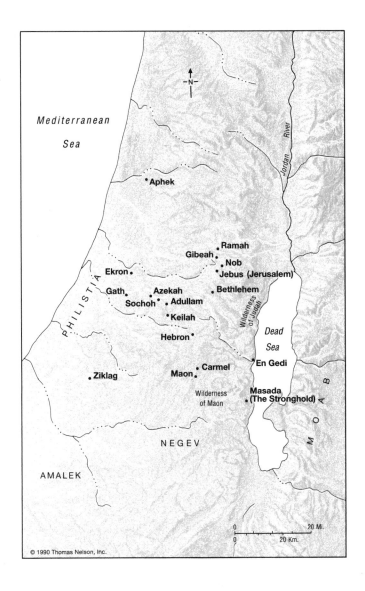

Nelson's Complete Book of Bible Maps and Charts © 1993 by Thomas Nelson, Inc.

2 SAMUEL

The book of 2 Samuel records the highlights of David's reign, first over the territory of Judah, and finally over the entire nation of Israel. It traces the ascension of David to the throne, his sins of adultery and murder, and the shattering consequences of those sins upon his family and the nation.

The two books of Samuel were originally one continuous account in the Hebrew text, but English translations (following the Greek and Latin translations) divide Samuel into two books.

Author

Like 1 Samuel, 2 Samuel is anonymous but was probably composed by an unnamed prophet who compiled written chronicles of prophets such as Nathan and Gad the seer (1 Chr. 29:29). In addition to these prophetic written sources, the compiler evidently used another source called the "Book of Jasher" (1:18).

Date

The date of the composition of 1 and 2 Samuel was sometime after the death of Solomon and the division of the kingdom (931 B.C.) but before the destruction of Samaria and the Assyrian captivity of the northern kingdom (722 B.C.). It is likely that Samuel was composed early in the divided kingdom, perhaps around 900 B.C.

Second Samuel records the major events of David's forty-year rule. His reign in Hebron begins in 1011 and ends in 1004 B.C. His thirty-three-year reign over the united Judah and Israel lasts from 1004 to 971 B.C.

Themes and Literary Structure

Second Samuel can be divided into three divisions: the triumphs of David (chs. 1—10), the transgressions of David (ch. 11), and the troubles of David (chs. 12—24).

The central character of 2 Samuel is David, around whom the entire book is

Continued on page 104

2 Samuel at a Glance

FOCUS	DAVID'S TRIUMPHS			DAVID'S TRANSGRESSIONS	DAVID'S TROUBLES	
REFERENCE	1:1 ——————— 6:1 ——————— 8:1		——————— 11:1	——————— 12:1	——————— 13:37 ——— 24:25	
DIVISION	POLITICAL TRIUMPHS	SPIRITUAL TRIUMPHS	MILITARY TRIUMPHS	SINS OF ADULTERY AND MURDER	TROUBLES IN DAVID'S HOUSE	TROUBLES IN THE KINGDOM
TOPIC	SUCCESS			SIN	FAILURE	
	OBEDIENCE			DISOBEDIENCE	JUDGMENT	
LOCATION	DAVID IN HEBRON	DAVID IN JERUSALEM				
TIME	7½ YEARS	33 YEARS				

Nelson's Complete Book of Bible Maps and Charts © 1993 by Thomas Nelson, Inc.

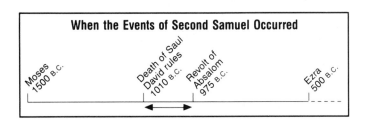

When the Events of Second Samuel Occurred

Moses 1500 B.C. — Death of Saul / David rules 1010 B.C. — Revolt of Absalom 975 B.C. — Ezra 500 B.C.

Continued from page 102

written. The key truth illustrated is the same as the theme of Deuteronomy: obedience to God brings blessing, and disobedience brings trouble and judgment. The first ten chapters describe the rewards of obedience as David's rule is extended first over Judah and then over all of Israel. David's crimes of adultery and murder, described in chapter 11, mark the turning point in the book. After this, David's life is a chronicle of trouble and misery—the death of an infant son, incest and murder among David's children, and rebellion against David's kingship.

Plot Development of 2 Samuel

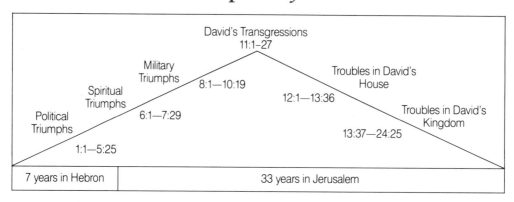

Although 2 Samuel shows that a person's obedience or disobedience to God has direct consequences for that person's life, it also demonstrates that despite these consequences God will rule and overrule so that His long-term purpose of world blessing and redemption may occur. Thus, for example, although David's sin with Bathsheba resulted in tragic loss for all concerned, it was Bathsheba who would give birth to Solomon.

God's long-term purpose of redemption is evident in the covenant God makes with David in 7:4–17 in which God promises David an eternal kingdom, throne, and seed. Although there are nine different dynasties in the northern kingdom of Israel, there is only one dynasty in Judah—the line of David. The promise of a permanent dynasty is fulfilled in Christ, the "Son of David" (Matt. 21:9; 22:45) who will sit upon the throne of David (Is. 9:7; Luke 1:32).

See map, "The Life of David," on page 106.

OUTLINE OF 2 SAMUEL

The Life of David

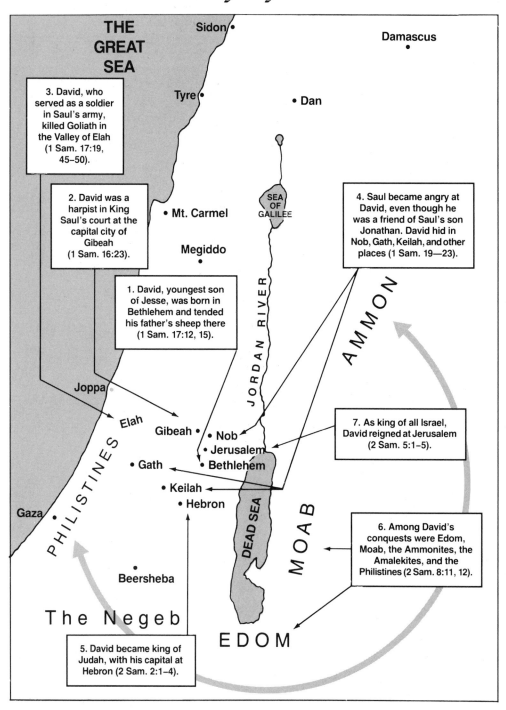

THE GREAT SEA

Sidon •

Damascus •

Tyre •

• Dan

3. David, who served as a soldier in Saul's army, killed Goliath in the Valley of Elah (1 Sam. 17:19, 45–50).

SEA OF GALILEE

4. Saul became angry at David, even though he was a friend of Saul's son Jonathan. David hid in Nob, Gath, Keilah, and other places (1 Sam. 19—23).

2. David was a harpist in King Saul's court at the capital city of Gibeah (1 Sam. 16:23).

• Mt. Carmel

Megiddo •

1. David, youngest son of Jesse, was born in Bethlehem and tended his father's sheep there (1 Sam. 17:12, 15).

JORDAN RIVER

AMMON

Joppa

Elah

Gibeah •

• Nob

• Jerusalem

• Bethlehem

7. As king of all Israel, David reigned at Jerusalem (2 Sam. 5:1–5).

PHILISTINES

• Gath

• Keilah ◄

• Hebron

Gaza •

DEAD SEA

MOAB

6. Among David's conquests were Edom, Moab, the Ammonites, the Amalekites, and the Philistines (2 Sam. 8:11, 12).

• Beersheba

The Negeb

EDOM

5. David became king of Judah, with his capital at Hebron (2 Sam. 2:1–4).

Nelson's Complete Book of Bible Maps and Charts © 1993 by Thomas Nelson, Inc.

The Expansion of David's Kingdom

Second Samuel records the expansion of David's kingdom from the territory of Judah, to all of Israel, and finally to the areas of Edom, Moab, Ammon, and Zobah and Syria as well.

The period of David's kingship over Judah was a time of conflict with Saul's son Ishbosheth and his general Abner (chs. 3—4). With the deaths of Ishbosheth and Abner, however, Israel acknowledged David as king (5:1–5), and David sought to establish a centrally located capital. David then captured the Jebusite stronghold on Mt. Zion and renamed it the City of David (5:6–10), thus beginning the long association of the Jewish people and the worship of God with the city of Jerusalem.

Following the capture of Jerusalem, David won crucial victories over Philistia (8:1; 21:15–22), Moab (8:2), Zobah and Syria (8:3–8), Ammon (10:6–14), and Syria (10:15–19).

See the following maps, "The City of David," and "David's Kingdom."

The City of David

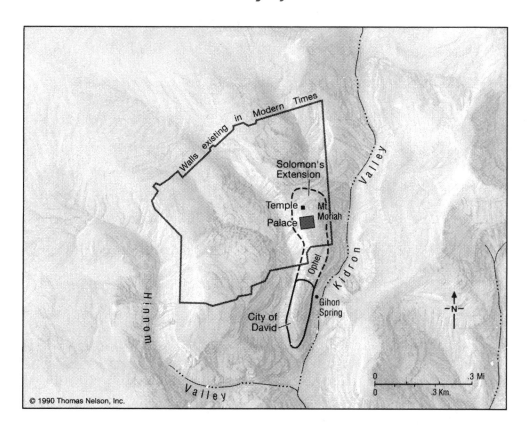

© 1990 Thomas Nelson, Inc.

David's Kingdom

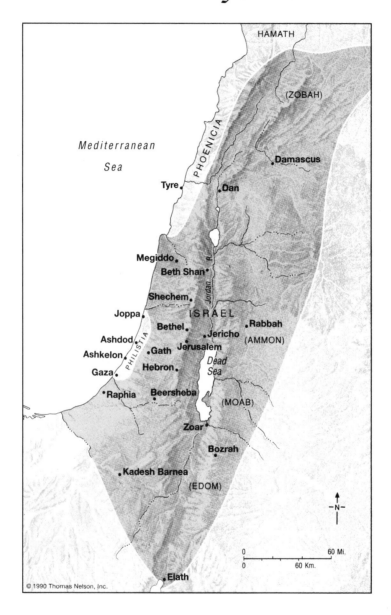

HAMATH

(ZOBAH)

Mediterranean

Sea

PHOENICIA

Damascus

Tyre

Dan

Megiddo

Beth Shan

Shechem

Joppa

ISRAEL

Bethel

Rabbah

Jericho

(AMMON)

Ashdod

Gath

Jerusalem

Ashkelon

Dead

Gaza

Hebron

Sea

Raphia

Beersheba

(MOAB)

Zoar

Bozrah

Kadesh Barnea

(EDOM)

Elath

© 1990 Thomas Nelson, Inc.

The Family of David

Though the continuation of David's line was part of the promise of the Davidic Covenant (7:4–17), his large family was a constant source of heartache and trouble throughout the latter part of 2 Samuel. David's family troubles included the death of Bathsheba's infant son as judgment for David's adultery (12:15–23), the incest of Amnon with Tamar, and Absalom's subsequent murder of Amnon (13:1–36). Perhaps most striking was the rebellion of David's son Absalom, who drove David from Jerusalem, took David's wives, and nearly wrested the kingdom from David (15:7—18:33).

The intrigue and hostility among the children of David's many wives and concubines was partially, and perhaps largely, due to David's polygamy. While common, polygamy was never successful because it violated the divine ordinance (Gen. 2:24).

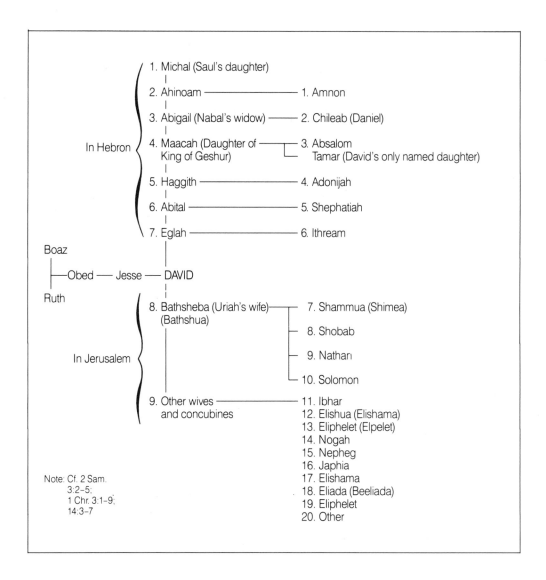

See page 110 for additional charts, "David's Triumphs" and "David's Troubles."

David's Triumphs

David was a man after God's own heart (1 Sam. 13:14), that is, his will was completely committed to the will of his Lord. As a dedicated servant of God, he was used by God to perform mighty acts for the sake of His chosen people Israel.

King of Judah (2:4)
King of Israel (5:3)
Conquers Jerusalem (5:7)
Returns ark (6:12)
Davidic covenant (7:16)
Defeats Philistines (8:1)
Defeats Moab (8:2)
Defeats Ammon (10:16)
Defeats Syria (10:19)

David's Troubles

Causes	Effects
Adultery (11:4)	Bathsheba bears a son (11:5)
Murder of Uriah (11:17)	Accused, repents, but the child dies (12:10, 13, 19)
Amnon's incest (13:14)	Amnon murdered (13:28, 29)
Absalom usurps throne (16:15, 16)	Absalom murdered (18:14, 15)
The census (24:2)	Plague (24:15)

Consistently illustrated in the life of David's household is the principle that a disobedient life is a troubled life.

Nelson's Complete Book of Bible Maps and Charts © 1993 by Thomas Nelson, Inc.

1 KINGS

The first half of 1 Kings traces the life of David's successor and son Solomon. Under his leadership Israel rose to the peak of her size and glory. Solomon's great accomplishments, including the unsurpassed splendor of the temple which he constructed in Jerusalem, brought him worldwide fame and respect. However, Solomon's zeal for God diminished in his later years, as pagan wives turned his heart away from wholehearted worship of God. As a result, the king with the divided heart leaves behind a divided kingdom, and 1 Kings then traces the twin histories of two sets of kings and two nations of disobedient people.

Like the books of Samuel, 1 and 2 Kings were originally one book. The division into two books was first made in the Greek translation of the Old Testament (the Septuagint) and then in the Latin Vulgate, and English translations have followed suit.

Author

The author of 1 and 2 Kings is unknown, although Jewish tradition ascribes the work to the prophet Jeremiah. All that can be said with certainty is that Kings was compiled from various sources and written from a prophetic perspective.

The author mentions three primary sources. The "book of the acts of Solomon" (11:41) appears to have contained annals, biographical data, and excerpts from the temple archives. The "book of the chronicles of the kings of Israel" (14:19; 15:7) appears to have recorded each king's political activities and was preserved in official state archives. The third source, the "book of the chronicles of the kings of Judah" (14:29; 15:7), was also an official state record preserved in the royal archives.

Date

The grammar and style of the Hebrew and the contents of the books of Kings indicate that this work was completed during the Babylonian captivity. Kings was completed after 561 B.C. since this is the date of the last recorded event (2 Kin. 25:27–30). Because there is no mention

Continued on page 113

1 Kings at a Glance

FOCUS	UNITED KINGDON			DIVIDED KINGDOM		
REFERENCE	1:1 ——————— 3:1 ——————— 9:1 ———			12:1 ——————— 15:1 ——————— 16:29 ——— 22:53		
DIVISION	ESTABLISHMENT OF SOLOMON	RISE OF SOLOMON	DECLINE OF SOLOMON	DIVISION OF THE KINGDOM	REIGNS OF VARIOUS KINGS	REIGN OF AHAB WITH ELIJAH
TOPIC	SOLOMON			MANY KINGS		
	KINGDOM IN TRANQUILITY			KINGDOMS IN TURMOIL		
LOCATION	JERUSALEM: CAPITAL OF UNITED KINGDOM			SAMARIA: CAPITAL OF ISRAEL JERUSALEM: CAPITAL OF JUDAH		
TIME	c. 40 YEARS			c. 90 YEARS		

Nelson's Complete Book of Bible Maps and Charts © 1993 by Thomas Nelson, Inc.

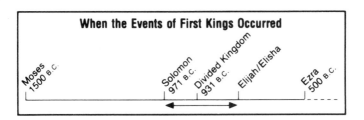

When the Events of First Kings Occurred

Moses 1500 B.C. — Solomon 971 B.C. — Divided Kingdom 931 B.C. — Elijah/Elisha — Ezra 500 B.C.

Continued from page 111

of Cyrus and his liberating edict of 539 B.C., Kings was probably completed prior to this last date.

First Kings covers the 120 years from the beginning of Solomon's reign in 971 B.C. through Ahaziah's reign ending in 851 B.C. The key date is 931 B.C., the year the kingdom was divided into the northern nation of Israel and the southern nation of Judah.

Themes and Literary Structure

The book of 1 Kings divides clearly into two main sections: the united kingdom under Solomon (chs. 1—11), and the divided kingdom (chs. 12—22).

First Kings provides a prophetically oriented evaluation of the spiritual and moral causes that led to the political and economic demise of the two kingdoms. The material is too selective to be considered a biography of the kings. For example, Omri was one of the northern kingdom's most important rulers from a political point of view, but because of his moral corruption, his achievements are dismissed in a mere eight verses (16:21–28). The lives of these kings are used to teach that faithfulness to the covenant and observance of God's law produces blessing, but apostasy is rewarded by divine judgment.

The first half of 1 Kings deals with the splendor of the Solomonic era. Solomon typifies Christ in a number of ways. His fabled wisdom points ahead to "Christ Jesus, who became for us wisdom from God" (1 Cor. 1:30). Solomon's fame, glory, wealth, and honor foreshadow Christ in His kingdom. Solomon's rulership brings knowledge, peace, and worship. However, despite Solomon's splendor, the Son of Man later says of His coming, "indeed a greater than Solomon *is* here" (Matt. 12:42).

Much stress in the books of Kings is placed upon the prophetic ministries of Elijah and Elisha, who served as the links between the earlier period and the era of the writing prophets.

See maps, "Solomon's Empire," on page 115, and "Solomon's Twelve Districts," on page 116.

OUTLINE OF 1 KINGS

Part One: The United Kingdom (1:1—11:43)

Solomon's Empire

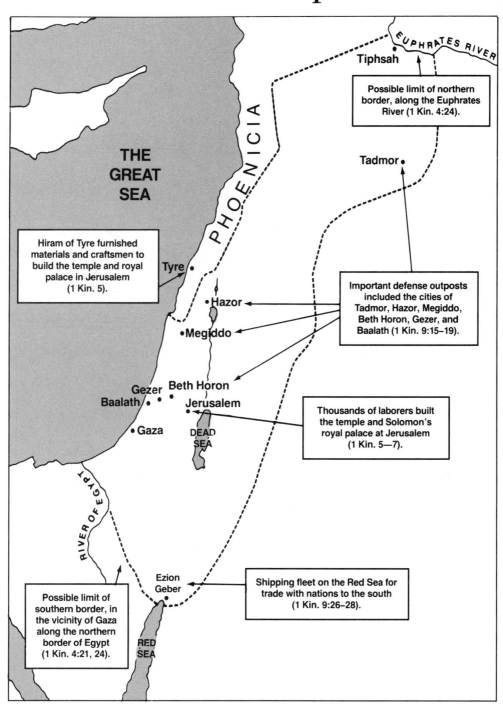

THE GREAT SEA

PHOENICIA

EUPHRATES RIVER

Tiphsah

Possible limit of northern border, along the Euphrates River (1 Kin. 4:24).

Tadmor

Hiram of Tyre furnished materials and craftsmen to build the temple and royal palace in Jerusalem (1 Kin. 5).

Tyre

Hazor

Megiddo

Important defense outposts included the cities of Tadmor, Hazor, Megiddo, Beth Horon, Gezer, and Baalath (1 Kin. 9:15–19).

Gezer   Beth Horon
Baalath
Jerusalem

Gaza

DEAD SEA

Thousands of laborers built the temple and Solomon's royal palace at Jerusalem (1 Kin. 5—7).

RIVER OF EGYPT

Ezion Geber

Shipping fleet on the Red Sea for trade with nations to the south (1 Kin. 9:26–28).

Possible limit of southern border, in the vicinity of Gaza along the northern border of Egypt (1 Kin. 4:21, 24).

RED SEA

Nelson's Complete Book of Bible Maps and Charts © 1993 by Thomas Nelson, Inc.

Solomon's Twelve Districts

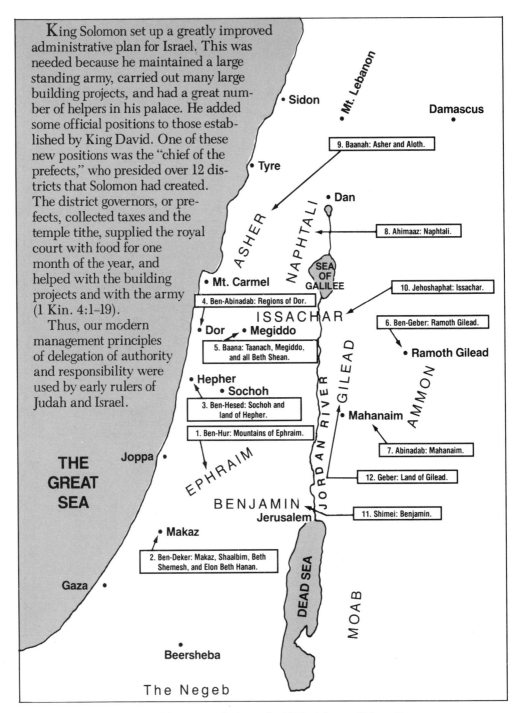

King Solomon set up a greatly improved administrative plan for Israel. This was needed because he maintained a large standing army, carried out many large building projects, and had a great number of helpers in his palace. He added some official positions to those established by King David. One of these new positions was the "chief of the prefects," who presided over 12 districts that Solomon had created. The district governors, or prefects, collected taxes and the temple tithe, supplied the royal court with food for one month of the year, and helped with the building projects and with the army (1 Kin. 4:1–19).

Thus, our modern management principles of delegation of authority and responsibility were used by early rulers of Judah and Israel.

Map labels:

- • Sidon
- Mt. Lebanon
- Damascus
- 9. Baanah: Asher and Aloth.
- • Tyre
- • Dan
- ASHER
- NAPHTALI
- 8. Ahimaaz: Naphtali.
- SEA OF GALILEE
- • Mt. Carmel
- 10. Jehoshaphat: Issachar.
- 4. Ben-Abinadab: Regions of Dor.
- ISSACHAR
- 6. Ben-Geber: Ramoth Gilead.
- • Dor • Megiddo
- 5. Baana: Taanach, Megiddo, and all Beth Shean.
- GILEAD
- • Ramoth Gilead
- AMMON
- • Hepher
- • Sochoh
- 3. Ben-Hesed: Sochoh and land of Hepher.
- JORDAN RIVER
- • Mahanaim
- 1. Ben-Hur: Mountains of Ephraim.
- 7. Abinadab: Mahanaim.
- THE GREAT SEA
- Joppa •
- EPHRAIM
- 12. Geber: Land of Gilead.
- BENJAMIN
- Jerusalem
- 11. Shimei: Benjamin.
- • Makaz
- 2. Ben-Deker: Makaz, Shaalbim, Beth Shemesh, and Elon Beth Hanan.
- DEAD SEA
- MOAB
- Gaza •
- • Beersheba
- The Negeb

Nelson's Complete Book of Bible Maps and Charts © 1993 by Thomas Nelson, Inc.

Jerusalem Under Solomon

The city of Jerusalem underwent considerable expansion during the reign of Solomon. According to 1 Kings 3:1, Solomon finished building "the wall all around Jerusalem." Archaeological evidence indicates that Solomon increased the size of the city from eleven to thirty-two acres; its total population increased several times over as well. Some of the population increase was due to Solomon's family alone. He had 700 wives and 300 concubines (11:3). The number of Solomon's children is not given but must have been very large as well.

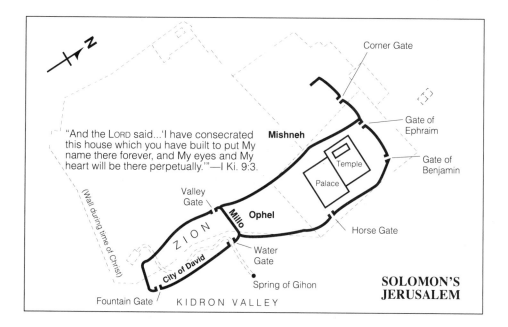

"And the LORD said...'I have consecrated this house which you have built to put My name there forever, and My eyes and My heart will be there perpetually.'"—I Ki. 9:3.

Mishneh

Temple

Palace

Valley Gate

Millo

Ophel

Horse Gate

Corner Gate

Gate of Ephraim

Gate of Benjamin

(Wall during time of Christ)

ZION

City of David

Water Gate

Spring of Gihon

Fountain Gate

KIDRON VALLEY

SOLOMON'S JERUSALEM

The Spread of Solomon's Fame

Solomon's influence in economic and political affairs was enhanced by the transportation and trade routes that intersected his kingdom.

See map on page 118.

The Plan of Solomon's Temple

Solomon's greatest legacy was the building of the temple. King David had wanted to build it, but was forbidden to do so by God because he had shed so much blood (1 Chr. 28:3). Thus, the task fell to Solomon, who was known as a man of peace. The building of the temple began in the spring of Solomon's fourth year (966 B.C.) and was completed seven years later (6:1–38). The temple was similar to the tabernacle, though twice its size. It was 90 feet long and

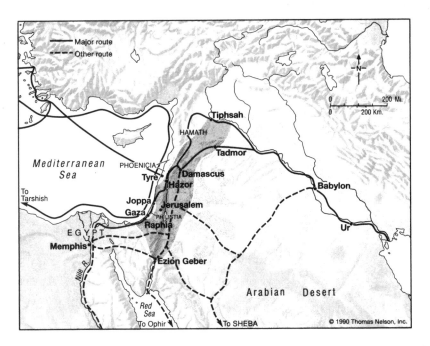

30 feet wide, and it contained the holy place and the Most Holy Place. Like the tabernacle, the temple faced toward the east, having the Most Holy Place at the extreme western end.

See chart, "Solomon's Temple," on page 119.

The Divided Kingdom

The glory of the united kingdom began to fade with the death of Solomon when his unwise son Rehoboam spoke harshly to the representatives of Israel who requested relief from the heavy taxation of Solomon's time (12:1–24). Rehoboam reigned over Judah to the south and Jeroboam became king of Israel to the north.

See map, "The Divided Kingdom," on page 120.

The Prophet Elijah

Elijah the prophet was from Tishbe in Gilead, but the precise location of this town is uncertain. There is no mention of his birth and parentage and his family background may even have been non-Israelite. Elijah's name, which means "Yahweh is my God," may be regarded as the motto of his life. His prophetic objective was to awaken Israel to the conviction that Yahweh alone is God. Elijah is pictured as a lonely figure "wearing a leather belt around his

Continued on page 121

Solomon's Temple

Solomon constructed the temple on Mt. Moriah, north of the ancient City of David. The temple was built according to plans that David received from the Lord and passed on to Solomon (1 Chr. 28:11–13, 19). The division into a sanctuary and inner sanctuary corresponds to the division of the tabernacle into the holy place and Most Holy Place.

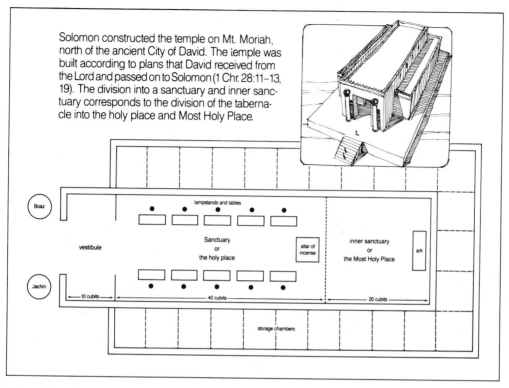

Boaz

lampstands and tables

vestibule

Sanctuary
or
the holy place

altar of
incense

inner sanctuary
or
the Most Holy Place

ark

Jachin

10 cubits | 40 cubits | 20 cubits

storage chambers

Nelson's Complete Book of Bible Maps and Charts © 1993 by Thomas Nelson, Inc.

The Divided Kingdom

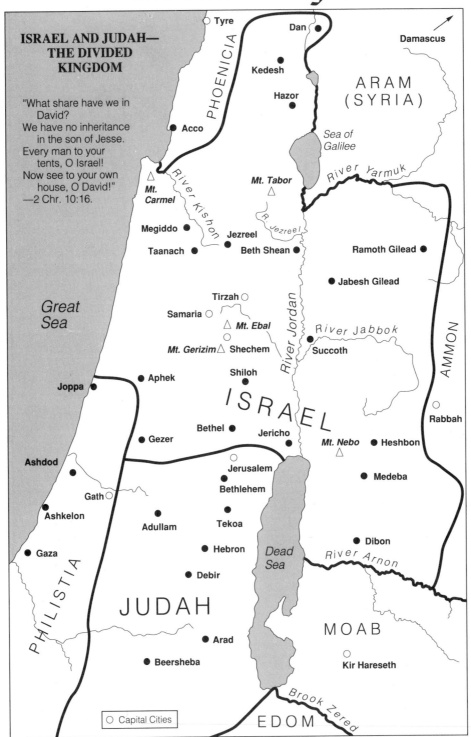

ISRAEL AND JUDAH—THE DIVIDED KINGDOM

"What share have we in David?
We have no inheritance in the son of Jesse.
Every man to your tents, O Israel!
Now see to your own house, O David!"
—2 Chr. 10:16.

Tyre

Dan

Damascus

PHOENICIA

Kedesh

Hazor

ARAM (SYRIA)

Acco

Sea of Galilee

Mt. Carmel

River Kishon

Mt. Tabor

River Yarmuk

Megiddo

Jezreel

R. Jezreel

Taanach

Beth Shean

Ramoth Gilead

Jabesh Gilead

Great Sea

Tirzah

Samaria

River Jordan

River Jabbok

Mt. Ebal

Mt. Gerizim

Shechem

Succoth

AMMON

Aphek

Shiloh

ISRAEL

Joppa

Gezer

Bethel

Jericho

Mt. Nebo

Heshbon

Rabbah

Ashdod

Jerusalem

Gath

Bethlehem

Medeba

Ashkelon

Adullam

Tekoa

Gaza

Hebron

Dead Sea

Dibon

River Arnon

PHILISTIA

Debir

JUDAH

MOAB

Arad

Kir Hareseth

Beersheba

Brook Zered

EDOM

○ Capital Cities

Nelson's Complete Book of Bible Maps and Charts © 1993 by Thomas Nelson, Inc.

Continued from page 118

waist" (2 Kin. 1:8). Elijah lived during the period of Ahab's reign, when the pagan worship of Baal was formally introduced into Israel (16:32).

Elijah's first act was to announce to Ahab that the true God was about to send a dreaded famine upon the country because of Ahab's religious sins (17:1). Baal, the Canaanite god of storm and fertility, was directly challenged by this prediction of drought.

When Elijah's career was over, he neither died nor was buried. While conversing with his successor, the prophet Elisha, Elijah was suddenly taken up in a chariot of fire and whirlwind into heaven (2 Kin. 2:1–12). Elijah is mentioned in Malachi 4:5 as the harbinger of the "day of the LORD" and as the herald of the Messiah, and this prophecy was fulfilled in the ministry of John the Baptist (Matt. 11:7–14; Luke 1:17).

See map, "The Life of Elijah," on page 123.

Elijah and Elisha

Elijah's victory on Mt. Carmel ended with the slaying of 450 prophets of Baal (18:20–40). His ministry spanned Canaan from the brook Cherith near his birthplace (17:1–7) to Zarephath where he performed the miracle that sustained the widow and her son, and as far south as Mt. Horeb in the Sinai Peninsula. In Samaria Elijah denounced King Ahab's injustice against Naboth of Jezreel (21:17–29). Near Jericho Elijah separated the waters of the Jordan River to cross over and subsequently was carried to heaven in a chariot of fire (2 Kin. 2:1–12).

Elisha healed Naaman of leprosy in the Jordan River (2 Kin. 5:1–19) and led the blinded Syrians to their defeat at Samaria (2 Kin. 6:8–23). In Damascus, Elisha prophesied the death of King Ben-Hadad of Syria and the succession of Hazael as king of Syria.

See map on page 122.

Locations in the Ministry
of Elijah and Elisha

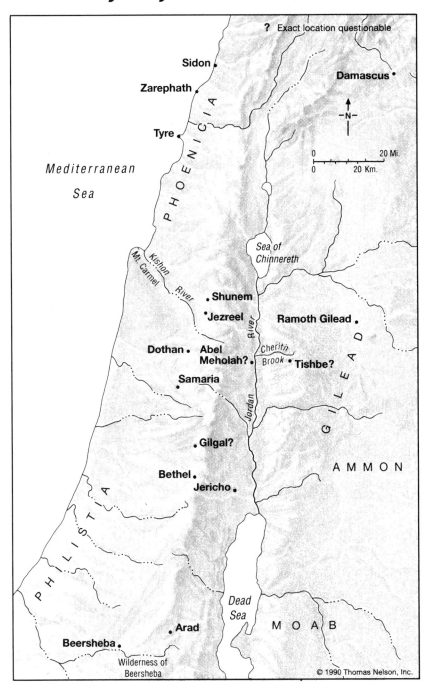

? Exact location questionable

Sidon

Damascus

Zarephath

—N—

Tyre

0   20 Mi.
0   20 Km.

Mediterranean

Sea

PHOENICIA

Sea of
Chinnereth

Mt. Carmel

Kishon River

Shunem

Jezreel

Ramoth Gilead

River

Dothan

Abel
Meholah?

Cherith
Brook

Tishbe?

Samaria

Jordan

G I L E A D

Gilgal?

A M M O N

Bethel

Jericho

P H I L I S T I A

Dead
Sea

M O A B

Arad

Beersheba

Wilderness of
Beersheba

© 1990 Thomas Nelson, Inc.

Nelson's Complete Book of Bible Maps and Charts © 1993 by Thomas Nelson, Inc.

The Life of Elijah

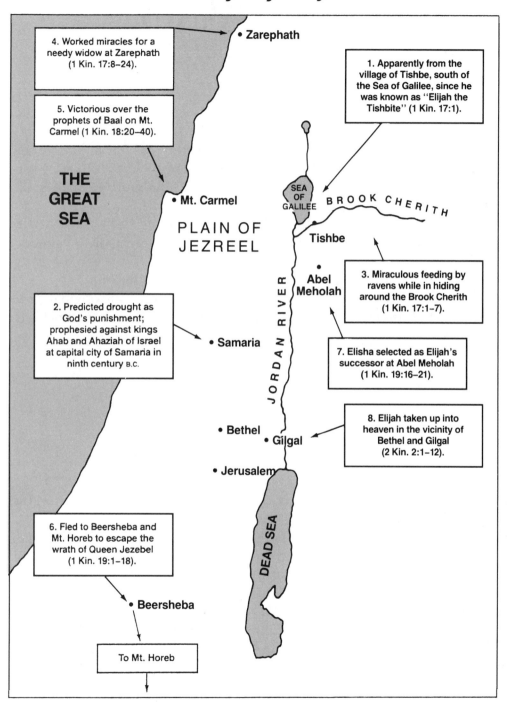

4. Worked miracles for a needy widow at Zarephath (1 Kin. 17:8–24).

• Zarephath

1. Apparently from the village of Tishbe, south of the Sea of Galilee, since he was known as "Elijah the Tishbite" (1 Kin. 17:1).

5. Victorious over the prophets of Baal on Mt. Carmel (1 Kin. 18:20–40).

THE GREAT SEA

SEA OF GALILEE

BROOK CHERITH

• Mt. Carmel

PLAIN OF JEZREEL

Tishbe

Abel Meholah

3. Miraculous feeding by ravens while in hiding around the Brook Cherith (1 Kin. 17:1–7).

JORDAN RIVER

2. Predicted drought as God's punishment; prophesied against kings Ahab and Ahaziah of Israel at capital city of Samaria in ninth century B.C.

• Samaria

7. Elisha selected as Elijah's successor at Abel Meholah (1 Kin. 19:16–21).

8. Elijah taken up into heaven in the vicinity of Bethel and Gilgal (2 Kin. 2:1–12).

• Bethel • Gilgal

• Jerusalem

6. Fled to Beersheba and Mt. Horeb to escape the wrath of Queen Jezebel (1 Kin. 19:1–18).

DEAD SEA

• Beersheba

To Mt. Horeb

Nelson's Complete Book of Bible Maps and Charts © 1993 by Thomas Nelson, Inc.

2 KINGS

Second Kings continues the drama begun in 1 Kings—the tragic history of two nations on a collision course with captivity. The author systematically traces the reigning monarchs of Israel and Judah, first by carrying one nation's history forward, then retracing the same period for the other.

Nineteen consecutive evil kings rule in Israel, leading to the captivity by Assyria. The picture is somewhat brighter in Judah, where godly kings occasionally emerge to reform the evils of their predecessors. In the end, however, sin outweighs righteousness and Judah is marched off to Babylon.

Like the books of Samuel and Chronicles, 1 and 2 Kings were originally one book. English translations have followed the division of the books first made in the Greek and Latin versions.

Author

See "Author" in 1 Kings.

Date

The composition of the books of Kings was completed during the Babylonian captivity.

Chapters 1—17 cover the 131 years from 853 B.C. (King Ahaziah of Israel) to 722 B.C. (the fall of Samaria and the Assyrian captivity of Israel). Chapters 18—25 record the 155 years from the beginning of Hezekiah's reign in 715 B.C. to the release of Jehoiachin in Babylon in 560 B.C. The united kingdom lasts for 112 years (1043–931 B.C.), the northern kingdom of Israel exists for another 209 years (931–722 B.C.), and the southern kingdom of Judah continues for an additional 136 years (722–586 B.C.). During this 457-year kingdom period, there are great shifts of world power. Egyptian and Assyrian power over Palestine fluctuates; Assyria rises to preeminence, declines, and is finally conquered by Babylon.

2 Kings at a Glance

FOCUS	DIVIDED KINGDOM			SURVIVING KINGDOM		
REFERENCE	1:1 ———— 9:1 ————		17:1 ———— 18:1	———— 22:1 ————	25:1 ————	25:30
DIVISION	MINISTRY OF ELISHA UNDER AHAZIAH AND JEHORAM	REIGNS OF TEN KINGS OF ISRAEL AND EIGHT KINGS OF JUDAH	FALL OF ISRAEL	REIGNS OF HEZEKIAH AND TWO EVIL KINGS	REIGNS OF JOSIAH AND FOUR EVIL KINGS	FALL OF JUDAH
TOPIC	ISRAEL AND JUDAH			JUDAH		
	AHAZIAH TO HOSHEA			HEZEKIAH TO ZEDEKIAH		
LOCATION	ISRAEL DEPORTED TO ASSYRIA			JUDAH DEPORTED TO BABYLONIA		
TIME	131 YEARS (853–722 B.C.)			155 YEARS (715–560 B.C.)		

Nelson's Complete Book of Bible Maps and Charts © 1993 by Thomas Nelson, Inc.

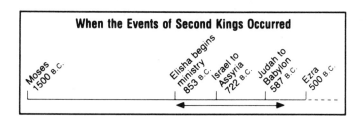

When the Events of Second Kings Occurred

Moses 1500 B.C. — Elisha begins ministry 853 B.C. — Israel to Assyria 722 B.C. — Judah to Babylon 587 B.C. — Ezra 500 B.C.

Themes and Literary Structure

 Second Kings traces the history of the divided kingdom in chapters 1—17 and the history of the surviving kingdom of Judah in chapters 18—25. As with 1 Kings, the narrative is somewhat difficult to follow, as the author switches back and forth between the northern and the southern kingdom.

The book is more than just a compilation of the politically important or socially significant events in Israel and Judah. Rather, 2 Kings is a selective history written with a theological purpose. The author selects and emphasizes the people and events that are morally and religiously significant and teaches that the decline and collapse of the two kingdoms occurred because of failure on the part of the rulers and people to heed the warnings of God's messengers. The spiritual climate of the nation determined its political and economic conditions. First and foremost, the books of Kings are covenant history written to explain to the Jewish exiles the reasons for the fall of the northern and southern kingdoms.

Second Kings presents God as the controller of history who reveals His plan and purpose for His people. God controls human affairs and those who obey the Lord enjoy His blessing while the disobedient experience God's discipline. Yet even the disobedience of His people cannot thwart God's redemptive purposes. Against all odds, the Davidic line of covenant promise is preserved (11:1–16), and the book concludes on a hopeful, forward-looking note with the release of David's royal descendant Jehoiachin from captivity in Babylon (25:27–30).

The prophets of Yahweh play a prominent role in 1 and 2 Kings as God uses them to remind the kings of their covenant responsibilities. The ministries of Elijah and Elisha in the northern kingdom are the most prominent, but many of the later writing prophets are mentioned as well. The certainty of God's prophetic word is highlighted as numerous fulfillments of prophecy and miracles performed by prophets are mentioned.

OUTLINE OF 2 KINGS

The Prophet Elisha

Coming from an apparently wealthy family, Elisha was anointed by Elijah as his successor and served as his assistant (1 Kin. 19:19–21). Elisha's own lengthy ministry began when Elijah was taken to heaven by a fiery chariot and a whirlwind (2 Kin. 2:11). Realizing his own need of divine assistance, Elisha requested a double portion of Elijah's prophetic spirit (2:9).

Like his predecessor Elijah, Elisha was intimately involved in the political affairs of Israel. In addition to calling the kings of Israel to repentance, Elisha was involved in the anointing of kings, and he often prophesied regarding military matters. Elisha was able to repeatedly reveal enemy plans to the king of Israel (6:12). The king of Israel even termed Elisha "the chariots of Israel and their horsemen" (13:14), a recognition of Elisha's great importance in Israel's success.

Elisha was known as a great worker of miracles and for helping those in need. Whether in causing a lost ax head to float (6:1–7), in feeding the hungry (4:42–44), in healing the Syrian general Naaman of leprosy (5:1–19), or in raising the son of the Shunammite woman from the dead (4:8–37), Elisha showed himself to be a compassionate friend of the people.

While Elijah was known for his ministry of forceful prophetic denunciations and is a type of John the Baptist (Matt. 11:14; 17:10–12; Luke 1:17), Elisha's ministry reminds us of Christ. Elijah generally lived apart from the people and stressed law, judgment, and repentance. Elisha lived among the people and emphasized grace, life, and hope.

See map, "Elisha's Ministry," on page 130.

Syrian Rulers

During the ministries of Elijah and Elisha, the major external military threat to the northern kingdom of Israel was Syria to the northeast. Sometimes called Arameans, the Syrians were military rivals of Israel from the time of Saul (1 Sam. 14:47) until Syria was overrun by the Assyrian empire in 732 B.C.

Continued on page 131

Elisha's Ministry

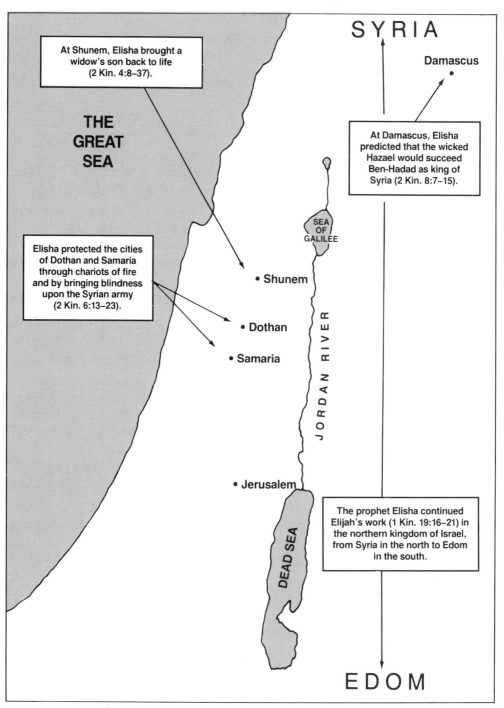

SYRIA

Damascus

At Damascus, Elisha predicted that the wicked Hazael would succeed Ben-Hadad as king of Syria (2 Kin. 8:7–15).

At Shunem, Elisha brought a widow's son back to life (2 Kin. 4:8–37).

THE GREAT SEA

SEA OF GALILEE

Elisha protected the cities of Dothan and Samaria through chariots of fire and by bringing blindness upon the Syrian army (2 Kin. 6:13–23).

• Shunem

• Dothan

JORDAN RIVER

• Samaria

• Jerusalem

The prophet Elisha continued Elijah's work (1 Kin. 19:16–21) in the northern kingdom of Israel, from Syria in the north to Edom in the south.

DEAD SEA

EDOM

Nelson's Complete Book of Bible Maps and Charts © 1993 by Thomas Nelson, Inc.

Continued from page 129

The Syrians were subject to Israel during the period when the empire of David and Solomon extended to the River Euphrates, but by the time of Ahab the Syrians were a persistent threat, and Ahab was finally killed fighting them (1 Kin. 20:1–34; 22:29–40). An extended siege of Samaria by Syria was only broken by divine intervention (6:24—7:20), and Syria was able to threaten Jerusalem of Judah during the time of King Joash (12:17–18).

Kings	Dates	Scripture References
Hezion (Rezon)	c. 990–930 B.C.	1 Kings 11:23, 25; 15:18
Tabrimmon	c. 930–885 B.C.	1 Kings 15:18
Ben-Hadad I	c. 885–860 B.C.	1 Kings 15:18, 20
Ben-Hadad II	c. 860–841 B.C.	1 Kings 20; 2 Kings 6:24; 8:7, 9, 14
Hazael	c. 841–801 B.C.	1 Kings 19:15, 17 2 Kings 8; 9:14, 15; 10:32; 12:17, 18; 13:3, 22, 24, 25
Ben-Hadad III	c. 807–780? B.C.	2 Kings 13:3, 24, 25
Rezin	c. 780?–732 B.C.	2 Kings 15:37; 16:5, 6, 9 (cf. Is. 7:1, 4, 8; 8:6; 9:11)

King Jehu's Black Obelisk

During the period of Old Testament history from about 900 to 700 B.C., the Assyrians were the dominant world power. One of the powerful Assyrian kings, Shalmaneser III (reigned 859–824 B.C.), erected a large stone monument on which he recorded his military victories. This impressive archaeological find, known as the Black Obelisk, contains a relief sculpture depicting the visit of King Jehu of Israel (reigned 841–814 B.C.) to pay tribute to Shalmaneser.

Placed outside the royal palace at Nimrud in Assyria, the monument is more than six feet high. Chiseled carefully in stone is a series of detailed drawings, with accompanying inscriptions that commemorate Shalmaneser's numerous military campaigns. The obelisk shows an event not mentioned in the Bible—Jehu bowing before Shalmaneser, with numerous Israelite servants and aids standing by with gifts for the Assyrian king.

Tribute, or compulsory payments to protect a weaker nation against a more powerful foe, was often levied by aggressor nations such as the Assyrians during Old Testament times.

After being anointed king of Israel by the prophet Elisha, Jehu eliminated all threats to his rule by killing all members of the family of Ahab, whom he succeeded (2 Kin. 9; 10). As a ruler, Jehu was a weak king who failed to eliminate Baal worship from the land.

The Black Obelisk is a valuable archaeological find, because it helps establish a date for Jehu's rule, as well as an overall chronology for this period of Israel's history. It also shows us what an Israelite king from this period must have looked like. This is the only image or drawing of an Israelite king that has been discovered by archaeologists.

Sennacherib's Prism

The monument known as Sennacherib's Prism is a fascinating artifact from Assyria's past. It gives a different account from the Bible about an important event in Israel's history—a siege against Jerusalem conducted by King Sennacherib of Assyria (ruled 705–681 B.C.) about 690 B.C. (Is. 36; 37).

The fifteen-inch-high clay prism contains well-preserved Assyrian script that verifies the attack on Jerusalem and King Hezekiah of Judah by Assyrian forces. "As to Hezekiah, the Jew, he did not submit to my yoke," the prism reads. "I laid siege to 46 of his strong cities, walled forts and to countless small cities in their vicinity, and conquered them. . . . [Hezekiah] I made a prisoner in Jerusalem, his royal residence, like a bird in a cage."

While Sennacherib's siege against Jerusalem is a verified historical fact, it is interesting that Sennacherib's account does not mention how the siege ended. This leads to suspicion among historians that the siege failed, since the Assyrians never mentioned their defeats in their official records—only their victories.

The biblical account indicates that Sennacherib suffered a crushing defeat in his siege of Jerusalem because of divine intervention. During the night, thousands of soldiers in the Assyrian army died through the action of the angel of the Lord (2 Kin. 19:35). Some scholars believe God used a deadly plague as an instrument of judgment against the enemies of His people.

Rulers of the ancient world used monuments such as this prism on which to record their exploits. These documents of stone and clay have survived for centuries in the rubble and ruin of ancient cities. They provide valuable insight into life in Bible times, confirming and, in many cases, adding valuable information about biblical events.

Assyrian Kings

Second Kings 15:19 provides the first direct mention in Scripture of any Assyrian king. "Pulu" (biblical "Pul") was the Babylonian name given to Tiglath-Pileser III (745–727 B.C.) after his conquest of Babylon. Tiglath-Pileser's campaign of 743 B.C. reached all the way to Israel, where he exacted tribute from Menahem. By this payment of tribute to the king of Assyria, Menahem became a vassal to the Assyrian ruler.

When Tiglath-Pileser III died in 727 B.C., his son Shalmaneser V (727–722 B.C.) succeeded him, and Hoshea of Israel took this as an opportunity to discontinue payment of tribute to Assyria. Hoshea foolishly made a pact with Egypt, which was now so weak and divided that it could not give Hoshea adequate support. In 725 B.C. Shalmaneser V marched against Israel and besieged the city of Samaria from 725–722 B.C. After three years of siege, Samaria fell and the days of Israel as a sovereign power were over.

Second Kings 18:17–37 describes the campaign by the Assyrian king Sennacherib (705–681 B.C.), the less capable son of Sargon II. Hezekiah of Judah had joined with Tyre and

Assur-nasirpal II	883–859 B.C.
Shalmaneser III	858–824 B.C.
Shamshi-Adad V	823–811 B.C.
Adad-nirari III	810–783 B.C.
Shalmaneser IV	782–773 B.C.
Assur-dan III	772–755 B.C.
Assur-nirari V	754–745 B.C.
Tiglath-Pileser III	745–727 B.C.
Shalmaneser V	727–722 B.C.
Sargon II	722–705 B.C.
Sennacherib	705–681 B.C.
Esarhaddon	681–669 B.C.
Ashurbanipal	668–627 B.C.

Egypt in an alliance against Assyria (2 Chr. 32:1–8). Sennacherib, in 701 B.C., proceeded to put down this revolt and moved against the cities of Judah.

Assyrian Campaigns Against Israel and Judah

From 734 B.C. to 732 B.C. Tiglath-Pileser III mounted one invasion against Judah and two against Israel.

Assyrian Campaigns Against Israel

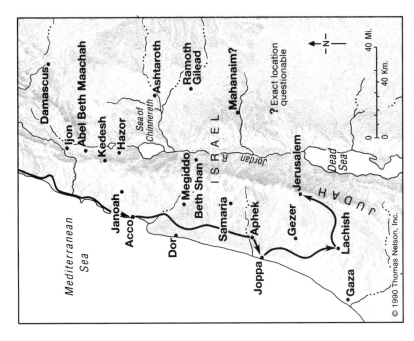

In 725 B.C. Shalmanesar V invaded Israel and marched on Samaria. Sargon II took Samaria in 722 B.C.

Assyrian Campaign Against Judah

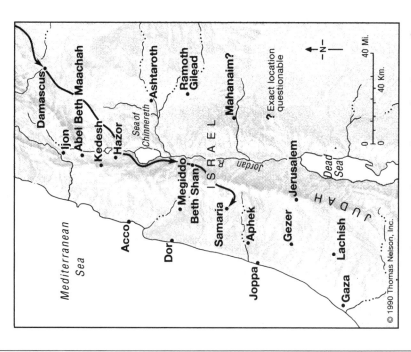

Sennacherib moved southward along the coastal plains to Lachish and camped against Jerusalem in 701 B.C.

The Assyrian Empire (650 B.C.)

This great (and cruel) empire covered the whole of the fertile crescent, with Jerusalem and Judah saved from its complete control by a miraculous defeat of its threatening army (2 Kin. 19).

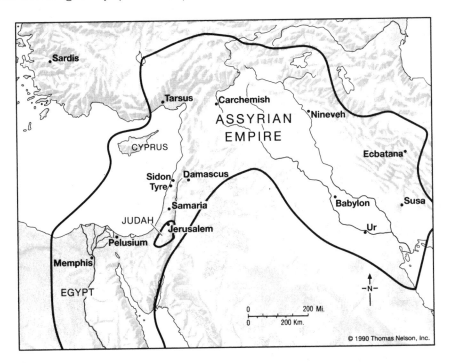

Jerusalem During Hezekiah's Time

The city of Jerusalem was further expanded in the time of Hezekiah, reaching a size of some 150 acres. In his efforts to fortify the city against Sennacherib, Hezekiah ordered the construction of a tunnel that would bring water from the spring of Gihon into the city proper. The tunnel was excavated through solid rock for a distance of almost 600 yards. When it was completed, it emerged just inside the southeastern corner of the old city, where what was later known as the Pool of Siloam was situated. This conduit, referred to in 2 Kings 20:20 and 2 Chronicles 32:30, was a remarkable engineering accomplishment, for the excavators worked with hand tools from opposite ends, meeting in the center.

See map, "Jerusalem in Hezekiah's Time," on page 136.

Babylonian Kings

Assyrian dominance of the ancient Near East came to an end with Babylonian victories at Nineveh (612 B.C.) by Nabopolassar and at Carchemish (605 B.C.)

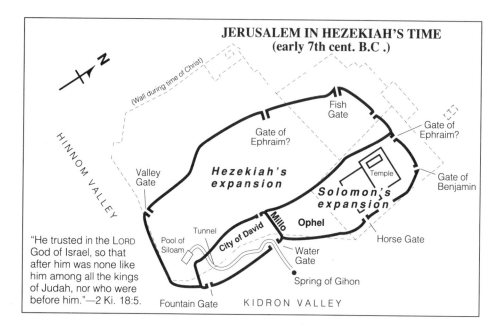

JERUSALEM IN HEZEKIAH'S TIME
(early 7th cent. B.C.)

(Wall during time of Christ)

Fish Gate

Gate of Ephraim?

Gate of Ephraim?

Valley Gate

HINNOM VALLEY

Hezekiah's expansion

Temple

Gate of Benjamin

Solomon's expansion

Millo

Ophel

Tunnel

City of David

Horse Gate

Pool of Siloam

Water Gate

"He trusted in the LORD God of Israel, so that after him was none like him among all the kings of Judah, nor who were before him."—2 Ki. 18:5.

Fountain Gate

Spring of Gihon

KIDRON VALLEY

by Nebuchadnezzar II. After defeating the Egyptians who had come to the aid of Assyria, Nebuchadnezzar immediately forced the submission of Judah's king Jehoiakim and other kings of the area. At this time (605 B.C.), certain young men of Jerusalem, including Daniel, were taken to exile in Babylon.

After Jehoiakim revolted, Jerusalem fell again to Nebuchadnezzar in 597 B.C. The temple was looted and the treasures were taken back to Babylon. A third Babylonian siege of Jerusalem followed Zedekiah's revolt (589 B.C.) and the city fell in July of 587 or 586 B.C.

Evil-Merodach, the son of Nebuchadnezzar, ruled Babylon only two years (562–560 B.C.). He released Judah's king Jehoiachin from prison in Babylon and gave the deposed king a place of privilege in the Babylonian court (25:27–30).

Nabopolassar	626–605 B.C.	Neriglissar	560–556 B.C.
Nebuchadnezzar II	605–562 B.C.	Labasi-Marduk	556 B.C.
Evil-Merodach	562–560 B.C.	Nabonidus (Belshazzar reigned as vice-regent)	555–539 B.C.

The Problem of Chronology

Three factors make the dating of the Kings material extremely difficult: (1) the coregency system, particularly in the southern kingdom, whereby a son officially began his reign during the lifetime of his father, with both father and son receiving credit for the years of coregency; (2) the use of both the "accession-year" system (whereby the year in which a king came to the throne was not counted as his first year) and the "nonaccession-year" system (whereby the remainder of the year in which a king was crowned was reckoned as his first year; and (3) the use of both the sacred-year (beginning with Nisan, the first month) and the civil-year (beginning with Tishri, the seventh month) methods of dating. Because of the complexity of the problems involved in the harmonization of the chronology of the Hebrew kings, many have concluded that the biblical dates are obviously contradictory and hopelessly beyond solution. Today, however, the chronological problems are basically solved, and the biblical dating has been demonstrated to be trustworthy and accurate.

See chart "The Divided Kingdom," on pages 138–140.

Nebuchadnezzar's Campaigns Against Judah

From 605 B.C. to 586 B.C. Judah suffered repeated Babylonian invasions. The final blow came from the southern approach to Jerusalem.

The Divided Kingdom

Southern Kingdom (931–586 B.C.)

King	Date	Biblical References	Prophets
(1) Rehoboam Son of Solomon 17 years	931–913 BC	1 Kin. 14:21–31; 2 Chr. 9:31—12:16	Shemaiah—2 Chr. 11:2–4; 12:5–7, 15 Iddo the Seer—2 Chr. 12:15
(2) Abijam (Abijah) Son of Rehoboam 3 years	913–911 BC	1 Kin. 15:1–8; 2 Chr. 13:1—14:1	Iddo the Seer—2 Chr. 13:22
(3) Asa Son of Abijam 41 years	911–870 BC	1 Kin. 15:9–24 2 Chr. 14:1—16:14	Azariah, the son of Oded—2 Chr. 15:1, 8 (see note in center column) Hanani—2 Chr. 16:7–10
(4) Jehoshaphat Son of Asa 25 years	870(873)–848 B.C.	1 Kin. 22:41–50; 2 Chr. 17:1—21:1	Jehu, the son of Hanani— 2 Chr. 19:2, 3 Jahaziel—2 Chr. 20:14–17 Eliezer—2 Chr. 20:37

Northern Kingdom (931–722 B.C.)

King	Date	Biblical References	Prophets
(1) Jeroboam I Son of Nebat 22 years	931–910 BC	1 Kin. 11:26–40; 12:1—14:20; 2 Chr. 10:1—11:4; 11:13–16; 13:2–20	Ahijah the Shilonite— 1 Kin. 11:29–39; 14:1–18 Man of God from Judah—1 Kin. 13:1–32; 2 Kin. 23:15–18 Old Prophet at Bethel— 1 Kin. 13:11–32; 2 Kin. 23:18 Iddo the Seer—2 Chr. 9:29
(2) Nadab Son of Jeroboam 2 years	910–909 BC	1 Kin. 15:25–31	
(3) Baasha Son of Ahijah 24 years	909–886 BC	1 Kin. 15:16–22, 27–29, 32–34; 16:1–7	Jehu, the son of Hanani—1 Kin. 16:1–7
(4) Elah Son of Baasha 2 years	886–885 BC	1 Kin. 16:8–14	
(5) Zimri Chariot Commander under Elah—7 days	885 BC	1 Kin. 16:9–12, 15–20	
(6) Omri Army Commander under Elah 12 years	885–874 BC	1 Kin. 16:16–18, 21–28	
(7) Ahab Son of Omri 22 years	874–853 BC	1 Kin. 16:29—22:40; 2 Chr. 18:1–34	Elijah—1 Kin. 17—21; 2 Kin. 1; 2 Elisha (servant of Elijah)— 1 Kin. 19:19–21 Micaiah the son of Imlah—1 Kin. 22:8–28; 2 Chr. 18:7–27

Southern Kingdom (931–586 BC)

King	Dates	Scripture	Prophets
(5) Jehoram (Joram) Son of Jehoshaphat 8 years	848(853)–841 BC	2 Kin. 8:16–24; 2 Chr. 21:1–20	Obadiah; Elijah—2 Chr. 21:12–15
(6) Ahaziah (Jehoahaz) Son of Jehoram 1 year	841 BC.	2 Kin. 8:25—9:29; 2 Chr. 22:1–9	
Queen Athaliah Daughter of Ahab; mother of Ahaziah 6 years	841–835 BC	2 Kin. 11:1–20; 2 Chr. 22:10—23:21	
(7) Joash (Jehoash) 40 years	835–796 BC	2 Kin. 11:21—12:21; 2 Chr. 24:1–27	Joel
(8) Amaziah Son of Joash 29 years	796–767 BC	2 Kin. 14:1–20; 2 Chr. 25:1–28	Unnamed Prophets—2 Chr. 25:7–9, 15, 16
(9) Uzziah (Azariah) Son of Amaziah 52 years	767(792)–740 BC	2 Kin. 15:1–7; 2 Chr. 26:1–23	Isaiah—called the year that Uzziah died; Zechariah—2 Chr. 26:5
(10) Jotham Son of Uzziah 16 years	740(750)–731 BC	2 Kin. 15:32–38; 2 Chr. 27:1–9	Isaiah; Micah
(11) Ahaz Son of Jotham 16 years	731(735)–715 BC	2 Kin. 16:1–20; 2 Chr. 28:1–27	Isaiah; Micah

Northern Kingdom (931–722 BC)

Unnamed Prophets—1 Kin. 18:4, 13; 20:28, 35–43; Elijah's Translation—2 Kin. 2:1–18

King	Dates	Scripture	Prophets
(8) Ahaziah Son of Ahab 2 years	853–852 BC	1 Kin. 22:51—2 Kin. 1:18; 2 Chr. 20:35–37	Elisha
(9) Joram (Jehoram) Son of Ahab 12 years	852–841 BC	2 Kin. 3:1—9:26	Elisha
(10) Jehu Son (or grandson) of Nimshi; an army officer under Ahab 28 years	841–814 BC	2 Kin. 9:1—10:36	Elisha
(11) Jehoahaz Son of Jehu 17 years	814–798 BC	2 Kin. 13:1–9	Elisha
(12) Jehoash (Joash) Son of Jehoahaz 16 years	798–782 BC	2 Kin. 13:10–13, 25; 14:8–16; 2 Chr. 25:17–24	Death of Elisha
(13) Jeroboam II Son of Jehoash 41 years	782 (793)–753 BC	2 Kin. 14:23–29	Jonah; Amos; Hosea
(14) Zechariah Son of Jeroboam II 6 months	753–752 B.C.	2 Kin. 15:8–12	Hosea
(15) Shallum Son of Jabesh 1 month	752 B.C.	2 Kin. 15:10, 13–15	Hosea
(16) Menahem Son of Gadi 10 years	752–742 BC	2 Kin. 15:14, 16–22	Hosea
(17) Pekahiah Son of Menahem 2 years	742–740 BC	2 Kin. 15:23–26	Hosea
(18) Pekah Son of Remaliah 20 years	740(752)–732 BC	2 Kin. 15:25, 27–31; 16:5; 2 Chr. 28:5, 6; Is. 7:1	Hosea; Oded the Prophet—2 Chr. 28:9–11

Nelson's Complete Book of Bible Maps and Charts © 1993 by Thomas Nelson, Inc.

Southern Kingdom (931–586 BC)

King	Date	Biblical References	Prophets
(12) Hezekiah Son of Ahaz 29 years	715 (729)–686 BC	2 Kin. 18:1–20:21; 2 Chr. 29:1–32:33; Is. 36:1–39:8	Isaiah Micah
(13) Manasseh Son of Hezekiah 55 years	686 (696)–642 BC	2 Kin. 21:1–18; 2 Chr. 33:1–20	Nahum Unnamed Prophets— 2 Kin. 21:10; 2 Chr. 33:18
(14) Amon Son of Manasseh 2 years	642–640 BC	2 Kin. 21:19–26; 2 Chr. 33:21–25	
(15) Josiah Son of Amon 31 years	640–609 BC	2 Kin. 22:1–23:30; 2 Chr. 34:1–35:27	Jeremiah Zephaniah Huldah the Prophetess— 2 Kin. 22:14–20; 2 Chr. 34:22–28
(16) Jehoahaz (Shallum) Son of Josiah 3 months	609 BC	2 Kin. 23:31–34; 2 Chr. 36:1–4; Jer. 22:1–12	Jeremiah
(17) Jehoiakim (Eliakim) Son of Josiah 11 years	609–598 BC	2 Kin. 23:34–24:7; 2 Chr. 36:4–8; Jer. 22:13–23; 26; 36	Jeremiah Habakkuk Daniel Urijah the son of Shemaiah Jer. 26:20
(18) Jehoiachin (Coniah) Son of Jehoiakim 3 months	598–597 BC	2 Kin. 24:8–17; 2 Chr. 36:9, 10; Jer. 22:24–30; 52:31–34	Jeremiah Daniel
(19) Zedekiah (Mattaniah) Son of Josiah 11 years	597–586 BC	2 Kin. 24:17–25:7; 2 Chr. 36:11–21; Jer. 39:1–10; 52:1–11	Jeremiah Daniel Ezekiel

586 BC—Fall of Jerusalem
(Southern Kingdom Goes into Captivity—Babylon)

Northern Kingdom (931–722 BC)

King	Date	Biblical References	Prophets
(19) Hoshea Son of Elah 9 years	732–722 BC	2 Kin. 15:30; 17:1–6; 18:9, 10	Hosea

722 BC—Fall of Samaria
(10 Northern Tribes Go into Captivity—Assyria)

NOTES: * Names in parentheses denote alternate names of the same king.
** Dates in parentheses denote coregencies, a period of rule in which the son occupied the throne with his father.
*** Prophets whose names appear in boldface letters are canonical prophets.

Nelson's Complete Book of Bible Maps and Charts © 1993 by Thomas Nelson, Inc.

1 AND 2 CHRONICLES

The books of 1 and 2 Chronicles cover the same period of Jewish history described in 2 Samuel through 2 Kings, though from a different perspective. While the books of Kings relate the history of Israel from the standpoint of captivity in Babylon, Chronicles presents the history of the Jews from the postexilic standpoint of those who have returned from captivity to the Land of Promise.

Like the books of Samuel and Kings, 1 and 2 Chronicles were originally a single continuous work. The two books were first separated by the translators of the Septuagint (Greek Old Testament). The name "Chronicles" comes from Jerome in his Latin Vulgate Bible (A.D. 385–405): *Chronicorum Liber*. He meant this title in the sense of "The Chronicles of the Whole of Sacred History."

Author

Although the author and date are not stated in the text, the Jewish tradition that Chronicles was penned by Ezra may be correct. Nevertheless, it is customary to speak of the author simply as "the chronicler." Some believe Chronicles, Ezra, and Nehemiah had the same author; the final verses of Chronicles (2 Chr. 36:22, 23) are repeated in Ezra 1:1–3.

Date

Internal evidence indicates that the Chronicles were probably composed sometime in the fifth century B.C. A postexilic date is underscored by the mention of the six generations following Zerubbabel (1 Chr. 3:17–21) and of the Persian coins known as "darics" (1 Chr. 29:7).

The books of Chronicles cover a wider space of time than any other work in Scripture. The genealogies and narrative of 1 Chronicles span the period from

Continued on page 143

1 Chronicles at a Glance

FOCUS	ROYAL LINE OF DAVID	REIGN OF DAVID				
REFERENCE	1:1 ——————— 10:1 ———	13:1 ——————— 18:1 ———————		21:1 ——————— 28:1 ——— 29:30			
DIVISION	GENEALOGIES OF DAVID AND ISRAEL	ACCESSION OF DAVID AS KING	ACQUISITION OF THE ARK	VICTORIES OF DAVID	PREPARATION FOR THE TEMPLE	LAST DAYS OF DAVID
TOPIC	GENEALOGY	HISTORY				
	ANCESTRY	ACTIVITY				
LOCATION	ISRAEL					
TIME	THOUSANDS OF YEARS	c. 33 YEARS				

Nelson's Complete Book of Bible Maps and Charts © 1993 by Thomas Nelson, Inc.

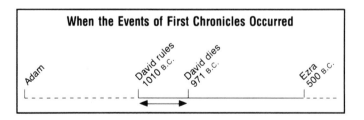

When the Events of First Chronicles Occurred

Adam — David rules 1010 B.C. — David dies 971 B.C. — Ezra 500 B.C.

Continued from page 141

Adam to the end of the life of David. Second Chronicles recounts the downfall of the Davidic dynasty from Solomon to the Exile.

Themes and Literary Structure

The Chronicles were written to the returned remnant who were rebuilding Jerusalem following their seventy-year Babylonian captivity. Because the returning exiles were originally from Judah, the religious and national heritage and history of the Southern kingdom (Judah) is presented by showing its unbroken connection with the patriarchal beginnings.

Chronicles is written from a priestly perspective. The primary historical theme centers around the priestly worship of Judah, from the time of Saul until the return of the Jewish nation to the land following the decree of Cyrus (538 B.C.). This religious history depicts the faithfulness and promises of God to His people, the power of the Word of God, and the central role of worship in the lives of God's people.

The temple in Jerusalem is the major unifying theme of 1 and 2 Chronicles. Much of the material found in Samuel and Kings is omitted from Chronicles because it does not develop this theme. For example, the kings of the northern kingdom are left out because of their rejection of temple worship at Jerusalem, while prominence is given to the reigns of Judah's temple restorers (Asa, Jehoshaphat, Joash, Hezekiah, and Josiah). The temple symbolizes God's presence among His people and reminds them of their high calling. It provides the spiritual link between their past and future.

The line and dynasty of David, recipient of the promises of the Davidic Covenant (1 Chr. 17:3–15), is important to Chronicles. The genealogies of 1 Chronicles 1—9 place a disproportionate emphasis on the tribes of Judah and Benjamin because Chronicles is not concerned with the Northern Kingdom but with the Southern Kingdom and the Davidic dynasty. They demonstrate God's keeping of His covenant promises in maintaining the Davidic line through the centuries. In keeping with the priestly interest of Chronicles, special attention is also paid to the tribe of Levi.

The whole book of 1 Chronicles, like 2 Samuel, is dedicated to the life of David. It begins with the genealogy of the royal line of David (chs. 1—9) before surveying key events of the reign of David (chs. 10—29).

See chart on page 144.

Samuel–Kings	Chronicles
• Prophetic Perspective	• Priestly Perspective
• Political History	• Religious History
• Wars Prominent	• Temple Prominent
• Record of Both Nations	• Record of Judah
• Continuing History of Nation	• Continuity of David's Line
• Man's Failure	• God's Faithfulness

OUTLINE OF 1 CHRONICLES

Second Chronicles begins with the reign of Solomon (chs. 1—9). While these chapters relate the grandeur of Solomon's kingdom, their primary concern is to describe the construction and dedication of the temple. The balance of 2 Chronicles (chs. 10—36) is a history of the Davidic dynasty, with particular attention to the history of temple worship. The book concludes with the edict of Cyrus of Persia ordering the rebuilding of the temple.

Other Bible charts, maps, and study helps relevant to the material in Chronicles may be found in the sections covering the books of Samuel and Kings.

OUTLINE OF 2 CHRONICLES

Continued on page 148

2 Chronicles at a Glance

FOCUS	REIGN OF SOLOMON			REIGNS OF THE KINGS OF JUDAH		
REFERENCE	1:1 ——————— 2:1 ——————— 8:1 ———————			10:1 ——————— 14:1 ———————		36:1 —— 36:23
DIVISION	INAUGURATION OF SOLOMON	COMPLETION OF THE TEMPLE	THE GLORY OF SOLOMON'S REIGN	THE DIVISION OF THE KINGDOM	THE REFORMS UNDER ASA, JEHOSHAPHAT, JOASH, HEZEKIAH, AND JOSIAH	THE FALL OF JUDAH
TOPIC	THE TEMPLE IS CONSTRUCTED			THE TEMPLE IS DESTROYED		
TOPIC	SPLENDOR			DISASTER		
LOCATION	JUDAH					
TIME	c. 40 YEARS			c. 393 YEARS		

Nelson's Complete Book of Bible Maps and Charts © 1993 by Thomas Nelson, Inc.

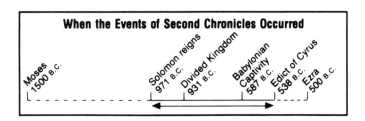

When the Events of Second Chronicles Occurred

Moses 1500 B.C.
Solomon reigns 971 B.C.
Divided Kingdom 931 B.C.
Babylonian Captivity 587 B.C.
Edict of Cyrus 538 B.C.
Ezra 500 B.C.

Continued from page 146

Part Two: The Reigns of the Kings of Judah (10:1—36:23)

The Temple

The temple, located in Jerusalem, was the center of the religious life of the Jewish people. In this sanctuary devoted to worship of the one true God, priests offered sacrifices to God to atone for the sins of the nation of Israel. Through temple services, the Jewish people pledged their lives to follow the laws and teachings of their creator.

Before the temple was built, the tabernacle was used as a place of worship by the Hebrew people. During much of their history, the tabernacle was moved from place to place to accompany the nation of Israel in their wanderings (Ex. 40). But after they settled in their permanent home in the Land of Promise, God commanded through His servant David that the temple be constructed. This more ornate structure, devoted to worship, would be a permanent fixture in their capital city (1 Chr. 28).

Three separate temples were actually built in Jerusalem across a period of about a thousand years in Jewish history. All three were built on the same site—on a hill known as Mount Moriah in the eastern section of the Holy City (2 Chr. 3:1).

The first temple, built by King Solomon about 960 B.C., stood on a platform about ten feet high with ten steps leading to an entrance flanked by two stone pillars. Thousands of common laborers and skilled craftsmen were involved in its construction (1 Kin. 6; 7; 2 Chr. 3; 4). This building was destroyed by the Babylonians when they captured Jerusalem in 586 B.C. But Cyrus, king of

Persia, authorized reconstruction of this building on the same site when he allowed the Jewish people to return to Jerusalem (Ezra 1). This structure, known as Zerubbabel's temple, was completed about 515 B.C. at the urging of the prophets Haggai and Zechariah (Ezra 6:13–15).

Several centuries later, Herod the Great, Roman ruler of Palestine, ordered construction of the third temple—an ornate, cream-colored building of stone and gold—to appease the Jewish people. This temple was the structure to which Jesus referred in speaking of His resurrection (John 2:19, 20). As He predicted, this temple was destroyed by the Romans about 40 years after His resurrection and ascension—in A.D. 70.

The accounts of Solomon's temple in the Old Testament suggest it had an inner courtyard, as well as an outer courtyard. The three main objects in the inner courtyard were (1) the bronze altar used for burnt offerings (1 Kin. 8:22, 64; 9:25); (2) the sea of cast bronze, which held water for ritual washings by the priests (1 Kin. 7:23–26); and (3) twelve oxen, apparently also cast bronze, which held the sea of bronze on their backs (1 Kin. 7:25).

In the inner courtyard was an area known as the holy place, which contained the golden incense altar, the table with showbread, five pairs of lampstands, and utensils used for offering sacrifices (1 Kin. 7:48–50). Beyond this area was a room known as the Most Holy Place, or the Holy of Holies, a restricted place which only the high priest could enter. Even he could go into this area only once a year—on the Day of Atonement when he went inside to make atonement for his own sins and then for the sins of the people (Lev. 16). In this room was the ark of the covenant, containing the stone tablets on which the Ten Commandments were written. God's presence was manifested in the Most Holy Place as a cloud (1 Kin. 8:5–11).

Jesus related to the temple in several ways. He showed respect for the temple and referred to it as "My Father's house" (John 2:16). His zeal led Him to purge the temple of merchants who were selling sacrificial animals, thus defiling the "house of prayer" (Mark 11:15–17). But as much as He respected the house of God, Jesus also taught that He was greater than the temple (Matt. 12:6).

His superiority to the temple was clearly shown when the veil of the temple was split from top to bottom at His death (Matt. 27:51). The veil hung before the most sacred place in the temple to keep out all persons except the Jewish high priest. The tearing of the veil symbolized that every believer has unhindered access to God through His Son Jesus Christ because of His sacrificial death on our behalf.

See chart, "Solomon's Temple," on page 119.

The Temples of the Bible

The Temple	Date	Description	Reference
The Tabernacle (Mobile Temple)	about 1444 B.C.	Detailed plan received by Moses from the Lord Constructed by divinely appointed artisans Desecrated by Nadab and Abihu	Ex. 25—30; Ex. 35:30—40:38; Lev. 10:1–7
Solomon's Temple	966–586 B.C.	Planned by David Constructed by Solomon Destroyed by Nebuchadnezzar	2 Sam. 7:1–29; 1 Kin. 8:1–66; Jer. 32:28–44
Zerubbabel's Temple	516–169 B.C.	Envisioned by Zerubbabel Constructed by Zerubbabel and the elders of the Jews Desecrated by Antiochus Epiphanes	Ezra 6:1–22; Ezra 3:1–8; 4:1–14; Matt. 24:15
Herod's Temple	19 B.C.–A.D. 70.	Zerubbabel's temple restored by Herod the Great Destroyed by the Romans	Mark 13:2, 14–23; Luke 1:11–20; 2:22–38; 2:42–51; 4:21–24; Acts 21:27–33
The Present Temple	Present Age.	Found in the heart of the believer The body of the believer is the Lord's only temple until the Messiah returns	1 Cor. 6:19, 20; 2 Cor. 6:16–18
The Temple of Revelation 11	Tribulation Period.	To be constructed during the Tribulation by the Antichrist To be desecrated and destroyed	Dan. 9:2; Matt. 24:15; 2 Thess. 2:4; Rev. 17:18
Ezekiel's (Millennial) Temple	Millennium.	Envisioned by the prophet Ezekiel To be built by the Messiah during His millennial reign	Ezek. 40:1—42:20; Zech. 6:12, 13
The Eternal Temple of His Presence	The Eternal Kingdom.	The greatest temple of all ("The Lord God Almighty and the Lamb are its temple") A spiritual temple	Rev. 21:22; Rev. 22:1–21

The temple (Gk. *hieron*) is a place of worship, a sacred or holy space built primarily for the national worship of God.

Prisoners for the Lord

PERSON	SITUATION
Joseph (Gen. 39:7–23; 41:1–45)	Refused to be seduced by his boss's wife, resulting in false accusations of sexual harassment and time in prison; eventually rose to leadership according to God's plan.
Samson (Judg. 16:21–31)	Allowed himself to be tricked by his lover Delilah into revealing the secret of his strength, resulting in arrest by the Philistines, who paraded him as a trophy until God enabled him to take revenge—and his own life in the process.
Micaiah (1 Kin. 22:1–38)	Refused to join other prophets in falsely predicting that Ahab would succeed in battle, resulting in his imprisonment; Ahab did die in battle.
Hanani (2 Chr. 16:7–10)	As a seer of the Lord, condemned King Asa for relying on the Syrians, for which he was put in prison.
Jeremiah (Jer. 37—38)	Prophesied that Judah would not be able to withstand a siege of the Chaldeans, then was imprisoned on a charge of desertion; later repeated his warning to King Zedekiah, and was put in a cistern; then warned Zedekiah a third time and was allowed to remain in the court of the prison until the nation fell to Babylon.
John the Baptist (Matt. 14:1–12)	Opposed the marriage of Herod Antipas to Herodias, wife of the tetrarch's half-brother and also his niece, for which John was imprisoned; later executed as a result of Herodias' trickery.
Peter and John (Acts 4:1–21)	Imprisoned as spokesmen of a new movement of Jesus' followers after a man was miraculously healed; released after being sternly warned not to teach about Jesus—a prohibition they immediately ignored.
Paul and Silas (Acts 16:16–40)	Delivered a young woman of Philippi both from demons and the power of her "employers," for which they were slandered, beaten, and jailed; miraculously released and later vindicated because of their Roman citizenship.
Paul (Acts 21:30—28:31)	Mobbed by antagonistic Jews, rescued by Roman soldiers, tried by regional rulers, and ultimately taken in chains to Rome as a prisoner of the empire.

EZRA

zra continues the Old Testament narrative of 2 Chronicles by showing how God fulfills His promise to return His people to the Land of Promise after seventy years of exile. Israel's "second exodus," this one from Babylon, is less impressive because only a remnant chooses to leave Babylon. Ezra relates the story of two returns from Babylon—the first led by Zerubbabel to rebuild the temple (chs. 1—6), and the second under the leadership of Ezra to rebuild the spiritual condition of the people (chs. 7—10).

Ezra and Nehemiah were treated as a unit in the original Hebrew and in the Greek translation known as the Septuagint. The two were separated in the Latin translation, and English translations have likewise treated them as separate works.

Author

Although Ezra is not specifically mentioned as the author, he is certainly the best candidate. Jewish tradition (the Talmud) attributes the book to Ezra, and portions of the work (7:28—9:15) are written in the first person, from Ezra's point of view. As in Chronicles, there is a strong priestly emphasis, and Ezra was a direct priestly descendant of Aaron through Eleazar, Phineas, and Zadok (7:1–5).

Date

Just as the Israelites were taken into exile in three successive stages (605, 597, 586 B.C.), they returned in three stages. The first occurred under the leadership of Zerubbabel (c. 538 B.C.). After considerable delay, this return resulted in the rebuilding of the temple (c. 520–516 B.C.), encouraged by the prophets Haggai and Zechariah. Ezra led the second return in the seventh year of Artaxerxes I (c. 458 B.C.). Nehemiah led the final return in the twentieth year of Artaxerxes I (c. 444 B.C.). Chronologically, the events of the book of Esther occur during a ten-to-twelve-year period (483–473 B.C.) between the first and second returns.

Continued on page 156

Ezra at a Glance

FOCUS	RESTORATION OF THE TEMPLE		REFORMATION OF THE PEOPLE	
REFERENCE	1:1 ———————— 3:1 ———————		7:1 ————————— 9:1 ———— 10:44	
DIVISION	FIRST RETURN TO JERUSALEM	CONSTRUCTION OF THE TEMPLE	SECOND RETURN TO JERUSALEM	RESTORATION OF THE PEOPLE
TOPIC	ZERUBBABEL		EZRA	
	FIRST RETURN OF 49,897		SECOND RETURN OF 1,754	
LOCATION	PERSIA TO JERUSALEM		PERSIA TO JERUSALEM	
TIME	22 YEARS (538–516 B.C.)		1 YEAR (458–457 B.C.)	

Nelson's Complete Book of Bible Maps and Charts © 1993 by Thomas Nelson, Inc.

When the Events of Ezra Occurred

David 1000 B.C. — Babylonian Captivity 587 B.C. — 1st return to Jerusalem 538 B.C. — Nehemiah's return to Jerusalem 444 B.C. — Jesus 4 B.C.

Continued from page 154

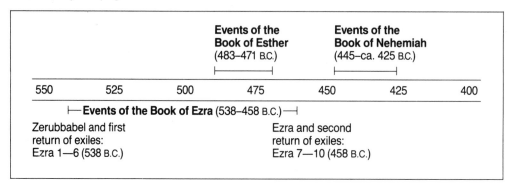

			Events of the Book of Esther (483–471 B.C.)	Events of the Book of Nehemiah (445–ca. 425 B.C.)		
550	525	500	475	450	425	400

├─**Events of the Book of Ezra** (538–458 B.C.)─┤

Zerubbabel and first
return of exiles:
Ezra 1—6 (538 B.C.)

Ezra and second
return of exiles:
Ezra 7—10 (458 B.C.)

Ezra (if he in fact is the author-compiler) probably wrote this book between 457 B.C. (the events of chs. 7—10) and 444 B.C. (Nehemiah's arrival in Jerusalem). During the period covered by the book of Ezra, Gautama Buddha (c. 560–480 B.C.) was in India, Confucius (551–479 B.C.) was in China, and Socrates (470–399 B.C.) was in Greece.

Themes and Literary Structure

 Ezra relates the first two returns from Babylon, the first led by Zerubbabel and the second led decades later by Ezra. Its two divisions are the restoration of the temple (chs. 1—6) and the reformation of the people (chs. 7—10).

The basic theme of Ezra is restoration—the restoration of the temple and the spiritual, moral, and social restoration of the returned remnant in Jerusalem under the leadership of Zerubbabel and Ezra. Both are undertaken despite opposition and difficulty.

The restoration of temple and people required a reassertion of the distinctive identity of Israel and her faith, together with separation from other peoples and pagan beliefs. This restoration was taking place in the context of the Persian empire, in which the dominant religious tendency was the merging of religious beliefs into one. The various peoples of the empire were encouraged to maintain their distinctive cultures, but without religious exclusivism. In this environment, the Jews experienced tremendous temptation to surrender all their previous claims to having an exclusive revelation from God. In addition, there was enormous temptation to surrender those behaviors which had been designed to separate them from the surrounding pagan cultures. In this context, the reestablishment of a temple worship purified of pagan religious influences and the purification of the people from intermarriage with other peoples were both necessary.

God's faithfulness is seen in the way He sovereignly protects His people in the midst of a powerful empire while they are in captivity. They prosper in their exile, and God raises up pagan kings who are sympathetic to their cause and encourage them to rebuild their homeland. God also provides zealous and capable leaders who direct the return and the rebuilding.

OUTLINE OF EZRA

The Return from Exile

When Cyrus the Persian captured Babylon in 539 B.C., government controls on captive peoples were loosened and the way was opened for exiled Judah to begin the return to her homeland. The ascension and victory of Cyrus fulfilled the prophecy of Isaiah 44:28—45:4. Three major expeditions made the journey: one in 538–537 B.C. under Zerubbabel, the second under Ezra in 458 B.C., and the last under Nehemiah in 444 B.C.

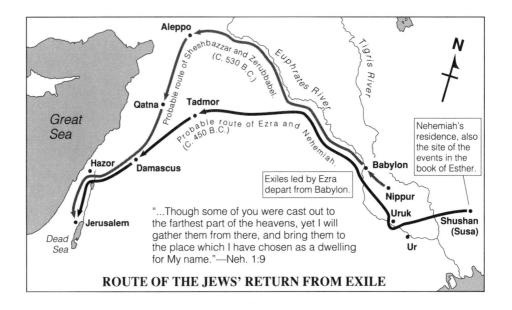

Probable route of Sheshbazzar and Zerubbabel. (C. 530 B.C.)

Probable route of Ezra and Nehemiah (C. 450 B.C.)

Euphrates River

Tigris River

Aleppo

Qatna • Tadmor

Great Sea

Hazor • Damascus

Jerusalem

Dead Sea

Nehemiah's residence, also the site of the events in the book of Esther.

Babylon

Exiles led by Ezra depart from Babylon.

Nippur

Uruk

Ur

Shushan (Susa)

"...Though some of you were cast out to the farthest part of the heavens, yet I will gather them from there, and bring them to the place which I have chosen as a dwelling for My name."—Neh. 1:9

ROUTE OF THE JEWS' RETURN FROM EXILE

NEHEMIAH

ehemiah, contemporary of Ezra and cupbearer to the king in the Persian palace, led the third and last return to Jerusalem after the Babylonian exile. Granted permission by the Persian king to return to his homeland, Nehemiah challenged his countrymen to rebuild the shattered walls of Jerusalem. In spite of opposition, the task was completed in only fifty-two days. By contrast, the task of reviving and reforming the people of God demanded years of Nehemiah's godly life and leadership.

The book of Nehemiah is a complement to the book of Ezra. It provides additional information about the religious and social reforms that took place in Judah and Jerusalem in the mid-fifth century B.C. The book derives its present title from the main character, Nehemiah, whose name appears in 1:1. Originally united with the book of Ezra in the Hebrew text, Nehemiah was treated as a separate book when the Scriptures were translated into Latin.

Author

Because Ezra and Nehemiah were treated as one book in the Hebrew text, and because the two books show certain similarities in style and outlook, many scholars have believed that Ezra and Nehemiah were originally compiled by the same person, probably Ezra. It is important that 1:1 describes the contents as "the words of Nehemiah." This assertion is supported by the narrative about Nehemiah being in the first person. Thus, if Ezra was the compiler, he was apparently quoting directly from the writings of Nehemiah.

Nehemiah held the very responsible position of cupbearer to King Artaxerxes. This was evidently more akin to being a personal advisor than merely something like a butler. That the king eventually made Nehemiah governor of Judah bears witness to his considerable administrative abilities. Frequently the cupbearer was also a eunuch, and this may explain why there is no reference to Nehemiah's family.

Nehemiah at a Glance

FOCUS	RECONSTRUCTION OF THE WALL		RESTORATION OF THE PEOPLE	
REFERENCE	1:1 —————— 3:1 —————	——— 8:1 —————	——— 11:1 —————	—— 13:31
DIVISION	PREPARATION TO RECONSTRUCT THE WALL	RECONSTRUCTION OF THE WALL	RENEWAL OF THE COVENANT	OBEDIENCE TO THE COVENANT
TOPIC	POLITICAL		SPIRITUAL	
	CONSTRUCTION		INSTRUCTION	
LOCATION	JERUSALEM			
TIME	19 YEARS (444–425 B.C.)			

Nelson's Complete Book of Bible Maps and Charts © 1993 by Thomas Nelson, Inc.

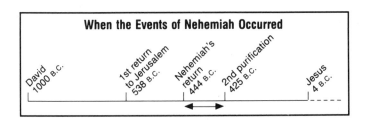

When the Events of Nehemiah Occurred

David 1000 B.C.   1st return to Jerusalem 538 B.C.   Nehemiah's return 444 B.C.   2nd purification 425 B.C.   Jesus 4 B.C.

Date

• DATE • Nehemiah is closely associated with the ministry of his contemporary, Ezra. As a priest, Ezra helped to bring spiritual revival; Nehemiah as governor helped to bring physical and political reconstruction and led the people in moral reform. Together, they combined to make an effective team in rebuilding the postexilic remnant. Malachi, the last Old Testament prophet, also ministered during this time to provide additional moral and spiritual direction.

The book of Nehemiah focuses on the events surrounding the third return from the Exile, in 444 B.C. Nehemiah served twice as governor of Judah. His first time as governor spanned twelve years (5:14), and ended when he returned to Babylon (13:6). He then returned to Jerusalem "after certain days." If the king was still Artaxerxes I, as seems likely, then Nehemiah's second governorship began prior to 424 B.C., when the king died. Thus, the book of Nehemiah was probably written between 430 and 420 B.C.

Themes and Literary Structure

The book of Nehemiah completes the historical account of God's people in the Old Testament, about four hundred years before the birth of the promised Messiah. Its two divisions are: the reconstruction of the wall (chs. 1—13), and the restoration of the people (chs. 8—13).

While Ezra deals with the religious restoration of Judah, Nehemiah is primarily concerned with Judah's political and geographical restoration. Great attention is devoted to the rebuilding of Jerusalem's walls, because Jerusalem was the spiritual and political center of Judah. Without walls, Jerusalem could hardly be considered a city at all.

Prominent in the book of Nehemiah, as in the rest of the Old Testament, is the concept of God's covenant with His people. The Old Testament treats Israel's history in terms of her faithfulness or disobedience to the covenant. Nehemiah 9:1—10:39 records a covenant renewal ceremony in which the people commit themselves to separate from the Gentiles in marriage and to obey God's commandments.

God's faithfulness to His people is highlighted by the extensive narrative of the rebuilding of the walls. This rebuilding was accomplished despite considerable odds against it: there was the question whether the Persian king would permit it, as well as the concerted opposition facing Nehemiah in Jerusalem from the Samaritans and the Ammonites. Despite nearly overwhelming difficulties, the rebuilding was completed in fifty-two days, and even Nehemiah's enemies conceded that the effort was the work of God (6:15–16).

Persian Kings

The events of the book of Ezra begin during the reign of Cyrus (c. 538). The book of Nehemiah fits within the reign of Artaxerxes I of Persia (465–24 B.C.). Esther was Artaxerxes' stepmother, and it is possible that she arranged Nehemiah's appointment as the king's cupbearer. Nehemiah left Persia in the twentieth year of Artaxerxes (2:1), returned to Persia in the thirty-second year of Artaxerxes (13:6), and left again for Jerusalem "after certain days" (13:6), perhaps about 425 B.C.

	Cyrus 559–530	Cambyses 530–522	Smerdis 522	Darius I 522–486	Xerxes I (Ahasuerus) (486–465)	Artaxerxes I 465–424	Xerxes II 424	Darius II 423–404
575	550	525		500	475	450	425	400

Nehemiah the Servant

An important and loyal servant of the king of Persia, Nehemiah was the cup-bearer whose work protected the king from poisoning. His duties of selecting and tasting the king's wine gave him constant access to the king. Nehemiah also proved himself to be an important and loyal servant of God and the Jewish people.

A Servant...	Because God...
Prays for his people (1:4)	*Preserves* His covenant (1:5)
Plans for his people (2:6–8)	*Places* ideas in his mind (2:12)
Perseveres against enemies for his people (4:9, 23)	*Perverts* their plans (4:15, 20)
Pleads for unity among his people (5:10, 11)	Is *pleased* with unity (5:9, 13)
Perceives falsehood and remains faithful (6:2, 8, 12)	*Proclaims* His name among the nations (6:16)

Nehemiah's Reconstruction Project

Many geographical landmarks in the city of Jerusalem are mentioned in the book of Nehemiah (3:12–18; 12:27–39). As reconstructed by Zerubbabel, Ezra, and Nehemiah, the postexilic city of Jerusalem was considerably smaller and less grand than the city which fell to Babylon in 586 B.C.

Jerusalem in Nehemiah's Time

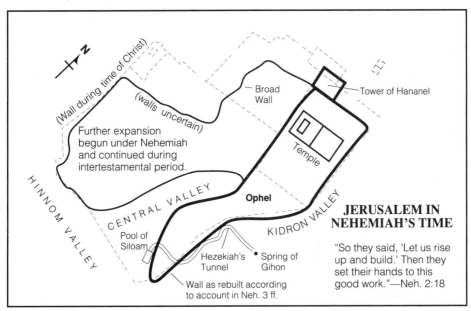

Nelson's Complete Book of Bible Maps and Charts © 1993 by Thomas Nelson, Inc.

ESTHER

God's hand of providence and protection on behalf of His people is evident throughout the book of Esther, even though the name of God does not appear once in the work. Haman's plot to destroy the Jews brings grave danger to God's people and is countered by the courage of Esther and the counsel of her wise cousin Mordecai, resulting in a great deliverance. The Jewish feast of Purim becomes an annual reminder of God's faithfulness on behalf of His people.

Author

While the text of Esther does not specify the author's identity, the writer's knowledge of Persian customs, the palace at Susa, and details of the events in the reign of Ahasuerus indicate that the author lived in Persia during this period. The obvious Jewish nationalism and knowledge further suggest that the author was Jewish. Ezra and Nehemiah have been suggested as possible authors, but the style of Esther differs markedly from Ezra and Nehemiah and any precise identification remains speculative.

Date

The events described in Esther occurred between 483–473 B.C. and fit between chapters 6 and 7 of Ezra, between the first return led by Zerubbabel and the second led by Ezra. That the author speaks of King Ahasuerus in the past tense (1:1) suggests that the book may have been written during the reign of Artaxerxes I (465–424 B.C.). Linguistically, the book may be dated to the latter half of the fifth or the early fourth century B.C.

Themes and Literary Structure

Historically, the book of Esther unveils a segment of Jewish history occurring during the Jewish captivity in Persia. It provides the only biblical portrait of the vast majority of Jews who chose to remain in Persia rather than return to Palestine.

Although there is little reason to doubt its historical character, the book of Esther is also a finely-crafted literary work in which the author presents a

Continued on page 166

Esther at a Glance

FOCUS	THREAT TO THE JEWS		TRIUMPH OF THE JEWS	
REFERENCE	1:1 ———————— 2:21 ———————		5:1 ———————— 8:4 ———————— 10:3	
DIVISION	SELECTION OF ESTHER AS QUEEN	FORMULATION OF THE PLOT BY HAMAN	TRIUMPH OF MORDECAI OVER HAMAN	TRIUMPH OF ISRAEL OVER HER ENEMIES
TOPIC	FEASTS OF AHASUERUS		FEASTS OF ESTHER AND PURIM	
	GRAVE DANGER		GREAT DELIVERANCE	
LOCATION	PERSIA			
TIME	10 YEARS (483–473 B.C.)			

Nelson's Complete Book of Bible Maps and Charts © 1993 by Thomas Nelson, Inc.

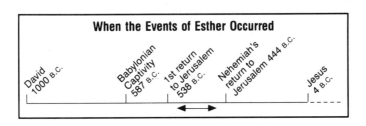

When the Events of Esther Occurred

David 1000 B.C. — Babylonian Captivity 587 B.C. — 1st return to Jerusalem 538 B.C. — Nehemiah's return to Jerusalem 444 B.C. — Jesus 4 B.C.

Continued from page 164
complicated plot of danger and deliverance with considerable skill. The book of Esther may be divided into two main sections: the threat to the Jews (chs. 1—4) and the triumph of the Jews (chs. 5—10).

Theologically, the theme of God's providential protection of His people pervades this book, although the name of God, or even the word for "God," is not found in the text—a fact that accounts for some of the later objections to the book's canonicity. Though God disciplines His people, He does not abandon them. The God of Israel is sovereign over history and His providence is evident on every page. Esther "happens" to be chosen queen; her cousin Mordecai "happens" to foil an assassination plot against the king; the king "happens" to read of Mordecai's deed at just the right time. The book implies that none of this is accidental, that God is firmly in control and is determined to keep His covenant promises to the children of Abraham.

The conduct of God's people is also important in Esther. The trouble comes to the Jews because Mordecai will not give worship to someone other than God. He will not surrender his commitment to God even to save himself and his people.

The theme of feasting is very prominent in Esther. A total of ten banquets are mentioned and crucial developments in the story typically happen at feasts (e.g., the disobedience of Vashti, Esther's attempt to save her people, the unmasking and condemnation of Haman). This banquet theme serves to highlight one important purpose of the book: an explanation of the origin of the Jewish Feast of Purim (9:18–32).

OUTLINE OF ESTHER

Part One: The Threat to the Jews (1:1—4:17)

Part Two: The Triumph of the Jews (5:1—10:3)

Persian Customs in the Book of Esther

The Book of Esther records events during the reign of King Ahasuerus (Xerxes) in the fifth century B.C. at Shushan (Susa), administrative capital of the Persian Empire. After the death of Darius I (the Persian king who had allowed any Jews who desired to return to their homeland to do so), his son Ahasuerus became king. Ahasuerus was the king who became dissatisfied with his queen, Vashti, and banished her, marrying Esther.

Royal Persian feasts were noted for their splendor and opulence. Esther describes the Persian custom of eating while reclining on beds or couches. All eating utensils were made of gold, "the vessels being diverse one from another" (1:7).

Special laws protected the Persian king. Esther 1:14 refers to the seven princes who "saw the king's face." These were the chief nobles who were his advisors. Only a person summoned by the king could visit him, a custom which signified his royalty, as well as protected him from would-be assassins.

Ruins of the palace of King Darius I at Persepolis.
Photo by Howard Vos

Esther feared going to Ahasuerus without being called, because the punishment for such a visit was death (4:11).

The Persian Empire boasted a well-organized postal system (3:13). The king's ring (8:8) was the signet ring with which official documents were signed. In ancient Persia documents were sealed in two ways: with a signet ring if they were written on papyrus, or with a cylinder seal if written on clay tablets. Among the objects excavated at the royal city of Persepolis (see photo, p. 167) was a cylinder seal, which belonged to King Xerxes.

The book of Esther also refers to "the laws of the Persians and the Medes" (1:19). This phrase describes the ironclad nature of the laws that governed the Persian Empire. Once a law was issued, it could not be changed or revoked—not even by the king himself.

Old Testament Women

One of the outstanding women of the Old Testament was Esther, a Jewish captive in Persia who saved her people from destruction by the schemer Haman (Esth. 1—10).

Other outstanding women of the Old Testament (for a New Testament list, see p. 337) include the following:

Name	Description	Biblical Reference
Bathsheba	Wife of David; mother of Solomon	2 Sam. 11:3, 27
Deborah	Judge who defeated the Canaanites	Judg. 4:4
Delilah	Philistine who tricked Samson	Judg. 16:4, 5
Dinah	Only daughter of Jacob	Gen. 30:21
Eve	First woman	Gen. 3:20
Gomer	Prophet Hosea's unfaithful wife	Hos. 1:2, 3
Hagar	Sarah's maid; mother of Ishmael	Gen. 16:3–16
Hannah	Mother of Samuel	1 Sam. 1
Jezebel	Wicked wife of King Ahab	1 Kin. 16:30, 31
Jochebed	Mother of Moses	Ex. 6:20
Miriam	Sister of Moses; a prophetess	Ex. 15:20
Naomi	Ruth's mother-in-law	Ruth 1:2, 4
Orpah	Ruth's sister-in-law	Ruth 1:4
Rachel	Wife of Jacob	Gen. 29:28
Rahab	Harlot who harbored Israel's spies; ancestor of Jesus	Josh. 2:3–1; Matt. 1:5
Ruth	Wife of Boaz and mother of Obed; ancestor of Jesus	Ruth 4:13, 17; Matt. 1:5
Sarah	Wife of Abraham; mother of Isaac	Gen. 11:29; 21:2, 3
Tamar	A daughter of David	2 Sam. 13:1
Zipporah	Wife of Moses	Ex. 2:21

Jewish Feasts

The Feast of Purim, which was established in the month of Adar—the last month of the sacred year—is a continual reminder of the heroism of Esther in risking her throne and life to save her people and to become God's channel for deliverance. The feast did not celebrate the destruction of the enemies, but rather the "resting" of the Jews from the oppression of their enemies. The days of Purim are characterized by feasting and gladness for deliverance and redemption through the providential care of God.

Jewish Feasts

Feast of	Month on Jewish Calendar	Day	Corresponding Month	References
Passover	Nisan	14	Mar.–Apr.	Ex. 12:1–14; Matt. 26:17–20
*Unleavened Bread	Nisan	15–21	Mar.–Apr.	Ex. 12:15–20
Firstfruits	Nisan or Sivan	16 6	Mar.–Apr. May–June	Lev. 23:9–14; Num. 28:26
*Pentecost (Harvest or Weeks)	Sivan	6 (50 days after barley harvest)	May–June	Deut. 16:9–12; Acts 2:1
Trumpets, *Rosh Hashanah*	Tishri	1, 2	Sept.–Oct.	Num. 29:1–6
Day of Atonement, *Yom Kippur*	Tishri	10	Sept.–Oct.	Lev. 23:26–32; Heb. 9:7
*Tabernacles (Booths or Ingathering)	Tishri	15–22	Sept.–Oct.	Neh. 8:13–18; John 7:2
Dedication (Lights), *Hanukkah*	Chislev	25 (8 days)	Nov.–Dec.	John 10:22
Purim (Lots)	Adar	14, 15	Feb.–Mar.	Esth. 9:18–32

*The three major feasts for which all males of Israel were required to travel to the Temple in Jerusalem (Ex. 23:14–19).

Nelson's Complete Book of Bible Maps and Charts © 1993 by Thomas Nelson, Inc.

WISDOM LITERATURE

The wisdom literature of the Old Testament consists of the books of Job, Proverbs, and Ecclesiastes, as well as some of the Psalms. The Hebrew word for wisdom is translated "skill for living," because the Jews regarded wisdom in very practical terms. This literature provided guidance for moral behavior and everyday living.

Hebrew wisdom literature, as distinguished from the wisdom writings of other cultures, was centered on God: "The fear of the LORD *is* the beginning of knowledge: *but* fools despise wisdom and instruction" (Prov. 1:7). In contrast, Egyptian wisdom, for example, focused on the wisdom of the sages and on disciplining oneself to accept the trials of life.

The three broad categories of wisdom literature in the Old Testament are (1) popular proverbs that express practical truths; (2) riddles or parables with a spiritual meaning; and (3) discussions of the problems of life.

The book of Proverbs provides wise sayings and observations designed to develop proper attitudes and godly behavior. Ecclesiastes offers a philosophical discussion of the emptiness of life without God (Eccl. 1:2, 14). Job is a classic examination of the problems of evil and human suffering. Its conclusion is that people can understand only what God chooses to reveal to them (Job 28:20–28).

Many of the Psalms, including 1, 4, 10, 14, 18, 19, 37, 49, 73, 90, and 112, are regarded as wisdom literature. A recurring theme in these Psalms is the problem of the prosperity of the wicked while the godly suffer. But the wise psalmist often returns to this refrain: "For evildoers shall be cut off: but those that wait upon the LORD, they shall inherit the earth" (Ps. 37:9).

Solomon, David's successor as king of Israel, was well known for his wisdom. God appeared to Solomon in a dream at the beginning of his reign and asked him what gift he wished above all else (1 Kin. 3:3–15). Solomon chose wisdom. Solomon apparently wrote many of the sayings in the book of Proverbs.

JOB

Set in the period of the patriarchs, the book of Job tells the story of a man who loses everything—his wealth, his family, and his health—and wrestles with the question, Why? The book begins with a heavenly debate between God and Satan, moves through three cycles of earthly debates between Job and his friends, and concludes with a dramatic divine diagnosis of Job's problems. In the end, Job acknowledges the sovereignty of God in his life and receives back more than he had before his trials.

The name "Job" appears in ancient Near Eastern texts, identifying a legendary wise man. Since there is no genealogical identification given for Job, some scholars believe the author is using a fictional character to make an important theological point. However, given the Bible's normal pattern of basing revelation on historical events, such an idea is questionable.

Author

The text of Job does not reveal the identity of its author, but the contents of the book indicate that its author was a profound thinker who treats some of the most crucial and difficult problems of human existence from a mature spiritual perspective. The author was also well-educated and familiar with wisdom literature motifs, nature, and foreign cultures.

Date

The dating of Job involves two issues: the date of the book's setting and the date of its composition. Although it is not possible to determine the precise date of the events described, several factors argue for a patriarchal date (2000–1800 B.C.): the absence of references to Israelite history or biblical law; Job's long life of over 100 years (42:16); Job's role as priest for his family, which was prohibited by Mosaic law (1:5); and the measurement of Job's wealth in terms of livestock (1:3).

Suggestions for the date of the book's composition range from the patriarchal era to the postexilic period. Most scholars today date the book between the Solomonic and exilic eras, and some points of contact between Job and Isaiah suggest that they may have been written about the same time.

Job at a Glance

FOCUS	DILEMMA OF JOB	DEBATES OF JOB					DELIVERANCE OF JOB
REFERENCE	1:1 ———— 3:1 ————	15:1 ————	22:1 ————	27:1 ————	32:1 ————	38:1 ——	42:17
DIVISION	CONTROVERSY OF GOD AND SATAN	FIRST CYCLE OF DEBATE	SECOND CYCLE OF DEBATE	THIRD CYCLE OF DEBATE	FINAL DEFENSE OF JOB	SOLUTION OF ELIHU	CONTROVERSY OF GOD WITH JOB
TOPIC	CONFLICT	DEBATE					REPENTANCE
	PROSE	POETRY					PROSE
LOCATION	LAND OF UZ (NORTH ARABIA)						
TIME	PATRIARCHAL PERIOD (c. 2000 B.C.)						

Nelson's Complete Book of Bible Maps and Charts © 1993 by Thomas Nelson, Inc.

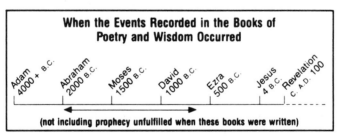

When the Events Recorded in the Books of Poetry and Wisdom Occurred

Adam 4000+ B.C. Abraham 2000 B.C. Moses 1500 B.C. David 1000 B.C. Ezra 500 B.C. Jesus 4 B.C. Revelation C. A.D. 100

(not including prophecy unfulfilled when these books were written)

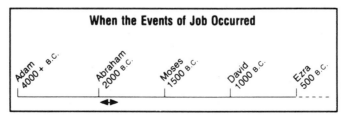

When the Events of Job Occurred

Adam 4000+ B.C. Abraham 2000 B.C. Moses 1500 B.C. David 1000 B.C. Ezra 500 B.C.

Themes and Literary Structure

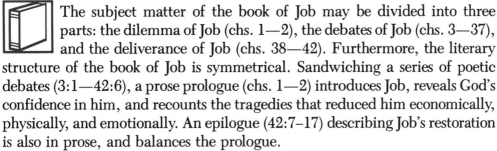

The subject matter of the book of Job may be divided into three parts: the dilemma of Job (chs. 1—2), the debates of Job (chs. 3—37), and the deliverance of Job (chs. 38—42). Furthermore, the literary structure of the book of Job is symmetrical. Sandwiching a series of poetic debates (3:1—42:6), a prose prologue (chs. 1—2) introduces Job, reveals God's confidence in him, and recounts the tragedies that reduced him economically, physically, and emotionally. An epilogue (42:7–17) describing Job's restoration is also in prose, and balances the prologue.

The basic question of the book is, "Why do the righteous suffer if God is loving and all-powerful?" Suffering itself is not the central theme; rather, the focus is on what Job learns from his suffering—the sovereignty of God over all creation. The debate in chapters 3—37 regards whether God would allow the innocent to suffer. The answer of Job's three friends—that there is a direct correlation between righteous conduct and health/prosperity—is shown to be inadequate. Elihu's claim that God can use suffering to purify the righteous is closer to the mark but is still incomplete. Finally, the direct conversation between God and Job shows that God is sovereign and worthy of worship in whatever He chooses to do. Job must learn to trust in the goodness and power of God, even in adversity, by enlarging his concept of God.

Job acknowledges a redeemer (19:25–27) and cries out for a mediator (9:33; 25:4; 33:23). The book raises problems and questions which are answered perfectly in Christ who identifies with our sufferings (Heb. 4:15). Christ is the believer's Life, Redeemer, Mediator, and Advocate.

OUTLINE OF JOB

Satan and Job's Friends

Much of the discussion in the book of Job concerns the relationship between human faithful obedience and divine blessing. Both Satan and Job's friends assume a direct correlation between the two—Satan argues that divine blessings elicit human obedience while Job's friends contend that obedience earns God's blessings and disobedience merits punishment. In contrast to these false views, the book of Job teaches that some sufferers are saints, that God is always worthy of the love and worship of His creation, whether or not He bestows blessings upon them, and that God always has a purpose in permitting suffering, though one may never fully comprehend it.

A Comparison of Satan's Theology with That of Job's Friends

Satan	Friends
IF Job is blessed by God, THEN he will be faithful.	IF Job is faithful, THEN he will be blessed.
OR	OR
IF Job is not blessed by God, THEN he will be unfaithful. (Satan accused God of bribing His followers.)	IF Job is unfaithful, THEN he will be punished.

God's Challenge to Job

The real answer to the problem of human suffering and divine sovereignty is found late in the book of Job, in the divine speeches (chs. 38—41). These speeches are sometimes misinterpreted, as if God merely bullies Job into submission without providing an answer. Job's repentance is due to his recognition of God's infinite greatness and of his own human finitude. A complete human explanation of the compatibility of divine sovereignty and goodness, and the existence of human suffering cannot be given because of the limitation of hu-

In the face of God's fearful challenge, Job could only humble himself:	
God's Challenge	Job's Response
First, Job's ignorance (38:1—40:2) • He was absent at creation • He cannot explain the forces of nature	Job admits his ignorance and becomes silent (40:3-5)
Second, Job's frailty (40:6—41:34) • He cannot overrule God's ways • He cannot control the forces of nature	Job confesses his presumption and repents (42:2-6)

man knowledge and the true character and extent of God's power over creation. But neither can it be demonstrated that the two are incompatible. Job finally finds rest in the realization that while God's ways are sometimes incomprehensible, He can always be trusted.

PSALMS

The book of Psalms is the largest and perhaps the most widely used book in the Bible. It explores the full range of human experiences in a very personal and practical way. Written over a lengthy period of Israel's history, the tremendous breadth of subject matter in the Psalms includes topics such as jubilation, war, peace, worship, judgment, messianic prophecy, praise, and lament. The Psalms were set to the accompaniment of stringed instruments and served as the temple hymnbook and devotional guide for the Jewish people.

The book of Psalms was gradually collected and came to be known as the *Sepher Tehillim* ("Book of Praises"), because almost every psalm contains some note of praise to God. The Septuagint (Greek Old Testament) uses the Greek term *Psalmoi* as a title for this book, meaning poems sung to the accompaniment of musical instruments, and this word is the basis for the English terms "psalter" and "psalm."

Author

No other book of the Bible has as many different authors as does Psalms. Seventy-three psalms are attributed to David in the superscriptions, and an additional two, Psalms 2 and 95, are ascribed to David in the New Testament. In addition to the seventy-five by David, twelve are ascribed to Asaph, a priest who headed the service of music. Ten were by the sons of Korah, a guild of singers and composers, and other psalms are ascribed to Solomon, Moses, Heman the Ezrahite, and Ethan the Ezrahite. Fifty of the psalms are anonymous, although some of these are traditionally ascribed to Ezra.

Date

The psalms were originally individual poems. With the passing of time these were collected to form smaller books and the book of Psalms in its present form comprises five of these smaller books. The earliest individual psalm is probably that of Moses (Ps. 90); the latest is

Continued on page 179

Psalms at a Glance

BOOK	BOOK I (1–41)	BOOK II (42–72)	BOOK III (73–89)	BOOK IV (90–106)	BOOK V (107–150)
CHIEF AUTHOR	DAVID	DAVID AND KORAH	ASAPH	ANONYMOUS	DAVID AND ANONYMOUS
NUMBER OF PSALMS	41	31	17	17	44
BASIC CONTENT	SONGS OF WORSHIP	HYMNS OF NATIONAL INTEREST		ANTHEMS OF PRAISE	
TOPICAL LIKENESS TO PENTATEUCH	GENESIS: MAN AND CREATION	EXODUS: DELIVERANCE AND REDEMPTION	LEVITICUS: WORSHIP AND SANCTUARY	NUMBERS: WILDERNESS AND WANDERING	DEUTERONOMY: SCRIPTURE AND PRAISE
CLOSING DOXOLOGY	41:13	72:18, 19	89:52	106:48	150:1–6
POSSIBLE COMPILER	DAVID	HEZEKIAH OR JOSIAH		EZRA OR NEHEMIAH	
POSSIBLE DATES OF COMPILATION	c. 1020–970 B.C.	c. 970–610 B.C.		UNTIL c. 430 B.C.	
SPAN OF AUTHORSHIP	ABOUT 1,000 YEARS (c. 1410–430 B.C.)				

Nelson's Complete Book of Bible Maps and Charts © 1993 by Thomas Nelson, Inc.

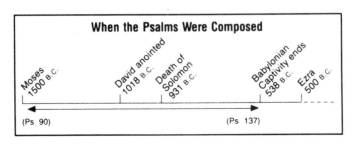

When the Psalms Were Composed

Moses 1500 B.C. — David anointed 1018 B.C. — Death of Solomon 931 B.C. — Babylonian Captivity ends 538 B.C. — Ezra 500 B.C.

(Ps. 90)   (Ps 137)

Continued from page 177

probably Psalm 137, which could not have been written before the sixth century B.C. Though many of the psalms were written and collected during the Davidic era, or shortly thereafter, the final compilation of Psalms was probably not complete until the latter half of the fifth century B.C. during the time of Ezra and Nehemiah (450–425 B.C.).

Themes and Literary Structure

The Psalter is really five books in one, and each book ends with a doxology. A number of different classification systems for psalm types have been developed, systems often based on the content or life-situation of the individual psalms. It is common to speak of psalms of lament, thanksgiving psalms, enthronement psalms, pilgrimage psalms, royal psalms, wisdom psalms, and imprecatory psalms (see page 182).

The poetry of the Psalms is unsurpassed. The one characteristic of Hebrew poetry most evident is parallelism, the relationship of one line or verse to another. Four of the most important types of Hebrew parallelism are: (1) synonymous parallelism, in which the second line of a couplet repeats the idea of the first line (e.g., 3:1; 24:1); (2) antithetic parallelism, where the thought of the second line is contrasted with that of the first line (e.g., 1:6; 90:6); (3) synthetic parallelism, in which the second line is a further development of the thought begun in the first line (e.g., 1:1; 19:7); (4) and emblematic parallelism, where the second line illustrates the thought of the first line, often by a simile (e.g., 42:1). Nine psalms are alphabetical or acrostic (Pss. 9, 10, 25, 34, 37, 111, 112, 119, 145). In acrostic psalms each successive line or group of lines begins with the successive letters of the Hebrew alphabet. The classic example of an acrostic poem is Psalm 119, in which each of the eight verses in a given stanza begins with the same letter.

OUTLINE OF PSALMS

Book One: Psalms 1—41

1. Two Ways of Life Contrasted
2. Coronation of the Lord's Anointed
3. Victory in the Face of Defeat
4. Evening Prayer for Deliverance
5. Morning Prayer for Guidance
6. Prayer for God's Mercy
7. Wickedness Justly Rewarded
8. God's Glory and Man's Dominion
9. Praise for Victory over Enemies
10. Petition for God's Judgment

Book Two: Psalms 42—72

62. Wait for God
63. Thirst for God
64. A Prayer for God's Protection
65. God's Provision Through Nature
66. Remember What God Has Done

67. God Shall Govern the Earth
68. God Is the Father of the Fatherless
69. Petition for God to Draw Near
70. Prayer for the Poor and Needy
71. Prayer for the Aged
72. The Reign of the Messiah

Book Three: Psalms 73—89

73. The Perspective of Eternity
74. Request for God to Remember His Covenant
75. "God Is the Judge"
76. The Glorious Might of God
77. When Overwhelmed, Remember God's Greatness
78. God's Continued Guidance in Spite of Unbelief
79. Avenge the Defilement of Jerusalem
80. Israel's Plea for God's Mercy
81. God's Plea for Israel's Obedience

82. Rebuke of Israel's Unjust Judges
83. Plea for God to Destroy Israel's Enemies
84. The Joy of Dwelling with God
85. Prayer for Revival
86. "Teach Me Your Way, O LORD"
87. Glorious Zion, City of God
88. Crying from Deepest Affliction
89. Claiming God's Promises in Affliction

Book Four: Psalms 90—106

90. "Teach Us to Number Our Days"
91. Abiding in "the Shadow of the Almighty"
92. It Is Good to Praise the Lord
93. The Majesty of God
94. Vengeance Belongs Only to God
95. Call to Worship the Lord
96. Declare the Glory of God
97. Rejoice! The Lord Reigns!
98. Sing a New Song to the Lord

99. "Exalt the LORD Our God"
100. "Serve the LORD with Gladness"
101. Commitments of a Holy Life
102. Prayer of an Overwhelmed Saint
103. Bless the Lord, All You People!
104. Psalm Rehearsing Creation
105. Remember, God Keeps His Promises
106. "We Have Sinned"

Types of Psalms

The book of Psalms is a collection of prayers, poems, and hymns that focus the worshiper's thoughts on God in praise and adoration. Parts of the book were used as a hymnal in the worship services of ancient Israel. The book contains 150 individual psalms, which may be grouped into the following types or categories.

   1. **Individual and communal lament psalms,** or prayers for God's deliverance. Psalms of the type are 3—7; 12; 13; 22; 25—28; 35; 38—40; 42—44; 51;

54—57; 59—61; 63; 64; 69—71; 74; 79; 80; 83; 85; 86; 88; 90; 102; 109; 120; 123; 130; and 140—143. These psalms speak to believers in moments of desperation and despair, when our need is for God's deliverance.

2. **Thanksgiving psalms,** consisting of praise to God for His gracious acts. This theme occurs in Psalms 8; 18; 19; 29; 30; 32—34; 36; 40; 41; 66; 103—106; 111; 113; 116; 117; 124; 129; 135; 136; 138; 139; 146—148; and 150. Every prayer we utter should include the element of thanksgiving. These psalms make us aware of God's blessings and lead us to express our thanks with feeling and conviction.

3. **Enthronement psalms,** which describe God's sovereign rule. Psalms of this type are 47; 93; and 96—99. Through these psalms we acknowledge God as powerful Creator and sovereign Lord over all His creation.

4. **Pilgrimage psalms,** which were sung by worshipers as they traveled to Jerusalem to celebrate the Jewish festivals. Pilgrimage psalms are 43; 46; 48; 76; 84; 87; and 120—134. These psalms can help us establish a mood of reverent worship.

5. **Royal psalms,** which portray the reign of the earthly king, as well as of the heavenly King of Israel. This theme is evident in Psalms 2; 18; 20; 21; 45; 72; 89; 101; 110; 132; and 144. These psalms can make us aware of our daily need to make Christ the sovereign ruler of our lives.

6. **Wisdom psalms,** which instruct the worshiper in the way of wisdom and righteousness. Individual wisdom psalms are 1; 37; and 119. These psalms are especially appropriate in times of decision when we are searching for God's will and direction in our lives.

7. **Imprecatory psalms,** in which the worshiper invokes God's wrath and judgment against his enemies. This theme occurs in Psalms 7; 35; 40; 55; 58; 59; 69; 79; 109; 137; 139; and 144. These psalms can help us be honest about our feelings toward people who have done us wrong and work our way through these feelings to a point of forgiveness.

Images of God in the Psalms	
Images of God as	*Reference in Psalms*
Shield	3:3; 28:7; 119:114
Rock	18:2; 42:9; 95:1
King	5:2; 44:4; 74:12
Shepherd	23:1; 80:1
Judge	7:11
Refuge	46:1; 62:7
Fortress	31:3; 71:3
Avenger	26:1
Creator	8:1, 6
Deliverer	37:39, 40
Healer	30:2
Protector	5:11
Provider	78:23–29
Redeemer	107:2

Messianic Psalms

Many of the psalms specifically anticipate the life and ministry of Jesus Christ, the Son of David, who came centuries later as the promised Messiah. The messianic prophecies in the psalms take a variety of forms and refer to Christ in a variety of ways. (1) Typical Messianic. The subject of the psalm is in some respects a type of Christ (see, e.g., Pss. 34:20; 69:4, 9). (2) Typical Prophetic. The psalmist uses language to describe his present experience, which points beyond his own life and becomes historically true only in Christ (e.g., Ps. 22). (3) Indirectly Messianic. At the time of composition the psalm refers to a king or the house of David in general but awaits final fulfillment in Christ (e.g., Pss. 2; 45; 72). (4) Purely Prophetic. Refers solely to Christ without reference to any other son of David (e.g., Ps. 110). (5) Enthronement. Anticipates the coming of Yahweh and the consummation of His kingdom, which will be fulfilled in the person of Christ (e.g., Pss. 96—99).

Psalm	Portrayal	Fulfilled
2:7	The Son of God	Matthew 3:17
8:2	Praised by children	Matthew 21:15, 16
8:6	Ruler of all	Hebrews 2:8
16:10	Rises from death	Matthew 28:7
22:1	Forsaken by God	Matthew 27:46
22:7, 8	Derided by enemies	Luke 23:35
22:16	Hands and feet pierced	John 20:27
22:18	Lots cast for clothes	Matthew 27:35, 36
34:20	Bones unbroken	John 19:32, 33, 36
35:11	Accused by false witnesses	Mark 14:57
35:19	Hated without cause	John 15:25
40:7, 8	Delights in God's will	Hebrews 10:7
41:9	Betrayed by a friend	Luke 22:47
45:6	The eternal King	Hebrews 1:8
68:18	Ascends to heaven	Acts 1:9–11
69:9	Zealous for God's house	John 2:17
69:21	Given vinegar and gall	Matthew 27:34
109:4	Prays for enemies	Luke 23:34
109:8	His betrayer replaced	Acts 1:20
110:1	Rules over His enemies	Matthew 22:44
110:4	A priest forever	Hebrews 5:6
118:22	The chief stone of God's building	Matthew 21:42
118:26	Comes in the name of the Lord	Matthew 21:9

PROVERBS

Proverbs provides God's detailed instructions for His people to deal successfully with the practical affairs of everyday life: how to relate to God, parents, children, neighbors, and government. Solomon, the principal author, uses a combination of poetry, parables, pithy questions, short stories, and wise maxims to give in strikingly memorable form the common sense and divine perspective necessary to handle life's challenges.

Because Solomon, the prototype of Israel's wise man, was the principal contributor, the Hebrew title of the book is *Mishle Shelomoh* ("Parables of Solomon"). The English title of the book is derived from the Latin *Liber Proverbiorum*, or "Book of Proverbs."

Author

Solomon's name appears at the beginning of the three sections he wrote: chapters 1—9; 10:1—22:16; chapters 25—29. According to 1 Kings 4:32, Solomon spoke three thousand proverbs, of which about 800 are included in Proverbs. It is likely that Solomon collected and edited proverbs other than his own (Eccl. 12:9).

Proverbs 22:17—24:34 consists of "the words of the wise" (22:17; 24:23). Some of these sayings are quite similar to those found in The Wisdom of Amenemope, a document of teachings on civil service by an Egyptian who probably lived between 1000 and 600 B.C. It is possible that Egyptian wisdom traditions borrowed certain aphorisms from Hebrew literature. In addition, Proverbs includes oracles by the unknown figures named Agur the son of Jakeh (30:1) and King Lemuel (31:1).

Date

Solomon's proverbs were written before 931 B.C., and his proverbs in chapters 25—29 were collected by Hezekiah about 230 years later. Thus portions of the book were completed no earlier than the time of the reign of Hezekiah and a reasonable date for completion is sometime in the fifth century B.C.

Continued on page 187

Proverbs at a Glance

FOCUS	PURPOSE OF PROVERBS	PROVERBS TO YOUTH	PROVERBS OF SOLOMON	PROVERBS OF SOLOMON (HEZEKIAH)	WORDS OF AGUR	WORDS OF LEMUEL
REFERENCE	1:1 ———	1:8 ———	10:1 ———	25:1 ———	30:1 ———	31:1 ——— 31:31
DIVISION	PURPOSE AND THEME	FATHER'S EXHORTATIONS	FIRST COLLECTION OF SOLOMON	SECOND COLLECTION OF SOLOMON	NUMERICAL PROVERBS	VIRTUOUS WIFE
TOPIC	PROLOGUE	PRINCIPLES OF WISDOM			EPILOGUE	
	COMMENDATION OF WISDOM	COUNSEL OF WISDOM			COMPARISONS OF WISDOM	
LOCATION	JUDAH					
TIME	c. 950–450 B.C.					

Nelson's Complete Book of Bible Maps and Charts © 1993 by Thomas Nelson, Inc.

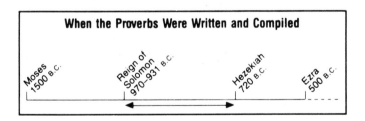

When the Proverbs Were Written and Compiled

Moses 1500 B.C. — Reign of Solomon 970–931 B.C. — Hezekiah 720 B.C. — Ezra 500 B.C.

Continued from page 185

Such wisdom literature was not unique to Israel, and is found in other countries of the ancient Near East. In Egypt, written examples can be found as early as 2700 B.C. Although the style was similar to Israel's wisdom literature, the proverbs and sayings of these countries differed from those of Israel in content because they lacked the character of the righteous standards of the Lord.

Themes and Literary Structure

The book of Proverbs may be divided into six segments: the purpose of Proverbs (1:1–7), the proverbs to the youth (1:8—9:18), the proverbs of Solomon (10:1—24:34), the proverbs of Solomon copied by Hezekiah's men (25:1—29:27), the words of Agur (30:1–33), and the words of King Lemuel (31:1–31).

Proverbs is one of the few biblical books that clearly spells out its purpose: to impart moral discernment and discretion (1:3–5), and to develop mental clarity and perception (1:2, 6). The "wisdom" of which Proverbs speaks is literally "skill" in living. Wisdom is more than shrewdness or intelligence. Instead, it relates to practical righteousness and moral acumen. Proverbs deals with the most fundamental skill of all: practical righteousness before God in every area of life.

Typical of the proverbs in the ancient Near East, many proverbs seem to have arisen in the context of the home. The term "son" occurs in forty-four verses in the book, "father" in fifteen, and "mother" in eleven. Husband and wife are admonished to be united joyfully in a clearly monogamous union (despite the polygamy practiced at the time, especially by Solomon). Both parents are directed to share in the training of the children and nurturing them in faith. Sins which attack the order of the home are straightforwardly exposed.

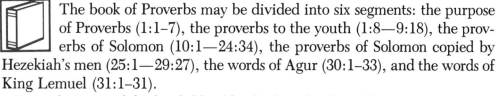

Wisdom is personified in the Proverbs and acts as God's dynamic Word. In the NT, Jesus becomes the Wisdom and Word of God.

Origin of Wisdom	Teaching of Wisdom	Value of Wisdom
In God (v. 22)	Prudence (vv. 5, 12)	Yields riches and honor (v. 18)
From everlasting (v. 23)	Understanding (v. 5)	Greater than gold and silver (v. 19)
Before all things (vv. 23–30)	Excellent things (v. 6)	The wise are blessed (vv. 32, 34)
	Truth (v. 7)	The wise find life (v. 35)
	Hatred of wickedness (v. 7)	The foolish love death (v. 36)
	Righteousness (v. 8)	
	Knowledge (v. 12)	
	Discretion (v. 12)	
	Fear of the Lord (v. 13)	

Many proverbs present a contrast between wisdom and folly. Wisdom is to be preferred to folly because of its divine origin and rich benefits. There are different kinds of fools, ranging from those who are naive and uncommitted to scoffers who arrogantly despise the way of God. The fool is not mentally deficient, but appears self-sufficient and orders life as if there is no God.

In Proverbs chapter 8, wisdom is personified and seen in its perfection. It is divine (8:22–31), it is the source of biological and spiritual life (8:35, 36), it is righteous and moral (8:8, 9), and it is available to all who will receive it (8:1–6, 32–35). This wisdom became incarnate in Christ "in whom is hidden all the treasures of wisdom and knowledge" (Col. 2:3; cf. 1 Cor. 1:30).

OUTLINE OF PROVERBS

Notable Teachers in Scripture

Moses	Renowned as the leader of Israel who first taught God's Law (Deut. 4:5).
Bezalel and Aholiab	Two master craftsmen who were gifted and called to teach others in the construction of the tabernacle (Ex. 35:30–35).
Samuel	The last of Israel's judges before the monarchy, who taught the people "the good and the right way" (1 Sam. 12:23).
David	Prepared his son Solomon to build and staff the temple (1 Chr. 28:9–21).
Solomon	Known for his outstanding wisdom, which he used to teach numerous subjects, including literature, botany, and zoology (1 Kin. 4:29–34).
Ezra	A scribe and priest who was committed not only to keeping the Law himself, but to teaching it to others (Ezra 7:10).
Jesus	Called Rabbi ("teacher," John 1:38; compare Matt. 9:11; 26:18; John 13:13), whose teaching revealed the good news of salvation (Eph. 4:20–21).
Barnabas	One of the teachers among the believers at Antioch (Acts 13:1), who had a lasting impact on Saul after his conversion to the faith (9:26–30).
Gamaliel	A renowned Jewish rabbi who was the teacher of Saul during his youth (Acts 22:3).
Paul	Perhaps the early church's most gifted teacher, known to have taught throughout the Roman world, notably at Antioch (Acts 13:1) and in the school of Tyrannus at Ephesus (19:9).
Priscilla and Aquila	Two believers who taught the way of God to a talented young orator named Apollos (Acts 18:26).
Apollos	A powerful teacher from Alexandria in Egypt, whose teaching paved the way for the gospel at Ephesus (Acts 18:24–26).
Timothy	Pastor-teacher of the church at Ephesus (1 Tim. 1:3; 2 Tim. 4:2).
Titus	Pastor-teacher of a church on the island of Crete (Titus 2:1–15).

ECCLESIASTES

cclesiastes is a profound and problematic book. It records an intense search for meaning and satisfaction in life on this earth, especially in view of all the injustice and apparent absurdities that surround us.

The name "Ecclesiastes" is derived from the Greek word *ekklesia* ("assembly") and means "one who addresses an assembly." This Greek term translates the Hebrew title *Qoheleth*, which is often rendered "Preacher" or "Teacher" in English.

Author

Because of the opening words of the book ("The words of the Preacher, the son of David, king in Jerusalem"), Ecclesiastes has traditionally been credited to Solomon, who is thought to have written it in his old age. The pessimistic tone that pervades the book would be in keeping with Solomon's spiritual state at that time (see 1 Kin. 11). Many scholars, however, date the book to a later period because of the character of the Hebrew (which appears to be from the exilic or postexilic period) and because of the theological problem posed by an apostate Solomon writing Holy Scripture. If Solomon did not compose the work, it may have had its origin in the time of Ezra (c. 450 B.C.).

Date

The question of the date of Ecclesiastes is bound up with the identity of the author (see above).

Themes and Literary Structure

The literary character of Ecclesiastes is complex. It seems to be a collection of various types of literature, all making the same general point. There are wise sayings (proverbs) as well as sections that are reflective and meditative. Over one third of the book is poetry, but narrative passages are also included.

Continued on page 192

Ecclesiastes at a Glance

FOCUS	THESIS: "ALL IS VANITY"		PROOF: "LIFE IS VAIN"		COUNSEL: "FEAR GOD"		
REFERENCE	1:1 ——— 1:4 ———	1:12 ——— 3:1 ———		7:1 ———	10:1 ———	12:9 ——— 12:14	
DIVISION	INTRODUCTION OF VANITY	ILLUSTRATIONS OF VANITY	PROOF FROM SCRIPTURE	PROOF FROM OBSERVATIONS	COPING IN A WICKED WORLD	COUNSEL FOR UNCERTAINTY	CONCLUSION: FEAR AND OBEY GOD
TOPIC	DECLARATION OF VANITY		DEMONSTRATION OF VANITY		FROM VANITY		
	SUBJECT		SERMONS		SUMMARY		
LOCATION	UNIVERSE: "UNDER THE SUN"						
TIME	c. 935 or c. 450 B.C.						

Nelson's Complete Book of Bible Maps and Charts © 1993 by Thomas Nelson, Inc.

Continued from page 190

Ecclesiastes is extremely difficult to synthesize and outline, and several alternate approaches have been proposed. A three-part schema is adopted here: (1) the thesis that all is vanity (1:1–11), (2) the proof that all is vanity (1:12—6:12), and (3) the counsel for living with vanity (7:1—12:14).

The purpose of Ecclesiastes is to demonstrate the thesis: "All is vanity" (1:2). This stands in contrast to the book of Proverbs, where an optimistic confidence assumes that life is fundamentally logical and consistent, with wise choices producing good results and foolish choices producing bad results. Ecclesiastes recognizes that this is frequently not the case. Here Ecclesiastes does not simply contradict Proverbs, but supplements it with a different but equally necessary perspective. There are inexplicable mysteries about life which defy easy solutions. Despite the unanswered questions, it is still best to fear God, keep His commandments, and thus enjoy life (3:12; 12:13).

In leaving certain difficult problems unsolved, Ecclesiastes poses profound questions regarding the meaning and coherence of life—questions that can be answered ultimately only in Jesus Christ, for only Christ can provide ultimate satisfaction, joy, and wisdom.

OUTLINE OF ECCLESIASTES

Part Three: The Counsel for Living with Vanity (7:1—12:14)

Wisdom from God

The author closes this book by stating that there is a God who will hold us accountable for the deeds of our lives. Life "under the sun" will be judged from a heavenly perspective. Thus the book ends on a positive and encouraging note, because one's accountability before God means that the course of our lives is of eternal significance. In spite of frequent observation and experience of life's apparent futility, the author exhorts his readers to grasp by faith the sovereignty, goodness, and justice of God and to enjoy all the facets of life as His gift.

See chart, "The Way of Wisdom," on page 194.

The Way of Wisdom

Without God "all is vanity":

Godless learning ⟶ cynicism (1:7, 8)
Godless greatness ⟶ sorrow (1:16–18)
Godless pleasure ⟶ disappointment (2:1, 2)
Godless labor ⟶ hatred of life (2:17)
Godless philosophy ⟶ emptiness (3:1–9)
Godless eternity ⟶ unfulfillment (3:11)
Godless life ⟶ depression (4:2, 3)
Godless religion ⟶ dread (5:7)
Godless wealth ⟶ trouble (5:12)
Godless existence ⟶ frustration (6:12)
Godless wisdom ⟶ despair (11:1–8)

The beginning of wisdom is the fear of God, a deeply serious attitude toward the commands of God.

GODLY FEAR ⟶ FULFILLMENT (12:13, 14)

Nelson's Complete Book of Bible Maps and Charts © 1993 by Thomas Nelson, Inc.

Song of Solomon

The Song of Solomon is a love song abounding in metaphors and oriental imagery. It depicts the wooing and wedding of a shepherdess by King Solomon and the joys and heartaches of wedded love. The book is arranged like scenes in a drama with three main speakers: the bride, the king, and a chorus (the daughters of Jerusalem).

Based on its first verse, this book is known by the titles "Song of Songs" and "Song of Solomon." In Latin the book is called *Canticles*, which means "songs."

Author

The book is traditionally attributed to Solomon, although some reject Solomonic authorship and consider the phrase "which is Solomon's" a dedication rather than a designation of authorship. If Solomon is the author, this book constitutes one of the 1,005 songs he is known to have composed (1 Kin. 4:32).

Date

Solomonic authorship demands a tenth-century B.C. date. Jewish tradition considers the book a product of Solomon's early years (cf. 6:8), before his excessive multiplying of wives and concubines due to political expediency and sensual indulgence. Those who reject Solomonic authorship date the book to the postexilic period, contending that certain Hebrew grammatical constructions suggest a relatively late date of origin.

Regardless of its exact date of composition, the Song of Solomon reflects the setting of Solomon's era, and the glory of the Solomonic period is essential to the symbolism of the work.

Song of Solomon at a Glance

FOCUS	BEGINNING OF LOVE		BROADENING OF LOVE	
REFERENCE	1:1 ——————— 3:6 ———		——— 5:2 ——————— 7:11 ——————— 8:14	
DIVISION	FALLING IN LOVE	UNITED IN LOVE	STRUGGLING IN LOVE	GROWING IN LOVE
TOPIC	COURTSHIP	WEDDING	PROBLEM	PROGRESS
	FOSTERING OF LOVE	FULFILLMENT OF LOVE	FRUSTRATION OF LOVE	FAITHFULNESS OF LOVE
LOCATION	ISRAEL			
TIME	c. 1 YEAR			

Nelson's Complete Book of Bible Maps and Charts © 1993 by Thomas Nelson, Inc.

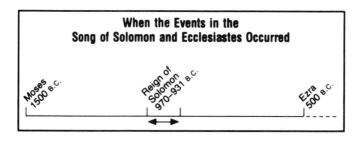

**When the Events in the
Song of Solomon and Ecclesiastes Occurred**

Moses 1500 B.C.   Reign of Solomon 970–931 B.C.   Ezra 500 B.C.

Themes and Literary Structure

 Like Ecclesiastes, this little book is not easily outlined, and various schemes can be used. It abounds with sudden changes of speakers, and they are not identified. The beginning of love is seen in 1:1—5:1, and the broadening of love is found in 5:2—8:14.

The Song is a type of Semitic wisdom literature, and it parallels the book of Proverbs in a number of ways. As is true of much Hebrew poetry, the book is characterized by parallelism, the stating and restating of an idea in close context. Key images in the book include wine, the garden, the kiss, various spices and fruits, the countryside or pastoral metaphors. Of special note is the fact that the name of God does not appear directly in the book.

The literary form and intent of the Song have been understood in a variety of ways which reduce to three basic approaches. The allegorical view understands the book as a poem describing the relationship between God and Israel or between Christ and the church. Each detail is seen as symbolic of deeper spiritual truth. The typological view differs from the allegorical by acknowledging the historical foundation and by finding analogy not in all subordinate details, but only in the main outlines. Proponents of this view acknowledge the mutual love between Solomon and the Shulamite, but go beyond that to consider the divine analogy with its more elevated and spiritual meaning as being the more important. The literal view takes the content of the song at face value. Some who interpret it in this way maintain that the poem is merely a secular love song expressing human romantic love at its best without spiritual lesson or theological content, but a literal interpretation need not mean that the book has no spiritual illustrations or application.

The poem may also be understood as depicting the ideal love relationship in marriage and so presenting a divine theology of marriage as expressed in the love between husband and wife in the physical area.

OUTLINE OF SONG OF SOLOMON

Geographic Locations

The text of the Song of Solomon mentions fifteen geographic locations from Lebanon and Syria in the north to Egypt in the south. The term "Shulamite," identifying the king's lover, appears only in 6:13 and may be derived from the town of Shunem which was southwest of the Sea of Galilee in the tribal area of Issachar.

See map, "Locations in the Song of Solomon," on page 199.

Couples in Love

Solomon and his bride show all of the affection and romance that people universally associate with being in love (Song 2:16). Theirs is one of a number of stories about romantic love told in the Bible.

Isaac and Rebekah (Gen. 24:1–67)	A father seeks and finds a wife for his son, and the young couple love each other deeply.
Jacob and Rachel (Gen. 29:1–30)	Jacob labors 14 years for his father-in-law in order to gain Rachel as his wife.
Boaz and Ruth (Ruth 3—4)	Legal technicalities bring together a Moabite widow and a wealthy landowner of Bethlehem, and through them a king is descended.
Elkanah and Hannah (1 Sam. 1—2)	A woman is loved by her husband despite being childless, and God eventually blesses her with the birth of a son, who becomes a mighty judge over Israel.
David and Michal (1 Sam. 18:20–30)	Genuine love is manipulated by a jealous king, but instead of ridding himself of his nemesis, the ruler gains a son-in-law.
Solomon and the Shulamite (Song of Solomon)	The commitments and delights of two lovers are told in a beautiful romantic poem.
Hosea and Gomer (Hos. 1:1—3:5)	God calls the prophet Hosea to seek out his adulterous spouse and restore the relationship despite what she has done.
Christ and the Church (Eph. 5:25–33)	Having won His bride's salvation from sin, Christ loves and serves her as His own body, thereby setting an example for human husbands everywhere.

Locations in the Song of Solomon

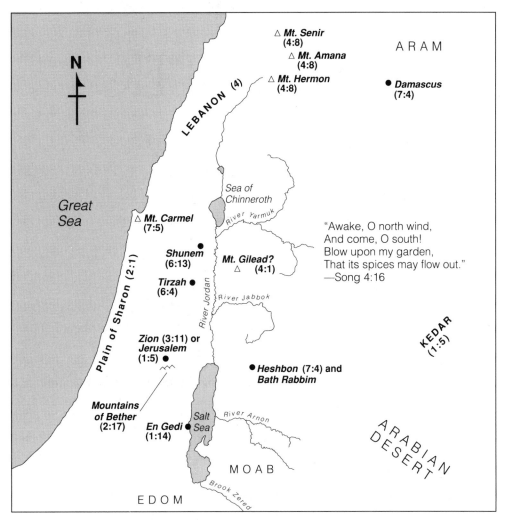

N

△ **Mt. Senir** (4:8)

△ **Mt. Amana** (4:8)

A R A M

△ **Mt. Hermon** (4:8)

● **Damascus** (7:4)

LEBANON (4)

Great Sea

Sea of Chinneroth

River Yarmuk

△ **Mt. Carmel** (7:5)

Shunem (6:13) ●

Mt. Gilead? △ (4:1)

"Awake, O north wind,
And come, O south!
Blow upon my garden,
That its spices may flow out."
—Song 4:16

Tirzah ● (6:4)

River Jordan

River Jabbok

Plain of Sharon (2:1)

Zion (3:11) or Jerusalem (1:5) ●

● **Heshbon** (7:4) and **Bath Rabbim**

KEDAR (1:5)

Mountains of Bether (2:17)

En Gedi ● (1:14)

Salt Sea

River Arnon

A R A B I A N D E S E R T

M O A B

Brook Zered

E D O M

Nelson's Complete Book of Bible Maps and Charts © 1993 by Thomas Nelson, Inc.

THE PROPHETIC BOOKS

The true prophets in the Old Testament were loyal servants of God and convinced foes of idolatry. They often risked their lives when confronting wicked kings and princes with the Word of God, and they poured their souls into their pleas that sinners repent and turn back to God.

In Israel, there was a long history of individuals who served as the Lord's messengers to the nation and to the world. Abraham functioned as a prophet when he interceded for a sinner (Gen. 20:7), but it was Moses whom the Lord first called and instructed in the ministerial role of a prophet (Ex. 3:1—4:17). Moses in fact was the greatest of the Old Testament prophets (Num. 12:6–8) and his experience as a prophet became a paradigm for later prophets as the vocabulary and relationships of the divine communication through Moses became standard for God's revelations to other 'rue prophets. Such terms as "send," "go," "speak," and "I will" were commonly used by the Lord to prophets, and they themselves frequently admonished their audiences to "hear" because "thus says the Lord."

Several elements often characterize the relationships between the Lord, the prophets, and their hearers: (1) the authority of the Lord over both the prophets and their audiences; (2) the obedience of the prophets, though sometimes with initial protest; (3) the authority of the prophets as representatives of the sovereign God; (4) the requirement of the audience to choose covenant obedience or disobedience; (5) the report of the prophet back to the Lord in the form of prayer.

The prophetic books are largely written in the style of Hebrew poetry. Although the prophets do not explain their choice of the poetic genre, it is likely they did so for at least several reasons: (1) poetry can speak powerfully to the will and emotions; the prophets did not wish simply to inform their audiences, but to move them to action as well. (2) Poetry, with its stress on symbolism and imagery is sometimes better suited than prose to convey the wonders of God and His character which are at the heart of the prophets' messages. (3) Poetry can speak about the meaning of future events without necessarily having to describe all details literally.

It is a mistake to think of the biblical prophets primarily as predictors of the future. To be sure, prediction was an essential part of their preaching, but their primary function was to call people to radical obedience and dependence upon God. The contents of prophetic messages were shaped by God's covenant with His people and by the particular historical circumstances of the individual prophet. The covenant was established to make Israel a holy nation that worshiped only the one true God. But the history of Israel was characterized by persistent rebellion against God, and these rebellions had a marked impact on how the prophetic messages were framed and presented. These messages often took the form of "lawsuits" initiated by God against His people for breach of covenant. The prophetic lawsuit typically included: (1) arraignment in the divine court; (2) accusations; (3) pronouncement of judicial sentence; (4) description of coming punishment; and (5) promise of restoration.

Samuel, Elijah, and Elisha were the most important prophets of the kingdom period (1050–586 B.C.), although a number of other prophets and prophetesses are mentioned in the historical books. The so-called "writing prophets" have left us sixteen books. Four of these prophets—Isaiah, Jeremiah, Ezekiel, and Daniel—are called the major prophets. Twelve others are represented by much shorter books and are called "minor prophets"—a reference to the length of their writings, not to their quality or importance.

See chart, "The Prophetic Books," on page 202. See map, "Places of the Prophets," on page 203.

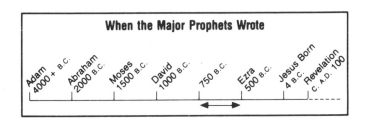

When the Major Prophets Wrote

Adam 4000+ B.C. | Abraham 2000 B.C. | Moses 1500 B.C. | David 1000 B.C. | 750 B.C. | Ezra 500 B.C. | Jesus Born 4 B.C. | Revelation c. A.D. 100

The Prophetic Books

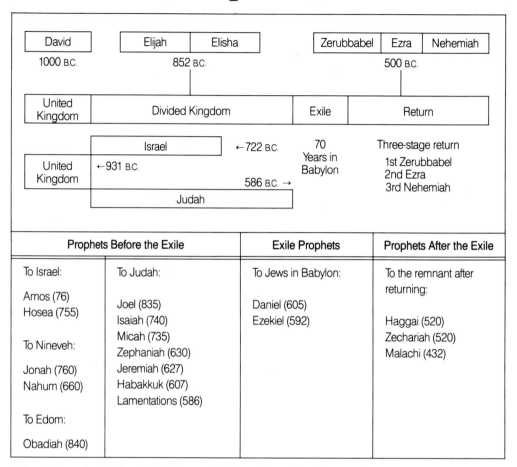

Prophets Before the Exile		Exile Prophets	Prophets After the Exile
To Israel: Amos (76) Hosea (755) To Nineveh: Jonah (760) Nahum (660) To Edom: Obadiah (840)	To Judah: Joel (835) Isaiah (740) Micah (735) Zephaniah (630) Jeremiah (627) Habakkuk (607) Lamentations (586)	To Jews in Babylon: Daniel (605) Ezekiel (592)	To the remnant after returning: Haggai (520) Zechariah (520) Malachi (432)

Nelson's Complete Book of Bible Maps and Charts © 1993 by Thomas Nelson, Inc.

Places of the Prophets

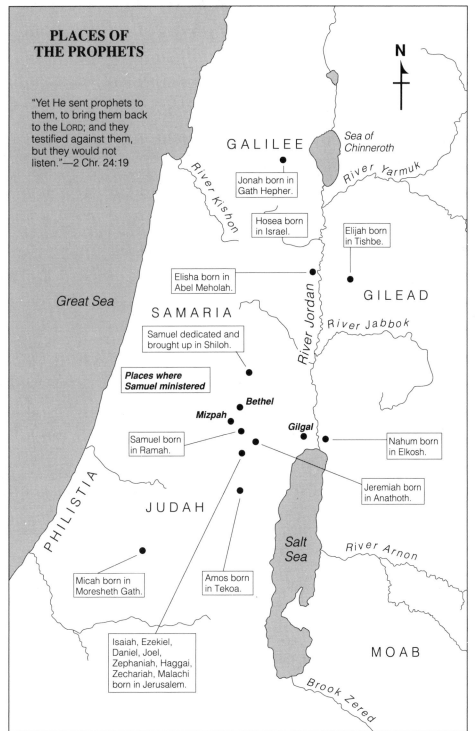

PLACES OF THE PROPHETS

"Yet He sent prophets to them, to bring them back to the LORD; and they testified against them, but they would not listen."—2 Chr. 24:19

N

GALILEE

Sea of Chinneroth

River Kishon

River Yarmuk

Jonah born in Gath Hepher.

Hosea born in Israel.

Elijah born in Tishbe.

Elisha born in Abel Meholah.

GILEAD

Great Sea

SAMARIA

River Jordan

River Jabbok

Samuel dedicated and brought up in Shiloh.

Places where Samuel ministered

Bethel

Mizpah

Gilgal

Samuel born in Ramah.

Nahum born in Elkosh.

Jeremiah born in Anathoth.

PHILISTIA

JUDAH

Salt Sea

River Arnon

Micah born in Moresheth Gath.

Amos born in Tekoa.

Isaiah, Ezekiel, Daniel, Joel, Zephaniah, Haggai, Zechariah, Malachi born in Jerusalem.

MOAB

Brook Zered

Nelson's Complete Book of Bible Maps and Charts © 1993 by Thomas Nelson, Inc.

ISAIAH

saiah has often been called "the prince of prophets" because of the majestic sweep of his book and the powerful way he depicts the themes of justice and redemption, culminating in the great prophecies of the Messiah and the messianic age. In this sense, Isaiah is like a miniature Bible. The first thirty-nine chapters are filled with judgment upon immoral and idolatrous people—both Judah and the surrounding nations. But the final twenty-seven chapters declare a message of hope and consolation.

The name *Isaiah*, from the Hebrew *yeshaiah*, means "Yahweh is Salvation," a term which aptly summarizes the contents of the book.

Author

Isaiah, the son of Amoz, is named as the author (1:1), and there is not even an allusion to any other writer. The unity of Isaiah has been challenged in the modern period by scholars who ascribe much of chapters 1—39 to the prophet Isaiah himself, but attribute chapters 40—55 (called "Deutero-Isaiah") to an unknown prophet in Babylon, and chapters 56—66 (called "Trito-Isaiah") to another unknown prophet in Palestine (c. 460–445 B.C.). Here it is argued that significant stylistic, historical, and theological differences distinguish chapters 1—39 from chapters 40—66, and that chapters 40—66 must further be divided into two sections reflecting a Babylonian exilic setting and a Palestinian postexilic setting, respectively.

Although the arguments against the unity of Isaiah have been impressive to some, strong arguments can also be marshalled in favor of the literary unity of the book. While some differences between sections do exist, the stylistic similarities throughout the book are greater than the alleged differences. These include similarities in thoughts, images, rhetorical ornaments, characteristic expressions, and local coloring. It is true that the first section is more terse and rational while the second is more flowing and emotional, but much of this is due to the different subject matter—the difference between condemnation and consolation.

Portions of the book are attributed to a period later than Isaiah, son of

Continued on page 206

Isaiah at a Glance

FOCUS	PROPHECIES OF CONDEMNATION				HISTORICAL PARENTHESIS	PROPHECIES OF COMFORT		
REFERENCE	1:1 —— 13:1 —— 24:1 —— 28:1 —————— 36:1 ——————— 40:1 ————— 49:1 ——— 58:1 – 66:24							
DIVISION	PROPHECIES AGAINST		PROPHECIES OF		HEZEKIAH'S SALVATION, SICKNESS, AND SIN	ISRAEL'S DELIVERANCE	ISRAEL'S DELIVERER	ISRAEL'S GLORIOUS FUTURE
	JUDAH	THE NATIONS	DAY OF LORD	JUDGMENT & BLESSING				
TOPIC	PROPHETIC				HISTORIC	MESSIANIC		
	JUDGMENT				TRANSITION	HOPE		
LOCATION	ISRAEL AND JUDAH							
TIME	c. 740–680 B.C.							

Nelson's Complete Book of Bible Maps and Charts © 1993 by Thomas Nelson, Inc.

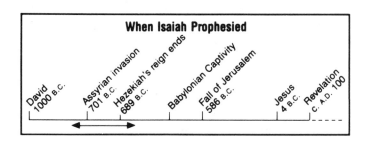

When Isaiah Prophesied

David 1000 B.C. — Assyrian invasion 701 B.C. — Hezekiah's reign ends 689 B.C. — Babylonian Captivity — Fall of Jerusalem 586 B.C. — Jesus 4 B.C. — Revelation c. A.D. 100

Continued from page 204

Amoz, because it is thought that the prophet could not have predicted the Babylonian exile and the return under Cyrus. This argument is based, however, on the dogmatic assumption that predictive prophecy is impossible. Such a theory cannot explain the presence of messianic prophecies that were fulfilled in the life of Christ. When all is said and done, the idea of a single author raises fewer difficulties than the theories of multiple authorship.

With good reason, then, it has been traditionally maintained that Isaiah, the son of Amoz, who prophesied in Jerusalem during the reigns of Uzziah, Jotham, Ahaz, and Hezekiah, is the author of the book that bears his name. The prophet was evidently from a distinguished Jewish family, and his education is evident in his impressive vocabulary and style. Isaiah apparently maintained close contact with the royal court, but his exhortations against alliances with foreign powers were not always well received. His wife was a prophetess and he fathered at least two sons (7:3; 8:3). Isaiah spent most of his time in Jerusalem, and Jewish tradition says that his persecutors sawed him in two during the reign of the evil king Manasseh (cf. Heb. 11:37).

Date

Isaiah's long ministry ranged from about 740 to 680 B.C. (1:1), and the book of Isaiah no doubt contains prophetic writings written throughout this period. He began his ministry near the end of Uzziah's reign (790–739 B.C.) and continued through the reigns of Jotham (739–731 B.C.), Ahaz (731–715 B.C.), and Hezekiah (715–686 B.C.). Isaiah outlived Hezekiah by a few years because 37:38 records the death of Sennacherib in 681 B.C. Hezekiah was succeeded in 686 B.C. by his wicked son Manasseh, who overthrew the worship of Yahweh and no doubt opposed the work of Isaiah.

During the time of Isaiah, Assyria was growing in power under Tiglath-Pileser, who turned toward the west after his conquests to the east, plucking up many of the smaller nations along the Mediterranean including the Northern Kingdom of Israel (722–21 B.C.). As a contemporary of Hosea and Micah, Isaiah prophesied during the last years of the Northern Kingdom but ministered to the Southern Kingdom which was following in the sins of her neighbor to the north. After the fall of Samaria and the Northern Kingdom, he warned Judah of judgment not by Assyria, the most immediate threat, but by Babylon.

Themes and Literary Structure

The book of Isaiah has three major sections: prophecies of condemnation (chs. 1—35), an historical parenthesis or interlude (chs. 36—39), and prophecies of comfort and consolation (chs. 40—66).

Isaiah's message is presented against the background of Israel's greatest period of prosperity after the "Golden Age" under David and Solomon. Prosperity, agricultural and commercial success, and military success were accompanied by immorality, excessive drinking, idolatry, oppression of the poor, greed, and the presence of false prophets who pandered to the desires of the people. In response to this situation, Isaiah stressed (1) salvation by faith (7:9; 28:16; 30:15), (2) the holiness of God and the need for ethical living (6:1–8; 37:23), (3) the offense of human sin and the certainty of divine judgment (chs. 1—35), and (4) the assurance of redemption for a repentant remnant (1:9, 19; 10:19–22; 46:3, 4; 65:8–10).

The basic theme of this book is found in Isaiah's name, which means "Salvation is of the Lord." The word "salvation" appears twenty-six times in Isaiah but only seven times in all the other prophets combined.

Of all the books in the Old Testament, only the Psalms contain a larger number of messianic prophecies than Isaiah. Isaiah sets forth every aspect of the glory and ministry of Christ: His incarnation (7:14; 9:6); His youth (7:15; 11:1; 53:2); His mild manner (42:2); His obedience (50:5); His message (61:1, 2); His miracles (35:5, 6); His sufferings, rejection, and vicarious death (50:6; 53:1–12); and His exaltation (52:13).

OUTLINE OF ISAIAH

The Coming Messiah

A striking example of the many messianic prophecies in Isaiah, 11:1–12 provides an accurate description of the coming Messiah and His kingdom. He was to be a descendant of King David (Matt. 1:1); He was to be filled with the Holy Spirit (cf. Matt. 3:16); He would be a merciful and righteous judge of mankind (Rev. 19:11). The Messiah's reign is described in terms of its universal significance. It is characterized by peace and reconciliation (Is. 11:6–9), the coming of the Gentiles to the Messiah (11:10), and the gathering of the faithful remnant of Israel (11:11–12).

Isaiah described the qualifications of the ideal King whose rule would contrast with the dark reign of King Ahaz. The role remained unfulfilled until the coming of Jesus the Messiah. "The kingdom of God is within you" was His message.

The Messiah		His Kingdom	
The Branch, a descendant of David, the stem of Jesse	11:1, 10	The Gentiles will seek Him	11:10
God's Spirit will rest upon Him	11:2	The remnant of Israel will be gathered	11:11–16
He will fear the Lord	11:3	There will be joy in God's salvation	12:1–6
He will judge the earth with righteousness	11:4, 5		

Judgment on the Nations

Like certain other Old Testament prophetic books, Isaiah contains a series of oracles against the foreign enemies of Israel and upon unfaithful elements within Israel itself (chs. 13—23). Beginning with Babylon, the future enemy that would destroy Judah (13:1—14:23), Isaiah goes on to prophesy judgment on Assyria (14:24–27), Philistia (14:28–32), Moab (15:1—16:14), Syria and Israel (17:1–11), all nations (17:12—18:7), Egypt (19:1—20:6), Babylon and her allies (21:1–16), Jerusalem and her unfaithful leaders (22:1–25), and the city of Tyre (23:1–18).

See map, "Judgment on the Nations," on page 211.

The Suffering Servant in Isaiah

The book of Isaiah presents four Servant Songs (42:1–4; 49:1–6; 50:4–9), which reach their conclusion in the final song of the Suffering Servant (52:13—53:12). This description of the Suffering Servant occupies a central place in the consolation section (chs. 40—66) and is presented in five stanzas, each of which provides a picture of the saving work of the Servant: His humiliation and exaltation (52:13–15); His experience of rejection (53:1–3); His vicarious suffering (53:4–6); His sacrificial death (53:7–9); His reconciling atonement and resurrection (53:10–12).

It is sometimes argued that the Suffering Servant song presents an ideal portrait of the people of Israel as a whole. The subject of the song cannot be reduced to such an ideal depiction, however, because it presents a concrete person who mediates between God and sinful human beings. Furthermore, the many correspondences between the Suffering Servant and the Person and work of Christ cannot be ignored.

See chart, "Fulfilled Prophecies from Isaiah," on page 212.

Judgment on the Nations

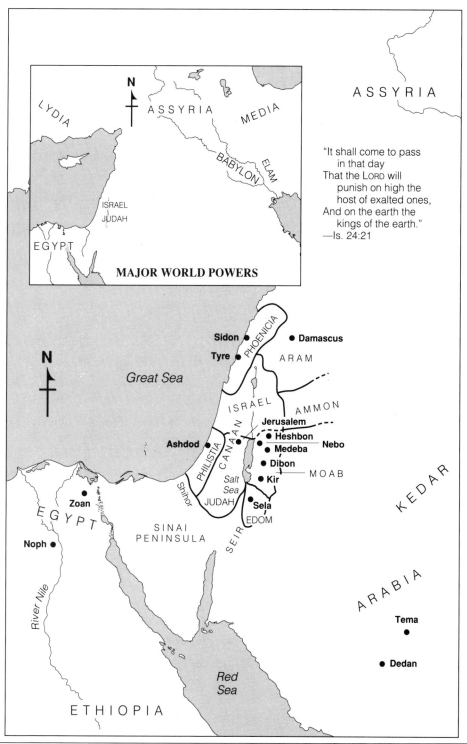

MAJOR WORLD POWERS

"It shall come to pass
    in that day
That the LORD will
    punish on high the
    host of exalted ones,
And on the earth the
    kings of the earth."
—Is. 24:21

Fulfilled Prophecies from Isaiah

The Prophecy	The Fulfillment
The Messiah . . .	Jesus Christ . . .
will be born of a virgin (Is. 7:14).	was born of a virgin named Mary (Luke 1:26–31).
will have a Galilean ministry (Is. 9:1, 2).	ministered in Galilee of the Gentiles (Matt. 4:13–16).
will be an heir to the throne of David (Is. 9:7).	was given the throne of His father David (Luke 1:32, 33).
will have His way prepared (Is. 40:3–5).	was announced by John the Baptist (John 1:19–28).
will be spat on and struck (Is. 50:6).	was spat on and beaten (Matt. 26:67).
will be exalted (Is. 52:13).	was highly exalted by God and the people (Phil. 2:9, 10).
will be disfigured by suffering (Is. 52:14; 53:2).	was scourged by the soldiers who gave Him a crown of thorns (Mark 15:15–19).
will make a blood atonement (Is. 53:5).	shed His blood to atone for our sins (1 Pet. 1:2).
will be widely rejected (Is. 53:1, 3).	was not accepted by many (John 12:37, 38).
will bear our sins and sorrows (Is. 53:4, 5).	died because of our sins (Rom. 4:25; 1 Pet. 2:24, 25).
will be our substitute (Is. 53:6, 8).	died in our place (Rom. 5:6, 8; 2 Cor. 5:21).
will voluntarily accept our guilt and punishment (Is. 53:7, 8).	was silent about our sin (Mark 15:4, 5; John 10:11; 19:30).
will be buried in a rich man's tomb (Is. 53:9).	was buried in the tomb of Joseph, a rich man from Arimathea (Matt. 27:57–60; John 19:38–42).
will save us who believe in Him (Is. 53:10, 11).	provided salvation for all who believe (John 3:16; Acts 16:31).
will die with transgressors (Is. 53:12).	was numbered with the transgressors (Mark 15:27, 28; Luke 22:37).
will heal the brokenhearted (Is. 61:1, 2).	healed the brokenhearted (Luke 4:18, 19).

JEREMIAH

The book of Jeremiah is the prophecy of a man divinely called in his youth from the priest-city of Anathoth. A heartbroken prophet with a heartbreaking message, Jeremiah labors for more than forty years proclaiming a message of doom to the stiff-necked people of Judah. Despised and persecuted by his countrymen, Jeremiah bathes his harsh prophecies in tears of compassion. His broken heart causes him to write a broken book, which is difficult to arrange chronologically or topically. But through his sermons and signs he faithfully declares that surrender to God's will is the only way to avoid calamity.

Author

The book clearly states that Jeremiah is its author (1:1). He dictated all his prophecies to his secretary Baruch from the beginning of his ministry until the fourth year of Jehoiakim, and later sections were also composed. Only chapter 52, a supplement which is almost identical to 2 Kings 24:18—25:30, was evidently not written by Jeremiah.

Jeremiah was the son of Hilkiah the priest and lived about two miles north of Jerusalem in the town of Anathoth. As an object lesson to Judah, he was not allowed to marry (16:2). Because of his unwelcome message of divine judgment to be brought about through Babylonian invasion, he was threatened and imprisoned. The prophet survived the Babylonian assault on the city and was later taken to Egypt where he died.

Date

According to 36:1–3, the writing of portions of Jeremiah may be dated with some precision to the fourth year of Jehoiakim (605 B.C.), when Jeremiah was commanded by God to write down the prophetic messages he had delivered to the people over the previous twenty years. This material apparently corresponds to chapters 1—20. The remaining chapters contain prophecies and historical accounts in topical rather than chronological order, covering the second twenty to twenty-five years of Jeremiah's ministry.

Continued on page 215

Jeremiah at a Glance

FOCUS	CALL OF JEREMIAH	PROPHECIES TO JUDAH				PROPHECIES TO THE GENTILES	FALL OF JERUSALEM
REFERENCE	1:1 ———— 2:1 ————	26:1 ————	30:1 ————	34:1 ————	46:1 ————		52:1 —— 52:34
DIVISION	PROPHETIC COMMISSION	CONDEMNATION OF JUDAH	CONFLICTS OF JEREMIAH	FUTURE RESTORATION OF JERUSALEM	PRESENT FALL OF JERUSALEM	CONDEMNATION OF NINE NATIONS	HISTORIC CONCLUSION
TOPIC	BEFORE THE FALL				THE FALL	AFTER THE FALL	
	CALL	MINISTRY					RETROSPECT
LOCATION	JUDAH					SURROUNDING NATIONS	BABYLON
TIME	c. 627–580 B.C.						

Nelson's Complete Book of Bible Maps and Charts © 1993 by Thomas Nelson, Inc.

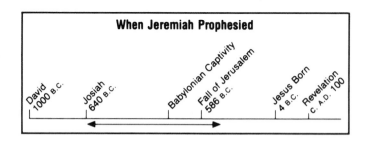

When Jeremiah Prophesied

David 1000 B.C. — Josiah 640 B.C. — Babylonian Captivity — Fall of Jerusalem 586 B.C. — Jesus Born 4 B.C. — Revelation C. A.D. 100

Continued from page 213

Jeremiah was a contemporary of Zephaniah, Habakkuk, Daniel, and Ezekiel, and his ministry stretched from c. 627 to c. 580 B.C. There were three stages in Jeremiah's ministry. From 627 to 605 B.C. he prophesied while Judah was threatened by Assyria and Egypt. From 605 to 586 B.C. he proclaimed God's judgment while Judah was threatened and besieged by Babylon. From 586 to about 580 B.C. he ministered in Jerusalem and Egypt after Judah's downfall.

Themes and Literary Structure

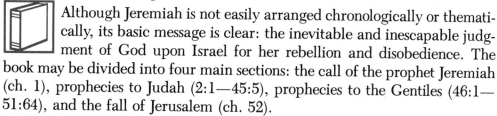 Although Jeremiah is not easily arranged chronologically or thematically, its basic message is clear: the inevitable and inescapable judgment of God upon Israel for her rebellion and disobedience. The book may be divided into four main sections: the call of the prophet Jeremiah (ch. 1), prophecies to Judah (2:1—45:5), prophecies to the Gentiles (46:1—51:64), and the fall of Jerusalem (ch. 52).

Often known as the "weeping prophet," Jeremiah faithfully proclaimed the divine condemnation of rebellious Judah for forty years. His sympathy and concern for his nation caused him to grieve deeply over the rebelliousness and imminent doom of his people.

Often Jeremiah desired to resign the prophetic office because of the harshness of his message and the unfriendly response that it elicited. It was Jeremiah's difficult task to confront a people who seemed to become more insanely confident as the peril grew. They believed that God would not let Jerusalem fall because they possessed the temple and the one true religion. Jeremiah was required to tell them that the terms of God's covenant mandated punishment for disobedience.

The well-known section on the new covenant (chs. 30—33) reflects Jeremiah's special interest in the covenant. All the prophets based their accusations and appeals on Israel's covenant relationship with God, but Jeremiah does so much more explicitly. He does not fault the content of the old covenant, but recognizes that it must be internalized if it is to be lived out. Thus he prophesies the coming of a new covenant—one that will be written on the hearts of God's people (31:31–34).

OUTLINE OF JEREMIAH

Part One: The Call of Jeremiah (1:1–19)

Jeremiah's Call

Like a number of other prophetic calls (cf. Is. 6), Jeremiah's call came as a result of a dialogue with God. Jeremiah would encounter many false prophets, and it was important that he have the assurance that his call came directly from God. Even though Jeremiah was young when God called him, the call was dependent upon the power of God, not upon human frailties such as age.

See chart, "The Call of Jeremiah," on page 218.

The Call of Jeremiah

Who?	The son of Hilkiah (1:1)
Where?	Anathoth in Benjamin (1:1)
When?	The reign of Josiah, 626 B.C. (1:2)
Why?	Ordained a prophet to the nations (1:5)
Origin?	Decided before his birth (1:5)
Jeremiah's response	"I am a youth" (1:6)
God corrects him	"I am with you" (1:7, 8)
God enables him	Given words of power (1:9, 10)

The dramatic character of Jeremiah's call highlights the principle that when God calls a person to a task, He also equips that person for the task. Like Jeremiah, we list our weaknesses and limitations. But God promises His enabling presence. Like Jeremiah, we anticipate fearful situations. But God promises His deliverance. God does not call us to a task He cannot help us to fulfill.

Nelson's Complete Book of Bible Maps and Charts © 1993 by Thomas Nelson, Inc.

Jeremiah's Journey to Egypt

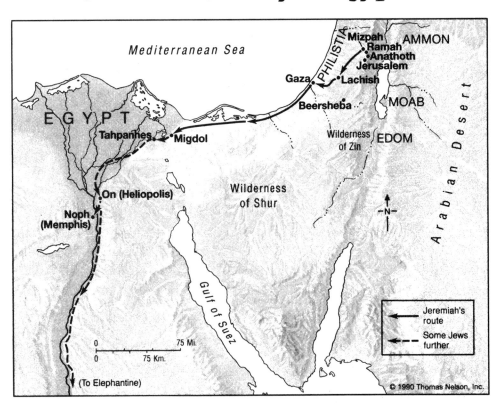

Babylonians Invade Palestine

Babylon overthrew Nineveh, the capital city of Assyria, in 612 B.C., and moved quickly to establish control over much of the ancient Near East. Defeating the Egyptians at the battle of Carchemish in 605 B.C., Nebuchadnezzar of Babylon moved against Palestine and deported important people such as Daniel to Babylon. Judah's king Jehoiakim thus became a Babylonian vassal, but he rejected Jeremiah's warnings in 601 B.C. and rebelled. Jehoiachin became Judah's next king in 597 B.C., but was replaced by Zedekiah three months later when Nebuchadnezzar captured Jerusalem and deported Jehoiachin to Babylon. Zedekiah was the last king of Judah; his attempted alliance with Egypt led to Nebuchadnezzar's occupation and overthrow of Jerusalem in 586 B.C.

Babylonians Invade Palestine

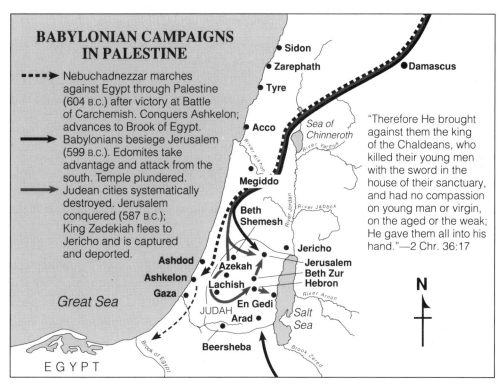

Nelson's Complete Book of Bible Maps and Charts © 1993 by Thomas Nelson, Inc.

LAMENTATIONS

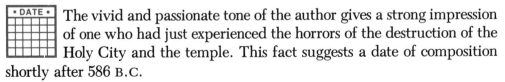

amentations describes the funeral of a city. It is a tearstained portrait of the once-proud Jerusalem, now reduced to rubble by the invading Babylonian hordes. In a five-poem dirge, the author expresses the deep emotion of one who has seen the slaughter of many of his people, the enslavement of others, and the abject despair of the few survivors.

Author

Traditionally, this book has been attributed to the prophet Jeremiah, though he is not named in the text. The Greek translation of the Old Testament (the Septuagint) names Jeremiah as the author, and early church fathers such as Origen and Jerome agreed. Its present location after the book of Jeremiah in the English text reflects this judgment. Stylistic similarities between the two books also indicate that Jeremiah was quite possibly the author.

Date

The vivid and passionate tone of the author gives a strong impression of one who had just experienced the horrors of the destruction of the Holy City and the temple. This fact suggests a date of composition shortly after 586 B.C.

Themes and Literary Structure

The five chapters of Lamentations consist of five mournful poems which can be entitled: (1) the destruction of Jerusalem, (2) the anger of Yahweh, (3) the prayer for mercy, (4) the siege of Jerusalem, (5) the prayer for restoration.

The five poems each comprise a chapter, and the first four have an acrostic structure—a literary form that follows the pattern of the alphabet: the first verse or group of verses begins with the first letter of the alphabet, the second with the second, and so forth. Of course, this structure is almost impossible to reproduce in translation.

The first four chapters (poems) are dirges, loaded with pain and agony,

Lamentations at a Glance

FOCUS	DESTRUCTION OF JERUSALEM	ANGER OF JEHOVAH	PRAYER FOR MERCY	SIEGE OF JERUSALEM	PRAYER FOR RESTORATION
REFERENCE	1:1 ————————	2:1 ————————	3:1 ————————	4:1 ————————	5:1 ——— 5:22
DIVISION	MOURNING CITY	BROKEN PEOPLE	SUFFERING PROPHET	RUINED KINGDOM	PENITENT NATION
TOPIC	GRIEF	CAUSE	HOPE	REPENTANCE	PRAYER
LOCATION	JERUSALEM				
TIME	c. 586 B.C.				

Nelson's Complete Book of Bible Maps and Charts © 1993 by Thomas Nelson, Inc.

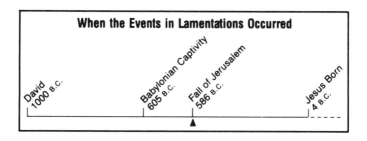

When the Events in Lamentations Occurred

David 1000 B.C. — Babylonian Captivity 605 B.C. — Fall of Jerusalem 586 B.C. — Jesus Born 4 B.C.

except for two brief outbursts of faith and hope in 3:19–42 and 3:55–60. Chapter 5 is not quite as intense, but even there the throb of deep hurt is present. Throughout the poems, one is aware of theological insights typical of Jeremiah. Sharp contrasts and vivid comparisons are often repeated, and figurative language is abundant.

The Theme of Renewal

Throughout the book, the author of Lamentations couples a recognition of human sin and its consequences with profound hope in God and prayers that God will lead His people back to Him along the path of sorrow, repentance, hope, and faith.

Sin ⟶ Suffering (1:8)
       Sorrow ⟶ Repentance (1:20)
              Prayer ⟶ Hope (3:19–24)
                    Faith ⟶ Restoration (5:21)

EZEKIEL

ritten by an exile carried to Babylon before the final assault on Jerusalem, Ezekiel uses prophecies, parables, signs, and symbols to dramatize God's message to His exiled people. Though they are like dry bones in the sun, God will reassemble them and breathe life into the nation once again. Present judgment will be followed by future glory.

The Hebrew name transliterated "Ezekiel" means "God Strengthens" or "Strengthened by God." The name occurs twice in this book and nowhere else in the Old Testament.

Author

The opening three verses name Ezekiel the son of Buzi as receiving the visions of God recorded in chapters 1—3. From there on, the book continues in the first person, no doubt referring to the same prophet Ezekiel. The unity of style, the phrases peculiar to Ezekiel but frequent to this book, and the constant attention to his great themes have convinced most scholars that the book is the result of Ezekiel's encounters with God.

Like Jeremiah, Ezekiel was a priest who was called to be a prophet of the Lord. His wife died as a sign to the exiled Jews that Jerusalem would not be spared (24:16–24). His prophetic ministry shows a priestly emphasis in his concern with the temple, priesthood, sacrifices, and the *Shekinah* (the glory of God manifested in the temple). Ezekiel was privileged to receive a number of striking visions and he was careful and artistic in his presentation.

Date

Ezekiel was carried off to exile in Babylon after the city fell a second time to Nebuchadnezzar in 597 B.C. His first vision is probably to be dated in the year 593–92 B.C. and the latest date given for an oracle is probably 571–70 B.C., making his ministry about twenty years long. The book as we now have it was probably completed shortly thereafter. The thirtieth year (1:1) is probably Ezekiel's age when he received his call, the age when

Continued on page 225

Ezekiel at a Glance

FOCUS	COMMISSION OF EZEKIEL			JUDGMENT ON JUDAH	JUDGMENT ON GENTILES	RESTORATION OF ISRAEL	
REFERENCE	1:1 —— 2:1 —————— 4:1 ————————— 25:1 ————————— 33:1 ———— 40:1 —— 48:35						
DIVISION	EZEKIEL SEES THE GLORY	EZEKIEL IS COMMISSIONED TO THE WORK	SIGNS, MESSAGES, VISIONS, AND PARABLES OF JUDGMENT	JUDGMENT ON SURROUNDING NATIONS	RETURN OF ISRAEL TO THE LORD	RESTORATION OF ISRAEL IN THE KINGDOM
TOPIC	BEFORE THE SIEGE (c. 592–587 B.C.)			DURING THE SIEGE (c. 586 B.C.)	AFTER THE SIEGE (c. 585–570 B.C.)		
	JUDAH'S FALL			JUDAH'S FOES	JUDAH'S FUTURE		
LOCATION	BABYLON						
TIME	c. 592–570 B.C.						

Nelson's Complete Book of Bible Maps and Charts © 1993 by Thomas Nelson, Inc.

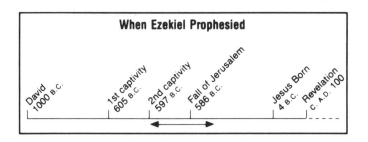

When Ezekiel Prophesied

David 1000 B.C. — 1st captivity 605 B.C. — 2nd captivity 597 B.C. — Fall of Jerusalem 586 B.C. — Jesus Born 4 B.C. — Revelation C. A.D. 100

Continued from page 223

priests entered fully into their temple duties. As exile had deprived Ezekiel of the privilege of serving as a temple priest, God graciously gave him the prophetic ministry recorded in this book.

This book is the easiest of the Old Testament books to date, because of Ezekiel's unique orderly sequence of dates. Each section of prophetic oracles begins with the year and day of the month. The prophet Ezekiel was a contemporary of both Jeremiah and Daniel, and some of his prophecies seem to be extensions of Jeremiah's message. Daniel is mentioned three times in the book (14:14, 20; 28:3).

Themes and Literary Structure

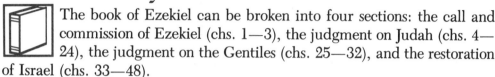
The book of Ezekiel can be broken into four sections: the call and commission of Ezekiel (chs. 1—3), the judgment on Judah (chs. 4—24), the judgment on the Gentiles (chs. 25—32), and the restoration of Israel (chs. 33—48).

Like the books of Daniel and Revelation, Ezekiel belongs to the genre of "apocalyptic" writings. Characteristics of this type of literature include the use of symbolism, visions, allegories, parables, and symbolic actions. Ezekiel uses many of these avenues of expression to impress upon his fellow exiles that God's judgment of Jerusalem was not yet finished. Jerusalem's cup of iniquity was finally running over; God's time for action had come. The certainty of divine judgment was symbolized by the departure of God's glory from the temple (8:1—11:25).

Ezekiel also stresses the certainty of God's judgment upon the nations surrounding Israel. It shows the full circle of judgment on the nations that surround Judah by following them in a clockwise circuit: Ammon, Moab, Edom, Philistia, Tyre, and Sidon (chs. 25—28). The oracles against the nations conclude with Egypt, a nation that would continue to exist but would never recover its former glory (29:15).

With the fall of Jerusalem, Ezekiel's attention turns to the future restoration of Israel. The vision of the valley of dry bones (37:1–14) vividly pictures the reanimation of the nation by the Spirit of God. The restoration of Israel is further developed as Ezekiel returns in a vision to the fallen city and is given detailed specifications for the reconstruction of the temple, the city, and the land (chs. 40—48). After an intricate description of the new outer court, inner court, and temple (chs. 40—42), Ezekiel views the return of the glory of the Lord to the temple from the east (43:1–12).

Ezekiel's eschatological visions of Israel's restoration clearly have a messianic dimension. The title "son of man" occurs some ninety times in Ezekiel and, while the title here is applied to Ezekiel himself, it was appropriated by Jesus as His favorite self-designation. Therefore, Ezekiel may be regarded as a type of Christ. As such, Ezekiel was empowered as a prophetic voice of the messianic age when the "Spirit of the LORD fell" upon him (11:5). The descent of the Holy Spirit upon Jesus at the Jordan River empowered Him to proclaim the advent of the messianic kingdom (Luke 4:18, 19). In addition, the vision of the Lord God as the divine Shepherd who gathers His scattered flock (34:11–16) evokes images of Jesus as the Good Shepherd (John 10:11–16). The restored sanctuary in the midst of a regathered people whose head is the King-priest, the Davidic Messiah (37:22–28), foreshadows the restored tabernacle of David, the church (Amos 9:11; Acts 15:16).

OUTLINE OF EZEKIEL

Scope of Ezekiel's Prophecies

The geographical scope of the prophetic visions in the book of Ezekiel is breathtaking. Written in exile in Babylon, Ezekiel's prophecies deal with Israel and the nations immediately surrounding her (chs. 25—32). Also mentioned are a variety of cities and areas of the ancient Mediterranean world (e.g., ch. 27). Perhaps most intriguing is the reference to Gog, an aggressive foreign ruler from the land of Magog, who is said to be the prince of Rosh, Meshech, and Tubal (38:1–2). Gog and his country Magog have not been satisfactorily identified. Magog may have been located in what is now modern Turkey because Tubal and Meshech are well attested in Greek and Assyrian records as located in this area.

See map, "Scope of Ezekiel's Prophecies," on page 232.

Ezekiel's Temple

Chapter 40 presents a detailed plan for a new temple complex in Jerusalem. Some interpret this prophecy as an exact blueprint of a physical temple to be constructed in or near Jerusalem during a future millennial (thousand-year) period. Others view Ezekiel's restored temple not as a blueprint, but as a vision that stresses the purity and spiritual vitality of the ideal place of worship and those who will worship there. Thus, it is not intended to refer to an earthly, physical fulfillment, but expresses the truth found in the name of the new city: THE LORD IS THERE (48:35).

See chart, "Ezekiel's Temple," on page 229.

Ezekiel's Vision of the Restoration of the Land

The boundaries of the restored nation of Israel approach the boundaries of the land as it was under David and Solomon. However, the area east of the Jordan—Gilead and Transjordan—will not be a part of this new inheritance. It was not part of the land that had been promised.

The tribes are not arranged as they were historically when the land was divided under Joshua (Josh. 13—19). God will do something new in the restoration.

The central portion of the land around Jerusalem will be set apart for religion and government.

To the north of the central district are seven tribes—Dan, Asher, Naphtali, Manasseh, Ephraim, Reuben, Judah.

To the south are the remaining five tribes—Benjamin, Simeon, Issachar, Zebulun, Gad.

See map, "Restoration of the Land," on page 233.

Ezekiel's Temple

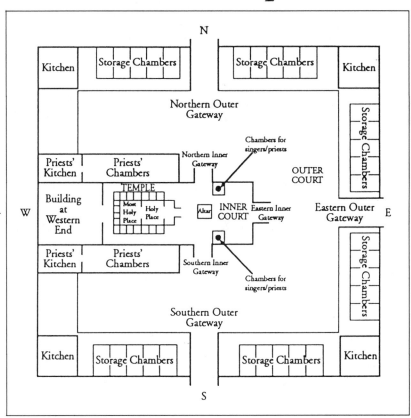

The Life and Times of Ezekiel

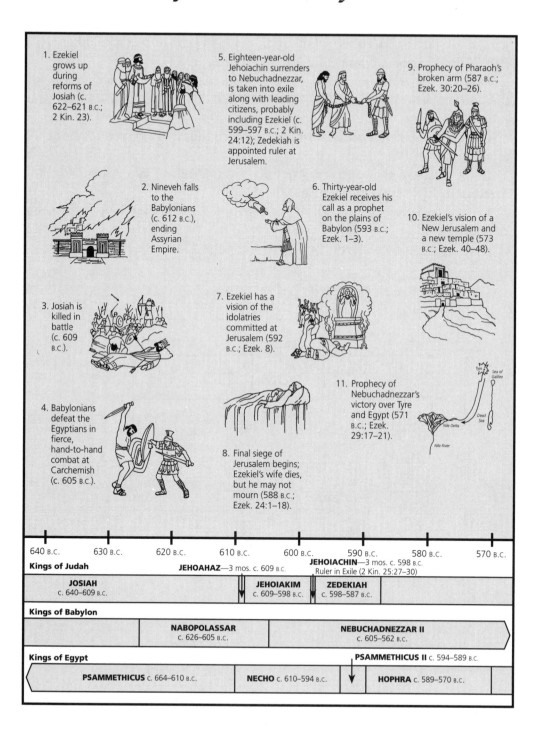

1. Ezekiel grows up during reforms of Josiah (c. 622–621 B.C.; 2 Kin. 23).

2. Nineveh falls to the Babylonians (c. 612 B.C.), ending Assyrian Empire.

3. Josiah is killed in battle (c. 609 B.C.).

4. Babylonians defeat the Egyptians in fierce, hand-to-hand combat at Carchemish (c. 605 B.C.).

5. Eighteen-year-old Jehoiachin surrenders to Nebuchadnezzar, is taken into exile along with leading citizens, probably including Ezekiel (c. 599–597 B.C.; 2 Kin. 24:12); Zedekiah is appointed ruler at Jerusalem.

6. Thirty-year-old Ezekiel receives his call as a prophet on the plains of Babylon (593 B.C.; Ezek. 1–3).

7. Ezekiel has a vision of the idolatries committed at Jerusalem (592 B.C.; Ezek. 8).

8. Final siege of Jerusalem begins; Ezekiel's wife dies, but he may not mourn (588 B.C.; Ezek. 24:1–18).

9. Prophecy of Pharaoh's broken arm (587 B.C.; Ezek. 30:20–26).

10. Ezekiel's vision of a New Jerusalem and a new temple (573 B.C.; Ezek. 40–48).

11. Prophecy of Nebuchadnezzar's victory over Tyre and Egypt (571 B.C.; Ezek. 29:17–21).

640 B.C.	630 B.C.	620 B.C.	610 B.C.	600 B.C.	590 B.C.	580 B.C.	570 B.C.

Kings of Judah

JEHOAHAZ—3 mos. c. 609 B.C.

JEHOIACHIN—3 mos. c. 598 B.C. Ruler in Exile (2 Kin. 25:27–30)

| JOSIAH c. 640–609 B.C. | JEHOIAKIM c. 609–598 B.C. | ZEDEKIAH c. 598–587 B.C. | |

Kings of Babylon

| NABOPOLASSAR c. 626–605 B.C. | NEBUCHADNEZZAR II c. 605–562 B.C. |

Kings of Egypt

PSAMMETHICUS II c. 594–589 B.C.

| PSAMMETHICUS c. 664–610 B.C. | NECHO c. 610–594 B.C. | HOPHRA c. 589–570 B.C. |

The Parables of Ezekiel

A parable is a truth wrapped in a memorable story or word picture. It could be fictional, dramatized, or the result of a vision. Jesus gave much of His teaching through parables (see "The Parables of Jesus Christ" at Luke 8:4). So did several of the Old Testament prophets, including Ezekiel.

1. The Wood of the Vine (Ezek. 15:1–8)
Symbolized the way in which Judah had become useless to the Lord and now served no other purpose than to be burned up in judgment.

2. The Foundling (Ezek. 16)
Illustrated the nation's betrayal of God's love and compassion.

3. The Eagles and the Cedar (Ezek. 17)
Illustrated the foolishness of King Zedekiah, whose rebellion would bring Nebuchadnezzar's troops to destroy Jerusalem.

4. The Fiery Furnace (Ezek. 22:17–22)
Explained the way in which God was going to purify His people through the "heat" of the siege of Jerusalem.

6. The Cooking Pot (Ezek. 24:1–14)
Symbolized the way in which God was going to "turn up the heat" on Jerusalem in order to cleanse it of its impurities.

5. The Two Harlots (Ezek. 23)
Symbolized the spiritual adultery of Israel and Judah.

7. The Shipwreck (Ezek. 27)
Illustrated the judgment that was going to fall on Tyre.

8. The Irresponsible Shepherds (Ezek. 34)
Signified the worthless leaders of Jerusalem and how God would deal with them.

9. The Dry Bones (Ezek. 37)
Symbolized the spiritual renewal of the nation of Israel.

Jeremiah and Zechariah were two other prophets who used parables to communicate their message. See Jer. 18:1–10 and Zech. 5:1–4.

Scope of Ezekiel's Prophecies

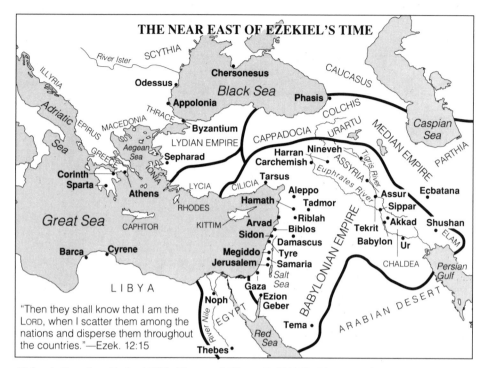

THE NEAR EAST OF EZEKIEL'S TIME

SCYTHIA

River Ister

ILLYRIA

Odessus

Chersonesus

Black Sea

CAUCASUS

Appolonia

Phasis

Adriatic Sea

EPIRUS

MACEDONIA

THRACE

Byzantium

COLCHIS

URARTU

Caspian Sea

MEDIAN EMPIRE

PARTHIA

LYDIAN EMPIRE

CAPPADOCIA

GREECE

Aegean Sea

Sepharad

Harran

Nineveh

ASSYRIA

IONIA

Carchemish

Tigris River

Corinth
Sparta

Tarsus

Euphrates River

Assur

Ecbatana

Athens

LYCIA

CILICIA

Aleppo

Sippar

Great Sea

RHODES

Hamath

Tadmor

Tekrit

Akkad

Shushan

CAPHTOR

KITTIM

Arvad

Riblah

Babylon

Ur

ELAM

Sidon

Biblos

Sidon

Damascus

Barca

Cyrene

Megiddo

Tyre

Jerusalem

Samaria

CHALDEA

Persian Gulf

BABYLONIAN EMPIRE

Salt Sea

LIBYA

Gaza

"Then they shall know that I am the
LORD, when I scatter them among the
nations and disperse them throughout
the countries."—Ezek. 12:15

Noph

Ezion
Geber

ARABIAN DESERT

River Nile

EGYPT

Tema

Red Sea

Thebes

Nelson's Complete Book of Bible Maps and Charts © 1993 by Thomas Nelson, Inc.

Restoration of the Land

HAMATH

• Zedad

Hazar Enan •

DAN

Berothah •

ASHER

MANSUATE

NAPHTALI

• Damascus

Mediterranean Sea

MANASSEH

KARNAIM

MEGIDDO

Sea of
Chinnereth

EPHRAIM

HAURAN

REUBEN

Jordan River

GILEAD

SAMARIA

JUDAH

AMMON

Jerusalem •

BENJAMIN

Dead Sea

SIMEON

PHILISTIA

ISSACHAR

MOAB

ZEBULUN

• Tamar

GAD

EDOM

• Meribah of
Kadesh

—N—

0   60 Mi.
0   60 Km.

© 1990 Thomas Nelson, Inc.

Nelson's Complete Book of Bible Maps and Charts © 1993 by Thomas Nelson, Inc.

DANIEL

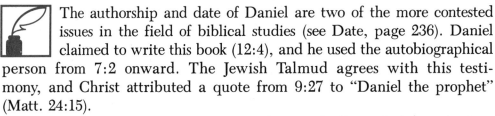

hree of the most famous stories in the Bible are recorded in the book of Daniel: Shadrach, Meshach, and Abed-Nego in the fiery furnace, the handwriting on the wall at Belshazzar's feast, and Daniel in the den of lions. Yet beyond these stories the book is a mystery to many—recording dreams, visions, and their interpretations which are difficult to understand. The central message of God's power and ultimate triumph is clear, however, and is as relevant today as it was in the time of Daniel.

The name "Daniel" means "God is my Judge," and the book is named after the author and principal character.

Author

The authorship and date of Daniel are two of the more contested issues in the field of biblical studies (see Date, page 236). Daniel claimed to write this book (12:4), and he used the autobiographical person from 7:2 onward. The Jewish Talmud agrees with this testimony, and Christ attributed a quote from 9:27 to "Daniel the prophet" (Matt. 24:15).

Daniel was a Jewish youth of noble birth carried off to Babylon in the first captivity under Nebuchadnezzar in 605 B.C. He became a member of the Babylonian royal service early in his captivity and spent most of his career as a high-ranking advisor to Nebuchadnezzar. Nebuchadnezzar's successors seem to have given Daniel less prominence, but after Babylon was conquered by the Persians, Daniel achieved considerable importance again under King Darius.

Daniel is one of the few well-known biblical characters about whom nothing negative is written. His life was characterized by faith, prayer, courage, consistency, and lack of compromise. This "greatly beloved" man (9:23; 10:11, 19) was mentioned three times by his sixth-century-B.C. contemporary Ezekiel as an example of righteousness.

Daniel at a Glance

FOCUS	HISTORY OF DANIEL	PROPHETIC PLAN FOR THE GENTILES				PROPHETIC PLAN OF ISRAEL		
REFERENCE	1:1 ——— 2:1 ———		5:1 ——— 6:1 ———		7:1 — 8:1 ———	9:1 ——— 10:1 — 12:13		
DIVISION	PERSONAL LIFE OF DANIEL	VISIONS OF NEBUCHADNEZZAR	VISION OF BELSHAZZAR	DECREE OF DARIUS	FOUR BEASTS	VISION OF RAM AND MALE-GOAT	VISION OF SEVENTY WEEKS	VISION OF ISRAEL'S FUTURE
TOPIC	DANIEL'S BACKGROUND	DANIEL INTERPRETS OTHERS' DREAMS				ANGEL INTERPRETS DANIEL'S DREAMS		
TOPIC	HEBREW	ARAMAIC				HEBREW		
LOCATION	BABYLON OR PERSIA							
TIME	c. 605–536 B.C.							

Nelson's Complete Book of Bible Maps and Charts © 1993 by Thomas Nelson, Inc.

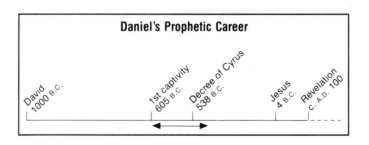

Daniel's Prophetic Career

David 1000 B.C. — 1st captivity 605 B.C. — Decree of Cyrus 538 B.C. — Jesus 4 B.C. — Revelation c. A.D. 100

Date

Babylon rebelled against the Assyrian Empire in 626 B.C., overthrew the Assyrian capital of Nineveh in 612 B.C., and became master of the ancient Near East when it defeated Egypt at the battle of Carchemish in 605 B.C. Later that year, the Babylonian king Nebuchadnezzar subdued Jerusalem and took prominent citizens of the city as hostages to Babylon, a group that included the young Daniel.

Daniel ministered for the full duration of the Babylonian captivity as a prophet and government official, and he continued on after Babylon was overcome by the Medes and Persians in 539 B.C. His prophetic ministry was directed to the gentile courts of Babylon and Persia, as well as to his Jewish countrymen. Zerubbabel led a return of the Jews to Jerusalem in the first year of Cyrus, and Daniel lived and ministered at least until the third year of Cyrus (536 B.C.; 10:1). Taking the statements of the book at face value, Daniel's book would appear to have been written by the ninth year of Cyrus (c. 530 B.C.).

Largely because of the extensive visions in Daniel concerning the empires which succeeded the Babylonian empire and a conviction that predictive prophecy is impossible, many critics have argued that Daniel is a fraudulent book written in the time of the Maccabees in the second century B.C., not in the sixth-century as the book claims. There are, however, strong reasons for accepting the sixth-century date.

The argument that predictive prophecy is impossible, and therefore that the sequence of empires depicted in chapters 7 and 8 was written during the second-century-B.C. period of Greek domination, involves a dogmatic rejection of the supernatural. Furthermore, this argument for a second-century date assumes that the four empire nations depicted are Babylonia, Media, Persia, and Greece. It is apparent, however, that Daniel speaks of a combined Medo-Persian empire (5:28), and that the description of the fourth empire fits Rome, which achieved dominance long after the alleged second-century-B.C. date of writing, rather than Greece.

Although it is claimed that the Aramaic portion of Daniel (chs. 2—7) is late Aramaic, recent studies have shown that Daniel's Aramaic is actually an example of early Imperial Aramaic—a form consistent with a sixth-century-B.C. date. In addition, the presence of fragments of the text of Daniel among the Dead Sea Scrolls—fragments which apparently date to the Maccabean period—does not allow sufficient time for a work supposedly written in the Maccabean period to have become widely accepted as Scripture.

Though some argue that there are historical errors in Daniel, and that these errors argue for a late date, recent evidence has demonstrated the historical accuracy of Daniel. While some questions remain, none pose an insuperable difficulty for a sixth-century-B.C. date.

Themes and Literary Structure

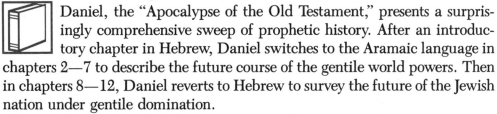

Daniel, the "Apocalypse of the Old Testament," presents a surprisingly comprehensive sweep of prophetic history. After an introductory chapter in Hebrew, Daniel switches to the Aramaic language in chapters 2—7 to describe the future course of the gentile world powers. Then in chapters 8—12, Daniel reverts to Hebrew to survey the future of the Jewish nation under gentile domination.

The theme of God's sovereign control in the affairs of world history clearly emerges and provides comfort to the future church, as well as to the Jews whose nation was destroyed by the Babylonians. The Babylonians, Persians, Greeks, and Romans will come and go, but God will establish His kingdom through His redeemed people forever.

Another theme of this book is the emphasis on separation to God, with Daniel as the ultimate example. From his decision not to eat the king's food (1:8–16), to his refusal to pray to the king (6:4–24), Daniel displayed such an uncompromising spirit that spectacular opportunities were opened for God to display His power on Daniel's behalf.

OUTLINE OF DANIEL

Dreams and Visions in Daniel

The future historical situation of God's people is communicated in prophetic visions of an image (ch. 2), four beasts (ch. 7), and two beasts (ch. 8). The dream of the image in chapter 2 and the vision of the four beasts in chapter 7 both refer to four successive gentile empires under which God's people would live: Babylon, Medo-Persia, Greece, and Rome.

The vision in chapter 8 deals with the experiences of God's people under the rule of the Medes and Persians, represented by the ram, and under the Greeks, represented by the goat. The "large horn" of 8:8 symbolizes Alexander the Great, who died at age 33 and whose kingdom was split into four parts ruled by four Greek generals—the "four notable horns" of 8:8. The "little horn" of 8:9 represents Antiochus IV Epiphanes who desecrated the temple in Jerusalem.

Correlation of Dreams and Visions in Daniel

	Image—Chapter 2	Beasts—Chapter 7	Beasts—Chapter 8	Kingdoms Represented
The Times of the Gentiles	Head of fine gold	Like a lion with eagle's wings		Babylon
	Chest and arms of silver	Like a bear	Ram with two horns	Medo–Persia
	Belly and thighs of bronze	Like a leopard with four wings and four heads	Male goat with one great horn, four horns and little horn	Greece
	Legs of iron, feet of iron and clay	Incomparable beast with ten horns and little horn		Rome
	Stone that becomes a great mountain	Messiah and saints receive the kingdom		Kingdom of God

Nelson's Complete Book of Bible Maps and Charts © 1993 by Thomas Nelson, Inc.

The Little Horns in Daniel

Although somewhat similar in description, the little horn of 7:8 is different from the little horn of 8:9. The little horn of 7:8 occurs in the context of the fourth kingdom (Rome), while the little horn of 8:9 appears in the context of the third kingdom (Greece). It is generally agreed that this second little horn refers to Antiochus IV Epiphanes who ruled Syria from 175 to 163 B.C. and who attacked Jerusalem and desecrated the temple.

The identity of the little horn of 7:8 is somewhat disputed. Many interpreters view this as a reference to the Antichrist who rules over a resurgent Roman empire of the future. Others interpret this as a reference to one of the ancient Roman caesars.

It is important to note that the little horns of chapters 7 and 8 are two distinct persons. Several factors make this distinction clear:	
Little Horn of Chapter 7	**Little Horn of Chapter 8**
Would come from Rome (fourth kingdom).	Would come from Greece (third kingdom).
Would be an eleventh horn, rooting up three of ten horns.	Would be a fifth horn, coming out of one of four horns.
Would persecute God's people for 42 months or 3½ years.	Would persecute God's people for 2,300 days or over 6 years.

Alexander's Greek Empire

(Daniel 2, 7, 8, 11)

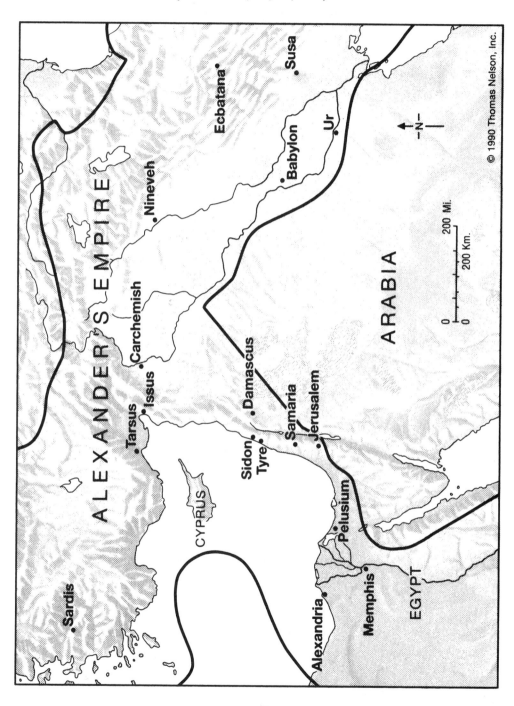

© 1990 Thomas Nelson, Inc.

HOSEA

The book of Hosea was written to a Northern Kingdom of Israel on the brink of disaster. Outwardly, the nation was enjoying a time of prosperity and growth; but inwardly, moral corruption and spiritual adultery permeated the lives of the people. The prophet Hosea was instructed by God to marry an unfaithful woman, and he found in his own life a vivid illustration of the unfaithfulness of God's people and the faithfulness of God. Hosea repeatedly echoes his threefold message: God abhors the sins of His people; judgment is certain; but God's love stands firm.

Hosea, whose name means "Salvation," has the same name as Israel's last king, Hoshea, even though the English Bible spells them differently.

Author

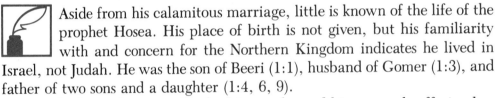

Aside from his calamitous marriage, little is known of the life of the prophet Hosea. His place of birth is not given, but his familiarity with and concern for the Northern Kingdom indicates he lived in Israel, not Judah. He was the son of Beeri (1:1), husband of Gomer (1:3), and father of two sons and a daughter (1:4, 6, 9).

Hosea had a real compassion for his people, and his personal suffering because of the behavior of his wife gave him insight into God's grief over Israel's sin. Thus, his words of coming judgment are passionate but tempered with a heart of tenderness.

Date

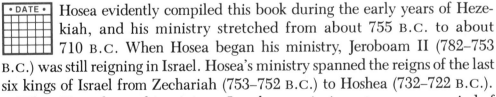

Hosea evidently compiled this book during the early years of Hezekiah, and his ministry stretched from about 755 B.C. to about 710 B.C. When Hosea began his ministry, Jeroboam II (782–753 B.C.) was still reigning in Israel. Hosea's ministry spanned the reigns of the last six kings of Israel from Zechariah (753–752 B.C.) to Hoshea (732–722 B.C.).

When Hosea began his ministry, Israel was enjoying a temporary period of political and economic prosperity under Jeroboam II. However, the nation began to crumble after Tiglath-Pileser II (745–727 B.C.) strengthened Assyria.

Continued on page 244

Hosea at a Glance

FOCUS	ADULTEROUS WIFE AND FAITHFUL HUSBAND			ADULTEROUS ISRAEL AND FAITHFUL LORD			
REFERENCE	1:1 ——— 2:2 ——————— 3:1 ——— 4:1 ——————— 6:4 ——————— 9:1 ——— 11:1 ——— 14:9						
DIVISION	PROPHETIC MARRIAGE	APPLICATION OF GOMER TO ISRAEL	RESTORATION OF GOMER	SPIRITUAL ADULTERY OF ISRAEL	REFUSAL OF ISRAEL TO REPENT	JUDGMENT OF ISRAEL BY GOD	RESTORATION OF ISRAEL TO GOD
TOPIC	MARRIAGE OF HOSEA			MESSAGE OF HOSEA			
	PERSONAL			NATIONAL			
LOCATION	NORTHERN KINGDOM OF ISRAEL						
TIME	c. 755–710 B.C.						

Nelson's Complete Book of Bible Maps and Charts © 1993 by Thomas Nelson, Inc.

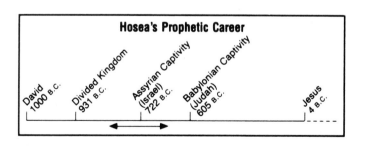

Hosea's Prophetic Career

David 1000 B.C. — Divided Kingdom 931 B.C. — Assyrian Captivity (Israel) 722 B.C. — Babylonian Captivity (Judah) 605 B.C. — Jesus 4 B.C.

Continued from page 242

The reigns of Israel's last six kings were relatively brief since four were murdered and a fifth was carried captive to Assyria. Confusion and decline characterized the last years of the Northern Kingdom, and her people refused to heed Hosea's warnings of imminent judgment.

Themes and Literary Structure

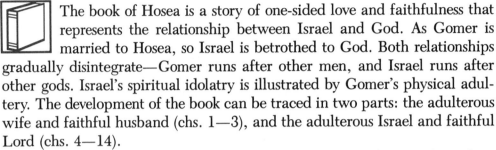

The book of Hosea is a story of one-sided love and faithfulness that represents the relationship between Israel and God. As Gomer is married to Hosea, so Israel is betrothed to God. Both relationships gradually disintegrate—Gomer runs after other men, and Israel runs after other gods. Israel's spiritual idolatry is illustrated by Gomer's physical adultery. The development of the book can be traced in two parts: the adulterous wife and faithful husband (chs. 1—3), and the adulterous Israel and faithful Lord (chs. 4—14).

Hosea's message reflects the terrible fascination of Israel with Baal worship. Baal means "husband" or "lord," and his worship involved fertility rites that included ritual prostitution. Baal was the other lover to whom the unfaithful Israel often turned.

Hosea provides one of the Old Testament's most eloquent expressions of God's mercy. It is embodied in the Hebrew word *hesed*, variously rendered "mercy," "loving-kindness," or "steadfast love." It involves loving loyalty to covenant commitments, well illustrated by the marriage vow. But from Hosea's perspective, God's faithful love would not permit Him to easily divorce His people.

See chart, "Israel's Apostasy and Hosea's Marriage," on page 245.

OUTLINE OF HOSEA

Israel's Apostasy and Hosea's Marriage

The stages of Israel's relationship with God are depicted in the prophecies of Jeremiah and Ezekiel, as well as in Hosea's relationship with Gomer.

Stage	Israel's Prophets	Hosea's Marriage
Betrothal	Jeremiah 2:2	Hosea 1:2
Marriage	Ezekiel 16:8–14	Hosea 1:3
Adultery	Jeremiah 5:7; Ezekiel 16:15–34	Hosea 3:1
Estrangement	Jeremiah 3:8–10; Ezekiel 16:35–52	Hosea 3:3, 4
Restoration	Ezekiel 16:53–63	Hosea 3:5

Nelson's Complete Book of Bible Maps and Charts © 1993 by Thomas Nelson, Inc.

What's in a Name?
(Hosea 1)

Names play a significant part in understanding Hosea, as the chart describes:

Name	Meaning
Jezreel (Hos. 1:4)	God Scatters
Lo-Ruhamah (Hos. 1:6)	Not Pitied
Lo-Amni (Hos. 1:9)	Not My People
Hosea (Hos. 1:1, related also to *Joshua*, Num. 13:16, and *Jesus*, Matt. 1:21)	Yahweh Is Salvation

JOEL

Disaster struck the Southern Kingdom of Judah in the form of a cloud of locusts. In a matter of hours, the fields were stripped bare, and the prophet Joel seized this opportunity to proclaim God's message. The plague of locusts is seen as a foreshadowing of the coming day of the Lord. In light of this, the book warns of approaching judgment, calls the people to repentance, and gives God's people hope of the coming day of salvation that will follow judgment.

The Hebrew name *Yo'el* means "Yahweh is God," a name appropriate to a book which emphasizes God's sovereign work in history.

Author

Although there are several other Joels in the Bible, the prophet Joel is known only from this book. Joel identifies himself as the son of Pethuel (1:1), and his frequent references to Zion and the house of the Lord suggest that he probably lived not far from Jerusalem. Because of his statements about the priesthood in 1:13, 14; and 2:17, some think Joel was a priest as well as a prophet. In any case, Joel was a clear, concise, and uncompromising preacher of repentance.

Date

Since the book includes no explicit time references, it cannot be dated with certainty. It has traditionally been dated c. 835 B.C., when Joash was placed upon the throne at the age of seven and Jehoiada the priest functioned as the real ruler (2 Kin. 11; 12). This period seems to fit the text of Joel since the influence of the priesthood appears to be strong and there is no mention of a king. Because of this priestly prominence, others argue that Joel is to be dated much later in the postexilic period.

Evidence also points to a sharing of material between Joel and Amos. Although some believe that Joel borrowed from Amos, it is more likely that Amos, an eighth-century prophet, borrowed from Joel. In addition, Joel's style is more like that of Hosea and Amos than that of the postexilic writers. Since

Continued on page 248

Joel at a Glance

FOCUS	DAY OF THE LORD IN RETROSPECT		DAY OF THE LORD IN PROSPECT	
REFERENCE	1:1 ——————— 1:13 —————————		2:1 ————————— 2:28 —————	3:21
DIVISION	PAST DAY OF THE LOCUST	PAST DAY OF THE DROUGHT	IMMINENT DAY OF THE LORD	ULTIMATE DAY OF THE LORD
TOPIC	HISTORICAL INVASION		PROPHETIC INVASION	
	PAST JUDGMENT ON JUDAH		FUTURE JUDGMENT AND RESTORATION OF JUDAH	
LOCATION	SOUTHERN KINGDOM OF JUDAH			
TIME	c. 835 B.C.			

Nelson's Complete Book of Bible Maps and Charts © 1993 by Thomas Nelson, Inc.

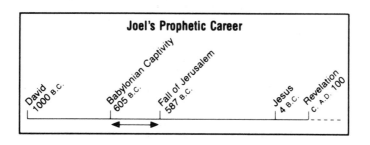

Joel's Prophetic Career

David 1000 B.C.

Babylonian Captivity 605 B.C.

Fall of Jerusalem 587 B.C.

Jesus 4 B.C.

Revelation c. A.D. 100

Continued from page 246

Joel does not mention idolatry, it may have been written after the purge of Baal worship early in the reign of Joash under Jehoiada the priest. As an early prophet in Judah, Joel would have been a contemporary of Elisha in Israel.

Themes and Literary Structure

The book of Joel is often considered to be the most polished literary work among the prophetic writings. His careful and well-developed imagery, especially in describing the locust plague in chapters 1 and 2, and the clear structure of the book support this contention. The book of Joel can be divided into two major sections: the day of the Lord in retrospect (ch. 1); and the day of the Lord in prospect (chs. 2; 3).

This brief book develops the crucial theme of the coming day of the Lord (1:15; 2:1, 2, 11, 31; 3:14, 18)—a time of awesome judgment upon people and nations that have rebelled against God. But it is also a time of future blessing upon those who have trusted in Him. The theme of disaster runs throughout the book (locust plagues, famine, raging fires, invading armies, celestial phenomena), but promises of hope are interspersed with the pronouncements of coming judgment.

OUTLINE OF JOEL

AMOS

The book of Amos addresses the excessive pursuit of luxury, self-indulgence, and oppression of the poor which characterized the period of prosperity and success in the Northern Kingdom of Israel under Jeroboam II. Amos's message of doom seemed incongruent with the elaborate trappings of that era. But with divinely given insight, he saw the corruption beneath the brilliantly colored exterior and announced that the nation was rotten to the core. The book stands as an eloquent witness against those who subordinate human need and dignity to the pursuit of wealth and pleasure.

The name "Amos" is derived from the Hebrew terms meaning "lift a burden." Thus, the name means "Burden" or "Burden-bearer." Amos lived up to the meaning of his name by bearing up under his divinely given burden of declaring judgment to rebellious Israel.

Author

Amos was not a "professional" prophet (7:14) like the more numerous institutional or cultic prophets of his day. From his rustic background at Tekoa, six miles south of Bethlehem in the Southern Kingdom of Judah, Amos was called by God to go to the Northern Kingdom to be His spokesman (7:15).

The prophet was a common man whose occupation was herding sheep, with supplementary income from tending sycamore fruit (7:14). His moral sensibilities were shocked by the perversions of Israel's worship that he observed at Bethel, one of the great national shrines.

Date

According to 1:1, Amos prophesied during the reigns of Uzziah, king of Judah (767–739 B.C.), and Jeroboam, king of Israel (782–753 B.C.), thus leaving a possible time-frame from 767 to 753 B.C. The prophecy of 7:9–11 seems to indicate a time late in the reign of Jeroboam and a probable date of writing is 760–753 B.C.

Amos ministered after the time of Joel and Jonah, and just before Hosea,

Continued on page 251

Amos at a Glance

FOCUS	EIGHT PROPHECIES	THREE SERMONS	FIVE VISIONS	FIVE PROMISES
REFERENCE	1:1 ———————————	3:1 ———————	7:1 ———————	9:11 ———— 9:15
DIVISION	JUDGMENT OF ISRAEL AND SURROUNDING NATIONS	SIN OF ISRAEL: PRESENT, PAST, AND FUTURE	PICTURES OF THE JUDGMENT OF ISRAEL	RESTORATION OF ISRAEL
TOPIC	PRONOUNCEMENTS OF JUDGMENT	PROVOCATIONS FOR JUDGMENT	FUTURE OF JUDGMENT	PROMISES AFTER JUDGMENT
	JUDGMENT			HOPE
LOCATION	SURROUNDING NATIONS	NORTHERN KINGDOM OF ISRAEL		
TIME	c. 760–753 B.C.			

Nelson's Complete Book of Bible Maps and Charts © 1993 by Thomas Nelson, Inc.

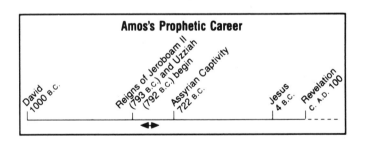

Amos's Prophetic Career

David 1000 B.C. — Reigns of Jeroboam II (793 B.C.) and Uzziah (792 B.C.) begin — Assyrian Captivity 722 B.C. — Jesus 4 B.C. — Revelation C. A.D. 100

Continued from page 249

Micah, and Isaiah. At this time Uzziah reigned over a prosperous and militarily successful Judah. In the north, Israel was ruled by the capable king Jeroboam II. Economic and military circumstances were almost ideal, but prosperity only increased the materialism, immorality, and injustice of the people. During these years, Assyria, Babylon, Syria, and Egypt were relatively weak. Thus, the people of Israel found it hard to imagine the coming disaster predicted by Amos—a disaster that occurred barely three decades later.

Themes and Literary Structure

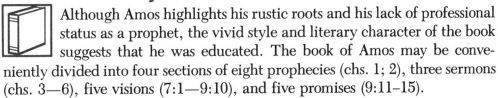 Although Amos highlights his rustic roots and his lack of professional status as a prophet, the vivid style and literary character of the book suggests that he was educated. The book of Amos may be conveniently divided into four sections of eight prophecies (chs. 1; 2), three sermons (chs. 3—6), five visions (7:1—9:10), and five promises (9:11–15).

The book of Amos is basically a message of judgment: prophecies of judgment on the nations, oracles and visions of divine judgment against Israel. Amos begins with a series of indictments against the seven neighbors of Israel, including Judah, and upon Israel herself (chs. 1; 2). Each foreign nation is to be punished for specific offenses either against Israel or some other nation. This judgment on the nations teaches that God is a universal monarch and all nations must answer to Him for their mistreatment of other nations and peoples.

The preaching of Amos stresses the righteousness and justice of God and His requirement that the human relationships of His people be characterized by righteousness and justice as well. The rich are condemned because of their oppression of the poor and for their religious hypocrisy. Religion is more than observing feast days and holding sacred assemblies; true religion demands righteous living, and the way people treat their neighbors reveals their relationship with God.

Amos ends the book on a note of consolation. After exile and judgment, God will restore His people to the land and bless them.

OUTLINE OF AMOS

The Preservation of the Remnant

In the eighth century B.C., Amos prophesied Israel's doom (8:1, 2), but he also declared the possibility of deliverance for the "remnant of Joseph" (5:15). Throughout history God has always preserved a remnant of His people, as the following chart shows.

People or Group	Reference
Noah and family in the Flood	Gen. 7:1
Joseph in Egypt during the famine	Gen. 45:7
Israel to their homeland	Deut. 4:27–31
7,000 who had not worshiped Baal	1 Kin. 19:18
Portion of Judah after captivity	Is. 10:20–23
Remnant to Zion	Mic. 2:12, 13
The church—both Jews and Gentiles	Rom. 9:22–27

OBADIAH

onsisting of only twenty-one verses, Obadiah is the shortest book in the Old Testament. It deals with the bitter rivalry between Edom, the descendants of Jacob's twin brother Esau, and the people of Israel. Obadiah, whose name means "Worshiper of Yahweh" or "Servant of Yahweh," pronounces condemnation against Edom and prophesies their total destruction because of their persistent opposition to God's chosen people.

Author

Obadiah was an obscure prophet who probably lived in the Southern Kingdom of Judah. Nothing is known of his hometown or family, but it is likely that he did not come from the kingly or priestly line because his father is not mentioned in 1:1.

Thirteen men named Obadiah are mentioned in the Old Testament, but none of these can be identified with any certainty as the author of this book.

Date

There are several views regarding the date of the book. Edom's cooperation with foreigners in sacking Jerusalem (vv. 10–14), which forms the historical background to the prophecy, could refer to a number of incidents, of which two are more likely. It may have occurred c. 850 B.C. in the reign of Jehoram (see 2 Chr. 21:8–10, 16, 17) during a period of revolt by Edom when Judah was also threatened by invading Philistines and Arabians. Also possible is a reference to Edomite complicity in the Babylonian capture of Jerusalem in 586 B.C. According to Psalm 137:7, the Edomites applauded the destruction of Jerusalem by Nebuchadnezzar. The case for this later date is also strengthened by the fact that Obadiah appears to quote from Jeremiah 49 (cf. vv. 1–4 with Jer. 49:14–16; vv. 5, 6 with Jer. 49:9, 10; v. 8 with Jer. 49:7; and v. 16 with Jer. 49:12). Thus, possible dates for the composition of Obadiah are c. 840 B.C., or between the fall of Jerusalem in 586 B.C. and the fall of Babylon to Cyrus in 539 B.C.

Obadiah at a Glance

FOCUS	JUDGMENT OF EDOM			RESTORATION OF ISRAEL
REFERENCE	1:1 ——————— 10	——————— 15	——————— 19	——————— 21
DIVISION	PREDICTIONS OF JUDGMENT	REASONS FOR JUDGMENT	RESULTS OF JUDGMENT	POSSESSION OF EDOM BY ISRAEL
TOPIC	DEFEAT OF ISRAEL			VICTORY OF ISRAEL
	PREDICTION OF JUDGMENT			PREDICTION OF POSSESSION
LOCATION	EDOM AND ISRAEL			
TIME	c. 890 B.C. or 586–539 B.C.			

Nelson's Complete Book of Bible Maps and Charts © 1993 by Thomas Nelson, Inc.

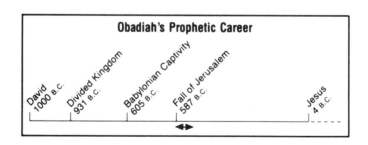

Obadiah's Prophetic Career

David 1000 B.C. — Divided Kingdom 931 B.C. — Babylonian Captivity 605 B.C. — Fall of Jerusalem 587 B.C. — Jesus 4 B.C.

Themes and Literary Structure

Though the shortest of the Old Testament books, Obadiah carries one of the strongest messages of judgment. Because of her long history of opposing God's people, Edom's fate is sealed, and there is no possibility of deliverance. God will bring total destruction upon Edom, and there will be no remnant. The book of Obadiah portrays Edom's day in the divine court, complete with arraignment, indictment, and sentence. This prophet of poetic justice describes how the Judge of the earth will overthrow the pride of Edom and restore the house of Jacob. The two sections of this short book are: the judgment of Edom (vv. 1–18) and the restoration of Israel (vv. 19–21).

The prophetic theme of the day of the Lord is prominent in verses 15–21. As in the prophecy of Joel, this climactic day brings both judgment and deliverance. For Edom, this is a pronouncement of doom (vv. 15, 16), but for Judah it will bring deliverance as they experience blessing and restoration to their land (vv. 17–21).

OUTLINE OF OBADIAH

I. The Predictions of Judgment on Edom . . . . vv. 1–9

II. The Reasons for the Judgment on Edom . . . . vv. 10–14

III. The Results of the Judgment on Edom . . . . vv. 15–18

IV. The Possession of Edom by Israel . . . . vv. 19–21

JONAH

God's loving concern for the Gentiles is not a truth disclosed only in the New Testament. More than seven centuries before Christ, God commissioned the Hebrew prophet Jonah to proclaim a message of repentance to the Assyrian city of Nineveh. Jewish nationalism, however, blinded both the prophet and covenant people to God's worldwide purposes of salvation. The story of Jonah is one of the clearest demonstrations in Scripture of God's love and mercy for all peoples.

Author

The book of Jonah has no stated author, though tradition ascribes it to Jonah, a prophet of the Northern Kingdom during the eighth century B.C. It is reasonable to suppose that Jonah himself would have recorded the unique experiences described in the book. This man, whose name means "dove," was the son of Amittai (1:1) and a native of Gath Hepher (2 Kin. 14:25) in Zebulun, a town about two miles north of Nazareth. Jonah is described in terms that point to his being a real person and his experiences actual and historical.

Date

Jonah was a contemporary of Jeroboam II of Israel (782–753 B.C.) who ministered after the time of Elisha and just before the time of Amos and Hosea. Israel was enjoying a period of resurgence and prosperity, and nationalistic fervor was probably high.

Assyria, a nation which had achieved a near-legendary reputation for cruelty, was in mild decline during these years, but it remained a threat. The repentance of Nineveh probably occurred in the reign of Ashurdan III (773–755 B.C.). Two plagues (765 and 759 B.C.) and a solar eclipse (763 B.C.) may have prepared the people for Jonah's message of judgment.

While some have argued that the book of Jonah was written in the post-exilic period in order to contradict the Jewish particularism of Ezra, Nehemiah, and Malachi, the teaching that God's plan includes the Gentiles is by no

Continued on page 258

Jonah at a Glance

FOCUS	FIRST COMMISSION OF JONAH				SECOND COMMISSION OF JONAH			
REFERENCE	1:1 ——— 1:4 ———		2:1 ——— 2:10 ———		3:1 ——— 3:5 ———		4:1 ——— 4:4 – 4:11	
DIVISION	DISOBEDIENCE TO THE FIRST CALL	JUDGMENT ON JONAH EXACTED	PRAYER OF JONAH IN THE FISH	DELIVERANCE OF JONAH FROM THE FISH	OBEDIENCE TO THE SECOND CALL	JUDGMENT ON NINEVEH AVERTED	PRAYER OF JONAH	REBUKE OF JONAH
TOPIC	GOD'S MERCY UPON JONAH				GOD'S MERCY UPON NINEVEH			
	"I WON'T GO."		"I WILL GO."		"I'M HERE."		"I SHOULDN'T HAVE COME."	
LOCATION	THE GREAT SEA				THE GREAT CITY			
TIME	c. 760 B.C.							

Nelson's Complete Book of Bible Maps and Charts © 1993 by Thomas Nelson, Inc.

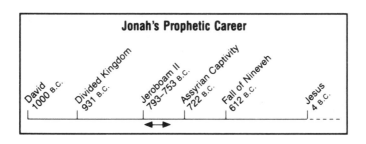

Jonah's Prophetic Career

David 1000 B.C. — Divided Kingdom 931 B.C. — Jeroboam II 793–753 B.C. — Assyrian Captivity 722 B.C. — Fall of Nineveh 612 B.C. — Jesus 4 B.C.

Continued from page 256

means unique to Jonah in the Old Testament (Gen. 9:27; 12:3; Lev. 19:33; Is. 2:2; Joel 2:28–32), and other arguments for a postexilic date are not persuasive.

Themes and Literary Structure

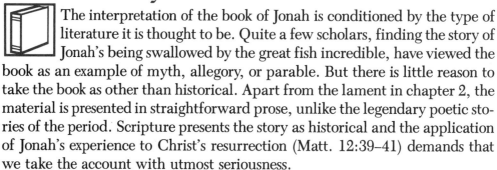

The interpretation of the book of Jonah is conditioned by the type of literature it is thought to be. Quite a few scholars, finding the story of Jonah's being swallowed by the great fish incredible, have viewed the book as an example of myth, allegory, or parable. But there is little reason to take the book as other than historical. Apart from the lament in chapter 2, the material is presented in straightforward prose, unlike the legendary poetic stories of the period. Scripture presents the story as historical and the application of Jonah's experience to Christ's resurrection (Matt. 12:39–41) demands that we take the account with utmost seriousness.

From a literary perspective, the book of Jonah displays remarkable structural symmetry and is developed by two parallel cycles that continually call for comparison. In addition, the book is rich in irony: the disobedience of the prophet is contrasted with the surprising faith of the mariners (ch. 1), and Jonah's petty concern for the plant contrasts with God's gracious care and concern for the people of pagan Nineveh (ch. 4).

The book of Jonah may be divided into the first commission of Jonah (chs. 1; 2) and the second commission of Jonah (chs. 3 and 4).

As already noted, the pervading theme in Jonah is God's gracious extension of His mercy to gentile nations, but other important themes are also evident. The sovereignty of God over life, elements, and circumstances is clearly stressed in the descriptions of the storm (1:4), the fish (1:17), the plant (4:6), and the worm (4:7).

The book of Jonah also served to challenge the nationalistic pride of Israel and her failure to comprehend the nature of her missionary task and the purpose of God to bestow his loving-kindness upon all peoples. The change in Jonah's own attitude is symbolic of the change God required of Israel as a whole.

Jonah's three-day experience in the belly of the fish also serves as a type of the death, burial, and resurrection of Christ (Matt. 12:39–41). Here it should be noted that the Hebrew idiom, "three days and three nights," only requires a portion of the first and third days.

OUTLINE OF JONAH

The Geography of Jonah

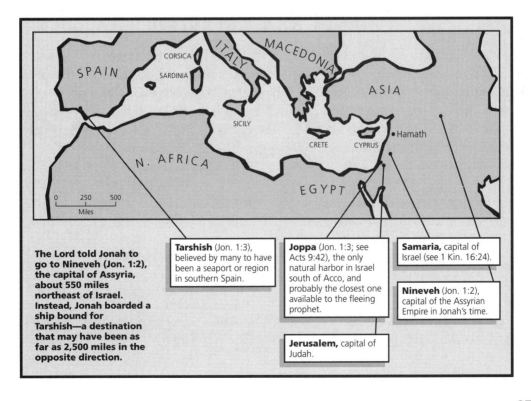

SPAIN

CORSICA

SARDINIA

ITALY

MACEDONIA

ASIA

SICILY

CRETE

CYPRUS

• Hamath

N. AFRICA

EGYPT

0　250　500
Miles

The Lord told Jonah to go to Nineveh (Jon. 1:2), the capital of Assyria, about 550 miles northeast of Israel. Instead, Jonah boarded a ship bound for Tarshish—a destination that may have been as far as 2,500 miles in the opposite direction.

Tarshish (Jon. 1:3), believed by many to have been a seaport or region in southern Spain.

Joppa (Jon. 1:3; see Acts 9:42), the only natural harbor in Israel south of Acco, and probably the closest one available to the fleeing prophet.

Samaria, capital of Israel (see 1 Kin. 16:24).

Nineveh (Jon. 1:2), capital of the Assyrian Empire in Jonah's time.

Jerusalem, capital of Judah.

Jonah and the Mariners

Chapter 1 provides an ironic contrast between Jonah and the mariners. In spite of the mariners' lack of past experience with the true God, they display more apparent sensitivity to God and more human compassion than does the prophet Jonah.

Jonah	The Mariners
He was a Hebrew with a rich history of YAHWEH God's faithfulness.	They were Gentiles with no history of YAHWEH God.
He was monotheistic, believing in the one true God. (v. 9)	They were polytheistic, worshiping many false gods.
He was rightly related to the true God.	They had no relationship with the true God.
He was spiritually insensitive, going in the wrong direction from God. (v. 5)	They were spiritually sensitive, moving in the right direction toward God. They prayed. (v. 5)
He was indifferent toward God's will in spite of knowing Him.	They were concerned before God in spite of little or no knowledge of Him.
He was uncompassionate toward Nineveh. (v. 3)	They were compassionate toward Jonah. (vv. 11–14)
Jonah was rebellious and therefore disciplined, but not destroyed. (v. 17)	They were brought to worship and commitment. (v. 16)

Nelson's Complete Book of Bible Maps and Charts © 1993 by Thomas Nelson, Inc.

Jonah and the Plant

Jonah's concern for the plant is contrasted with God's concern for Nineveh. God stresses to Jonah that the prophet neither created nor sustained the plant about which he was so concerned. The many thousands of Ninevites, however, were created and constantly sustained by God. And God, who knows when a sparrow falls, is even concerned for the cattle of the city. Jonah's perspective was not what it should have been because it was not the same as God's.

God and Nineveh	Jonah and the Plant
God cared for the people of Nineveh	Jonah cared for a plant
God was concerned for the welfare of others	Jonah was concerned for himself
God created all that was in Nineveh	Jonah did not create the plant
God tended Nineveh	Jonah did nothing for the plant
The people of Nineveh are of *eternal* significance	The plant was most *temporal*
God's concern was and is for human life	Jonah's concern was for personal comfort and selfish personal interest
God's concern for Nineveh is proper and displays his love	Jonah's concern for a plant rather than for people is improper; it displays selfishness and an improper perspective on life

Nelson's Complete Book of Bible Maps and Charts © 1993 by Thomas Nelson, Inc.

MICAH

Burdened by the abusive treatment of the poor, the book of Micah rebukes anyone who would use social status or political power for personal gain. One third of Micah exposes the sins of his countrymen, another third pictures the punishment God is about to send, and the final third holds out the hope of restoration once that discipline has ended. Through it all, God's righteous demands upon His people are clear: "To do justly, to love mercy, and to walk humbly with your God" (6:8).

Author

The prophet Micah, whose name means "Who is like the Lord?" was one of the eighth-century prophets, together with Hosea, Amos, Isaiah, and Jonah, and he is mentioned in Jeremiah 26:18. Micah's home was Moresheth Gath (1:14), a town probably located about 20 miles southwest of Jerusalem.

Like Amos, Micah was a man of the country who had time for thought and clear vision. Blessed with Amos's passion for justice and Hosea's heart of love, Micah's spirit burned with indignation over how the city dwellers oppressed the peasants. Yet his teaching is not entirely unique; he echoes great truths proclaimed by his predecessors and contemporaries, especially Isaiah of Jerusalem.

Date

The first verse indicates that Micah prophesied in the days of Jotham (739–731 B.C.), Ahaz (731–715 B.C.) and Hezekiah (715–686 B.C.), kings of Judah. Although Micah deals primarily with Judah, he also addresses the Northern Kingdom of Israel and predicts the fall of Samaria (1:6). Much of his ministry, therefore, took place before the Assyrian captivity of Israel in 722 B.C. His strong denunciations of idolatry and immorality also suggest that his ministry largely preceded the sweeping religious reforms of Hezekiah. Thus, Micah's prophecies ranged from about 735 to 710 B.C.

During the ministry of Micah, the kingdom of Israel continued to crumble inwardly and outwardly until its collapse in 722 B.C. The Assyrian empire

Continued on page 263

Micah at a Glance

FOCUS	PREDICTION OF JUDGMENT		PREDICTION OF RESTORATION			PLEA FOR REPENTANCE		
REFERENCE	1:1 ——— 3:1 ———		4:1 ——— 4:6 ———		5:2 ———	6:1 ——— 6:10 ———		7:7 ——— 7:20
DIVISION	JUDGMENT OF PEOPLE	JUDGMENT OF LEADERSHIP	PROMISE OF COMING KINGDOM	PROMISE OF COMING CAPTIVITIES	PROMISE OF COMING KING	FIRST PLEA OF GOD	SECOND PLEA OF GOD	PROMISE OF FINAL SALVATION
TOPIC	PUNISHMENT		PROMISE			PARDON		
	RETRIBUTION		RESTORATION			REPENTANCE		
LOCATION	JUDAH—ISRAEL							
TIME	c. 735–710 B.C.							

Nelson's Complete Book of Bible Maps and Charts © 1993 by Thomas Nelson, Inc.

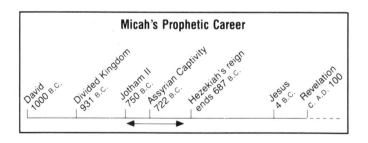

Micah's Prophetic Career

David 1000 B.C. — Divided Kingdom 931 B.C. — Jotham II 750 B.C. — Assyrian Captivity 722 B.C. — Hezekiah's reign ends 687 B.C. — Jesus 4 B.C. — Revelation C. A.D. 100

Continued from page 261

reached the zenith of its power and became a constant threat to Judah. Babylon was still under Assyrian domination, and Micah's prediction of a future Babylonian captivity for Judah (4:10) must have seemed unlikely.

Themes and Literary Structure

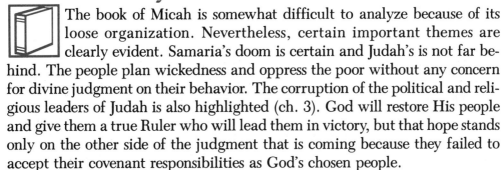 The book of Micah is somewhat difficult to analyze because of its loose organization. Nevertheless, certain important themes are clearly evident. Samaria's doom is certain and Judah's is not far behind. The people plan wickedness and oppress the poor without any concern for divine judgment on their behavior. The corruption of the political and religious leaders of Judah is also highlighted (ch. 3). God will restore His people and give them a true Ruler who will lead them in victory, but that hope stands only on the other side of the judgment that is coming because they failed to accept their covenant responsibilities as God's chosen people.

The book may be divided into three sections: the prediction of judgment (chs. 1—3), the prediction of restoration (chs. 4 and 5), and the plea for repentance (chs. 6 and 7).

The prediction of Micah 5:2 that the Messiah would be born in the city of Bethlehem is one of the clearest and most important of all Old Testament messianic prophecies. In addition, Micah 2:12, 13; 4:1–8; and 5:4, 5 offer vivid descriptions of the righteous reign of Christ over the whole world.

OUTLINE OF MICAH

NAHUM

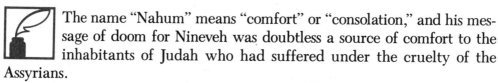

In contrast to his predecessor Jonah, whose ministry resulted in the repentance of the Ninevites, the prophet Nahum proclaims the downfall of the great Assyrian city of Nineveh. The Ninevites have forgotten their revival and have returned to their habits of violence, idolatry, and arrogance. As a result, Babylon will so destroy the city that no trace of it will remain—a prophecy fulfilled in painful detail.

Author

The name "Nahum" means "comfort" or "consolation," and his message of doom for Nineveh was doubtless a source of comfort to the inhabitants of Judah who had suffered under the cruelty of the Assyrians.

According to 1:1, the prophet was called the "Elkoshite." Although the precise location of Elkosh is unknown, many scholars believe that Elkosh was a town in southern Judah (later called Elcesei) between Jerusalem and Gaza. This would make Nahum a prophet of the Southern Kingdom and may explain his interest in the triumph of Judah (1:15; 2:2).

Date

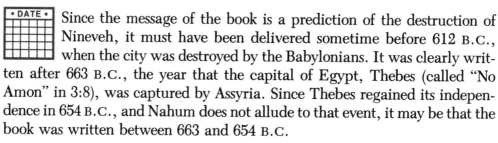

Since the message of the book is a prediction of the destruction of Nineveh, it must have been delivered sometime before 612 B.C., when the city was destroyed by the Babylonians. It was clearly written after 663 B.C., the year that the capital of Egypt, Thebes (called "No Amon" in 3:8), was captured by Assyria. Since Thebes regained its independence in 654 B.C., and Nahum does not allude to that event, it may be that the book was written between 663 and 654 B.C.

Nahum at a Glance

FOCUS	DESTRUCTION OF NINEVEH DECREED		DESTRUCTION OF NINEVEH DESCRIBED		DESTRUCTION OF NINEVEH DESERVED	
REFERENCE	1:1 ——— 1:9	——— 2:1	——— 2:3	——— 3:1	——— 3:12	——— 3:19
DIVISION	GENERAL PRINCIPLES OF DIVINE JUDGMENT	DESTRUCTION OF NINEVEH AND DELIVERANCE OF JUDAH	THE CALL TO BATTLE	DESCRIPTION OF THE DESTRUCTION OF NINEVEH	REASONS FOR THE DESTRUCTION OF NINEVEH	INEVITABLE DESTRUCTION OF NINEVEH
TOPIC	VERDICT OF VENGEANCE		VISION OF VENGEANCE		VINDICATION OF VENGEANCE	
	WHAT GOD WILL DO		HOW GOD WILL DO IT		WHY GOD WILL DO IT	
LOCATION	IN JUDAH AGAINST NINEVEH, CAPITAL OF ASSYRIA					
TIME	c. 660 B.C.					

Nelson's Complete Book of Bible Maps and Charts © 1993 by Thomas Nelson, Inc.

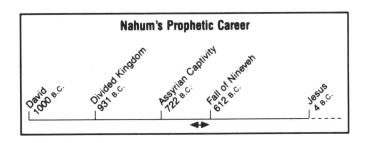

Nahum's Prophetic Career

David 1000 B.C. — Divided Kingdom 931 B.C. — Assyrian Captivity 722 B.C. — Fall of Nineveh 612 B.C. — Jesus 4 B.C.

Themes and Literary Structure

Nahum single-mindedly proclaims the doom of the Assyrian capital of Nineveh. Among the reasons for the condemnation of the city are the inhumanities of the Assyrian army (2:12), and the vices of the city (3:4). The nature of God, specifically His wrath, His holiness, His justice, and His power, makes it inevitable that His enemies will perish (1:2–10).

The brief book of Nahum can be divided into three parts: the destruction of Nineveh decreed (ch. 1), the destruction of Nineveh described (ch. 2), and the destruction of Nineveh deserved (ch. 3).

OUTLINE OF NAHUM

HABAKKUK

The prophet Habakkuk ministered during the death throes of the nation of Judah. Although repeatedly called to repentance, the nation stubbornly refused to change her sinful ways. Asking how long this intolerable situation would continue, Habakkuk is told by God that the Babylonians will be His chastening rod on the nation—an announcement that sends the prophet to his knees. Though perplexed, Habakkuk acknowledges that the just in any generation shall live by faith (2:4), not by sight, and he concludes by praising God's wisdom even though he doesn't fully understand God's ways.

Author

The author of this book is the prophet Habakkuk, about whom little is known apart from his name, which is derived from the Hebrew word meaning "embrace" or "embracer." The fact that he is called a "prophet" (1:1; 3:1) may suggest that he was a member of a professional prophetic guild. In addition, the musical reference at the conclusion of the book indicates that Habakkuk may have been a priest connected with the temple worship in Jerusalem.

Date

Although the book of Habakkuk includes no reference to the reign of a king, internal evidence indicates a date between the death of King Josiah (609 B.C.) and the beginning of the Babylonian captivity (605 B.C.). The only explicit time references in Habakkuk are to the Babylonian invasion as an imminent event (1:6; 2:1; 3:16). The deplorable conditions of the people (1:2–4) imply a date after the untimely death of Josiah at the Battle of Megiddo (609 B.C.) and early in the wicked reign of King Jehoiakim (609–597 B.C.).

A contemporary of Zephaniah and Jeremiah, Habakkuk warned of God's approaching judgment through the approaching Babylonians. This prophecy was fulfilled in 605 B.C. when Nebuchadnezzar deported ten thousand of Jerusalem's prominent citizens to Babylon.

Habakkuk at a Glance

FOCUS	PROBLEMS OF HABAKKUK				PRAISE OF HABAKKUK
REFERENCE	1:1 ——————— 1:5	——————— 1:12	——————— 2:2	——————— 3:1	——————— 3:19
DIVISION	FIRST PROBLEM OF HABAKKUK	FIRST REPLY OF GOD	SECOND PROBLEM OF HABAKKUK	SECOND REPLY OF GOD	PRAYER OF PRAISE OF HABAKKUK
TOPIC	FAITH TROUBLED				FAITH TRIUMPHANT
	WHAT GOD IS DOING				WHO GOD IS
LOCATION	THE NATION OF JUDAH				
TIME	c. 607 B.C.				

Nelson's Complete Book of Bible Maps and Charts © 1993 by Thomas Nelson, Inc.

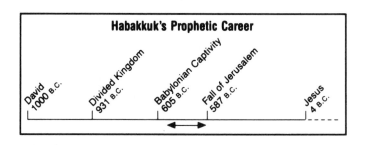

Habakkuk's Prophetic Career

David 1000 B.C. — Divided Kingdom 931 B.C. — Babylonian Captivity 605 B.C. — Fall of Jerusalem 587 B.C. — Jesus 4 B.C.

Themes and Literary Structure

 The book of Habakkuk may be conveniently divided into two portions: the problems or perplexity of Habakkuk (chs. 1 and 2), and the praise of Habakkuk (ch. 3).

Realizing Israel's iniquity and need for punishment, Habakkuk is perplexed with the moral dilemma of how a holy God could employ the even more wicked Babylonians to chastise His children. God's response is twofold: He reaffirms His basic moral nature which implies that everyone must eventually face judgment for their offenses (2:2–22). God also gives Habakkuk a vision of His infinite glory, a vision somewhat reminiscent of the one given in Job 38—41. These two responses are enough to reestablish Habakkuk's faith in God.

Habakkuk also stresses God's sovereign freedom as God to accomplish His good ends in His own way. In spite of appearances to the contrary, God is still on the throne as the Lord of history and the Ruler of the nations.

The book of Habakkuk depicts the prophet's struggle of faith, and in so doing the centrality of faith in the lives of God's people is highlighted. This faith which can endure despite unfavorable outward circumstances comes to beautiful expression in 3:16–19.

OUTLINE OF HABAKKUK

Living by Faith

In what seems to be merely an incidental contrast between the arrogance of the Babylonians and the humble submission of the righteous to God, Habakkuk states a fundamental principle of the gospel: "The just shall live by his faith." When Paul (Rom. 1:17; Gal. 3:11) and the writer of Hebrews (Heb. 10:38) quote this verse, they merely apply the principle laid down by the prophet regarding the importance of faith in man's relationship to God.

The prophet's response to the difficult questions put to him: The just shall live by faith.	
Question 1:	Why does God not respond to the wrong and injustice in the land (1:2–4)?
Answer:	He is about to respond by using Babylon as a tool of judgment (1:5–11).
Question 2:	Why does God use the wicked Babylonians to punish those more righteous than themselves (1:12, 13)?
Answer:	God has chosen this plan of action (2:2, 3). The just person will live by faith in God (2:4). Woe to the unrighteous (2:6–20).

ZEPHANIAH

The book of Zephaniah repeatedly hammers home the message that the day of the Lord, judgment day, is coming when the malignancy of sin will be dealt with. Israel and her gentile neighbors will soon experience the crushing hand of God's wrath. But after the chastening process is complete, blessing will come in the person of the Messiah.

Author

Normally the genealogy of a prophet is traced no further than his father. Zephaniah, however, traces his ancestry back four generations in order to demonstrate his royal lineage as the great-great-grandson of King Hezekiah (1:1). Thus, he was a distant relative of King Josiah and those to whom he addresses his prophecy.

Apparently Zephaniah lived in the city of Jerusalem because he refers to the city as "this place" (1:4), and he also describes the topography with intimate familiarity.

Date

Zephaniah fixes the time of his prophecy "in the days of Josiah son of Amon, king of Judah" (1:1). Josiah reigned from 640 to 609 B.C., and 2:13 indicates that the destruction of Nineveh (612 B.C.) was still in the future. Thus, the book of Zephaniah can be dated between 640 and 612 B.C.

Because Josiah's religious reforms began c. 628 B.C., and because Zephaniah catalogs lists of sins prevalent prior to the reforms (1:3–13; 3:1–7), the time of Zephaniah may be dated more precisely as occurring c. 635 to 625 B.C. Zephaniah's forceful prophecy may even have been a factor in the reforms that took place.

Zephaniah at a Glance

FOCUS	JUDGMENT IN THE DAY OF THE LORD					SALVATION IN THE DAY OF THE LORD	
REFERENCE	1:1 ———— 1:4 ————	2:4 ————	3:1 ————	3:8 ————		3:9 ———— 3:14 —— 3:20	
DIVISION	JUDGMENT ON THE WHOLE EARTH	JUDGMENT ON THE NATION OF JUDAH	JUDGMENT ON THE NATIONS SURROUNDING JUDAH	JUDGMENT ON THE CITY OF JERUSALEM	JUDGMENT ON THE WHOLE EARTH	PROMISE OF CONVERSION	PROMISE OF RESTORATION
TOPIC	DAY OF WRATH					DAY OF JOY	
	JUDGMENT ON JUDAH					RESTORATION FOR JUDAH	
LOCATION	JUDAH AND THE NATIONS						
TIME	c. 630 B.C.						

Nelson's Complete Book of Bible Maps and Charts © 1993 by Thomas Nelson, Inc.

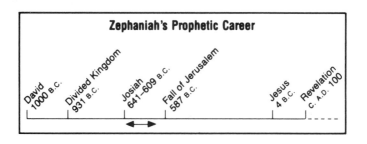

Zephaniah's Prophetic Career

David 1000 B.C. — Divided Kingdom 931 B.C. — Josiah 641–609 B.C. — Fall of Jerusalem 587 B.C. — Jesus 4 B.C. — Revelation c. A.D. 100

Themes and Literary Structure

On the whole, Zephaniah is a fierce and grim book of warning about the coming day of the Lord. Desolation, darkness, and ruin will strike Judah and the nations because of the wrath of God upon sin. Zephaniah moves three times from the general to the specific: (1) from universal judgment to judgment upon Judah (1:1—2:3); from judgment upon surrounding nations to judgment upon Jerusalem (2:4—3:7); and from judgment and cleansing of all nations to the restoration of Israel (3:8–20). The two broad divisions of the book are the judgment in the day of the Lord (1:1—3:8), and the salvation in the day of the Lord (3:9–20).

As with Amos some one hundred years earlier, the theme of the coming day of the Lord is central for Zephaniah. This day of the Lord is seen as having two components: judgment that results in the destruction of Judah by foreign armies, but also restoration and hope for the people of God. Zephaniah sees this second aspect of the day of the Lord as a terminal event, bringing history to a close. Thus the message shares some characteristics with apocalyptic literature that portrays the end times.

OUTLINE OF ZEPHANIAH

HAGGAI

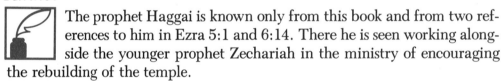

Haggai is second only to Obadiah in brevity among the Old Testament books, but this strong and frank series of four brief sermons accomplishes its intended effect. The work on the temple had ceased and the people had become more concerned with the beautification of their own houses than with the building of the central sanctuary of God. Because of their misplaced priorities, their future labors cannot be blessed by God. Only when the people put the Lord first by completing the task He set before them will His hand of blessing once again be upon them.

Author

The prophet Haggai is known only from this book and from two references to him in Ezra 5:1 and 6:14. There he is seen working alongside the younger prophet Zechariah in the ministry of encouraging the rebuilding of the temple.

Haggai returned from Babylon with Zerubbabel and evidently lived in Jerusalem. Some interpret 2:3 to mean that he was born in Judah before the 586 B.C. destruction of the first temple and was one of the small company who could remember the splendor of the former temple. This would mean that Haggai was about seventy-five years old when he prophesied in 520 B.C. It is equally likely, however, that he was born in Babylon during the captivity.

Date

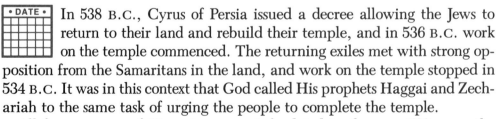

In 538 B.C., Cyrus of Persia issued a decree allowing the Jews to return to their land and rebuild their temple, and in 536 B.C. work on the temple commenced. The returning exiles met with strong opposition from the Samaritans in the land, and work on the temple stopped in 534 B.C. It was in this context that God called His prophets Haggai and Zechariah to the same task of urging the people to complete the temple.

All four sermons of Haggai are precisely dated in the year 520 B.C., the second year of the reign of Darius I (521–486 B.C.), king of Persia. The first was delivered on the first day of the Hebrew month of Elul (August-

Continued on page 276

Haggai at a Glance

FOCUS	COMPLETION OF THE LATTER TEMPLE	GLORY OF THE LATTER TEMPLE	PRESENT BLESSINGS OF OBEDIENCE	FUTURE BLESSINGS THROUGH PROMISE
REFERENCE	1:1 —————————— 2:1	————————— 2:10	———————— 2:20	———————— 2:23
DIVISION	"CONSIDER YOUR WAYS . . . MY HOUSE THAT IS IN RUINS."	"THE GLORY OF THIS LATTER TEMPLE SHALL BE GREATER."	"FROM THIS DAY I WILL BLESS YOU."	"I WILL SHAKE HEAVEN AND EARTH."
TOPIC	THE TEMPLE OF GOD		THE BLESSINGS OF GOD	
	FIRST REBUKE (PRESENT)	FIRST ENCOURAGEMENT (FUTURE)	SECOND REBUKE (PRESENT)	SECOND ENCOURAGEMENT (FUTURE)
LOCATION	JERUSALEM			
TIME	SEPTEMBER 1 520 B.C.	OCTOBER 21 520 B.C.	DECEMBER 24 520 B.C.	DECEMBER 24 520 B.C.

Nelson's Complete Book of Bible Maps and Charts © 1993 by Thomas Nelson, Inc.

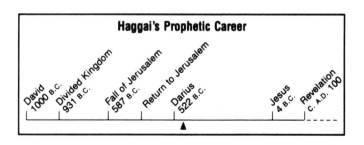

Continued from page 274

September), the second on the first day of Tishri (September-October), and the last two on the twenty-fourth day of Kislev (November-December). Later, the messages were compiled into what is now known as the book of Haggai.

Haggai, along with Zechariah and Malachi, faced a different situation than had the pre-exilic prophets. Those earlier prophets confronted a people who tended to depend upon physical ceremonies and buildings rather than upon a true relationship with God marked by obedience. In contrast, the postexilic prophets ministered to a discouraged and apathetic people who were tempted to believe that nothing they did made any difference from a religious stand-point. The destruction of Jerusalem had humbled a once-proud people and they were influenced by the Persian view of all religions as equal in value.

As a result, the returning Jews saw little reason to pay careful attention to their distinctive laws and practices, and they felt no need to be overly concerned about rebuilding the temple. Of course, the dangers of this situation were profound. In short order, the Jews would be assimilated into the pagan culture around them; the revelatory heritage would be lost, and the messianic line of promise extinguished. The postexilic prophets were faced with the task of encouraging the people to distinguish themselves from the other peoples by the character of their obedience, and this obedience had to begin with the rebuilding of the temple and the reestablishment of the Mosaic laws.

Themes and Literary Structure

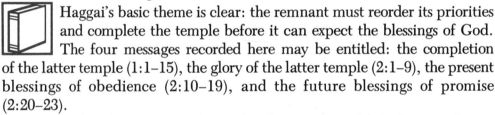 Haggai's basic theme is clear: the remnant must reorder its priorities and complete the temple before it can expect the blessings of God. The four messages recorded here may be entitled: the completion of the latter temple (1:1–15), the glory of the latter temple (2:1–9), the present blessings of obedience (2:10–19), and the future blessings of promise (2:20–23).

The promise of Haggai 2:9 points ahead to the crucial role the second temple was to have in God's redemptive plan. Herod the Great later spent years enlarging and enriching this temple, and it was filled with the glory of God incarnate every time Christ came to Jerusalem.

The Messiah is also portrayed in the person of Zerubbabel (2:23), who becomes the center of the messianic line, sealing both branches together.

See chart, "Zerubbabel," on page 277.

Zerubbabel

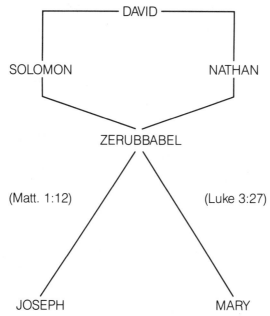

Nelson's Complete Book of Bible Maps and Charts © 1993 by Thomas Nelson, Inc.

The Temples of the Scriptures

The Book of Haggai consists of four brief sermons urging the people to re-establish proper priorities and to complete construction of the temple under Zerubbabel. The various temples of the Bible and their significance are described below:

(1) *Solomon's Temple.* The construction of this temple by Solomon was a fulfillment of David's desire to build a "house for the LORD"—a desire which he was never to realize in his lifetime (2 Sam. 7:1–29). The temple was built after the death of David and dedicated by his son (1 Kin. 8:1ff). This temple was destroyed by the armies of Nebuchadnezzar at the fall of Jerusalem in 586 B.C. (Jer. 32:28–44).

(2) *Zerubbabel's Temple.* This is the one under construction during the ministry of the prophet Zechariah. It was completed and dedicated in 516 B.C. (Ezra 6:1–22). It was constructed under the direction of Zerubbabel (Ezra 3:1–8; 4:1–14) who was a descendant of David (1 Chr. 3:19). This temple was desecrated in 169 B.C. by Antiochus Epiphanes.

(3) *Herod's Temple.* Restoration of Zerubbabel's temple began in 19 B.C. under the administration of Herod the Great. The temple was nearing completion in A.D. 70, after nearly 90 years of renovation and enlargement, when it was destroyed by the Romans. Since this time there has been no temple in Jerusalem.

(4) *The Present Temple.* There is a temple in which the Lord reigns at present. According to 1 Cor. 6:19 and 2 Cor. 6:16–18 the present temple of the Lord is the heart of the believer. There the Lord reigns until the day when the Messiah will return and set up His earthly kingdom and the millennial temple.

(5) *The Temple of Revelation 11.* This temple will be constructed during the Tribulation by the Antichrist. It is mentioned in 2 Thess. 2:4 as the site for the abomination of desolation mentioned by Daniel the prophet (Dan. 9:2) and Jesus (Matt. 24:15). This temple will be destroyed with the kingdom of the Antichrist (see Rev. 17; 18).

(6) *The Millennial Temple.* This is the temple that is described in detail in Ezek. 40:1—42:20. It is this temple that the prophet Zechariah has in view in 6:12, 13. It will be built by the Messiah Himself, who will rule in it as the righteous Priest-King of His own millennial kingdom (6:13).

(7) *The Eternal Temple of His Presence.* This temple is presented in Rev. 21:22. John says there will be no physical temple in the eternal kingdom because ". . . the Lord God Almighty and the Lamb are its temple." This temple will be the greatest of all and it will be the focus of the eternal kingdom as it is presented in Rev. 21:22.

ZECHARIAH

For a dozen years or more, the task of rebuilding the temple had been half completed. The prophet Zechariah was commissioned by God to encourage the people to complete this important task. Rather than exhorting them with strong words of rebuke, Zechariah offered a very positive goal: the temple must be built, for someday the glory of the Messiah would inhabit it.

Author

Zechariah, whose name means "Yahweh Remembers," was one of the postexilic prophets and a contemporary of Haggai. The name "Zechariah" was a popular one in the Old Testament, being shared by no fewer than twenty-nine Old Testament characters.

As the son of Berechiah and grandson of Iddo, he came from one of the priestly families of the tribe of Levi. He was born in Babylon and was brought by his grandfather to Palestine when the Jewish exiles rerturned under Zerubbabel.

Date

Zechariah was a younger contemporary of Haggai the prophet, Zerubbabel the governor, and Joshua the high priest. The historical setting for chapters 1—8 is the same as that of Haggai (520–518 B.C.). Work was resumed on the temple in 520 B.C. and the project was completed in 516 B.C.

Chapters 9—14 are undated, but stylistic differences and references to Greece (9:13) indicate a date of between 480 and 470 B.C. This would mean that Darius I (521–486 B.C.) had passed from the scene and had been succeeded by Xerxes (486–464 B.C.), the king who made Esther queen of Persia.

Themes and Literary Structure

Zechariah uses a series of eight visions, four messages, and two burdens to portray God's future plans for His covenant people. The first eight chapters were written to encourage the remnant while they were rebuilding the temple; the last six chapters were written after the com-

Continued on page 281

Zechariah at a Glance

FOCUS	EIGHT VISIONS			FOUR MESSAGES	TWO BURDENS	
REFERENCE	1:1 ——— 1:7 ———		6:9 ——— 7:1 ———		9:1 ——— 12:1 ———	14:21
DIVISION	CALL TO REPENTANCE	EIGHT VISIONS	CROWNING OF JOSHUA	QUESTION OF FASTING	FIRST BURDEN: REJECTION OF THE MESSIAH	SECOND BURDEN: REIGN OF THE MESSIAH
TOPIC	PICTURES			PROBLEM	PREDICTION	
	ISRAEL'S FORTUNE			ISRAEL'S FASTINGS	ISRAEL'S FUTURE	
LOCATION	JERUSALEM					
TIME	WHILE BUILDING THE TEMPLE (520–518 B.C.)				AFTER BUILDING THE TEMPLE (c. 480–470 B.C.)	

Nelson's Complete Book of Bible Maps and Charts © 1993 by Thomas Nelson, Inc.

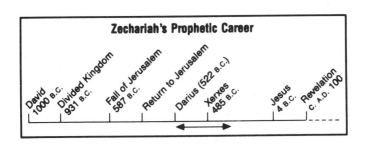

Zechariah's Prophetic Career

David 1000 B.C. — Divided Kingdom 931 B.C. — Fall of Jerusalem 587 B.C. — Return to Jerusalem — Darius (522 B.C.) — Xerxes 485 B.C. — Jesus 4 B.C. — Revelation c. A.D. 100

Continued from page 279

pletion of the temple to anticipate Israel's coming Messiah. Zechariah moves from gentile domination to messianic rule, from persecution to peace, and from uncleanness to holiness.

The last six chapters are not clearly tied to a specific historical situation in the life of the prophet but look forward to the events leading up to and including the coming messianic age. Here the rise of Greece, the advent and rejection of the Messiah, and the final triumph of the Messiah are foretold.

OUTLINE OF ZECHARIAH

Zechariah's Visions

The book of Zechariah includes a series of visions with vivid but mysterious symbols, together with the appearance of an angel who interprets the visions but leaves some of the symbols unexplained. These visions mix the work of the Messiah in both advents, and like the other prophets, Zechariah sees only the peaks of God's program without the intervening valleys.

Zechariah's Visions

The visions of Zechariah had historical meaning for his day, but they also have meaning for all time. God will save His people and bring judgment on the wicked.

Vision	Significance
Man and horses among the myrtle trees (1:8)	The Lord will again be merciful to Jerusalem (1:14, 16, 17).
Four horns, four craftsmen (1:18–20)	Those who scattered Judah are cast out (1:21).
Man with measuring line (2:1)	God will be a protective wall of fire around Jerusalem (2:3–5).
Cleansing of Joshua (3:4)	The Servant, the Branch, comes to save (3:8, 9).
Golden lampstand and olive trees (4:2, 3)	The Lord empowers Israel by His Spirit (4:6).
Flying scroll (5:1)	Dishonesty is cursed (5:3).
Woman in the basket (5:6, 7)	Wickedness will be removed (5:9).
Four chariots (6:1)	The spirits of heaven execute judgment on the whole earth (6:5, 7).

Nelson's Complete Book of Bible Maps and Charts © 1993 by Thomas Nelson, Inc.

MALACHI

M alachi, a prophet in the days of Nehemiah, directed his message of judgment to a people plagued with corrupt priests, wicked practices, and a false sense of security. Using the question-and-answer method, Malachi probes deeply into their problems of hypocrisy, infidelity, mixed marriages, divorce, false worship, and arrogance.

For four hundred years after Malachi's ringing condemnations, God remained silent. Only with the coming of John the Baptist (3:1) does God again communicate with His people through a prophet's voice.

Author

The name "Malachi" means "My Messenger." Although some have considered it a title rather than a name, this is unlikely since such a usage would be unique among the prophets. Unknown to us apart from the superscription to this book, Malachi was the last of the Old Testament prophets and the author of this final book of the Old Testament.

Date

Although an exact date cannot be established for Malachi, internal evidence can be used to deduce an approximate date. The use of the Persian term for governor, *pechah* (1:8), indicates that the book was written during the Persian domination of Israel. The temple had been rebuilt, since sacrifices were being offered in the temple (1:7–10). In addition, Malachi's oracle addressed the same problems that Nehemiah faced: corrupt priests (1:6—2:9; cf. Neh. 13:1–9), neglect of tithes and offerings (3:7–12; cf. Neh. 13:10–13), and intermarriage with pagan wives (2:10–16; cf. Neh. 13:23–28). Nehemiah had come to Jerusalem in 444 B.C. to rebuild the city walls, but returned to Persia in 432 B.C. On his return to Palestine (c. 425 B.C.), Nehemiah dealt with the sins described in Malachi. Thus it is likely that Malachi proclaimed his message while Nehemiah was absent between 432 and 425 B.C.

Malachi at a Glance

FOCUS	PRIVILEGE OF THE NATION	POLLUTION OF THE NATION		PROMISE TO THE NATION		
REFERENCE	1:1 ———————— 1:6 ——————— 2:10 ——————— 3:16 ——————— 4:1 ——————— 4:4 ———— 4:6					
DIVISION	LOVE OF GOD FOR THE NATION	SIN OF THE PRIESTS	SIN OF THE PEOPLE	BOOK OF REMEMBRANCE	COMING OF CHRIST	COMING OF ELIJAH
TOPIC	PAST	PRESENT		FUTURE		
	CARE OF GOD	COMPLAINT OF GOD		COMING OF GOD		
LOCATION	JERUSALEM					
TIME	c. 432–425 B.C.					

Nelson's Complete Book of Bible Maps and Charts © 1993 by Thomas Nelson, Inc.

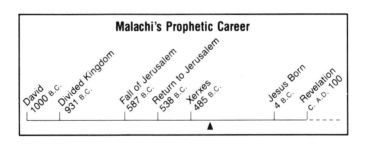

Malachi's Prophetic Career

David 1000 B.C. — Divided Kingdom 931 B.C. — Fall of Jerusalem 587 B.C. — Return to Jerusalem 538 B.C. — Xerxes 485 B.C. — Jesus Born 4 B.C. — Revelation c. A.D. 100

Themes and Literary Structure

 The people of Israel had become disillusioned and doubtful. Internally they wondered if God's messianic promises would ever be fulfilled and whether it was worth serving God after all. Externally, these attitudes were manifested in empty ritual, cheating on tithes and offerings, and indifference to the moral and ceremonial law.

Malachi challenges these problems and attitudes and calls the people to a new commitment and obedience. The book of Malachi may be divided into three main parts: the privilege of the nation (1:1–5), the pollution of the nation (1:6—3:15), and the promise to the nation (3:16—4:6).

OUTLINE OF MALACHI

The Coming of Christ

The last two chapters of the last book of the Old Testament contain dramatic prophecies of the coming of the Lord and of John the Baptist. Israel flocked to the Jordan River four hundred years later when "the voice of one crying in the wilderness: 'Prepare the way of the LORD'" (Matt. 3:3; cf. Mal. 3:1) appeared, thus breaking the long period of prophetic silence.

See chart, "The Coming of Christ," on page 286.

The Coming of Christ

Malachi's Prophecy	Confirmed in the New Testament
As Messenger of the covenant, Christ comes to His temple (3:1) and purifies His people (3:3).	Christ cleanses the temple (John 2:14–17) and sanctifies His people (Heb. 13:12).
His coming brings judgment (4:1).	Those whose names are not in the Book of Life are cast into the lake of fire (Rev. 20:11–15).
As the Sun of Righteousness, Christ heals His people (4:2).	Christ heals the multitudes; ultimately all sickness will pass away (Matt. 12:15; Rev. 21:4).
His forerunner prepares for the coming of the Lord (3:1; 4:5).	John the Baptist announces Christ (Matt. 11:10–14).

INTERTESTAMENTAL PERIOD

Bridging the Testaments

The map below shows Palestine as a subject region within four successive world empires, beginning with the Assyrian Empire in 750 B.C. and concluding with Alexander's Greek Empire of 331–146 B.C. After his death in 323 B.C., Alexander's leading generals divided the empire and established their own dynasties. Two of these controlled Palestine: first the kingdom of Ptolemy, which held Palestine from 323 B.C. until 198 B.C. when, by battle, it was lost to the kingdom of Seleucus. Then the Syrian Seleucids ruled until the strengthening revolt of the Jewish Hasmonean family (later called the Maccabees) gained complete independence in 143 B.C. Jewish independence of Judea lasted until the Romans occupied the region under general Pompey in 63 B.C. The Romans continued to occupy the whole of Palestine throughout all of New Testament history. Maps illustrating these shifts of political power over Palestine may be found on pages 288–291.

Succession of Four World Empires

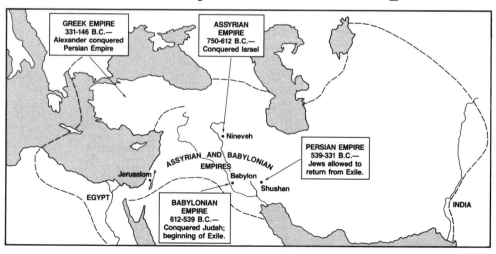

Ptolemaic Control of Palestine

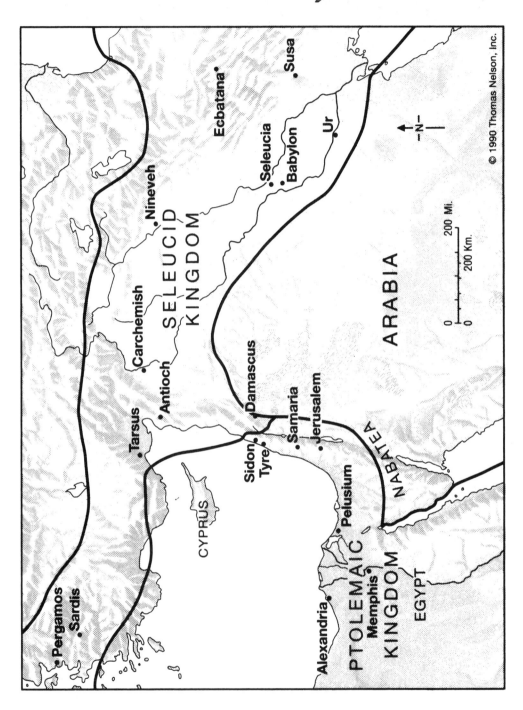

© 1990 Thomas Nelson, Inc.

Seleucid Control of Palestine

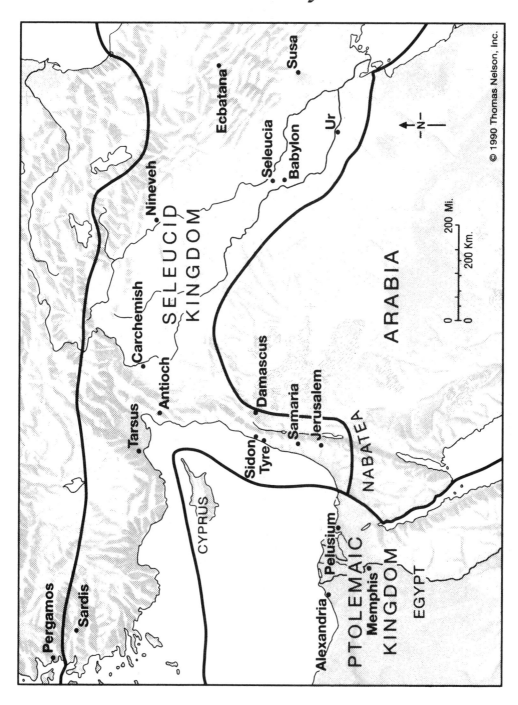

© 1990 Thomas Nelson, Inc.

Expansion of Palestine Under the Maccabees

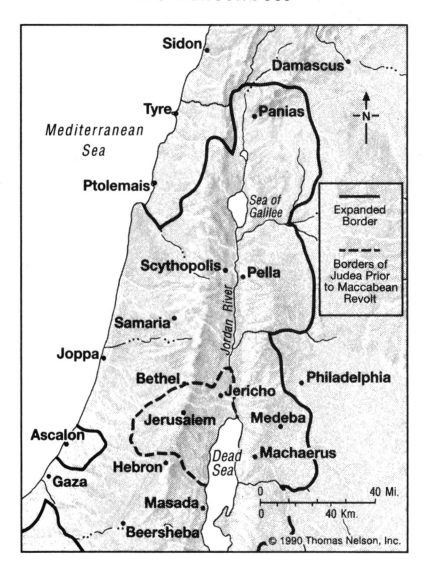

Sidon

Damascus

Tyre

Panias

—N—

Mediterranean Sea

Ptolemais

Sea of Galilee

Expanded Border

- - - Borders of Judea Prior to Maccabean Revolt

Scythopolis

Pella

Jordan River

Samaria

Joppa

Bethel

Philadelphia

Jericho

Jerusalem

Medeba

Ascalon

Machaerus

Hebron

Dead Sea

Gaza

0   40 Mi.

0   40 Km.

Masada

Beersheba

© 1990 Thomas Nelson, Inc.

Roman Control of Palestine

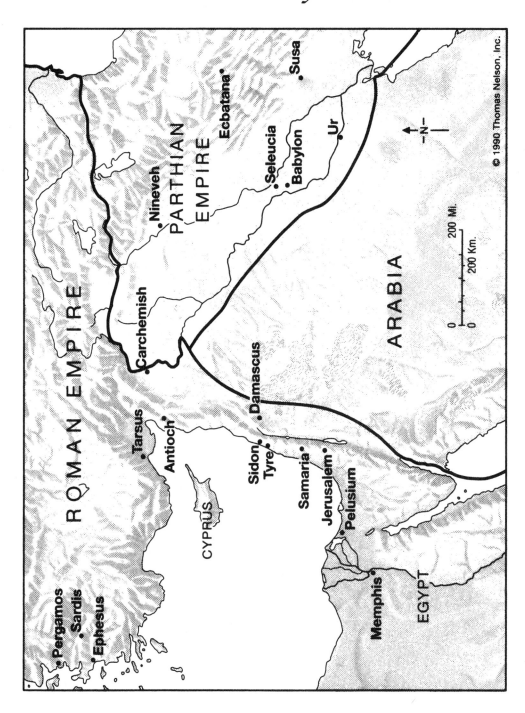

© 1990 Thomas Nelson, Inc.

PARTHIAN EMPIRE

ROMAN EMPIRE

ARABIA

EGYPT

CYPRUS

Susa

Ecbatana

Nineveh

Seleucia

Babylon

Ur

Carchemish

Damascus

Tarsus

Antioch

Sidon

Tyre

Samaria

Jerusalem

Pelusium

Memphis

Pergamos

Sardis

Ephesus

200 Mi.

200 Km.

THE NEW TESTAMENT

THE FOUR GOSPELS

The four Gospels—Matthew, Mark, Luke, and John—tell us about the life of Jesus. Yet they are not true biographies. They say little about Jesus' family background and youth, and nothing about His physical appearance. They concentrate almost totally on the three years of Jesus' ministry, but even here they do not give enough information to reconstruct a complete history of those years. Rather, attention is focused on the Person of Jesus and His teachings, and all four Gospels climax with Jesus' death and resurrection, and the events associated with them.

Matthew, Mark, and Luke are called the "Synoptic Gospels." The term "Synoptic" means they view the life of Jesus from a common perspective. After introducing Jesus in different ways depending on their purpose, they record the ministry of John the Baptist, the baptism and temptation of Jesus, His ministries in Galilee and in Judea, His final week in Jerusalem, His death and resurrection. In the Synoptic record Jesus characteristically refers to Himself as the Son of Man, and He proclaims the kingdom of God.

Despite the similarities in the Synoptic accounts, these Gospels vary in what material they include and in the arrangement of specific events. Furthermore, each Gospel was written to emphasize certain aspects of Jesus' Person and work. Matthew emphasizes that Jesus is the true Messiah and the object of Old Testament prophecy and expectation. Mark's fast-moving account was written to appeal to Roman Christians, and Luke's Gospel is addressed to a cultured Gentile and stresses Jesus' concern for all kinds of people.

The Gospel of John differs from the Synoptics in a number of ways. It tells more about Jesus' early ministry in Judea. John also records long thematic discourses by Jesus instead of the shorter sayings typical of the Synoptic accounts. In John, Jesus refers to Himself as God's Son and speaks of salvation as eternal life. More than the Synoptics, John includes theological reflection on the meaning of Jesus' life and death.

See chart, "Why Four Gospels?," on page 296. *Continued on page 297*

Why Four Gospels?

Gospel	Matthew	Mark	Luke	John
Audience	Jews	Romans	Hellenists	Greek World
Portrait of Jesus	Jesus is the **Messiah/King** who fulfills Old Testament prophecy and expectations	Jesus is the authoritative Son of God	Jesus is the perfect **Son of Man** who came to save and minister to all people through the power of the Holy Spirit and prayer	Jesus is the fully **divine Son of God** in whom we should believe to receive eternal life (the "I AM" of God)
Key Verses	Matthew 1:1; 16:16; 20:28	Mark 1:1; 8:27; 10:45; 15:34	Luke 19:10	John 20:31
Key Words	Fulfilled	Immediately	Son of Man	Believe; Eternal Life

Nelson's Complete Book of Bible Maps and Charts © 1993 by Thomas Nelson, Inc.

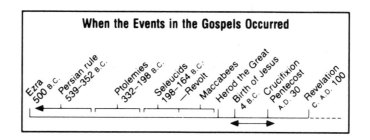

When the Events in the Gospels Occurred

Ezra 500 B.C. — Persian rule 539–352 B.C. — Ptolemies 332–198 B.C. — Seleucids 198–164 B.C.; —Revolt — Maccabees — Herod the Great — Birth of Jesus 4 B.C. — Crucifixion — Pentecost A.D. 30 — Revelation C. A.D. 100

Continued from page 295

The question of the literary relationship between the Synoptic Gospels is not easily answered. In general, the Synoptics follow the same general outline and record similar material. Sometimes the accounts are almost identical, but at other times important differences are observed. This phenomenon is called the "synoptic problem," and a number of theories have been advanced to explain the literary relationship of these three Gospels.

1. Some suggest that the writers of the three Synoptic Gospels drew their material from an earlier Gospel which has not been preserved.

2. Others have argued that oral tradition regarding the deeds and teachings of Jesus became fixed very early and that the similarities we see in the Synoptic Gospels are due to their dependence upon oral tradition. This theory is, however, insufficient to account for the possible existence of early written sources (see Luke 1:1–4), and the evident variations in form and content.

3. The most popular current theory maintains that Mark was the first Gospel and that Matthew and Luke utilized Mark as well as other sources in composing their own works. Some scholars who affirm Marcan priority hold to a "two-source theory," in which Matthew and Luke also utilize another source commonly called "Q," from the German word *Quelle*, meaning "source." This second source is said to account for about 250 verses (mostly teaching material) common to Matthew and Luke but not found in Mark.

Other theories of Marcan priority hold that Matthew and Luke utilized multiple sources in addition to Mark. In a "four-source theory," an M-source is postulated to account for material unique to Matthew, and an L-source for material peculiar to Luke.

4. Following a view widely supported by the early church fathers, some argue that Matthew was the first of the Synoptics. Luke, which utilized Matthew, is usually viewed as second; and Mark is third, being an abbreviated combination of Matthew and Luke. The preaching of Peter is also seen as a significant influence on Mark's Gospel.

See chart, "Three Synoptic Gospel Source Theories," on page 298. On the following pages, see also the charts "The Miracles of Jesus Christ" and "The Parables of Jesus Christ." Text continues on page 301.

Three Synoptic Gospel Source Theories

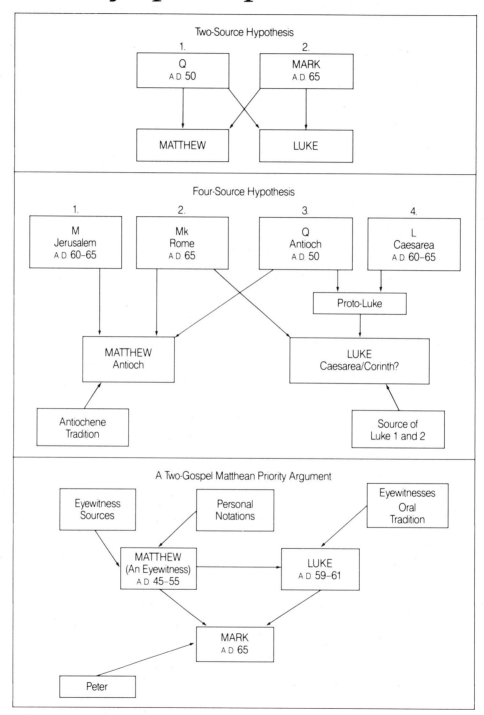

Two-Source Hypothesis

1.
Q
A.D. 50

2.
MARK
A.D. 65

MATTHEW

LUKE

Four-Source Hypothesis

1.
M
Jerusalem
A.D. 60–65

2.
Mk
Rome
A.D. 65

3.
Q
Antioch
A.D. 50

4.
L
Caesarea
A.D. 60–65

Proto-Luke

MATTHEW
Antioch

LUKE
Caesarea/Corinth?

Antiochene
Tradition

Source of
Luke 1 and 2

A Two-Gospel Matthean Priority Argument

Eyewitness
Sources

Personal
Notations

Eyewitnesses
Oral
Tradition

MATTHEW
(An Eyewitness)
A.D. 45–55

LUKE
A.D. 59–61

MARK
A.D. 65

Peter

Nelson's Complete Book of Bible Maps and Charts © 1993 by Thomas Nelson, Inc.

The Miracles of Jesus Christ

Miracle	Matthew	Mark	Luke	John
1. Cleansing a Leper	8:2	1:40	5:12	
2. Healing a Centurion's Servant (of paralysis)	8:5		7:1	
3. Healing Peter's Mother-in-Law	8:14	1:30	4:38	
4. Healing the Sick at Evening	8:16	1:32	4:40	
5. Stilling the Storm	8:23	4:35	8:22	
6. Demons Entering a Herd of Swine	8:28	5:1	8:26	
7. Healing a Paralytic	9:2	2:3	5:18	
8. Raising the Ruler's Daughter	9:18, 23	5:22, 35	8:40, 49	
9. Healing the Hemorrhaging Woman	9:20	5:25	8:43	
10. Healing Two Blind Men	9:27			
11. Curing a Demon-Possessed, Mute Man	9:32			
12. Healing a Man's Withered Hand	12:9	3:1	6:6	
13. Curing a Demon-Possessed, Blind and Mute Man	12:22		11:14	
14. Feeding the Five Thousand	14:13	6:30	9:10	6:1
15. Walking on the Sea	14:25	6:48		6:19
16. Healing the Gentile Woman's Daughter	15:21	7:24		
17. Feeding the Four Thousand	15:32	8:1		
18. Healing the Epileptic Boy	17:14	9:17	9:38	
19. Temple Tax in the Fish's Mouth	17:24			
20. Healing Two Blind Men	20:30	10:46	18:35	
21. Withering the Fig Tree	21:18	11:12		
22. Casting Out an Unclean Spirit		1:23	4:33	
23. Healing a Deaf-Mute		7:31		
24. Healing a Blind Man at Bethsaida		8:22		
25. Escape from the Hostile Multitude			4:30	
26. Catch of Fish			5:1	
27. Raising of a Widow's Son at Nain			7:11	
28. Healing the Infirm, Bent Woman			13:11	
29. Healing the Man with Dropsy			14:1	
30. Cleansing the Ten Lepers			17:11	
31. Restoring a Servant's Ear			22:51	
32. Turning Water into Wine				2:1
33. Healing the Nobleman's Son (of fever)				4:46
34. Healing an Infirm Man at Bethesda				5:1
35. Healing the Man Born Blind				9:1
36. Raising of Lazarus				11:43
37. Second Catch of Fish				21:1

Nelson's Complete Book of Bible Maps and Charts © 1993 by Thomas Nelson, Inc.

The Parables of Jesus Christ

Parable	Matthew	Mark	Luke
1. Lamp Under a Basket	5:14–16	4:21, 22	8:16, 17 11:33–36
2. A Wise Man Builds on Rock and a Foolish Man Builds on Sand	7:24–27		6:47–49
3. Unshrunk (New) Cloth on an Old Garment	9:16	2:21	5:36
4. New Wine in Old Wineskins	9:17	2:22	5:37, 38
5. The Sower	13:3–23	4:2–20	8:4–15
6. The Tares (Weeds)	13:24–30		
7. The Mustard Seed	13:31, 32	4:30–32	13:18, 19
8. The Leaven	13:33		13:20, 21
9. The Hidden Treasure	13:44		
10. The Pearl of Great Price	13:45, 46		
11. The Dragnet	13:47–50		
12. The Lost Sheep	18:12–14		15:3–7
13. The Unforgiving Servant	18:23–35		
14. The Laborers in the Vineyard	20:1–16		
15. The Two Sons	21:28–32		
16. The Wicked Vinedressers	21:33–45	12:1–12	20:9–19
17. The Wedding Feast	22:2–14		
18. The Fig Tree	24:32–44	13:28–32	21:29–33
19. The Wise and Foolish Virgins	25:1–13		
20. The Talents	25:14–30		
21. The Growing Seed		4:26–29	
22. The Absent Householder		13:33–37	
23. The Creditor and Two Debtors			7:41–43
24. The Good Samaritan			10:30–37
25. A Friend in Need			11:5–13
26. The Rich Fool			12:16–21
27. The Watchful Servants			12:35–40
28. The Faithful Servant and the Evil Servant			12:42–48
29. The Barren Fig Tree			13:6–9
30. The Great Supper			14:16–24
31. Building a Tower and a King Making War			14:25–35
32. The Lost Coin			15:8–10
33. The Lost Son			15:11–32
34. The Unjust Steward			16:1–13
35. The Rich Man and Lazarus			16:19–31
36. Unprofitable Servants			17:7–10
37. The Persistent Widow			18:1–8
38. The Pharisee and the Tax Collector			18:9–14
39. The Minas			19:11–27

Nelson's Complete Book of Bible Maps and Charts © 1993 by Thomas Nelson, Inc.

Harmonizing the Gospels

A precise historical chronology, both internal and external, for the events described in the Gospels is difficult to determine. There is some uncertainty with regard to both the external historical events and the relationships between some events depicted in the Gospels themselves. For this reason, the Harmony of the Gospels presented here, together with the historical dates assigned, should be regarded as approximate.

Such uncertainties should not surprise us, however, for the Gospels do not pretend to be complete biographies of Jesus. The Gospel writers do give some historical markers, but their primary intention is to present the saving Person and work of Jesus Christ. While we may have full confidence in the historical character of the events described, there is much that the Gospels do not tell us (cf. John 21:25).

Traditionally, the life of Jesus was dated from 1 B.C. to A.D. 33. More recently, the birth of Jesus has been reckoned by many scholars c. 5–6 B.C. Suggestions for the date of Jesus' death range from A.D. 27 to A.D. 33, with the Passover period of A.D. 30 being perhaps the most probable.

The birth of Jesus probably took place a year or two prior to the death of Herod the Great in 4 B.C. (cf. Matt. 2:1–23). There is considerable uncertainty regarding the census under Quirinius (Luke 2:2), usually dated c. A.D. 7. Some have suggested that Quirinius may have governed Syria twice, or that the census which took place at the time of Jesus' birth was the initial registration stage of a census completed during the time of Quirinius.

Luke 3:1 dates the beginning of John the Baptist's ministry to the "fifteenth year of the reign of Tiberius Caesar," a date of some uncertainty (either A.D. 26 or 29, depending on the system of reckoning). According to Luke 3:23, Jesus began His ministry when He was "about thirty years of age." While the Synoptic accounts of Jesus' ministry could take as little as a year, the record in John of Jesus' Passover visits to Jerusalem indicates a ministry length of about three years (though some argue for a two-year period of ministry). Thus, if Jesus' ministry began in A.D. 27, a three-year ministry yields a date for the crucifixion and resurrection in A.D. 30.

Harmony of the Gospels

Date	Event	Location	Matthew	Mark	Luke	John
INTRODUCTIONS TO JESUS CHRIST						
	(1) Luke's Introduction				1:1–4	
	(2) Pre-fleshly state of Christ					1:1–18
	(3) Genealogy of Jesus Christ		1:1–17		3:23–38	
BIRTH, INFANCY, AND ADOLESCENCE OF JESUS AND JOHN THE BAPTIST						
7 B.C.	(1) Announcement of Birth of John	Jerusalem (Temple)			1:5–25	
7 or 6 B.C.	(2) Announcement of Birth of Jesus to the Virgin	Nazareth			1:26–38	
c. 5 B.C.	(3) Song of Elizabeth to Mary	⎰ Hill Country ⎱ of Judea			1:39–45	
	(4) Mary's Song of Praise				1:46–56	
5 B.C.	(5) Birth, Infancy, and Purpose for Future of John the Baptist	Judea			1:57–80	
	(6) Announcement of Jesus' Birth to Joseph	Nazareth	1:18–25			
5–4 B.C.	(7) Birth of Jesus Christ	Bethlehem	1:24, 25		2:1–7	
	(8) Proclamation by the Angels	⎰ Near ⎱ Bethlehem			2:8–14	
	(9) The Visit of Homage by Shepherds	Bethlehem			2:15–20	
	(10) Jesus' Circumcision	Bethlehem			2:21	
4 B.C.	(11) First Temple Visit with Acknowledgments by Simeon and Anna	Jerusalem			2:22–38	
	(12) Visit of the Wise Men	⎰ Jerusalem & ⎱ Bethlehem	2:1–12			
	(13) Flight into Egypt and Massacre of Innocents	⎧ Bethlehem, ⎨ Jerusalem & ⎩ Egypt	2:13–18			
	(14) From Egypt to Nazareth with Jesus		2:19–23		2:39	
Afterward A.D. 7–8	(15) Childhood of Jesus	Nazareth			2:40, 51	
	(16) Jesus, 12 Years Old, Visits the Temple	Jerusalem			2:41–50	
Afterward	(17) 18-Year Account of Jesus' Adolescence and Adulthood	Nazareth			2:51, 52	
TRUTHS ABOUT JOHN THE BAPTIST						
C. A.D. 25–27	(1) John's Ministry Begins	Judean Wilderness	3:1	1:1–4	3:1, 2	1:19–28
	(2) Man and Message		3:2–12	1:2–8	3:3–14	
	(3) His Picture of Jesus		3:11, 12	1:7, 8	3:15–18	1:26, 27
	(4) His Courage		14:4–12		3:19, 20	
BEGINNING OF JESUS' MINISTRY						
C. A.D. 27	(1) Jesus Baptized	Jordan River	3:13–17	1:9–11	3:21–23	
	(2) Jesus Tempted	Wilderness	4:1–11	1:12, 13	4:1–13	
	(3) Calls First Disciples	Beyond Jordan				1:29–34
	(4) The First Miracle	Cana in Galilee				1:35–51 2:1–11
	(5) First Stay in Capernaum	(Capernaum is "His" city)				2:12
A.D. 27	(6) First Cleansing of the Temple	Jerusalem				2:13–22
	(7) Received at Jerusalem	Judea				2:23–25

Date	Event	Location	Matthew	Mark	Luke	John
A.D. 27	(8) Teaches Nicodemus about Second Birth	Judea				3:1–21
	(9) Co-Ministry with John	Judea				3:22–30
	(10) Leaves for Galilee	Judea	4:12	1:14	4:14	4:1–4
	(11) Samaritan Woman at Jacob's Well	Samaria				4:5–42
	(12) Returns to Galilee			1:15	4:15	4:43–45

THE GALILEAN MINISTRY OF JESUS

Date	Event	Location	Matthew	Mark	Luke	John
A.D. 27–29						
A.D. 27	(1) Healing of the Noble-man's Son	Cana				4:46–54
	(2) Rejected at Nazareth	Nazareth			4:16–30	
	(3) Moved to Capernaum	Capernaum	4:13–17			
	(4) Four Become Fishers of Men	Sea of Galilee	4:18–22	1:16–20	5:1–11	
	(5) Demoniac Healed on the Sabbath Day	Capernaum		1:21–28	4:31–37	
	(6) Peter's Mother-in-Law Cured, Plus Others	Capernaum	8:14–17	1:29–34	4:38–41	
C. A.D. 27	(7) First Preaching Tour of Galilee	Galilee	4:23–25	1:35–39	4:42–44	
	(8) Leper Healed and Response Recorded	Galilee	8:1–4	1:40–45	5:12–16	
	(9) Paralytic Healed	Capernaum	9:1–8	2:1–12	5:17–26	
	(10) Matthew's Call and Reception Held	Capernaum	9:9–13	2:13–17	5:27–32	
	(11) Disciples Defended via a Parable	Capernaum	9:14–17	2:18–22	5:33–39	
A.D. 28	(12) Goes to Jerusalem for Second Passover; Heals Lame Man	Jerusalem				5:1–47
	(13) Plucked Grain Precipitates Sabbath Controversy	En Route to Galilee	12:1–8	2:23–28	6:1–5	
	(14) Withered Hand Healed Causes Another Sabbath Controversy	Galilee	12:9–14	3:1–6	6:6–11	
	(15) Multitudes Healed	Sea of Galilee	12:15–21	3:7–12	6:17–19	
	(16) Twelve Apostles Selected After a Night of Prayer	{Near {Capernaum		3:13–19	6:12–16	
	(17) Sermon on the Mt.	{Near {Capernaum	5:1—7:29		6:20–49	
	(18) Centurion's Servant Healed	Capernaum	8:5–13		7:1–10	
	(19) Raises Widow's Son from Dead	Nain			7:11–17	
	(20) Jesus Allays John's Doubts	Galilee	11:2–19		7:18–35	
	(21) Woes Upon the Privileged		11:20–30			
	(22) A Sinful Woman Anoints Jesus	Simon's House, Capernaum			7:36–50	
	(23) Another Tour of Galilee	Galilee			8:1–3	
	(24) Jesus Accused of Blasphemy	Capernaum	12:22–37	3:20–30	11:14–23	
	(25) Jesus' Answer to a Demand for a Sign	Capernaum	12:38–45		{11:24–26, { 29–36	
	(26) Mother, Brothers Seek Audience	Capernaum	12:46–50	3:31–35	8:19–21	

Nelson's Complete Book of Bible Maps and Charts © 1993 by Thomas Nelson, Inc.

Date	Event	Location	Matthew	Mark	Luke	John
A.D. 28	(27) Famous Parables of Sower, Seed, Tares, Mustard Seed, Leaven, Treasure, Pearl, Dragnet, Lamp Told	By Sea of Galilee	13:1–52	4:1–34	8:4–18	
	(28) Sea Made Serene	Sea of Galilee	8:23–27	4:35–41	8:22–25	
	(29) Gadarene Demoniac Healed	{E. Shore of Galilee	8:28–34	5:1–20	8:26–39	
	(30) Jairus' Daughter Raised and Woman with Hemorrhage Healed		9:18–26	5:21–43	8:40–56	
	(31) Two Blind Men's Sight Restored		9:27–31			
	(32) Mute Demoniac Healed		9:32–34			
	(33) Nazareth's Second Rejection of Christ	Nazareth	13:53–58	6:1–6		
	(34) Twelve Sent Out		9:35—11:1	6:7–13	9:1–6	
	(35) Fearful Herod Beheads John	Galilee	14:1–12	6:14–29	9:7–9	
Spring A.D. 29	(36) Return of 12, Jesus Withdraws, 5000 Fed	{Near Bethsaida Sea of Galilee	14:13–21	6:30–44	9:10–17	6:1–14 6:15–21
	(37) Walks on the Water		14:22–33	6:45–52		
	(38) Sick of Gennesaret Healed	Gennesaret	14:34–36	6:53–56		
	(39) Peak of Popularity Passes in Galilee	Capernaum				{6:22–71 7:1
A.D. 29	(40) Traditions Attacked		15:1–20	7:1–23		
	(41) Aborted Retirement in Phoenicia: Syro-Phoenician Healed	Phoenicia	15:21–28	7:24–30		
	(42) Afflicted Healed	Decapolis	15:29–31	7:31–37		
	(43) 4000 Fed	Decapolis	15:32–39	8:1–9		
	(44) Pharisees Increase Attack	Magdala	16:1–4	8:10–13		
	(45) Disciples' Carelessness Condemned; Blind Man Healed		16:5–12	8:14–26		
	(46) Peter Confesses Jesus Is the Christ	{Near Caesarea Philippi	16:13–20	8:27–30	9:18–21	
	(47) Jesus Foretells His Death	{Caesarea Philippi	16:21–26	8:31–38	9:22–25	
	(48) Kingdom Promised		16:27, 28	9:1	9:26, 27	
	(49) The Transfiguration	{Mountain Unnamed	17:1–13	9:2–13	9:28–36	
	(50) Epileptic Healed	{Mt. of Transfiguration	17:14–21	9:14–29	9:37–42	
	(51) Again Tells of Death, Resurrection	Galilee	17:22, 23	9:30–32	9:43–45	
	(52) Taxes Paid	Capernaum	17:24–27			
	(53) Disciples Contend About Greatness; Jesus Defines; also Patience, Loyalty, Forgiveness	Capernaum	18:1–35	9:33–50	9:46–62	
	(54) Jesus Rejects Brothers' Advice	Galilee				7:2–9
c. Sept. A.D. 29	(55) Galilee Departure and Samaritan Rejection		19:1		9:51–56	7:10
	(56) Cost of Discipleship		8:18–22		9:57–62	

LAST JUDEAN AND PEREAN MINISTRY OF JESUS

Date	Event	Location	Matthew	Mark	Luke	John
A.D. 29–30 Oct. A.D. 29	(1) Feast of Tabernacles	Jerusalem				7:2, 10–52
	(2) Forgiveness of Adulteress	Jerusalem				{7:53— 8:11

Nelson's Complete Book of Bible Maps and Charts © 1993 by Thomas Nelson, Inc.

Date	Event	Location	Matthew	Mark	Luke	John
A.D. 29	(3) Christ—the Light of the World	Jerusalem				8:12–20
	(4) Pharisees Can't Meet the Prophecy Thus Try to Destroy the Prophet	{Jerusalem— Temple				8:21–59
	(5) Man Born Blind Healed; Following Consequences	Jerusalem				9:1–41
	(6) Parable of the Good Shepherd	Jerusalem				10:1–21
	(7) The Service of the Seventy	{Probably Judea			10:1–24	
	(8) Lawyer Hears the Story of the Good Samaritan	Judea (?)			10:25–37	
	(9) The Hospitality of Martha and Mary	Bethany			10:38–42	
	(10) Another Lesson on Prayer	Judea (?)			11:1–13	
	(11) Accused of Connection with Beelzebub				11:14–36	
	(12) Judgment Against Lawyers and Pharisees				11:37–54	
	(13) Jesus Deals with Hypocrisy, Covetousness, Worry, and Alertness				12:1–59	
	(14) Repent or Perish				13:1–5	
	(15) Barren Fig Tree				13:6–9	
	(16) Crippled Woman Healed on Sabbath				13:10–17	
Winter A.D. 29	(17) Parables of Mustard Seed and Leaven	{Probably Perea			13:18–21	
	(18) Feast of Dedication	Jerusalem				10:22–39
	(19) Withdrawal Beyond Jordan					10:40–42
	(20) Begins Teaching Return to Jerusalem with Special Words About Herod	Perea			13:22–35	
	(21) Meal with a Pharisee Ruler Occasions Healing Man with Dropsy; Parables of Ox, Best Places, and Great Supper				14:1–24	
	(22) Demands of Discipleship	Perea			14:25–35	
	(23) Parables of Lost Sheep, Coin, Son				15:1–32	
	(24) Parables of Unjust Steward, Rich Man and Lazarus				16:1–31	
	(25) Lessons on Service, Faith, Influence				17:1–10	
	(26) Resurrection of Lazarus	{Perea to Bethany				11:1–44
	(27) Reaction to It: Withdrawal of Jesus					11:45–54
A.D. 30	(28) Begins Last Journey to Jerusalem via Samaria & Galilee	{Samaria, Galilee			17:11	
	(29) Heals Ten Lepers				17:12–19	
	(30) Lessons on the Coming Kingdom				17:20–37	
	(31) Parables: Persistent Widow, Pharisee and Tax Collector				18:1–14	
	(32) Doctrine on Divorce		19:1–12	10:1–12		

Nelson's Complete Book of Bible Maps and Charts © 1993 by Thomas Nelson, Inc.

Date	Event	Location	Matthew	Mark	Luke	John
A.D. 30	(33) Jesus Blesses Children: Objections	Perea	19:13–15	10:13–16	18:15–17	
	(34) Rich Young Ruler	Perea	19:16–30	10:17–31	18:18–30	
	(35) Laborers of the 11th Hour		20:1–16			
	(36) Foretells Death and Resurrection	{Near Jordan	20:17–19	10:32–34	18:31–34	
	(37) Ambition of James and John		20:20–28	10:35–45		
	(38) Blind Bartimaeus Healed	Jericho		10:46–52	18:35–43	
	(39) Interview with Zacchaeus	Jericho			19:1–10	
	(40) Parable: the Minas	Jericho			19:11–27	
	(41) Returns to Home of Mary and Martha	Bethany				{11:55— 12:1
	(42) Plot to Kill Lazarus	Bethany				12:9–11

JESUS' FINAL WEEK OF WORK AT JERUSALEM

Date	Event	Location	Matthew	Mark	Luke	John
Spring A.D. 30						
Sunday	(1) Triumphal Entry	Bethany, Jerusalem, Bethany	21:1–9	11:1–11	19:28–44	12:12–19
Monday	(2) Fig Tree Cursed and Temple Cleansed	{Bethany to Jerusalem	21:10–19	11:12–18	19:45–48	
	(3) The Attraction of Sacrifice	Jerusalem				12:20–50
Tuesday	(4) Withered Fig Tree Testifies	{Bethany to Jerusalem	21:20–22	11:19–26		
	(5) Sanhedrin Challenges Jesus. Answered by Parables: Two Sons, Wicked Vinedressers and Marriage Feast	Jerusalem	{21:23— 22:14	{11:27— 12:12	20:1–19	
	(6) Tribute to Caesar	Jerusalem	22:15–22	12:13–17	20:20–26	
	(7) Sadducees Question the Resurrection	Jerusalem	22:23–33	12:18–27	20:27–40	
	(8) Pharisees Question Commandments	Jerusalem	22:34–40	12:28–34		
	(9) Jesus and David	Jerusalem	22:41–46	12:35–37	20:41–44	
	(10) Jesus' Last Sermon	Jerusalem	23:1–39	12:38–40	20:45–47	
	(11) Widow's Mite	Jerusalem		12:41–44	21:1–4	
	(12) Jesus Tells of the Future	Mt. Olives	24:1–51	13:1–37	21:5–36	
	(13) Parables: Ten Virgins, Talents, The Day of Judgment	Mt. Olives	25:1–46			
	(14) Jesus Tells Date of Crucifixion		26:1–5	14:1, 2	22:1, 2	
	(15) Anointing by Mary at Simon's Feast	Bethany	26:6–13	14:3–9		12:2–8
	(16) Judas Contracts the Betrayal		26:14–16	14:10, 11	22:3–6	
Thursday	(17) Preparation for the Passover	Jerusalem	26:17–19	14:12–16	22:7–13	
Thursday P.M.	(18) Passover Eaten, Jealousy Rebuked	Jerusalem	26:20	14:17	{22:14–16, 24–30	
	(19) Feet Washed	Upper Room				13:1–20
	(20) Judas Revealed, Defects	Upper Room	26:21–25	14:18–21	22:21–23	13:21–30
	(21) Jesus Warns About Further Desertion; Cries of Loyalty	Upper Room	26:31–35	14:27–31	22:31–38	13:31–38
	(22) Institution of the Lord's Supper	Upper Room	26:26–29	14:22–25	22:17–20	

Nelson's Complete Book of Bible Maps and Charts © 1993 by Thomas Nelson, Inc.

Date	Event	Location	Matthew	Mark	Luke	John
Thursday P.M.	(23) Last Speech to the Apostles and Intercessory Prayer	Jerusalem				{14:1— 17:26
Thursday- Friday	(24) The Grief of Gethsemane	Mt. of Olives	{26:30, 36–46	{14:26, 32–42	22:39–46	18:1
Friday	(25) Betrayal, Arrest, Desertion	Gethsemane	26:47–56	14:43–52	22:47–53	18:2–12
	(26) First Examined by Annas	Jerusalem				{18:12–14, 19–23
	(27) Trial by Caiaphas and Council; Following Indignities	Jerusalem	{26:57, 59–68	{14:53, 55–65	{22:54, 63–65	18:24
	(28) Peter's Triple Denial	Jerusalem	{26:58, 69–75	{14:54, 66–72	22:54–62	{18:15–18, 25–27
	(29) Condemnation by the Council	Jerusalem	27:1	15:1	22:66–71	
	(30) Suicide of Judas	Jerusalem	27:3–10			
	(31) First Appearance Before Pilate	Jerusalem	{27:2, 11–14	15:1–5	23:1–7	18:28–38
	(32) Jesus Before Herod	Jerusalem			23:6–12	
	(33) Second Appearance Before Pilate	Jerusalem	27:15–26	15:6–15	23:13–25	{18:39— 19:16
	(34) Mockery by Roman Soldiers	Jerusalem	27:27–30	15:16–19		
	(35) Led to Golgotha	Jerusalem	27:31–34	15:20–23	23:26–33	19:16, 17
	(36) 6 Events of First 3 Hours on Cross	Calvary	27:35–44	15:24–32	23:33–43	19:18–27
	(37) Last 3 Hours on Cross	Calvary	27:45–50	15:33–37	23:44–46	19:28–30
	(38) Events Attending Jesus' Death		27:51–56	15:38–41	{23:45, 47–49	
	(39) Burial of Jesus	Jerusalem	27:57–60	15:42–46	23:50–54	19:31–42
	(40) Tomb Sealed	Jerusalem	27:61–66		23:55, 56	
Friday- Saturday	(41) Women Watch	Jerusalem		15:47		

THE RESURRECTION THROUGH THE ASCENSION

A.D. **30**

Date	Event	Location	Matthew	Mark	Luke	John
Dawn of First Day (Sunday, ''Lord's Day'')	(1) Women Visit the Tomb	Near Jerusalem	28:1–10	16:1–8	24:1–11	
	(2) Peter and John See the Empty Tomb				24:12	20:1–10
	(3) Jesus' Appearance to Mary Magdalene	Jerusalem		16:9–11		20:11–18
	(4) Jesus' Appearance to the Other Women	Jerusalem	28:9, 10			
	(5) Guards' Report of the Resurrection		28:11–15			
Sunday Afternoon	(6) Jesus' Appearance to Two Disciples on Way to Emmaus			16:12, 13	24:13–35	
Late Sunday	(7) Jesus' Appearance to Ten Disciples Without Thomas	Jerusalem			24:36–43	20:19–25
One Week Later	(8) Appearance to Disciples with Thomas	Jerusalem				20:26–31
During 40 Days until Ascension	(9) Jesus' Appearance to Seven Disciples by Sea of Galilee	Galilee				21:1–25
	(10) Great Commission	Mt. Olivet	28:16–20	16:14–18	24:44–49	
	(11) The Ascension			16:19, 20	24:50–53	

Nelson's Complete Book of Bible Maps and Charts © 1993 by Thomas Nelson, Inc.

The Herodian Dynasty

Herod was the family name of several Roman rulers who served as provincial governors of Palestine and surrounding regions during New Testament times.

The first Herod, known as Herod the Great, was the Roman ruler of Palestine during the days of the Roman Emperor Caesar Augustus when Jesus was born in Bethlehem (Matt. 2:1; Luke 3:1). All the other different Herods mentioned in the New Testament were the sons or grandsons of this Herod.

Herod the Great (ruled 37–4 B.C.), was known as a master builder, organizer, and developer, although his policies were considered cruel and ruthless by the Jewish people. His most notable achievement was the rebuilding of the temple in Jerusalem—a project that required almost fifty years. He also rebuilt and enlarged the city of Caesarea into a port city on the Mediterranean Sea. Caesarea served as the Roman provincial capital for Palestine during the New Testament era. The magnificent aqueducts that he built at this city are still visible today.

Herod's son Antipas succeeded him as Roman governor of Galilee and Perea (Matt. 14:1). Antipas was responsible for the imprisonment and death of John the Baptist (Luke 3:19, 20; Matt. 14:1–12).

Herod the Great's grandson Agrippa was named ruler over all of Palestine by the Roman emperor Caligula. Agrippa is known as a persecutor of early Christians. He had James put to death and had Peter arrested. Because of his cruelty and blasphemy, Agrippa was slain by an angel of the Lord (Acts 12).

In A.D. 50, Agrippa's son, known as Agrippa II, was made ruler of the king of Chalcis's territory. Later he was given Abilene, Trachonitis, Acra, and important parts of Galilee and Perea. The only reference to this Herod in the New Testament occurs in Acts 25:13—26:32, which deals with Paul's imprisonment in Caesarea. Agrippa listened to Paul's defense, but the apostle appealed to Rome. Agrippa had no power to set him free.

The other two Herods mentioned in the New Testament are Herod Archelaus (Matt. 2:22) and Herod Philip (Luke 3:1). Both of these rulers were sons of Herod the Great; they ruled parts of the territory previously administered by their father.

Family Tree of Herod

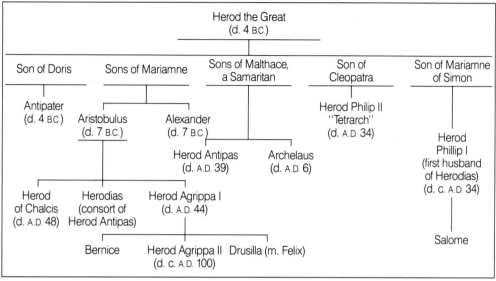

Herod the Great
(d. 4 B.C.)

Son of Doris	Sons of Mariamne	Sons of Malthace, a Samaritan	Son of Cleopatra	Son of Mariamne of Simon

Antipater
(d. 4 B.C.)

Aristobulus
(d. 7 B.C.)

Alexander
(d. 7 B.C.)

Herod Antipas
(d. A.D. 39)

Archelaus
(d. A.D. 6)

Herod Philip II
"Tetrarch"
(d. A.D. 34)

Herod Phillip I
(first husband of Herodias)
(d. c. A.D. 34)

Herod of Chalcis
(d. A.D. 48)

Herodias
(consort of Herod Antipas)

Herod Agrippa I
(d. A.D. 44)

Salome

Bernice

Herod Agrippa II
(d. c. A.D. 100)

Drusilla (m. Felix)

Nelson's Complete Book of Bible Maps and Charts © 1993 by Thomas Nelson, Inc.

The Plan of Herod's Temple

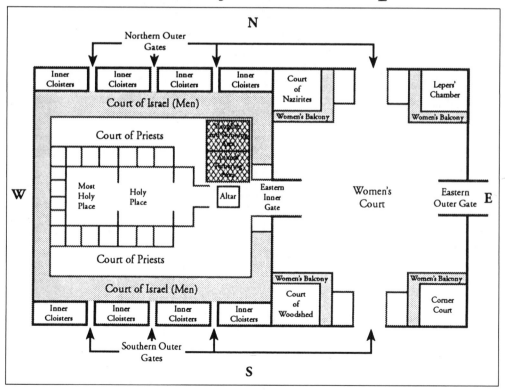

New Testament Political Rulers

Roman Emperor	Rulers of Palestine		
	Herod the Great (37–4 B.C.)		
	Judea	Galilee and Perea	Other Provinces
Augustus Caesar (31 B.C.–A.D. 14)	Archelaus (4 B.C.–A.D. 6)	Herod Antipas (4 B.C.–A.D. 39)	Herod Philip II (4 B.C.–A.D. 34)
	Coponius (A.D. 6–8)		
	Ambivius (A.D. 9–12)		
	Annius Rufus (A.D. 12–15)		
Tiberius Caesar (A.D. 14–37)	Valerius Gratus (A.D. 15–26)		
	Pontius Pilate (A.D. 26–36)		
Caligula (A.D. 37–41)	Marcellus (A.D. 37)		
	Herod Agrippa I (A.D. 37–44)		
Claudius (A.D. 41–54)	Cuspius Fadus (A.D. 44–46)		
	Tiberius Alexander (A.D. 46–48)		
	Ventidius Cumanus (A.D. 48–52)	Herod Agrippa II (Began to rule in A.D. 34 in other provinces and in A.D. 39 in Galilee and Perea.)	
	M. Antonius Felix (A.D. 52–60)		
Nero (A.D. 54–68)	Porcius Festus (A.D. 60–62)		
	Clodius Albinus (A.D. 62–64)		
Galbo, Otho, Vitellius (A.D. 68–69)	Gessius Florus (A.D. 64–66)		
Vespasian (A.D. 69–79)	Jewish Revolt (A.D. 66–70)		
Titus (A.D. 79–81)			
Domitian (A.D. 81–96)			

Nelson's Complete Book of Bible Maps and Charts © 1993 by Thomas Nelson, Inc.

MATTHEW

The Gospel of Matthew is appropriately located at the beginning of the New Testament. This is not because it was the first New Testament book, or even the earliest Gospel, to be written. Rather, more than any of the other Gospels it emphasizes Jesus' relation to the Old Testament. Thus it serves as a bridge, connecting the two Testaments as promise and fulfillment.

Author

The earliest manuscripts of the first Gospel do not identify an author, and some modern scholars reject Matthew as the author. However, since the second century A.D., church tradition has recognized Matthew, the disciple of Jesus and apostle, as its writer.

Before his call to follow Jesus (9:9–13), Matthew occupied the unpopular post of tax collector in Capernaum for the Roman government. As a trained tax collector, Matthew was probably accustomed to taking notes and keeping records of what went on around him. The Jewish character of this Gospel fits well with such an author.

Date

Some have suggested a date as early as A.D. 50, and Matthew was first quoted by one of the church fathers around A.D. 110. The precise dating depends, to some extent, on the relationship of Matthew to Mark and Luke (see "The Four Gospels" on page 295).

The two expressions "to this day" (27:8) and "until this day" (28:15) indicate that a substantial period of time has passed since the events described in the book, but they also point to a probable date prior to the destruction of Jerusalem in A.D. 70. The Jewish flavor of this Gospel is another argument for a date prior to A.D. 70. If Matthew depended upon Mark's Gospel as a source, the date of Mark would determine the earliest possible date for Matthew, and a likely time frame for this book is A.D. 58–68. It may have been written in Palestine or Syrian Antioch.

Continued on page 313

Matthew at a Glance

FOCUS	OFFER OF THE KING				REJECTION OF THE KING		
REFERENCE	1:1 ——— 4:12	——— 8:1	——— 11:2	——— 16:13	——— 20:29	——— 28:1 – 28:20	
DIVISION	PRESENTATION OF THE KING	PROCLAMATION OF THE KING	POWER OF THE KING	PROGRESSIVE REJECTION OF THE KING	PREPARATION OF THE KING'S DISCIPLES	PRESENTATION AND REJECTION OF THE KING	PROOF OF THE KING
TOPIC	TEACHING THE THRONGS				TEACHING THE TWELVE		
	CHRONOLOGICAL	THEMATIC		CHRONOLOGICAL			
LOCATION	BETHLEHEM AND NAZARETH	GALILEE				JUDEA	
TIME	c. 4 B.C.—A.D. 33						

Nelson's Complete Book of Bible Maps and Charts © 1993 by Thomas Nelson, Inc.

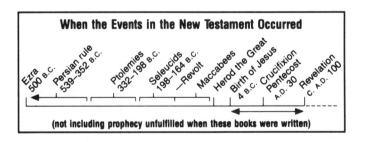

When the Events in the New Testament Occurred

Ezra 500 B.C. · Persian rule 539–352 B.C. · Ptolemies 332–198 B.C. · Seleucids 198–164 B.C. —Revolt · Maccabees · Herod the Great · Birth of Jesus 4 B.C. · Crucifixion · Pentecost A.D. 30 · Revelation C. A.D. 100

(not including prophecy unfulfilled when these books were written)

Themes and Literary Structure

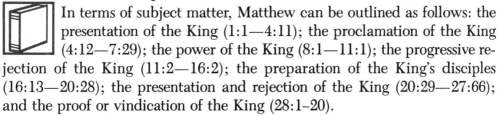 In terms of subject matter, Matthew can be outlined as follows: the presentation of the King (1:1—4:11); the proclamation of the King (4:12—7:29); the power of the King (8:1—11:1); the progressive rejection of the King (11:2—16:2); the preparation of the King's disciples (16:13—20:28); the presentation and rejection of the King (20:29—27:66); and the proof or vindication of the King (28:1-20).

An important key to the literary structure of Matthew is found in the phrase "when Jesus had ended" (7:28; 11:1; 13:53; 19:1; 26:1), which is used to conclude the five key discourses of the book: the Sermon on the Mount (5:3—7:27), Instruction of the Disciples (10:5-42), Parables of the Kingdom (13:3-52), Terms of Discipleship (18:3-35), and the Olivet Discourse (24:4—25:46). This fivefold structure, common in Judaism (e.g., the Pentateuch), may reveal Matthew's purpose of showing Jesus as the fulfillment of the prophecy regarding the coming prophet like Moses (Deut. 18:15).

Matthew was placed first in the canon of New Testament books by the early church because it is a natural bridge between the Testaments. Matthew presents Jesus as Israel's promised messianic King and royal descendant of David. To show that Jesus fulfills the qualifications for the Messiah, Matthew uses more Old Testament quotations and allusions than any other New Testament book (almost 130). Often used in this Gospel is the phrase "that what was spoken through the prophet might be fulfilled," which appears nine times in Matthew and not once in the other Gospels.

Matthew emphasizes Jesus as a teacher. He was especially an authoritative interpreter of the Law of Moses and of the will of God (4:23; 5:2; 7:28, 29).

Matthew is the only Gospel to mention the church explicitly (16:18; 18:17), and the phrase "kingdom of heaven" occurs thirty-two times in this Gospel but nowhere else in the New Testament.

The narrative of Matthew includes some events not mentioned or without precise parallel in the other Gospels—e.g., the visit of the wise men (2:1-12), the flight to Egypt (2:12-23), and the Sermon on the Mount (5:1—7:29).

Fulfillment of prophecy was involved when Joseph and Mary went to Egypt (2:15; cf. Hos. 11:1) after the visit of the wise men. Matthew intends that his readers see an implicit link between Jesus and Israel (the Son who emerges from Egypt, Hos. 11:1). Many suggest that, by employing Hosea 11:1 in 2:15, Matthew implies that Jesus recapitulates the history of Israel, and embodies in Himself the future of Israel as the people of God.

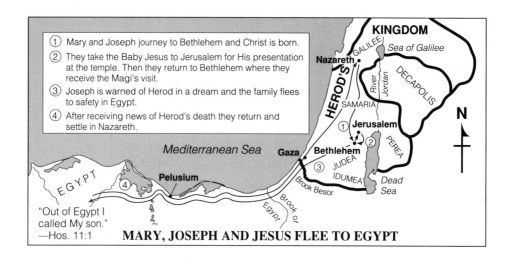

① Mary and Joseph journey to Bethlehem and Christ is born.

② They take the Baby Jesus to Jerusalem for His presentation at the temple. Then they return to Bethlehem where they receive the Magi's visit.

③ Joseph is warned of Herod in a dream and the family flees to safety in Egypt.

④ After receiving news of Herod's death they return and settle in Nazareth.

"Out of Egypt I called My son."
—Hos. 11:1

MARY, JOSEPH AND JESUS FLEE TO EGYPT

OUTLINE OF MATTHEW

Part One: The Presentation of the King (1:1—4:11)

Part Two: The Proclamation of the King (4:12—7:29)

The Sermon on the Mount

Jesus' long discourse known as the Sermon on the Mount (Matt. 5—7) is so named because He taught His disciples and the crowds that followed Him from a mountainside at the beginning of His public ministry (Matt. 5:1). The traditional site of the Sermon is marked today by a beautiful little church, the Chapel on the Mount of Beatitudes, one of the major stopping points for tourists who visit the Holy Land.

The central theme of the Sermon is summarized in Matthew 5:48, "You shall be perfect, just as your Father in heaven is perfect." The word *perfect* does not refer to sinless or moral perfection. It indicates completeness, wholeness, maturity—being all that God wants a person to be. This goal, although we never attain it in this life, should continually challenge us to greater service for the Lord.

The ten major sections of the Sermon on the Mount are as follows:

1. The Beatitudes (5:3–12): The blessed rewards of living as citizens of Christ's kingdom.

2. The lessons of salt and light (5:13–16): The effects of Christian living on the world.

3. True righteousness (5:17–48): The deeper meaning of the law of God.

4. Practice without hypocrisy (6:1–18): The right motives for giving, praying, and fasting.

5. The Christian's concerns (6:19–34): Serving God with singleness of purpose and putting the concerns of His kingdom first are actions that free us from anxiety over lesser things.

6. Warning against judgment (7:1–6): The dangers of judging others harshly and carelessly.

7. Invitation to prayer (7:7–12): The blessings and privileges of prayer.

8. The two ways (7:13, 14): Choose the narrow way, not the broad way that leads to destruction.

9. A tree and its fruit (7:15–20): "By their fruits you will know them."

10. The importance of deeds (7:21–29): To obey God is far better than talking about your obedience.

The Baptism of Jesus

All three Synoptic Gospels record the baptism and temptation of Jesus (Matt. 3:13—4:11; Mark 1:9–13; Luke 3:21, 22; 4:1–13). In His baptism, Jesus identified with the people He came to save. In addition, He received the blessing of His Heavenly Father, and was empowered by the Holy Spirit for His messianic work. Immediately after His baptism, Jesus was led by the Spirit into the wilderness to be tempted by the devil. It was necessary for Jesus, as the sinless Second Adam, to face His adversary at the outset of His ministry and victoriously to demonstrate His victory over temptation.

The map on page 319 traces the possible route taken by Jesus to leave Nazareth, go to the site of John's baptisms, and then enter the wilderness of Judea.

Jesus' Galilean Ministry

The Synoptic Gospels give considerable prominence to the ministry of Jesus in Galilee. An area of mixed population, Galilee was known as "Galilee of the Gentiles" (Matt. 4:15), and its Jewish inhabitants, with their distinctive manner of speech (Matt. 26:69, 73), were often despised by the Jews of Judea.

Though born in the Judean city of Bethlehem, Jesus was raised in the Gali-

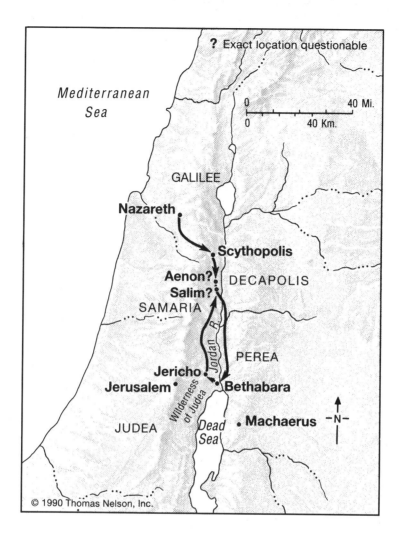

lean town of Nazareth. The town of Capernaum became the headquarters for Jesus' Galilean ministry and most of His disciples were from the region of Galilee.

See map, "Galilean Ministry," on page 321. See also map, "Events in Christ's Ministry," on page 352.

Jesus' Ministry Beyond Galilee

Although Jesus' ministry was directed primarily to Jews (Matt. 15:24), all four Gospels record instances where He ministered to Gentiles. The immediate reason for Jesus' excursion into gentile territory was the opposition of the Jewish

Continued on page 322

The Life of Jesus

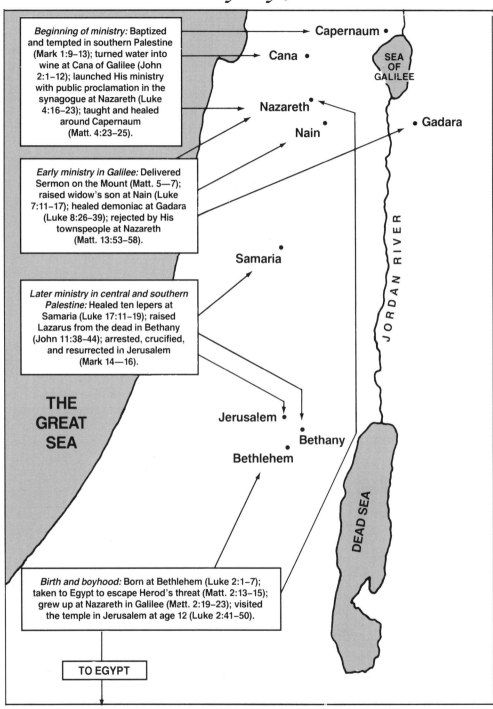

Beginning of ministry: Baptized and tempted in southern Palestine (Mark 1:9–13); turned water into wine at Cana of Galilee (John 2:1–12); launched His ministry with public proclamation in the synagogue at Nazareth (Luke 4:16–23); taught and healed around Capernaum (Matt. 4:23–25).

Early ministry in Galilee: Delivered Sermon on the Mount (Matt. 5—7); raised widow's son at Nain (Luke 7:11–17); healed demoniac at Gadara (Luke 8:26–39); rejected by His townspeople at Nazareth (Matt. 13:53–58).

Later ministry in central and southern Palestine: Healed ten lepers at Samaria (Luke 17:11–19); raised Lazarus from the dead in Bethany (John 11:38–44); arrested, crucified, and resurrected in Jerusalem (Mark 14—16).

Birth and boyhood: Born at Bethlehem (Luke 2:1–7); taken to Egypt to escape Herod's threat (Matt. 2:13–15); grew up at Nazareth in Galilee (Matt. 2:19–23); visited the temple in Jerusalem at age 12 (Luke 2:41–50).

Capernaum •

Cana •

SEA OF GALILEE

Nazareth •

Nain •

• Gadara

JORDAN RIVER

Samaria •

THE GREAT SEA

Jerusalem •

• Bethany

Bethlehem •

DEAD SEA

TO EGYPT

Nelson's Complete Book of Bible Maps and Charts © 1993 by Thomas Nelson, Inc.

Galilean Ministry

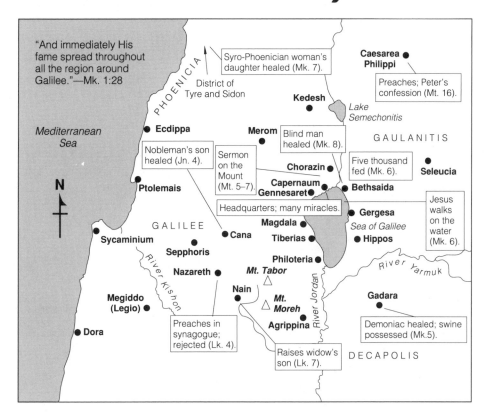

"And immediately His fame spread throughout all the region around Galilee."—Mk. 1:28

Mediterranean Sea

PHOENICIA

District of Tyre and Sidon

Syro-Phoenician woman's daughter healed (Mk. 7).

Caesarea Philippi

Preaches; Peter's confession (Mt. 16).

Kedesh

Lake Semechonitis

● Ecdippa

Merom ●

Blind man healed (Mk. 8).

GAULANITIS

Nobleman's son healed (Jn. 4).

Sermon on the Mount (Mt. 5–7).

Chorazin ●

Five thousand fed (Mk. 6).

Seleucia

Ptolemais

Capernaum ●
Gennesaret ●

● Bethsaida

Headquarters; many miracles.

● Gergesa

Jesus walks on the water (Mk. 6).

GALILEE

Magdala ●

Sea of Galilee

● Cana

Tiberias ●

● Hippos

Sycaminium

Sepphoris

Philoteria ●

River Kishon

Nazareth ●

Mt. Tabor △

Megiddo (Legio) ●

Nain ●

Mt. Moreh △

River Jordan

River Yarmuk

Gadara ●

Demoniac healed; swine possessed (Mk.5).

● Dora

Agrippina ●

Preaches in synagogue; rejected (Lk. 4).

Raises widow's son (Lk. 7).

DECAPOLIS

N

Continued from page 319

leaders, but His ministry there also served to anticipate the extension of the gospel to the Gentiles after Pentecost.

Near Tyre, Jesus cast out a demon from the daughter of a Syro-Phoenician woman (Mark 7:24–30). Peter made his great confession at Caesarea Philippi (Matt. 16:13–19). Jesus returned to Galilee via the Decapolis region, crossing the Jordan River south of the Sea of Galilee.

Places of Central Palestine

In 19:1—20:34, Matthew records the final ministry of Jesus in the central Palestine region of Judea. Beginning on the east side of the Jordan, Jesus moved toward the city of Jerusalem and the climax of His redemptive work.

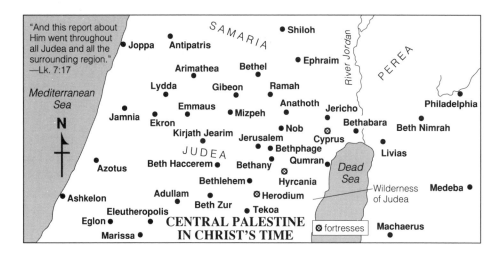

Last Journey to Jerusalem

Although Jesus made a number of trips to Jerusalem (treated in greater detail in the Gospel of John), the Synoptic Gospels emphasize Jesus' final journey to Jerusalem, where He would suffer for the sins of humanity and rise again in victory over death.

During this journey from Galilee to Jerusalem, Jesus instructed His disciples on the meaning of true Christian discipleship and told them of His coming passion.

Events of Holy Week

The Gospel writers devoted many pages to the events leading up to the crucifixion of Jesus. The final week of His earthly ministry began with the triumphal entry into Jerusalem and the "Hosannas" from the crowd that changed to cries of "Crucify Him" before the week was over. Jesus apparently spent most of the week teaching in the temple area during the day. His evenings were spent in the home of Mary, Martha, and Lazarus in Bethany. Significant events during this week included the plot of the Sanhedrin, Jesus' betrayal and arrest, the trials of Jesus, His journey to Golgotha down the Jerusalem street known today as the Via Dolorosa, and the resurrection. After His resurrection, Jesus ministered another forty days before His ascension.

Day	Event	Biblical Reference
Sunday	The triumphal entry into Jerusalem	Mark 11:1–11
Monday	Cleanses the temple in Jerusalem	Mark 11:15–19
Tuesday	The Sanhedrin challenges Jesus' authority	Luke 20:1–8
	Jesus foretells the destruction of Jerusalem and His Second Coming	Matt. 24; 25
	Mary anoints Jesus at Bethany	John 12:2–8
	Judas bargains with the Jewish rulers to betray Jesus	Luke 22:3–6
Thursday	Jesus eats the Passover meal with His disciples and institutes the Memorial Supper	John 13:1–30 Mark 14:22–26
	Prays in Gethsemane for His disciples	John 17
Friday	His betrayal and arrest in the Garden of Gethsemane	Mark 14:43–50
	Jesus questioned by Annas, the former high priest	John 18:12–24
	Condemned by Caiaphas and the Sanhedrin	Mark 14:53–65
	Peter denies Jesus three times	John 18:15–27
	Jesus is formally condemned by the Sanhedrin	Luke 22:66–71
	Judas commits suicide	Matt. 27:3–10
	The trial of Jesus before Pilate	Luke 23:1–5
	Jesus' appearance before Herod Antipas	Luke 23:6–12
	Formally sentenced to death by Pilate	Luke 23:13–25
	Jesus is mocked and crucified between two thieves	Mark 15:16–27
	The veil of the temple is torn as Jesus dies	Matt. 27:51–56
	His burial in the tomb of Joseph of Arimathea	John 19:31–42
Sunday	Jesus is raised from the dead	Luke 24:1–9

Christ's Trial and Crucifixion

After His triumphal entry into Jerusalem, Jesus encountered the opposition of the priests, Sadduces, Pharisees, and scribes. Following His arrest in the Garden of Gethsemane, the three religious and three civil trials culminated in His crucifixion outside the city wall.

See map, "Christ's Trial and Crucifixion," on page 324.

Christ's Trial and Crucifixion

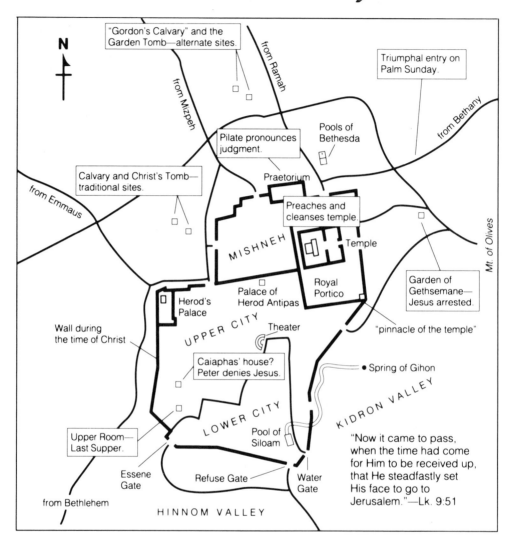

"Gordon's Calvary" and the Garden Tomb—alternate sites.

Triumphal entry on Palm Sunday.

from Ramah

from Mizpeh

from Bethany

Pools of Bethesda

Pilate pronounces judgment.

Calvary and Christ's Tomb— traditional sites.

from Emmaus

Praetorium

Preaches and cleanses temple.

MISHNEH

Temple

Garden of Gethsemane— Jesus arrested.

Royal Portico

Mt. of Olives

Palace of Herod Antipas

Herod's Palace

Wall during the time of Christ

UPPER CITY

Theater

"pinnacle of the temple"

Caiaphas' house? Peter denies Jesus.

Spring of Gihon

KIDRON VALLEY

LOWER CITY

Upper Room— Last Supper.

Pool of Siloam

Essene Gate

Refuse Gate

Water Gate

from Bethlehem

HINNOM VALLEY

"Now it came to pass, when the time had come for Him to be received up, that He steadfastly set His face to go to Jerusalem."—Lk. 9:51

Resurrection Appearances

Ten distinct resurrection appearances of Christ prior to His ascension can be documented in Scripture, in addition to the appearance of the glorified Christ to Paul on the Damascus road. Such repeated attestation points to the centrality of the resurrection for New Testament believers—the certainty of Christ's resurrection provides the firm guarantee of the final resurrection of believers (1 Cor. 15:12–23).

See map, "The Resurrection," below. See also chart, "Appearances of the Risen Christ," on page 392. See also map, "The Resurrection," on page 355.

The Resurrection

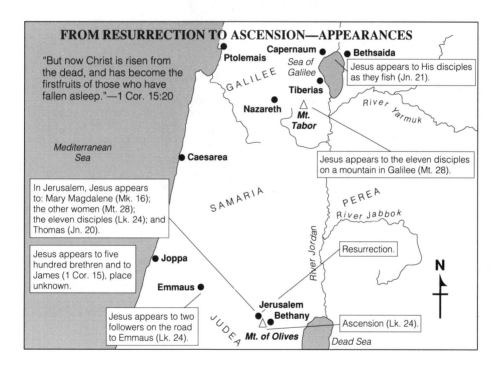

FROM RESURRECTION TO ASCENSION—APPEARANCES

"But now Christ is risen from the dead, and has become the firstfruits of those who have fallen asleep."—1 Cor. 15:20

Jesus appears to His disciples as they fish (Jn. 21).

Jesus appears to the eleven disciples on a mountain in Galilee (Mt. 28).

In Jerusalem, Jesus appears to: Mary Magdalene (Mk. 16); the other women (Mt. 28); the eleven disciples (Lk. 24); and Thomas (Jn. 20).

Jesus appears to five hundred brethren and to James (1 Cor. 15), place unknown.

Resurrection.

Ascension (Lk. 24).

Jesus appears to two followers on the road to Emmaus (Lk. 24).

The Land of the Gospels

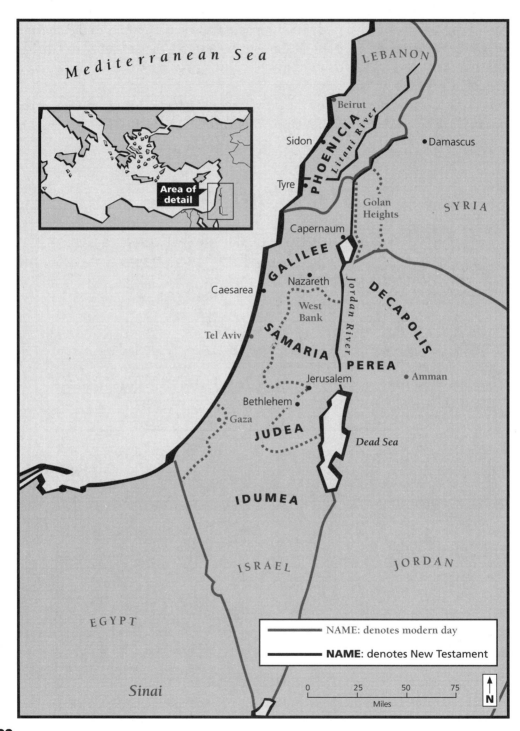

Mediterranean Sea

LEBANON

Beirut

PHOENICIA

Litani River

Sidon

•Damascus

Tyre

SYRIA

Golan
Heights

Capernaum

GALILEE

Nazareth

DECAPOLIS

Caesarea

West
Bank

Jordan River

Tel Aviv

SAMARIA

PEREA

•Amman

Jerusalem

Bethlehem

JUDEA

Dead Sea

•Gaza

IDUMEA

ISRAEL

JORDAN

EGYPT

NAME: denotes modern day

NAME: denotes New Testament

Sinai

| 0 | 25 | 50 | 75 |
Miles

N

Area of
detail

MARK

Mark, the shortest of the four Gospels, tells us more about the actions than the teachings of Jesus. Most of the events recorded also appear in Matthew and Luke, but Mark narrates them with greater detail and vividness. His direct, fast-moving style carries the reader swiftly to the central event of the gospel—Jesus' death and resurrection.

Author

Mark's Gospel, like the other Gospels, is technically anonymous in that the author does not identify himself. However, the clear testimony of the early church fathers is that this book was written by John Mark, whose family figured prominently in the early Jerusalem church (Acts 12:12). Mark was a companion of Paul and Barnabas on their first missionary journey (Acts 12:25; 13:13). Although Paul refused to take Mark on his second journey (Acts 15:37, 38), Mark was later reconciled to Paul (Col. 4:10) and associated with Peter (1 Pet. 5:13).

Date

Many scholars believe that Mark was the first of the four Gospels, but there is uncertainty over its date. Because of the prophecy about the destruction of the temple (13:2), it should be dated before A.D. 70, but early traditions disagree as to whether it was written before or after the martyrdom of Peter (c. A.D. 64). The probable range for this book is A.D. 55–68.

Mark was evidently directed to a Roman readership, and early tradition indicates that it originated in Rome. That may be why Mark omitted a number of items that would not have been meaningful to Gentiles, such as the genealogy of Christ, fulfilled prophecy, references to the Law, and certain Jewish customs found in the other Gospels. Mark also interprets Aramaic words (3:17; 5:41; 7:34; 15:22) and used a number of Latin terms in place of their Greek equivalents (4:21; 6:27, 42; 15:15, 16, 39).

Mark at a Glance

FOCUS	TO SERVE			TO SACRIFICE	
REFERENCE	1:1 ——————— 2:13 ——————— 8:27		——————— 11:1 ——————— 16:1 ——————— 16:20		
DIVISION	PRESENTATION OF THE SERVANT	OPPOSITION TO THE SERVANT	INSTRUCTION BY THE SERVANT	REJECTION OF THE SERVANT	RESURRECTION OF THE SERVANT
TOPIC	SAYINGS AND SIGNS			SUFFERINGS	
	c. 3 YEARS		c. 6 MONTHS	8 DAYS	
LOCATION	GALILEE AND PEREA			JUDEA AND JERUSALEM	
TIME	c. A.D. 29–33				

Nelson's Complete Book of Bible Maps and Charts © 1993 by Thomas Nelson, Inc.

Themes and Literary Structure

 Mark structures his Gospel around various geographical movements of Jesus, which are climaxed by His death and subsequent resurrection. After the introduction, Mark narrates the public ministry of Jesus in Galilee (1:14—8:30), on the way to Judea (8:31—10:52), and in Jerusalem (11:1—13:37), culminating in the passion (14:1—15:47) and the resurrection (ch. 16).

The shortest and simplest of the four Gospels, Mark gives a vivid and fast-moving account of the ministry of Christ. The distinctive word of this book is the Greek term *euthus*, translated "immediately" or "straightway," and it appears more often in this brief Gospel than in the rest of the New Testament books combined. Christ is constantly moving toward a goal that is hidden to almost all.

Mark highlights the power and authority of Jesus, the eternal Son of God, as a teacher (1:22), and over Satan and unclean spirits (1:27; 3:19–30), sin (2:1-12), the Sabbath (2:27, 28; 3:1–6), nature (4:35–41; 6:45–52), disease (5:21-34), death (5:35–43), legalistic tradition (7:1–13, 14–20), and the temple (11:15–18).

Almost forty percent of this Gospel is devoted to a detailed account of the last eight days of Jesus' life, climaxing in His resurrection. In many ways, Mark emphasizes the passion and resurrection as the gauge by which the whole of Jesus' ministry may be measured.

The "Messianic Secret" in Mark

On several occasions in the Gospel of Mark Jesus tells someone not to tell, either who He is or what they have seen that would demonstrate who He is. This is called the Messianic Secret. Why did Jesus want to keep His identity as the Messiah a secret?

- To avoid being considered just a "miracle worker." Note that many of these commands follow miracles. Jesus did not want people to follow Him just to see Him do tricks. He came as the Son of God to bring salvation and forgiveness from sin, not just physical healing and miracles.
- To avoid undue publicity which would hinder His mobility and ministry to His disciples. Note the result of the leper's disobedience in 1:45.
- To avoid the mistaken notion of the type of Messiah He came to be. He came to suffer and serve and sacrifice Himself, not simply to display His power (cf. 10:45).
- To avoid the premature death that increased popularity could bring.

Following His transfiguration, which displayed His glory to the disciples, Jesus tells them not to speak of this event "till the Son of Man had risen from the dead" (9:9). Following His resurrection and vindication, the identity of Messiah and the character of His mission is properly understood in its full scope. After the resurrection, all believers are sent into the world "to tell" (cf. Matt. 28:7, 8, 18–20; Mark 16:7; Luke 24:9, 44–47).

OUTLINE OF MARK

The Roman Empire in New Testament Times

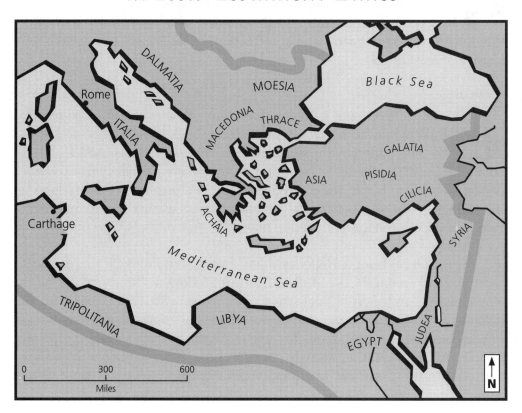

LUKE

T|he first of a two-part work (the second being the book of Acts), the Gospel of Luke is the longest and most literary of the four Gospels. Presenting Jesus' ancestry, birth, and early life before moving carefully through His ministry, death, and resurrection, Luke is also the most comprehensive of the Gospels.

Author

The third Gospel is anonymous, but scholars generally agree that Luke wrote both this Gospel and the book of Acts. The author has been identified by the so-called "we passages" in Acts (Acts 16:10–17; 20:5—21:18; 27:1—28:16). The author of Acts writes primarily from a third-person viewpoint, but in these passages changes abruptly to the first person, indicating that he was personally present and was a traveling companion of Paul. Since Luke is not mentioned in any of the "we passages," he is likely that companion.

Luke may have been a Hellenistic Jew, but it is more likely that he was a Gentile. In Colossians 4:10–14, Paul lists three fellow workers who are "of the circumcision" and then he includes Luke's name with two Gentiles. It has been suggested that Luke may have been a Greek physician to a Roman family (it was common for Greek slaves to serve as physicians) who at some point was set free. Ancient tradition strongly supports Luke as the author of Luke-Acts, and one strand of ancient tradition maintains that Luke was from Syrian Antioch, remained unmarried, and died at the age of eighty-four.

Date

Regarding the date of the composition of Luke, scholarship generally divides into two positions. Those favoring a later date place the writing after A.D. 70 because of their claim that 21:20 indicates that the fall of Jerusalem had already taken place (this position assumes that genuine predictive prophecy is impossible).

Biblical evidence points to A.D. 58–63 as the most likely time of writing.

Continued on page 336

Luke at a Glance

FOCUS	INTRODUCTION OF THE SON OF MAN	MINISTRY OF THE SON OF MAN	REJECTION OF THE SON OF MAN	CRUCIFIXION AND RESUR-RECTION OF THE SON OF MAN
REFERENCE	1:1 ———————— 4:14 ————————— 9:51 ———————— 19:28 ———————— 24:53			
DIVISION	ADVENT	ACTIVITIES	ANTAGONISM AND ADMONITION	APPLICATION AND AUTHENTICATION
TOPIC	SEEKING THE LOST			SAVING THE LOST
	MIRACLES PROMINENT		TEACHING PROMINENT	
LOCATION	ISRAEL	GALILEE	ISRAEL	JERUSALEM
TIME	c. 4 B.C.–A.D. 33			

Nelson's Complete Book of Bible Maps and Charts © 1993 by Thomas Nelson, Inc.

Continued from page 334

Luke was written earlier than Acts, its companion volume, and the last chapter of Acts recounts events that occurred c. A.D. 63 (and probably concludes as it does because the events were contemporary). If Acts was written during Paul's Roman imprisonment (c. A.D. 63), the Gospel of Luke may have been composed during Paul's two-year incarceration in Caesarea, prior to the journey to Rome.

Themes and Literary Structure

 Luke contains much in common with the other Synoptic Gospels—Matthew and Mark—but about half of Luke's material is exclusively his own. In particular, Luke highlights Jesus' final journey from Galilee to Jerusalem. This special section, often called the "travelogue" (9:51—19:27) contains many parables not otherwise recorded.

A distinguishing feature of Luke's Gospel is its emphasis on the universality of the Christian message. Jesus is not just the Jewish Messiah, but the Savior of the whole world (2:32; 24:27). In presenting Jesus as the Savior of all people, Luke pays particular attention to Jesus' ministry to the poor, the outcasts, and to women.

See chart, "New Testament Women," on page 337.

The humanity and compassion of Jesus are repeatedly stressed in Luke's Gospel. Luke gives the most complete account of Christ's ancestry, birth, and development. He is the ideal Son of Man who identified with the sorrow and plight of sinful humanity in order to carry our sorrows and accomplish the work of salvation. Jesus alone fulfills the ideal of human perfection. This perfection is particularly demonstrated in Jesus' response to temptation—where the first Adam failed, Jesus as the second Adam triumphed (4:1–13).

Temptation: The Two Adams Contrasted

Both Adam and Christ faced three aspects of temptation. Adam yielded, bringing upon humankind sin and death. Christ resisted, resulting in justification and life.		
1 John 2:16	**Genesis 3:6** **First Adam**	**Luke 4:1–13** **Second Adam—Christ**
"the lust of the flesh"	"the tree was good for food"	"command this stone to become bread"
"the lust of the eyes"	"it was pleasant to the eyes"	"the devil...showed Him all the kingdoms"
"the pride of life"	"a tree desirable to make one wise"	"throw Yourself down from here"

Continued on page 338

New Testament Women

Mary, the virgin mother of Jesus, has a place of honor among the women of the New Testament. She is an enduring example of faith, humility, and service (Luke 1:26–56).
Other notable women of the New Testament include the following:

Name	Description	Biblical Reference
Anna	Recognized Jesus as the long-awaited Messiah	Luke 2:36–38
Bernice	Sister of Agrippa before whom Paul made his defense	Acts 25:13
Candace	A queen of Ethiopia	Acts 8:27
Chloe	Woman who knew of divisions in the church at Corinth	1 Cor. 1:11
Claudia	Christian of Rome	2 Tim. 4:21
Damaris	Woman of Athens converted under Paul's ministry	Acts 17:34
Dorcas (Tabitha)	Christian in Joppa who was raised from the dead by Peter	Acts 9:36–41
Drusilla	Wife of Felix, governor of Judea	Acts 24:24
Elizabeth	Mother of John the Baptist	Luke 1:5, 13
Eunice	Mother of Timothy	2 Tim. 1:5
Herodias	Queen who demanded the execution of John the Baptist	Matt. 14:3–10
Joanna	Provided for the material needs of Jesus	Luke 8:3
Lois	Grandmother of Timothy	2 Tim. 1:5
Lydia	Converted under Paul's ministry in Philippi	Acts 16:14
Martha and Mary	Sisters of Lazarus; friends of Jesus	Luke 10:38–42
Mary Magdalene	Woman from whom Jesus cast out demons	Matt. 27:56–61; Mark 16:9
Phoebe	A servant, perhaps a deaconess, in the church at Cenchrea	Rom. 16:1, 2
Priscilla	Wife of Aquila; laborer with Paul at Corinth and Ephesus	Acts 18:2, 18, 19
Salome	Mother of Jesus' disciples James and John	Matt. 20:20–24
Sapphira	Held back goods from the early Christian community	Acts 5:1
Susanna	Provided for the material needs of Jesus	Luke 8:3

Nelson's Complete Book of Bible Maps and Charts © 1993 by Thomas Nelson, Inc.

Continued from page 336

This Gospel has more references to prayer than do the other Gospels. Luke especially emphasizes the prayer life of Jesus, recording seven occasions on which Jesus prayed that are not found elsewhere. In addition, this Gospel abounds in notes of praise and thanksgiving.

OUTLINE OF LUKE

Part Four: The Crucifixion and Resurrection
of the Son of Man (19:28—24:53)

The Genealogies of Jesus

Both Matthew and Luke present genealogies of Jesus (Matt. 1:1–17; Luke 3:23–38), though with some differences. Matthew traces Jesus' lineage back to Abraham while Luke reveals the universal nature of His mission by tracing His lineage back to Adam. There are also certain differences in the names; these differences may be explained by one of the following possibilities: (1) The operation of the law of levirate marriage (Deut. 25:5) suggests that one genealogy (either Luke's or Matthew's) gives the legal descent and the other the physical descent; or (2) both Joseph and Mary were descended from David by different branches of the family. Thus it may be that Matthew gives Joseph's descent, which is the legal descent of Jesus, while Luke gives Mary's descent, which is the actual connection of Jesus with the race that He came to save.

See chart, "Genealogy of Jesus," on page 342.

Jesus and the Twelve

Jesus chose twelve apostles to serve with Him during His ministry and to provide leadership for the church after His ascension. Twelve probably were selected because this number corresponds to the twelve tribes of Old Testament Israel.

Chosen by Jesus after He prayed all night (Luke 6:12–16), the Twelve included two sets of fishermen brothers, a tax collector, and a traitor. Among the Twelve, Peter, James, and John were particularly close to the Master.

The terms *disciple* and *apostle* are often used interchangeably in referring to these men. But a disciple is a learner or follower, while an apostle generally refers to a person who is sent with a special message or commission (John 13:16). The Twelve were definitely apostles; when Jesus called them, He had a specific mission in mind for them—to carry on His work after He ended His earthly ministry.

The original Twelve were chosen from among those people whom Jesus knew personally (Acts 1:21, 22). They had an inadequate understanding of Jesus' mission and the necessity for His death (Matt. 15:16). Jesus was patient with the immature apostles, although He occasionally rebuked them (Luke 9:55). After they were empowered by the Holy Spirit at Pentecost, the apostles were filled with new boldness and understanding. They became powerful witnesses in Jerusalem and surrounding regions, in spite of harsh persecution. Many were martyred for their faith.

As listed in Matthew 10:1–4 (also see Mark 3:13–19; Luke 6:12–16; Acts 1:13), the Twelve were: (1) Simon Peter (Cephas), leader of the apostles; (2) Andrew, brother of Simon; (3) James, son of Zebedee and brother of John;

Continued on page 343

Genealogy of Jesus

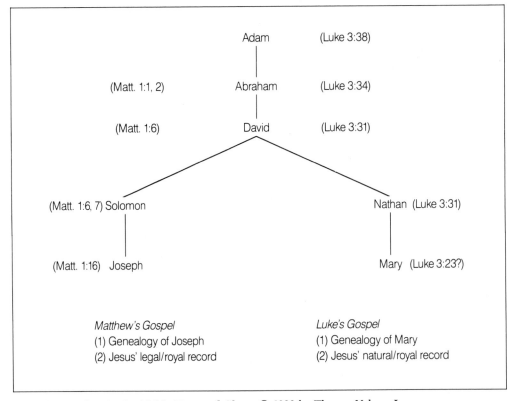

Adam   (Luke 3:38)

(Matt. 1:1, 2)   Abraham   (Luke 3:34)

(Matt. 1:6)   David   (Luke 3:31)

(Matt. 1:6, 7) Solomon   Nathan (Luke 3:31)

(Matt. 1:16)   Joseph   Mary (Luke 3:23?)

Matthew's Gospel
(1) Genealogy of Joseph
(2) Jesus' legal/royal record

Luke's Gospel
(1) Genealogy of Mary
(2) Jesus' natural/royal record

Continued from page 341

(4) John, the beloved apostle; (5) Philip, from Bethsaida; (6) Bartholomew (probably Nathanael), from Cana of Galilee; (7) Matthew (Levi), tax collector; (8) Thomas (Didymus, which means "Twin"), from Galilee; (9) Simon the Canaanite, probably Simon the Zealot, from Galilee; (10) James, the son of Alphaeus; (11) Lebbaeus, or Thaddaeus; and (12) Judas Iscariot, who betrayed Jesus.

Matthias was chosen by the apostles to replace Judas after the ascension of Jesus (Acts 1:26).

See chart, "The Twelve Apostles," on page 344.

The Twelve Apostles

Matthew 10:2–4	Mark 3:16–19	Luke 6:14–16	Acts 1:13
Simon Peter	Simon Peter	Simon Peter	Simon Peter
Andrew	James	Andrew	John
James	John	James	James
John	Andrew	John	Andrew
Philip	Philip	Philip	Philip
Bartholomew	Bartholomew	Bartholomew	Thomas
Thomas	Matthew	Matthew	Bartholomew
Matthew	Thomas	Thomas	Matthew
James	James	James	James
(of Alphaeus)	(of Alphaeus)	(of Alphaeus)	(of Alphaeus)
Thaddaeus[1]	Thaddaeus	Simon (the Zealot)	Simon (the Zealot)
Simon	Simon	Judas	Judas
(the Cananite)[2]	(the Cananite)	(of James)	(of James)
Judas Iscariot	Judas Iscariot	Judas Iscariot	....

Matthew and Mark have the name Thaddaeus while Luke, in his two lists (Luke 6 and Acts 1), has Judas (of James). Some think Judas may have been his original name and that it was changed later to Thaddaeus (meaning perhaps "warm-hearted") in order to avoid the stigma attached to the name Judas Iscariot.

"The Cananite" is a transliteration which probably represents an Aramaic word meaning "Zealous."

It is interesting that all four lists begin with Simon Peter and end with Judas Iscariot (except the Acts 1 list, for Judas had already killed himself). Also, the names would appear to be in groups of four. Peter, Andrew, James, and John are always in the first group—though not always in that order—and Philip, Bartholomew, Thomas, and Matthew are in the second group in all four lists.

In all four lists, Peter's name heads the first group, Philip heads the second, and James (of Alphaeus) heads the third. John's Gospel does not contain a listing of the apostles.

Nelson's Complete Book of Bible Maps and Charts © 1993 by Thomas Nelson, Inc.

JOHN

The Gospel of John has long held a place of high honor and devotion among Christians. The profundity of its message—focusing on the mystery of the Person of Christ and the incarnation, His relationship to the Father, and the importance of belief in Christ—together with the relative simplicity of its construction makes it frequently the first portion of Scripture to be translated into another language.

Author

While the Gospel of John does not specifically designate its author, many factors support the long-held belief that he was John the apostle, the brother of James and son of Zebedee. According to 20:21, 24, this Gospel was written by "the disciple whom Jesus loved," and, of the inner circle of Jesus' disciples (Peter, James, and John), John is the only probable candidate. That the author was a Palestinian Jew and an eyewitness of the events he describes also supports Johannine authorship.

Early written sources and persistent tradition about the apostle John point to Ephesus as the most likely place for the origin of the Gospel. John is believed to have lived and worked in the area of Ephesus for many years, and a tomb discovered there is reputed to be his. In addition, several key terms and ideas contained in the Gospel would have been especially fitting for this area of Asia Minor.

Date

The church father Irenaeus explicitly testifies that John wrote the Gospel while residing in Ephesus (A.D. 66–98), and there is little reason to challenge a date within this period. Although some scholars in the past have argued that John's Gospel was composed during the middle of the second century A.D., the discovery in Egypt of a papyrus fragment of the Gospel of John dating to c. A.D. 125 makes a first-century date almost certain.

John at a Glance

FOCUS	INCARNATION OF THE SON OF GOD	PRESENTATION OF THE SON OF GOD	OPPOSITION TO THE SON OF GOD	PREPARATION OF THE DISCIPLES	CRUCIFIXION AND RESURRECTION OF THE SON OF GOD
REFERENCE	1:1 ———— 1:19 ———— 5:1 ———— 13:1 ———— 18:1 ———— 21:25				
DIVISION	INTRODUCTION TO CHRIST	REVELATION OF CHRIST	REJECTION OF CHRIST	REVELATION OF CHRIST	REJECTION OF CHRIST
TOPIC	SEVEN MIRACLES			UPPER ROOM DISCOURSE	SUPREME MIRACLE
	THAT YOU MIGHT BELIEVE			THAT YOU MIGHT HAVE LIFE	
LOCATION	ISRAEL				
TIME	A FEW YEARS			A FEW HOURS	A FEW WEEKS

Nelson's Complete Book of Bible Maps and Charts © 1993 by Thomas Nelson, Inc.

Themes and Literary Structure

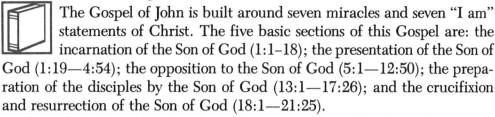 The Gospel of John is built around seven miracles and seven "I am" statements of Christ. The five basic sections of this Gospel are: the incarnation of the Son of God (1:1–18); the presentation of the Son of God (1:19—4:54); the opposition to the Son of God (5:1—12:50); the preparation of the disciples by the Son of God (13:1—17:26); and the crucifixion and resurrection of the Son of God (18:1—21:25).

That John's Gospel is significantly different from the Synoptic Gospels (Matthew, Mark, and Luke) has been noticed from the earliest days of church history. It is probable that John wrote after the Synoptics had been completed, and that he was aware of them. That being the case, John wrote to supplement the Synoptics and to provide a theological interpretation of the Person and work of Christ especially suited for his Hellenistic audience.

Unlike the Synoptics, which present Jesus' teaching in the form of short sayings and parables, John presents Jesus' teaching in the form of longer theological discourses: the discourse on the bread of life (6:41–59), the good shepherd and His sheep (10:1–30), the vine and the branches (15:1–8), and the priestly prayer (17:1–26). In these discourses, contrasting pairs of ideas are frequently utilized, such as light/darkness, belief/unbelief, love/hate, and earthly/heavenly. In contrast to the Synoptic Gospels' focus upon the Galilean ministry, John emphasizes events in Judea and he records three or four Passover visits by Jesus to Jerusalem.

Although the Synoptics are full of the raw material for Christological doctrine, John displays a more intense conviction of the centrality of the Person of Christ. For John, the activity of Christ is not understandable apart from the fact that He is the Messiah, the Son of God, and God Himself (1:1–18). This emphasis upon the Person of Jesus is highlighted by John's inclusion of seven "I am" sayings.

The "I AM" Statements

Twenty-three times in all we find our Lord's meaningful "I AM" (*ego eimi*, Gk.) in the Greek text of this Gospel (4:26; 6:20, 35, 41, 48, 51; 8:12, 18, 24, 28, 58; 10:7, 9, 11, 14; 11:25; 13:19; 14:6; 15:1, 5; 18:5, 6, 8). In several of these He joins His "I AM" with seven tremendous metaphors which are expressive of His saving relationship toward the world.

"I AM the Bread of life" (6:35, 41, 48, 51).
"I AM the Light of the world" (8:12).
"I AM the Door of the sheep" (10:7, 9).
"I AM the Good Shepherd" (10:11, 14).
"I AM the Resurrection and the Life" (11:25).
"I AM the Way, the Truth, the Life" (14:6).
"I AM the true Vine" (15:1, 5).

Also, in stressing the work of Father, Son, and Holy Spirit in accomplishing salvation, John's Gospel presents components of the Christian doctrine of the Trinity (e.g., 16:13–15).

OUTLINE OF JOHN

Titles of Christ

In addition to the "I am" sayings of Jesus, the Gospel of John also provides us with a number of beloved titles of Christ such as "Bread of Life," "The Good Shepherd," "Lamb of God," and "Light of the World."

See chart, "Titles of Christ," on page 351.

See also map, "Galilean Ministry," on page 321.

Titles of Christ

The two most popular titles or names Christians use in speaking of our Lord are *Jesus*, a translation of the Hebrew word *Joshua*, which means "YAHWEH Is Salvation," and *Christ*, a transliteration of the Greek term *Christos*, meaning "Anointed One" or "Messiah." Following are some other significant names or titles for Christ used in the New Testament. Each title expresses a distinct truth about Jesus and His relationship to believers.

Name or Title	Significance	Biblical Reference
Adam, Last Adam	First of the new race of the redeemed	1 Cor. 15:45
Alpha and Omega	The beginning and ending of all things	Rev. 21:6
Bread of Life	The one essential food	John 6:35
Chief Cornerstone	A sure foundation for life	Eph. 2:20
Chief Shepherd	Protector, sustainer, and guide	1 Pet. 5:4
Firstborn from the Dead	Leads us into resurrection and eternal life	Col. 1:18
Good Shepherd	Provider and caretaker	John 10:11
Great Shepherd of the Sheep	Trustworthy guide and protector	Heb. 13:20
High Priest	A perfect sacrifice for our sins	Heb. 3:1
Holy One of God	Sinless in His nature	Mark 1:24
Immanuel (God With Us)	Stands with us in all of life's circumstances	Matt. 1:23
King of Kings, Lord of Lords	The Almighty, before whom every knee will bow	Rev. 19:16
Lamb of God	Gave His life as a sacrifice on our behalf	John 1:29
Light of the World	Brings hope in the midst of darkness	John 9:5
Lord of Glory	The power and presence of the living God	1 Cor. 2:8
Mediator between God and Men	Brings us into God's presence redeemed and forgiven	1 Tim. 2:5
Only Begotten of the Father	The unique, one-of-a-kind Son of God	John 1:14
Prophet	Faithful proclaimer of the truths of God	Acts 3:22
Savior	Delivers from sin and death	Luke 1:47
Seed of Abraham	Mediator of God's covenant	Gal. 3:16
Son of Man	Identifies with us in our humanity	Matt. 18:11
The Word	Present with God at the creation	John 1:1

Nelson's Complete Book of Bible Maps and Charts © 1993 by Thomas Nelson, Inc.

Events in Christ's Ministry

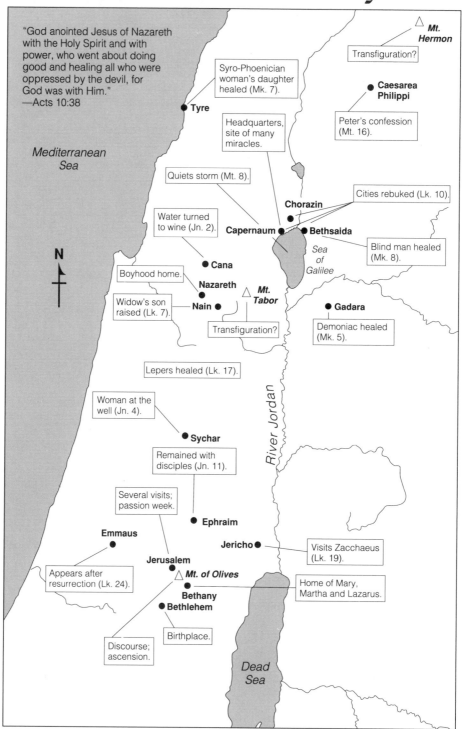

"God anointed Jesus of Nazareth with the Holy Spirit and with power, who went about doing good and healing all who were oppressed by the devil, for God was with Him."
—Acts 10:38

△ **Mt. Hermon**

Transfiguration?

● **Caesarea Philippi**

Peter's confession (Mt. 16).

Syro-Phoenician woman's daughter healed (Mk. 7).

● **Tyre**

Mediterranean Sea

Headquarters, site of many miracles.

Quiets storm (Mt. 8).

Cities rebuked (Lk. 10).

Chorazin

Water turned to wine (Jn. 2).

Capernaum ● ● **Bethsaida**

Blind man healed (Mk. 8).

Sea of Galilee

N

● **Cana**

Boyhood home.

Nazareth

△ *Mt. Tabor*

Widow's son raised (Lk. 7). **Nain** ●

Transfiguration?

● **Gadara**

Demoniac healed (Mk. 5).

Lepers healed (Lk. 17).

Woman at the well (Jn. 4).

● **Sychar**

Remained with disciples (Jn. 11).

River Jordan

Several visits; passion week.

● **Ephraim**

Emmaus

Jericho ●

Visits Zacchaeus (Lk. 19).

Appears after resurrection (Lk. 24).

Jerusalem

△ *Mt. of Olives*

Home of Mary, Martha and Lazarus.

Bethany
● **Bethlehem**

Discourse; ascension.

Birthplace.

Dead Sea

High Priestly Prayer

The longest recorded prayer of Jesus, called the "High Priestly Prayer," is found in John 17:1-26. After voicing a triumphant declaration of victory in 16:33 ("I have overcome the world"), Jesus proceeds to pray for Himself, for His disciples, and for future believers. Facing His hour of deepest travail, Jesus looks forward to the blessed results of His victory over sin and death—the gathering of the redeemed, and the love and unity that God and the redeemed will share (17:20–26).

Jesus Prays		
(1) For Himself: (vv. 1–5)	(2) For His disciples: (vv. 6–19)	(3) For future believers: (vv. 20–26)
He affirms the glory of the Cross (vv. 1, 2)	He prays for their knowledge (vv. 6–9)	He prays for their oneness (vv. 20–22)
He expresses the very essence of eternal life (vv. 3, 4)	He prays for their perseverance (vv. 10–12)	He prays for their perfect unity (v. 23)
He rejoices in the shared glory of the Father (v. 5)	He prays for their joy (v. 13)	He prays for their future presence with Him (vv. 24, 25)
	He prays for their sanctification (vv. 14–17)	He prays for their mutual love (v. 26)
	He prays for their mission (vv. 18, 19)	

The Death of Jesus

John's Gospel presents Jesus' death as the fulfillment of Old Testament prophecy (e.g., 18:8, 9) and as an event appointed by His Father (18:11). In this

	Aspect of Jesus' Death	Old Testament Reference
The Jews viewed Jesus' death as a scandal. The church understood His death as fulfillment of Old Testament prophecy.	In obedience to His Father (18:11)	Psalm 40:8
	Announced by Himself (18:32; see 3:14)	Numbers 21:8, 9
	In the place of His people (18:14)	Isaiah 53:4–6
	With evildoers (19:18)	Isaiah 53:12
	In innocence (19:6)	Isaiah 53:9
	Crucified (19:18)	Psalm 22:16
	Buried in a rich man's tomb (19:38–42)	Isaiah 53:9

Gospel, Jesus also characteristically refers to His death, resurrection, and ascension as a unit, using the term *glorify* (e.g., 17:1–5). The Father glorified the Son by sustaining Him through His death and resurrecting Him to life; the Son glorified the Father by willingly offering Himself for our salvation.

Resurrection Appearances

The Gospel of John records details of several postresurrection appearances of the Lord not found, or only briefly alluded to, in the Synoptic Gospels. These include the appearance to the doubting disciple Thomas (20:24), the appearance to the disciples at the Sea of Galilee (21:1–14), and the restoration of Peter (21:15–23).

See map, "The Resurrection," on page 355.
See also map, "The Resurrection," on page 325.

Important Events in a Tiny Place

Though probably written in the great city of Ephesus in the province of Asia Minor, across the Aegean Sea from Greece, the Gospel of John is set exclusively in the seemingly insignificant area of faraway Palestine. Nevertheless, John shows that the events described in the book are of universal significance, and he writes in order that those who read his work "may believe that Jesus is the Christ" and that they "may have life in His name" (20:31).

See map, "Palestine," on page 356.

The Signs and Their Meanings

Turns water into wine (John 2:1–12)	Jesus is the source of life.
Heals a nobleman's son (John 4:46–54)	Jesus is master over distance.
Heals a lame man at the pool of Bethesda (John 5:1–17)	Jesus is master over time.
Feeds 5,000 (John 6:1–14)	Jesus is the bread of life.
Walks on water, stills a storm (John 6:15–21)	Jesus is master over nature.
Heals a man blind from birth (John 9:1–41)	Jesus is the light of the world.
Raises Lazarus from the dead (John 11:17–45)	Jesus has power over death.

The Resurrection

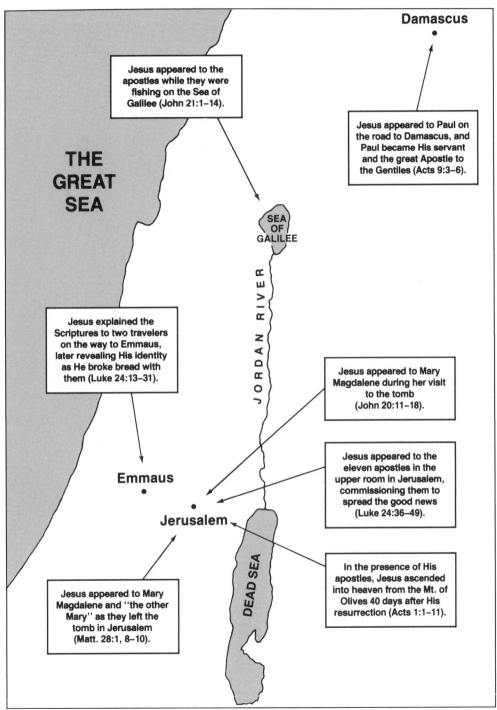

Jesus appeared to the apostles while they were fishing on the Sea of Galilee (John 21:1–14).

Damascus

Jesus appeared to Paul on the road to Damascus, and Paul became His servant and the great Apostle to the Gentiles (Acts 9:3–6).

THE GREAT SEA

SEA OF GALILEE

JORDAN RIVER

Jesus explained the Scriptures to two travelers on the way to Emmaus, later revealing His identity as He broke bread with them (Luke 24:13–31).

Jesus appeared to Mary Magdalene during her visit to the tomb (John 20:11–18).

Jesus appeared to the eleven apostles in the upper room in Jerusalem, commissioning them to spread the good news (Luke 24:36–49).

Emmaus

Jerusalem

DEAD SEA

In the presence of His apostles, Jesus ascended into heaven from the Mt. of Olives 40 days after His resurrection (Acts 1:1–11).

Jesus appeared to Mary Magdalene and "the other Mary" as they left the tomb in Jerusalem (Matt. 28:1, 8–10).

Nelson's Complete Book of Bible Maps and Charts © 1993 by Thomas Nelson, Inc.

Palestine

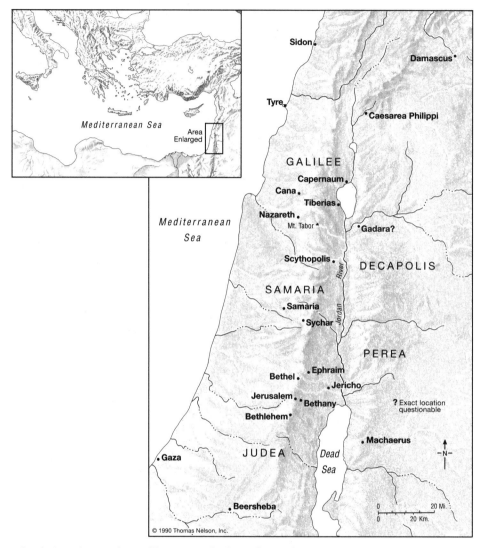

Nelson's Complete Book of Bible Maps and Charts © 1993 by Thomas Nelson, Inc.

ACTS

Jesus' last recorded words have come to be known as the Great Commission: "You shall be witnesses to Me in Jerusalem, and in all Judea and Samaria, and to the end of the earth" (1:8). The book of Acts is the story of the men and women who took that commission seriously and began to spread the gospel of Christ to the most remote corners of the known world.

Author

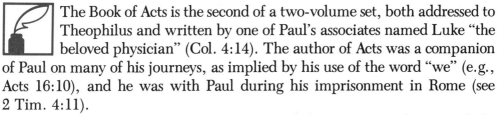

The Book of Acts is the second of a two-volume set, both addressed to Theophilus and written by one of Paul's associates named Luke "the beloved physician" (Col. 4:14). The author of Acts was a companion of Paul on many of his journeys, as implied by his use of the word "we" (e.g., Acts 16:10), and he was with Paul during his imprisonment in Rome (see 2 Tim. 4:11).

Luke 1:3, 4 offers a clue to the author's purpose: to provide "an orderly account . . . that you may know the certainty of those things in which you were instructed." Luke was a researcher and chronicler of events for the benefit of his friend Theophilus and for the general reader.

Date

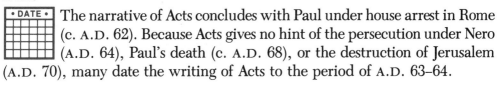

The narrative of Acts concludes with Paul under house arrest in Rome (c. A.D. 62). Because Acts gives no hint of the persecution under Nero (A.D. 64), Paul's death (c. A.D. 68), or the destruction of Jerusalem (A.D. 70), many date the writing of Acts to the period of A.D. 63–64.

Themes and Literary Structure

Each section of the book (chs. 1—7; 8—12; 13—28) focuses on a particular audience, a key personality, and a significant phase in the expansion of the gospel message.

The resurrected Christ is the central theme of the sermons and defenses in Acts. The Old Testament Scriptures, the historical resurrection, the apostolic testimony, and the convicting power of the Holy Spirit all bear witness that

Continued on page 359

Acts at a Glance

FOCUS	WITNESS IN JERUSALEM		WITNESS IN JUDEA AND SAMARIA	WITNESS TO THE END OF THE EARTH	
REFERENCE	1:1 ———————— 3:1 ————————		8:5 ————————————	13:1 —————————— 21:17 — 28:31	
DIVISION	POWER OF THE CHURCH	PROGRESS OF THE CHURCH	EXPANSION OF THE CHURCH	PAUL'S THREE JOURNEYS	PAUL'S TRIALS
TOPIC	JEWS		SAMARITANS	GENTILES	
	PETER		PHILIP	PAUL	
LOCATION	JERUSALEM		JUDEA AND SAMARIA	UTTERMOST PART	
TIME	2 YEARS (A.D. 33–35)		13 YEARS (A.D. 35–48)	14 YEARS (A.D. 48–62)	

Nelson's Complete Book of Bible Maps and Charts © 1993 by Thomas Nelson, Inc.

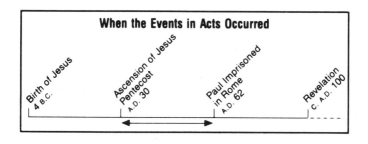

When the Events in Acts Occurred

Birth of Jesus 4 B.C.

Ascension of Jesus Pentecost A.D. 30

Paul Imprisoned in Rome A.D. 62

Revelation c. A.D. 100

Continued from page 357

Jesus is both Lord and Christ (2:22–36; 10:34–43) and the only way of salvation (4:12).

The growth of the church is highlighted in Acts. While there are four accounts of the life of Jesus, this is the only book that carries on the story from His ascension to the period of the New Testament epistles. Thus, Acts is the historical link between the Gospels and the epistles and was written to trace the development of the body of Christ over the one-generation transition from a primarily Jewish to a predominantly gentile membership. This apologetic work presents Christianity as distinct from Judaism but also as its fulfillment.

Throughout the book, there is emphasis on the activity of the Holy Spirit and the power of Jesus' resurrection. Because of Luke's strong emphasis on the ministry of the Holy Spirit, this book could be regarded as "the Acts of the Spirit of Christ working in and through the Apostles."

OUTLINE OF ACTS

The Nations of Pentecost

Pentecost, a Jewish feast also known as the Feast of Weeks, marked the completion of the barley harvest. On this annual holiday about 50 days after the resurrection of Jesus, Jewish people from throughout the Roman Empire were gathered in the city of Jerusalem to observe this great religious holiday. When the Holy Spirit was poured out on the apostles, they began to speak with "other tongues," and these people from other nations understood them perfectly (Acts 2:5–13). This map shows the different regions of the Roman Empire represented in Jerusalem on the Day of Pentecost.

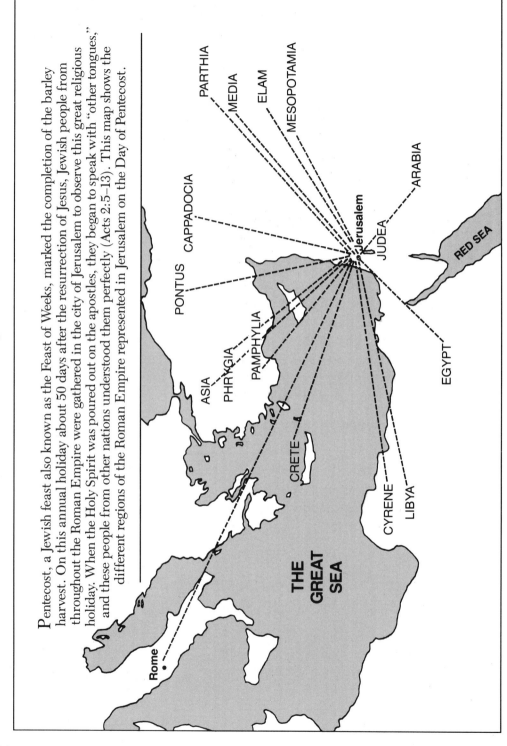

Nelson's Complete Book of Bible Maps and Charts © 1993 by Thomas Nelson, Inc.

Major Sermons in Acts

Several important sermons and speeches are recorded in the Book of Acts. Over twenty are included, with the majority coming from Peter (7 total) and Paul (11 total). Below are listed the more significant, together with the theme and text location.

Speech	Theme	Biblical Reference
Peter to crowds at Pentecost	Peter's explanation of the meaning of Pentecost	Acts 2:14–40
Peter to crowds at the temple	The Jewish people should repent for crucifying the Messiah	Acts 3:12–26
Peter to the Sanhedrin	Testimony that a helpless man was healed by the power of Jesus	Acts 4:5–12
Stephen to the Sanhedrin	Stephen's rehearsal of Jewish history, accusing the Jews of killing the Messiah	Acts 7
Peter to Gentiles	Gentiles can be saved in the same manner as Jews	Acts 10:28–47
Peter to church at Jerusalem	Peter's testimony of his experiences at Joppa and a defense of his ministry to the Gentiles	Acts 11:4–18
Paul to synagogue at Antioch	Jesus was the Messiah in fulfillment of Old Testament prophecies	Acts 13:16–41
Peter to Jerusalem council	Salvation by grace available to all	Acts 15:7–11
James to Jerusalem council	Gentile converts do not require circumcision	Acts 15:13–21
Paul to Ephesian elders	Remain faithful in spite of false teachers and persecution	Acts 20:17–35
Paul to crowd at Jerusalem	Paul's statement of his conversion and his mission to the Gentiles	Acts 22:1–21
Paul to Sanhedrin	Paul's defense, declaring himself a Pharisee and a Roman citizen	Acts 23:1–6
Paul to King Agrippa	Paul's statement of his conversion and his zeal for the gospel	Acts 26
Paul to Jewish leaders at Rome	Paul's statement about his Jewish heritage	Acts 28:17–20

Philip's Travels

Philip was the second of the seven deacons appointed in 6:5, 6. Two journeys by Philip are recorded in 8:5–13 and 8:26–40. During his first, the city of Samaria was evangelized with great success. On the second, he preached to the Ethiopian eunuch on the road to Gaza before continuing on from Azotus to Caesarea.

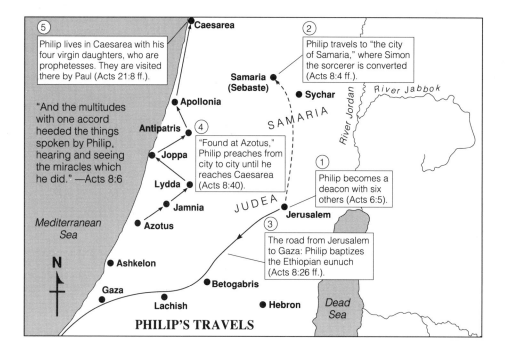

Caesarea
⑤ Philip lives in Caesarea with his four virgin daughters, who are prophetesses. They are visited there by Paul (Acts 21:8 ff.).

② Philip travels to "the city of Samaria," where Simon the sorcerer is converted (Acts 8:4 ff.).

Samaria (Sebaste)

Sychar

River Jordan

River Jabbok

SAMARIA

Apollonia

"And the multitudes with one accord heeded the things spoken by Philip, hearing and seeing the miracles which he did." —Acts 8:6

Antipatris

④ "Found at Azotus," Philip preaches from city to city until he reaches Caesarea (Acts 8:40).

Joppa

Lydda

① Philip becomes a deacon with six others (Acts 6:5).

Jamnia

JUDEA

Mediterranean Sea

Azotus

Jerusalem

N

③ The road from Jerusalem to Gaza: Philip baptizes the Ethiopian eunuch (Acts 8:26 ff.).

Ashkelon

Betogabris

Gaza

Lachish

Hebron

Dead Sea

PHILIP'S TRAVELS

Peter's Travels

The first twelve chapters of Acts are largely concerned with the apostle Peter. The early leader of the Jewish-Christian church in Jerusalem, Peter was also instrumental in the extension of the gospel message to the Gentiles through his response to the vision of the clean and unclean animals in chapter 10.

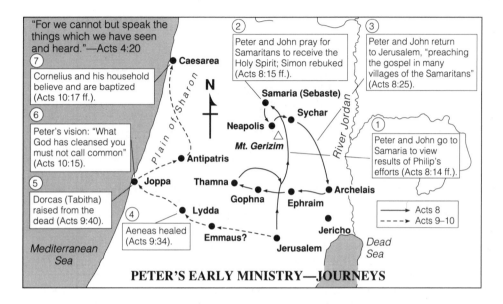

"For we cannot but speak the things which we have seen and heard."—Acts 4:20

⑦ Cornelius and his household believe and are baptized (Acts 10:17 ff.).

⑥ Peter's vision: "What God has cleansed you must not call common" (Acts 10:15).

⑤ Dorcas (Tabitha) raised from the dead (Acts 9:40).

④ Aeneas healed (Acts 9:34).

② Peter and John pray for Samaritans to receive the Holy Spirit; Simon rebuked (Acts 8:15 ff.).

③ Peter and John return to Jerusalem, "preaching the gospel in many villages of the Samaritans" (Acts 8:25).

① Peter and John go to Samaria to view results of Philip's efforts (Acts 8:14 ff.).

Caesarea
Plain of Sharon
N
Samaria (Sebaste)
Sychar
Neapolis
Mt. Gerizim
River Jordan
Antipatris
Joppa
Thamna
Gophna
Ephraim
Archelais
Lydda
Emmaus?
Jericho
Jerusalem
Mediterranean Sea
Dead Sea

→ Acts 8
---→ Acts 9–10

PETER'S EARLY MINISTRY—JOURNEYS

Dreams and Visions

In New Testament times, God often used dreams (when a person was asleep) and visions (when a person was awake) to make His will known. Particularly in the book of Acts, church leaders such as Peter and Paul received guidance through visions for future ministry.

Personality	Message of Dream	Biblical Reference
Joseph	Three separate dreams: (1) assured of Mary's purity (2) warned to flee to Egypt (3) told to return to Nazareth	Matt. 1:20 Matt. 2:13 Matt. 2:19–23
Wise men	Warned of Herod's plot against the baby Jesus	Matt. 2:12
VISIONS		
Personality	Message of Vision	Biblical Reference
Paul	Converted to Christianity in a blinding vision of Christ on the Damascus road	Acts 9:3–9
Ananias	Instructed to minister to Saul in Damascus	Acts 9:10–16
Cornelius	Instructed to ask Peter to come to Joppa	Acts 10:3–6
Peter	Told to eat unclean animals—a message to accept the Gentiles	Acts 10:9–18, 28
Paul	Beckoned to do missionary work in the province of Macedonia	Acts 16:9
Paul	Assured of God's presence in Corinth	Acts 18:9, 10
Paul	Promised God's presence during his trip to Rome	Acts 23:11
Paul	Viewed the glories of the third heaven	2 Cor. 12:1–4
John	Received series of visions of future	Rev. 4:1—22:11

Peter and Paul Compared

In Acts 12:25, Luke's literary attention turns from Peter to Paul, and from the predominantly Jewish-Christian church to the Gentile-Christian church. Paul's status and role as a true Apostle is highlighted by the parallels between his ministry and Peter's. See chart, "The Life of Paul," on page 368.

Peter	Paul
Heals a man lame from birth (3:1–11)	Heals a man lame from birth (14:8–18)
Heals people by his shadow (3:15, 16)	Heals people by handkerchiefs or aprons (19:11, 12)
Success is a cause for Jewish jealousy (5:17)	Success is a cause for Jewish jealousy (13:45)
Confronts Simon, a sorcerer (8:9–24)	Confronts Bar-Jesus, a sorcerer (13:6–11)
Raises Tabitha (Dorcas) to life (9:36–41)	Raises Eutychus to life (20:9–12)
Is jailed and freed miraculously by God (12:3–19)	Is jailed and freed miraculously by God (16:25–34)

Paul's Ministry

The second half of Acts is devoted almost exclusively to the ministry of the apostle Paul. Formerly a persecutor of the church, Saul, soon to be renamed Paul, was converted by a vision of the risen Christ on the road to Damascus (9:1–19). During the course of the three missionary journeys and the journey to captivity in Rome covered in Acts, Paul took the message of the gospel throughout much of the Roman Empire and even to its very heart—the city of Rome itself. See chart, "The Career of the Apostle Paul," on page 369.

The Life of Paul

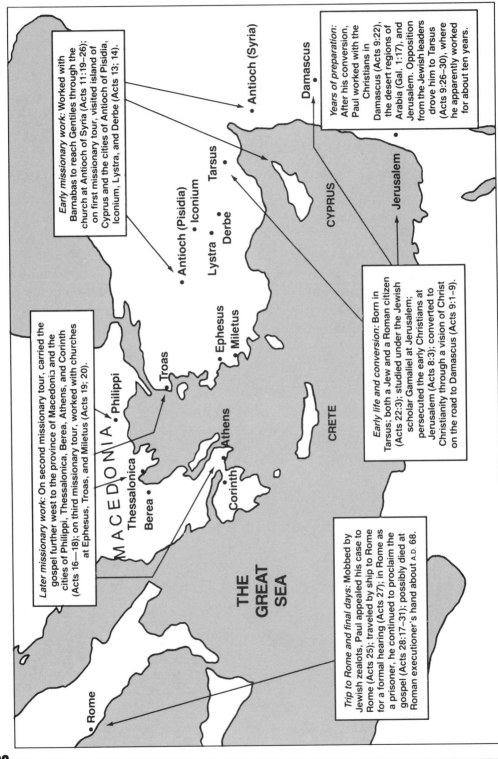

Early missionary work: Worked with Barnabas to reach Gentiles through the church at Antioch of Syria (Acts 11:19–26); on first missionary tour, visited island of Cyprus and the cities of Antioch of Pisidia, Iconium, Lystra, and Derbe (Acts 13: 14).

Years of preparation: After his conversion, Paul worked with the Christians in Damascus (Acts 9:22), the desert regions of Arabia (Gal. 1:17); and Jerusalem. Opposition from the Jewish leaders drove him to Tarsus (Acts 9:26–30), where he apparently worked for about ten years.

Early life and conversion: Born in Tarsus; both a Jew and a Roman citizen (Acts 22:3); studied under the Jewish scholar Gamaliel at Jerusalem; persecuted the early Christians at Jerusalem (Acts 8:3); converted to Christianity through a vision of Christ on the road to Damascus (Acts 9:1–9).

Later missionary work: On second missionary tour, carried the gospel further west to the province of Macedonia and the cities of Philippi, Thessalonica, Berea, Athens, and Corinth (Acts 16—18); on third missionary tour, worked with churches at Ephesus, Troas, and Miletus (Acts 19; 20).

Trip to Rome and final days: Mobbed by Jewish zealots, Paul appealed his case to Rome (Acts 25); traveled by ship to Rome for a formal hearing (Acts 27); in Rome as a prisoner, he continued to proclaim the gospel (Acts 28:17–31); possibly died at Roman executioner's hand about A.D. 68.

Antioch (Syria)

Damascus

Tarsus

Antioch (Pisidia)
Iconium
Lystra
Derbe

CYPRUS

Jerusalem

MACEDONIA Philippi

Troas

Thessalonica
Berea

Ephesus
Miletus

Athens

Corinth

CRETE

THE GREAT SEA

Rome

Nelson's Complete Book of Bible Maps and Charts © 1993 by Thomas Nelson, Inc.

The Career of the Apostle Paul

Origin:	Tarsus in Cilicia (Acts 22:3) Tribe of Benjamin (Phil. 3:5)
Training:	Learned tentmaking (Acts 18:3) Studied under Gamaliel (Acts 22:3)
Early Religion:	Hebrew and Pharisee (Phil. 3:5) Persecuted Christians (Acts 8:1–3; Phil. 3:6)
Salvation:	Met the risen Christ on the road to Damascus (Acts 9:1–8) Received the infilling of the Holy Spirit on the street called Straight (Acts 9:17)
Called to Missions:	Church at Antioch was instructed by the Holy Spirit to send out Paul to the work (Acts 13:1–3) Carried the gospel to the Gentiles (Gal. 2:7–10)
Roles:	Spoke up for the church at Antioch at the council of Jerusalem (Acts 15:1–35) Opposed Peter (Gal. 2:11–21) Disputed with Barnabas about John Mark (Acts 15:36–41)
Achievements:	Three extended missionary journeys (Acts 13—20) Founded numerous churches in Asia Minor, Greece, and possibly Spain (Rom. 15:24, 28) Wrote letters to numerous churches and various individuals which now make up one-fourth of our New Testament
End of Life:	Following arrest in Jerusalem, was sent to Rome (Acts 21:27; 28:16–31) According to Christian tradition, released from prison allowing further missionary work in Macedonia; rearrested, imprisoned again in Rome, and beheaded outside of the city

Nelson's Complete Book of Bible Maps and Charts © 1993 by Thomas Nelson, Inc.

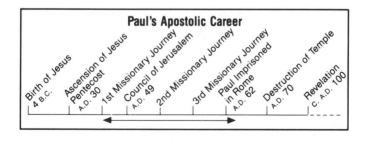

Paul's First and Second Journeys

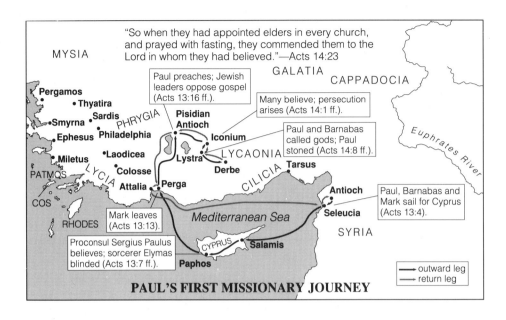

PAUL'S FIRST MISSIONARY JOURNEY

"So when they had appointed elders in every church, and prayed with fasting, they commended them to the Lord in whom they had believed."—Acts 14:23

Paul preaches; Jewish leaders oppose gospel (Acts 13:16 ff.).

Many believe; persecution arises (Acts 14:1 ff.).

Paul and Barnabas called gods; Paul stoned (Acts 14:8 ff.).

Paul, Barnabas and Mark sail for Cyprus (Acts 13:4).

Mark leaves (Acts 13:13).

Proconsul Sergius Paulus believes; sorcerer Elymas blinded (Acts 13:7 ff.).

MYSIA · GALATIA · CAPPADOCIA · Euphrates River · Pergamos · Thyatira · Smyrna · Sardis · PHRYGIA · Philadelphia · Ephesus · Laodicea · Miletus · Colosse · PATMOS · LYCIA · Pisidian Antioch · Iconium · Lystra · LYCAONIA · Derbe · Tarsus · CILICIA · Antioch · Seleucia · SYRIA · Attalia · Perga · Mediterranean Sea · COS · RHODES · CYPRUS · Salamis · Paphos

— outward leg
— return leg

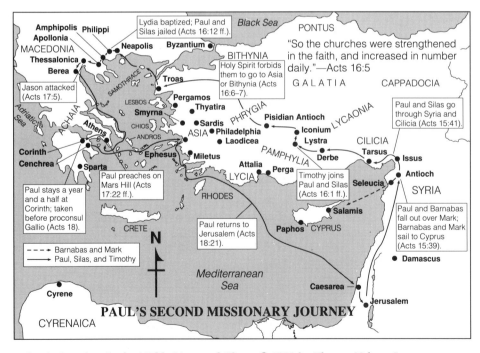

PAUL'S SECOND MISSIONARY JOURNEY

Lydia baptized; Paul and Silas jailed (Acts 16:12 ff.).

"So the churches were strengthened in the faith, and increased in number daily."—Acts 16:5

Holy Spirit forbids them to go to Asia or Bithynia (Acts 16:6–7).

Jason attacked (Acts 17:5).

Paul and Silas go through Syria and Cilicia (Acts 15:41).

Paul preaches on Mars Hill (Acts 17:22 ff.).

Paul stays a year and a half at Corinth; taken before proconsul Gallio (Acts 18).

Timothy joins Paul and Silas (Acts 16:1 ff.).

Paul returns to Jerusalem (Acts 18:21).

Paul and Barnabas fall out over Mark; Barnabas and Mark sail to Cyprus (Acts 15:39).

Black Sea · PONTUS · Amphipolis · Philippi · Apollonia · MACEDONIA · Neapolis · Byzantium · Thessalonica · Berea · BITHYNIA · Troas · GALATIA · CAPPADOCIA · SAMOTHRACE · LESBOS · Pergamos · Thyatira · PHRYGIA · Pisidian Antioch · Smyrna · Sardis · Iconium · LYCAONIA · Adriatic Sea · ACHAIA · CHIOS · ASIA · Philadelphia · Lystra · CILICIA · Athens · ANDROS · Laodicea · PAMPHYLIA · Derbe · Tarsus · Issus · Corinth · Ephesus · Miletus · Attalia · Perga · Antioch · Cenchrea · Sparta · LYCIA · Seleucia · SYRIA · RHODES · Salamis · Damascus · CRETE · Paphos · CYPRUS · N · Mediterranean Sea · Caesarea · Cyrene · Jerusalem · CYRENAICA

- - - ▸ Barnabas and Mark
——▸ Paul, Silas, and Timothy

Nelson's Complete Book of Bible Maps and Charts © 1993 by Thomas Nelson, Inc.

Paul's Third and Fourth Journeys

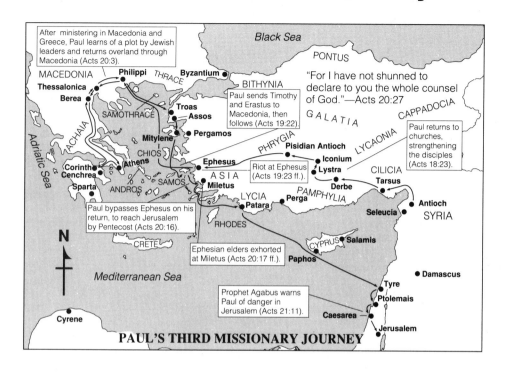

After ministering in Macedonia and Greece, Paul learns of a plot by Jewish leaders and returns overland through Macedonia (Acts 20:3).

Paul sends Timothy and Erastus to Macedonia, then follows (Acts 19:22).

"For I have not shunned to declare to you the whole counsel of God."—Acts 20:27

Paul returns to churches, strengthening the disciples (Acts 18:23).

Riot at Ephesus (Acts 19:23 ff.).

Paul bypasses Ephesus on his return, to reach Jerusalem by Pentecost (Acts 20:16).

Ephesian elders exhorted at Miletus (Acts 20:17 ff.).

Prophet Agabus warns Paul of danger in Jerusalem (Acts 21:11).

Black Sea
PONTUS
BITHYNIA
GALATIA
CAPPADOCIA
LYCAONIA
CILICIA
PHRYGIA
MACEDONIA
Philippi
THRACE
Byzantium
Thessalonica
Berea
Troas
Assos
SAMOTHRACE
Mitylene
Pergamos
CHIOS
Athens
Corinth
Cenchrea
Sparta
ANDROS
SAMOS
Miletus
Ephesus
Pisidian Antioch
Iconium
Lystra
Derbe
Tarsus
ASIA
LYCIA
Patara
Perga
PAMPHYLIA
RHODES
Antioch
Seleucia
SYRIA
Adriatic Sea
ACHAIA
CRETE
CYPRUS
Salamis
Paphos
Mediterranean Sea
Tyre
Ptolemais
Caesarea
Jerusalem
Damascus
Cyrene

N

PAUL'S THIRD MISSIONARY JOURNEY

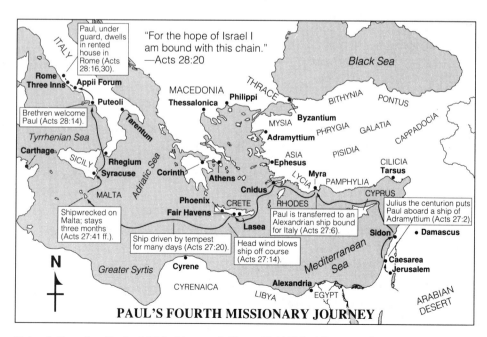

Paul, under guard, dwells in rented house in Rome (Acts 28:16,30).

"For the hope of Israel I am bound with this chain."—Acts 28:20

Brethren welcome Paul (Acts 28:14).

Shipwrecked on Malta; stays three months (Acts 27:41 ff.).

Ship driven by tempest for many days (Acts 27:20).

Head wind blows ship off course (Acts 27:14).

Paul is transferred to an Alexandrian ship bound for Italy (Acts 27:6).

Julius the centurion puts Paul aboard a ship of Adramyttium (Acts 27:2).

ITALY
Rome
Three Inns
Appii Forum
Puteoli
Tarentum
Tyrrhenian Sea
Carthage
SICILY
Rhegium
Syracuse
MALTA
Corinth
Athens
Phoenix
Fair Havens
CRETE
Lasea
Cnidus
RHODES
Greater Syrtis
Cyrene
CYRENAICA
LIBYA
Alexandria
EGYPT
Black Sea
MACEDONIA
Philippi
Thessalonica
THRACE
BITHYNIA
PONTUS
MYSIA
Byzantium
PHRYGIA
GALATIA
CAPPADOCIA
Adramyttium
PISIDIA
ASIA
Ephesus
Myra
LYCIA
PAMPHYLIA
CILICIA
Tarsus
CYPRUS
Sidon
Damascus
Caesarea
Jerusalem
Mediterranean Sea
ARABIAN DESERT
Adriatic Sea

N

PAUL'S FOURTH MISSIONARY JOURNEY

Nelson's Complete Book of Bible Maps and Charts © 1993 by Thomas Nelson, Inc.

New Testament Deliverances

In New Testament times Christian believers were often delivered from grim circumstances through a miraculous display of God's power. Paul and Silas, for example, were beaten and imprisoned as troublemakers because of their preaching in Philippi. While they prayed and sang during the night, the prison was shaken by an earthquake and they were released to continue their work (Acts 16:16–40). God's power to deliver is still available today for those who will exercise faith and seek His will in their lives.

Here are several other specific instances of God's miraculous deliverance of people of faith in New Testament times:

Name	God's Action	Biblical Reference
Gadarene with unclean spirit	Delivered from demon possession by Jesus	Mark 5:1–15
Lazarus	Raised from the dead by Jesus	John 11:38–44
Jesus	Raised from the dead after three days in the grave	Luke 24:1–7 John 20:1–10
Apostles	Freed from prison by an angel	Acts 5:17–20
Dorcas	Raised from the dead by Peter	Acts 9:36–41
Peter	Released from prison by an angel	Acts 12:1–11
Eutychus	Revived by Paul after his fall from a window	Acts 20:1–12
Paul	Delivered from a pressing burden (unnamed) in Asia	2 Cor. 1:8–11
Paul	Delivered unharmed to the island of Malta after a shipwreck	Acts 28:1

New Testament Journeys

The most famous traveler of the New Testament was the apostle Paul. The account of his journey to Rome in a Roman grain ship gives many insights into sea travel in New Testament times (Acts 27). Caught in a winter storm, the ship and its passengers ran aground on the island of Malta, or Melita, off the coast of Sicily. After three months and a break in the bad weather, they continued to Rome in a second ship which sailed from Alexandria, Egypt (Acts 28:11).

Other famous journeys of New Testament personalities include the following:

Personality	Description of Journey	Biblical Reference
Wise men	From the East (Persia?) to Bethlehem to worship the newborn Jesus	Matt. 2:1–12
Joseph and Mary	From Nazareth to Bethlehem, where Jesus was born	Luke 2:4
Mary, Joseph, and Jesus	Fled to Egypt to escape Herod's threat; returned to Nazareth after Herod's death	Matt. 2:13–23
Philip	From Jerusalem to Samaria to preach to the Samaritans; from Samaria into the desert to witness to the Ethiopian eunuch; from the desert to Caesarea	Acts 8:5 Acts 8:26 Acts 8:40
Paul	From Jerusalem to Damascus to arrest the early Christians	Acts 9
Peter	From Joppa to Caesarea to meet Cornelius and preach to the Gentiles	Acts 10
Barnabas	From Jerusalem to Antioch to work with the gentile converts	Acts 11:19–26
Paul and Barnabas	Paul's first missionary tour from Antioch to numerous places, including the island of Cyprus and the cities of Attalia, Perga, Antioch of Pisidia, Inconium, Lystra, and Derbe	Acts 13; 14
Paul and Silas	Paul's second missionary tour from Antioch to numerous cities, including Tarsus, Troas, Neapolis, Philippi, Amphipolis, Thessalonica, Berea, Athens, Corinth, and Ephesus	Acts 15—18
Paul	Paul's third missionary tour from Antioch to numerous cities; new locations visited on this tour included Assos, Mitylene, Miletus, Cos, Patara, Myra, and the island of Rhodes in the Aegean Sea off the coast of Asia Minor	Acts 18—21

Paul's Prison Experiences

Paul's first lengthy imprisonment, recorded in Acts 21:27—28:31, resulted from false accusations by Jews in Jerusalem that Paul had brought a Gentile into the temple area (21:28, 29). Because he was a Roman citizen, Paul was offered protection by the Roman authorities from the Jerusalem mob and was transported under guard to Caesarea (23:11–35). After hearings before the Jewish Sanhedrin (22:30—23:10), the Roman governor Felix (24:1–21), the succeeding governor Festus (25:1–12), and King Agrippa (25:13—26:32), Paul was taken to Rome (27:1—28:16). The book of Acts closes with Paul under house arrest in Rome awaiting his hearing before the emperor (28:17–31).

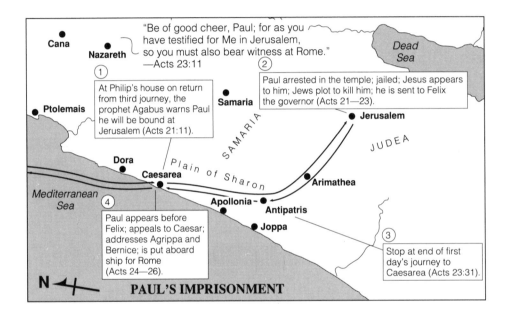

Early Christian Churches

From evidence in the Pastoral Epistles (1 and 2 Timothy; Titus), it appears that Paul was released from the Roman imprisonment recorded in Acts. He continued his ministry and perhaps ventured as far west as Spain (cf. Rom. 15:24). By the end of the first century, the church was well established in the eastern Mediterranean region and there were active mission efforts to the east and west.

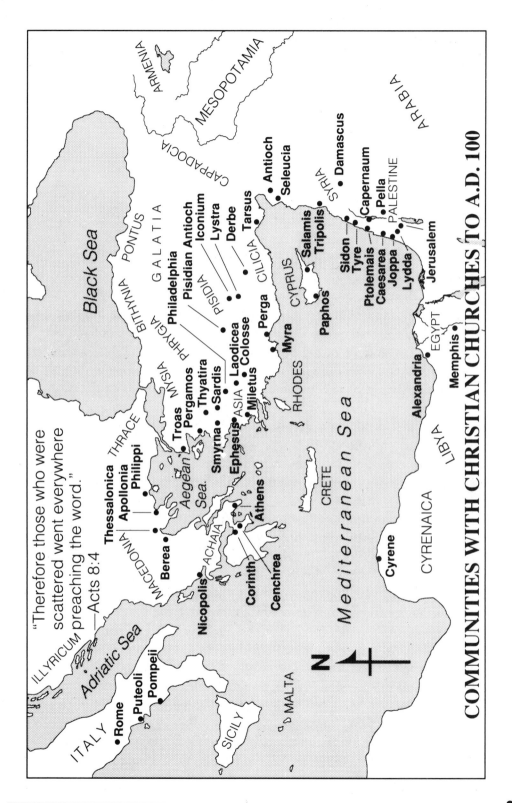

"Therefore those who were scattered went everywhere preaching the word."
—Acts 8:4

COMMUNITIES WITH CHRISTIAN CHURCHES TO A.D. 100

The Epistles of Paul

etters were a common form of communication in the first century. Paul wrote them to encourage, warn, and instruct the churches he had founded (1 and 2 Corinthians, Galatians, Ephesians, Philippians, 1 and 2 Thessalonians). He also wrote letters to churches that he had not visited (Romans, Colossians) and to individuals (1 and 2 Timothy, Titus, Philemon). Through his letters, Paul's ministry was extended not only to those directly addressed in his writing, but also to readers of the Bible throughout the centuries.

There is a pattern to Paul's letters. In the introduction he identifies himself and his addressees, then sends them greetings. The introduction is often followed by thanksgiving and intercession for the readers. Next he usually deals with doctrinal questions and then with their application to life. Paul normally closes with greetings from his companions and with added greetings to various people in the churches to which he writes. His letters conclude with a benediction.

Paul's greetings are unique. The normal Greek greeting was similar to their word for "grace." "Peace" was the usual Jewish greeting. Paul combines the two in a specifically Christian form: "Grace to you and peace from God the Father and our Lord Jesus Christ" (Gal. 1:3). God's grace in Christ brings reconciliation with God, harmony among people, and wholeness of life.

Paul's burden for the addressees is revealed in his thanksgivings for the spiritual progress of his readers (e.g., 1 Thess. 1:2–10) and his intercessions for their continued growth (e.g., Phil. 1:8–11). In Galatians, where Paul was deeply concerned about his converts following false teachers, he skips the thanksgiving and intercession, going directly to the problem at hand.

Paul's letters cover both doctrinal and practical issues. In Romans, practical application (12:1—15:32) most clearly follows doctrinal discussion (1:16—11:36). In Philippians, on the other hand, doctrinal discussion and practical application are mixed together. In 1 Corinthians Paul seems to be answering a series of questions sent to him from Corinth.

The last three letters written by the apostle Paul (1 Timothy, 2 Timothy, and Titus) are known as the Pastoral Epistles—so named because they deal with matters pertaining to pastors and their congregations. The epistles of 1 Timothy and Titus are our earliest guides to church organization; they are noted for their lists of qualifications for pastors and deacons in the early church. All three of these epistles emphasize sound doctrine and challenge believers to good works.

Paul's closing benedictions always include a wish for God's grace to be with his readers: "The grace of our Lord Jesus Christ be with you all" (Rom. 16:24; 1 Cor. 16:23; Phil. 4:23; 1 Thess. 5:28; 2 Thess. 3:18). He begins and ends with the unspeakable gift of God's grace in Christ.

The Influence of Paul

The witness of the apostle Paul began early in Damascus and in Tarsus, the city of his birth. Missionary travels then took him throughout the provinces of Galatia, Asia, Macedonia, and Achaia. Even while under custody in Caesarea and imprisoned in Rome, Paul testified of his salvation in Christ.

See also maps, "Paul's First and Second Journeys" on page 370 and "Paul's Third and Fourth Journeys" on page 371. See also charts, "Time Line of Paul's Epistles" on page 378 and "Survey of Paul's Epistles" on page 379.

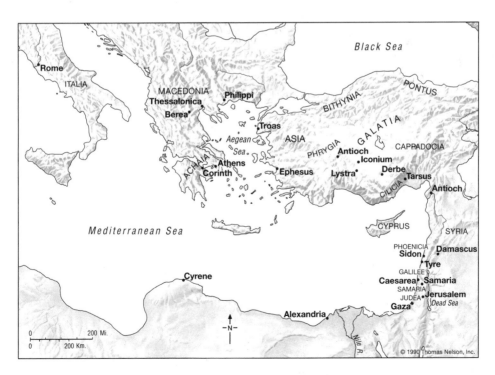

© 1990 Thomas Nelson, Inc.

Time Line of Paul's Epistles

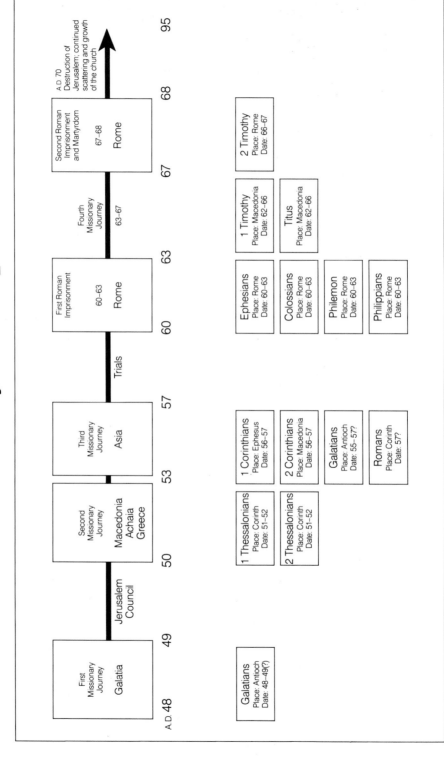

Nelson's Complete Book of Bible Maps and Charts © 1993 by Thomas Nelson, Inc.

Survey of Paul's Epistles

Book	No. of Chapters	Theme	Place Written	Date Written	Recipients
Romans	16	The Righteousness of God	Corinth	Winter 57	Beloved of God in Rome, called to be saints (1:1)
1 Corinthians	16	Solving Divisions and Disorders	Ephesus	56–57	Church of God at Corinth, those sanctified in Christ Jesus (1:2)
2 Corinthians	13	The Ministry of Reconciliation	Macedonia	56–57	Church of God at Corinth with all the saints in Achaia (1:1)
Galatians	6	Freedom in Christ	Antioch(?)	48–49 or 55–57	Churches of Galatia (1:2)
Ephesians	6	The Church: The Body of Christ	Rome	60–63	Saints of Ephesus, faithful in Christ Jesus (1:1)
Philippians	4	Joyful Christian Living	Rome	60–63	Saints in Christ Jesus in Philippi with the bishops and deacons (1:1)
Colossians	4	The Cosmic Christ	Rome	60–63	Saints and faithful brethren in Christ at Colosse (1:2)
1 Thessalonians	5	The Coming of Christ	Corinth	51–52	Church of the Thessalonians in God the Father and the Lord Jesus Christ (1:1)
2 Thessalonians	3	The Day of the Lord	Corinth	51–52	Church of the Thessalonians in God our Father and the Lord Jesus Christ (1:1)
1 Timothy	6	Pastoral Advice	Macedonia(?)	62–66	Timothy, a true son in the faith (1:2)
2 Timothy	4	A Farewell Word of Encouragement	Rome	66–67	Timothy, a beloved son (1:2)
Titus	3	A Christian Conduct Manual	Macedonia(?)	63–66	Titus, a true son in our common faith (1:4)
Philemon	1	Receiving a Slave as a Brother	Rome	60–63	Philemon, our beloved friend and fellow laborer (1:1)

Nelson's Complete Book of Bible Maps and Charts © 1993 by Thomas Nelson, Inc.

ROMANS

omans is theologically the most important of all the epistles written by
Paul, and it contains his most comprehensive and logical presentation
of the gospel. This book has repeatedly played important roles through
the history of the church. Augustine, a theologian of the fourth century, was
converted by reading Romans. Similarly, in the sixteenth century the book of
Romans inspired Martin Luther when he discovered in it the truth of justification by faith. Centuries later, John Wesley's heart was "strangely warmed"
when he heard Luther's preface to this epistle read aloud.

Author

There is overwhelming agreement among scholars that the apostle
Paul wrote this foundational New Testament book. The vocabulary,
style, logic, and theological development are consistent with Paul's
other epistles. Paul dictated the letter to a secretary named Tertius (16:22),
who was allowed to add his own greeting.

While Pauline authorship is unquestioned, the unity of the epistle has been a
matter of debate. Some have argued that chapter 16 was originally separate
from the letter, but was appended at a later date. It is simpler, however, to
understand the list of greetings in this final chapter as Paul's effort as a
stranger to the Roman church to list their mutual friends.

Date

That Paul himself had not yet visited Rome at the time Romans was
written is apparent in 1:13. The epistle is to be dated during the third
missionary journey when he engaged in the collection of a fund for
the church in Jerusalem. When he wrote 2 Corinthians, traveling from Ephesus to Corinth, the collection was still incomplete (2 Cor. 8:1–9). At the time he
wrote to the church at Rome, this collection seems to have been completed
(15:26–28). Therefore, we assume Paul wrote the epistle to the Romans from
Corinth where he stayed for three months in A.D. 57 at the end of his third
missionary journey, before he traveled to Jerusalem (15:25; Acts 20:2, 3).

See map, "Paul's Third and Fourth Journeys," on page 371.

Romans at a Glance

FOCUS	REVELATION OF GOD'S RIGHTEOUSNESS			VINDICATION OF GOD'S RIGHTEOUSNESS			APPLICATION OF GOD'S RIGHTEOUSNESS	
REFERENCE	1:1 —————— 3:21 —————— 6:1 —————— 9:1 ——— 9:30 ——— 11:1 ————— 12:1 ——— 14:1 – 16:27							
DIVISION	NEED FOR GOD'S RIGHTEOUSNESS	IMPUTATION OF GOD'S RIGHTEOUSNESS	DEMONSTRATION OF GOD'S RIGHTEOUSNESS	ISRAEL'S PAST: ELECTION	ISRAEL'S PRESENT: REJECTION	ISRAEL'S FUTURE: RESTORATION	CHRISTIAN DUTIES	CHRISTIAN LIBERTIES
TOPIC	SIN	SALVATION	SANCTIFICATION	SOVEREIGNTY			SERVICE	
	DOCTRINAL						BEHAVIORAL	
LOCATION	PROBABLY WRITTEN IN CORINTH							
TIME	C. A.D. 57							

Nelson's Complete Book of Bible Maps and Charts © 1993 by Thomas Nelson, Inc.

Themes and Literary Structure

The key phrase of this epistle is found in 1:17: "the righteousness of God." This phrase encapsulates the very heart of the epistle. Romans is written, therefore, to show how sinful men and women can receive the righteousness of God through faith in Jesus Christ. The theme of divine righteousness that runs through the book is reflected in the following outline: the revelation of the righteousness of God (chs. 1—8); the vindication of the righteousness of God (chs. 9—11); and the application of the righteousness of God (chs. 12—16).

Within the context of his overarching theme of the righteousness of God, Paul discusses the need of sinful humanity for God's righteousness (1:18—3:20), the imputation of Christ's righteousness to sinful human beings in justification (3:21—5:21), and the sanctification of the redeemed (6:1—8:39). In addition Paul discusses God's righteousness as revealed in His faithfulness to His covenant promises to Israel (9:1—11:36), and the righteousness that Christians are to display before each other and before the world (12:1—16:27).

In his sweeping presentation of God's plan of salvation, Paul moves from condemnation to glorification and from theological truth to practical behavior. Key words, such as righteousness, faith, law, all, and sin, each appear at least sixty times in this epistle.

OUTLINE OF ROMANS

The City of Rome

Rome was founded in 753 B.C., and by the time of Paul it was the greatest city in the world with over one million inhabitants. It was full of magnificent buildings, but the majority of people were slaves; opulence and squalor co-existed in this imperial city.

The church in Rome was well-known (1:8), and it had been established for several years by the time of this letter. The believers there were numerous, and evidently they met in several places (16:1–16). The Roman historian Tacitus referred to the Christians who were persecuted under Nero in A.D. 64 as "an immense multitude."

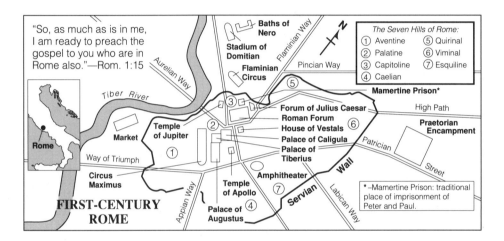

Christian Living

Although the theological depth of Paul's epistle to the Romans is profound, the apostle does not neglect the practical aspects of the Christian life. Given what God has done for us and in us through Jesus Christ, Paul exhorts each believer to honor God with lives of sacrificial obedience that are "holy, acceptable to God" (12:1).

See chart, "The Christian Life," on page 385.

The Christian Life

Description of the Christian	Result
Presents himself to God (12:1)	Becomes a sacrifice that is living, holy, and pleasing to God (12:1)
Receives transformation by a renewed mind (12:2)	Discovers and displays the will of God (12:2)
Has spiritual gifts according to grace from God (12:6–8)	Uses spiritual gifts as part of Christ's body (12:6)
Honors civil law (13:1)	Honors God (13:1)
Loves others (13:8)	Fulfills God's law (13:8)
Pursues peace (14:19)	Serves to edify all (14:19)
Becomes like-minded toward others (15:5)	Glorifies God with others (15:6)

Nelson's Complete Book of Bible Maps and Charts © 1993 by Thomas Nelson, Inc.

Kingdom-Style Mentoring

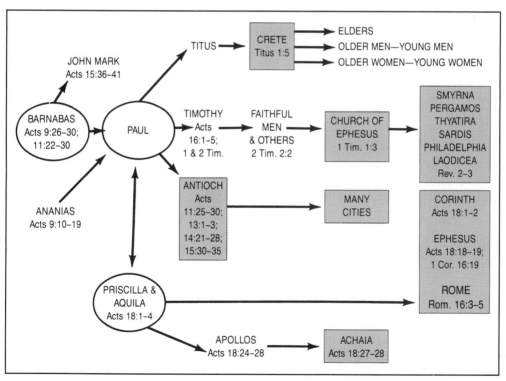

Nelson's Complete Book of Bible Maps and Charts © 1996 by Thomas Nelson, Inc.

1 CORINTHIANS

irst Corinthians reveals the problems, pressures, and struggles of a church called out of a pagan society. Paul addresses a variety of problems in the lifestyle of the Corinthian Christians: factions, lawsuits, immorality, questionable practices, abuse of the Lord's Supper, and spiritual gifts. In addition to words of discipline, Paul shares words of counsel in answer to questions raised by the Corinthians.

Author

Pauline authorship of 1 Corinthians is almost universally accepted. In addition to the explicit statements of the epistle (1:1; 16:21), the vocabulary and teachings of the text point to Paul the apostle to the Gentiles. References to this letter in extra-biblical literature can be found as early as A.D. 95, when Clement of Rome mentions 1 Corinthians as having been written by Paul.

Date

First Corinthians was probably written during Paul's third missionary journey in A.D. 56 or 57, with 2 Corinthians being written some six to eighteen months later. Paul had founded the church at Corinth during an eighteen-month stay in the city (A.D. 51–52).

The Corinth which Paul knew had been founded as a Roman colony during the century before Christ. It was strategically located in the Roman province of Achaia on a narrow strip of land between the Aegean Sea and the Adriatic Sea, with two adjoining ports. Corinth's location made it a center for trade routes passing from east to west, and the resulting prosperity brought both luxury and immorality. "To live like a Corinthian" meant to live in gross immorality, and many pagan temples located in Corinth encouraged this licentious way of life through temple prostitution.

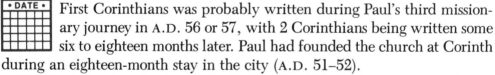

1 Corinthians at a Glance

FOCUS	ANSWER TO CHLOE'S REPORT OF DIVISIONS		ANSWER TO REPORT OF FORNICATION			ANSWER TO LETTER OF QUESTIONS				
REFERENCE	1:1 —— 1:18 —— 5:1 — 6:1 —— 6:12 —— 7:1 —— 8:1 —— 11:2 — 15:1 — 16:1 —— 16:24									
DIVISION	REPORT OF DIVISIONS	REASON FOR DIVISIONS	INCEST	LITIGATION	IMMORALITY	MARRIAGE	OFFERINGS TO IDOLS	PUBLIC WORSHIP	RESUR-RECTION	COLLECTION FOR JERUSALEM
TOPIC	DIVISIONS IN THE CHURCH		DISORDER IN THE CHURCH			DIFFICULTIES IN THE CHURCH				
	CONCERN		CONDEMNATION			COUNSEL				
LOCATION	WRITTEN IN EPHESUS									
TIME	C. A.D. 56									

Nelson's Complete Book of Bible Maps and Charts © 1993 by Thomas Nelson, Inc.

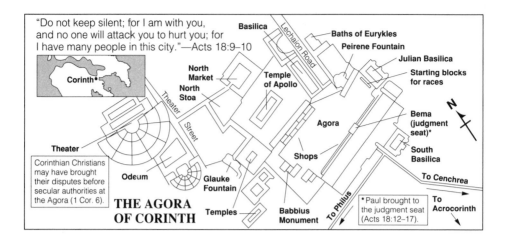

THE AGORA OF CORINTH

"Do not keep silent; for I am with you, and no one will attack you to hurt you; for I have many people in this city."—Acts 18:9–10

Corinth

Corinthian Christians may have brought their disputes before secular authorities at the Agora (1 Cor. 6).

* Paul brought to the judgment seat (Acts 18:12–17).

Themes and Literary Structure

This epistle is quite orderly in its approach as it sequentially addresses a group of problems that have come to Paul's attention. Paul also gives a series of perspectives on various questions and issues raised by the Corinthians in a letter. The three divisions of 1 Corinthians are: (1) the answer to Chloe's report of divisions (chs. 1—4); (2) answer to the report of fornication and disorder (chs. 5—6); and (3) answer to the letter of questions (chs.7—16).

As he prepares to deal with the serious problems present in the Corinthian church early on in the epistle, Paul proclaims the relevance and sufficiency of Christ for every area of the believer's life. Christ Jesus "became for us wisdom from God—and righteousness and sanctification and redemption" (1:30).

In dealing with the sexual immorality that had arisen in the Corinthian church, Paul stresses the importance of church discipline and purity (5:9–13). Here the apostle also indicates that a primary goal of such discipline is the restoration of the wayward.

The relationship of Christian liberty and Christian love is also explored. Paul writes that "all things are lawful for me, but all things are not helpful" (6:12), and chapter 13 contains the most extensive and profound teaching on the self-giving character of Christian love.

In addition, 1 Corinthians contains extensive doctrinal instruction on the place of spiritual gifts in the church (chs. 12—14), and on the nature of the resurrection body (ch. 15).

Spiritual Gifts

The New Testament provides us with several lists of spiritual gifts. No one list is exhaustive, and the contents of each list depend on the specific purpose of the author. In Romans 12, Paul deals with the gifts in general terms, while in 1 Corinthians 12 Paul stresses the gifts which build up the church as a whole rather than the more spectacular gifts, such as tongues, which may confer individual benefit but were subject to abuse by the Corinthian Christians.

See chart, "New Testament Lists of Spiritual Gifts," on page 391.

The Way of Love

Paul valued the gift of prophecy highly (see 14:1), and the Corinthians placed a premium on spectacular gifts such as speaking in tongues, as well as on the gifts of understanding spiritual mysteries and faith to do dramatic miracles. Yet even these spiritual gifts do us no good in God's sight unless we live in love.

Love is...	Without Love...	Love is Greater Than...
Patient, kind, unselfish, truthful, hopeful, enduring (vv. 4–7) Not envious, proud, self-centered, rude, or provoked to anger (vv. 4, 5)	Tongues are mere noise (v. 1) Prophecy, mysteries, knowledge, and faith amount to nothing (v. 2) Good deeds are unprofitable (v. 3)	Prophecies, which will fail (v. 8) Tongues, which will cease (v. 8) Knowledge, which will vanish (v. 8)
Love is one of the dynamic terms Paul uses to speak of the holy life enabled by the fullness of the Holy Spirit. It encompasses motive and deed. Love is characteristic of the mature believer.		

New Testament Lists of Spiritual Gifts

Romans 12:6–8	1 Cor. 12:8–10	1 Cor. 12:28–30	Eph. 4:11	1 Peter 4:9–11
Prophecy	Word of Wisdom	Apostleship	Apostleship	Speaking
Serving	Word of Knowledge	Prophecy	Prophecy	Serving
Teaching	Faith	Teaching	Evangelism	
Exhortation	Healings	Miracles	Pastor/Teacher	
Giving	Miracles	Healing		
Leading	Prophecy	Helping		
Showing Mercy	Discerning of Spirits	Administrating		
	Tongues	Tongues		
	Interpretation of Tongues	Interpretation of Tongues		

Nelson's Complete Book of Bible Maps and Charts © 1993 by Thomas Nelson, Inc.

The Work of the Holy Spirit

In the beginning
  • Active and present at creation, hovering over the unordered conditions (Gen. 1:2)

In the Old Testament
  • The origin of supernatural abilities (Gen. 41:38)
  • The giver of artistic skill (Ex. 31:2–5)
  • The source of power and strength (Judg. 3:9, 10)
  • The inspiration of prophecy (1 Sam. 19:20, 23)
  • The equipper of God's messenger (Mic. 3:8)

In Old Testament prophecy
  • The cleansing of the heart for holy living (Ezek. 36:25–29)

In salvation
  • Regenerates the believer (Titus 3:5)
  • Indwells the believer (Rom. 8:9–11)
  • Sanctifies the believer (2 Thess. 2:13)

In the New Testament
  • Declares the truth about Christ (John 16:13, 14)
  • Endows with power for gospel proclamation (Acts 1:8)
  • Pours out God's love in the heart (Rom. 5:5)
  • Makes intercession (Rom. 8:26)
  • Imparts gifts for ministry (1 Cor. 12:4–11)
  • Enables the fruit of holy living (Gal. 5:22, 23)
  • Strengthens the inner being (Eph. 3:16)

In the written Word
  • Inspired the writing of Scripture (2 Tim. 3:16; 2 Pet. 1:21)

Resurrection Appearances

The Corinthians also had problems with the doctrine of the resurrection, which Paul sought to correct in chapter 15. Here his historical and theological defense of the resurrection includes teaching on the fact of Christ's resurrection, the temporal relationship between Christ's resurrection and the believer's, and the nature of the resurrected body. The Corinthians probably had been struggling over this issue because the idea of a resurrected body had little place in Greek thought, which tended to exalt the spiritual over the physical.

See charts "Appearances of the Risen Christ" below and "Resurrection Options" on page 393. See also map, "The Resurrection," on page 355.

Appearances of the Risen Christ

Central to Christian faith is the bodily resurrection of Jesus. By recording the resurrection appearances, the New Testament leaves no doubt about this event.

- In or around Jerusalem
  To Mary Magdalene
  (John 20:11–18)
  To the other women
  (Matt. 28:8–10)
  To Peter
  (Luke 24:34)
  To ten disciples
  (Luke 24:36–43; John 20:19–25)
  To the Eleven, including Thomas
  (John 20:26–29)
  At His ascension
  (Luke 24:50–53; Acts 1:4–12)

- To the disciples on the Emmaus road
  (Luke 24:13–35)

- In Galilee
  (Matt. 28:16–20; John 21:1–24)

- To five hundred people
  (1 Cor. 15:6)

- To James and the apostles
  (1 Cor. 15:7)

- To Paul on the road to Damascus
  (Acts 9:1–6; 18:9, 10; 22:1–8; 23:11; 26:12–18; 1 Cor. 15:8)

Nelson's Complete Book of Bible Maps and Charts © 1993 by Thomas Nelson, Inc.

Resurrection Options

The resurrection of Jesus has been interpreted as:

1. A Great Hoax (the resurrection is *false*).
2. Mythology (the resurrection is *fiction*).
3. **The Supreme Event of History (the resurrection is *fact*).**

The following theories have been proposed to explain the empty tomb and the post-Resurrection appearances of Christ:

Theory	Explanation
1. **Swoon**	Jesus did not actually die.
2. **Spirit**	Jesus' spirit returned but not His body.
3. **Vision**	The disciples hallucinated.
4. **Legend/Myth**	The resurrection is only a myth or story with a teaching point. A real Jesus is probable, but not really necessary.
5. **Stolen Body**	The body was stolen by (1) the Jews, (2) the Romans, (3) the disciples (Matt. 28:11–15), or (4) Joseph of Arimathea (John 19:38ff.).
6. **Wrong Tomb**	The disciples went to the wrong tomb, found it empty, and erroneously concluded that Jesus had risen.
7. **Deliberate Lie for Profit**	The disciples fabricated the resurrection story for profit.
8. **Mistaken Identity**	The disciples mistook for Jesus someone who looked like Him.
9. **A Literal, Bodily Resurrection**	Jesus was raised from the dead, historically and bodily, by the supernatural power of God (1 Cor. 15:3ff.).

Nelson's Complete Book of Bible Maps and Charts © 1993 by Thomas Nelson, Inc.

Ethics for Witnessing

(1) We are Christians, called by God to honor Jesus Christ with our lives, abiding by biblically defined ethical standards in every area of life, public and private. This includes our efforts to persuade coworkers and others to believe the good news about Jesus Christ.

(2) Wherever we live and work, we seek to follow the mandate, motives, message, and model of Jesus, who still pursues and reclaims those lost in sin and rebelling against Him.

(3) We believe all people are created in God's image with the capacity to relate to their Creator and Redeemer. We disdain any effort to influence people which depersonalizes them or deprives them of their inherent value as persons.

(4) Since we respect the value of persons, we believe all are worthy of hearing about Jesus Christ. We also affirm the right of every person to survey other religious options. People are free to choose a different belief system than Christianity.

(5) We affirm the role and right of Christians to share the gospel of Christ in the marketplace of ideas. However, this does not justify any means to fulfill that end. We reject coercive techniques or manipulative appeals, especially those that play on emotions and discount or contradict reason or evidence. We will not bypass a person's critical faculties, prey upon psychological weaknesses, undermine a relationship with one's family or religious institution, or mask the true nature of Christian conversion. We will not intentionally mislead.

(6) We respect the individual integrity, intellectual honesty, and academic freedom of others, both believers and skeptics, and so we proclaim Christ without hidden agendas. We reveal our own identity, purpose, theological positions, and sources of information. We will use no false advertising and seek no material gain from presenting the gospel.

(7) We invite people of other religious persuasions to join us in true dialogue. We acknowledge our humanness—that we Christians are just as sinful, needy, and dependent on the grace of God as anyone else. We seek to listen sensitively in order to understand, and thus rid our witness of any stereotypes or fixed formulae which block honest communication.

(8) As our "brothers' keepers," we accept our responsibility to admonish any Christian brother or sister who presents the message of Christ in a way that violates these ethical guidelines.

2 CORINTHIANS

Since Paul's first letter, the Corinthian church had been swayed by false teachers who stirred the people against Paul. They claimed he was fickle, proud, unimpressive in appearance and speech, dishonest, and unqualified as an apostle of Jesus Christ. Paul sent Titus to Corinth to deal with these difficulties, and upon his return, rejoiced to hear of the Corinthians' change of heart. Paul wrote this letter to express his thanksgiving for the repentant majority and to appeal to the rebellious minority to accept his authority. Throughout the book he defends his conduct, character, and calling as an apostle of Jesus Christ.

Author

External and internal evidence amply support the Pauline authorship of this letter. As with Romans, the problem with 2 Corinthians is the question of its unity. Many have suggested that chapters 10—13 were not a part of this letter in its original form because of their contrast, in tone and subject matter, with chapters 1—9. Among those who deny the unity of the epistle, the most popular solution is that chapters 10—13 belong to a letter by Paul, now lost, which is referred to in 2:4. It is more reasonable, however, to explain the difference in tone between chapters 1—9 and 10—13 as due to the change in focus from the repentant majority to the rebellious minority.

Date

• DATE • Paul wrote 2 Corinthians from Macedonia during his third missionary journey, probably in A.D. 56 or 57. It was written perhaps six months to a year after 1 Corinthians. See map, "Paul's Third and Fourth Journeys," on page 371.

Many scholars believe that 2 Corinthians was, in actuality, the fourth letter Paul wrote to the Corinthian believers. In 1 Corinthians 5:9, Paul speaks of an earlier epistle, and after writing 1 Corinthians, Paul visited Corinth in what has been termed the "sorrowful visit" (2:1; cf. 13:1). After this visit (his third to the city), Paul wrote a "sorrowful letter" (2:4), which has also been lost.

Continued on page 397

2 Corinthians at a Glance

FOCUS	EXPLANATION OF PAUL'S MINISTRY			COLLECTION FOR THE SAINTS		VINDICATION OF PAUL'S APOSTLESHIP		
REFERENCE	1:1 —— 2:14 ——	6:11 ——		8:1 ——	8:7 ——	10:1 —— 11:1 ——		12:14 — 13:14
DIVISION	HIS CHANGE OF PLANS	PHILOSOPHY OF MINISTRY	EXHORTATIONS TO THE CORINTHIANS	EXAMPLE OF THE MACEDONIANS	EXHORTATION TO THE CORINTHIANS	ANSWERS HIS ACCUSERS	DEFENDS HIS APOSTLESHIP	ANNOUNCES HIS UPCOMING VISIT
TOPIC	CHARACTER OF PAUL			COLLECTION FOR SAINTS		CREDENTIALS OF PAUL		
	EPHESUS TO MACEDONIA: CHANGE OF ITINERARY			MACEDONIA: PREPARATION FOR VISIT		TO CORINTH: IMMINENT VISIT		
LOCATION	WRITTEN IN MACEDONIA							
TIME	C. A.D. 56							

Continued from page 395

Titus carried this letter to Corinth and then on his return gave good news to Paul when they met in Macedonia (7:6–8). In relief and thanksgiving, Paul then wrote 2 Corinthians from Macedonia.

Themes and Literary Structure

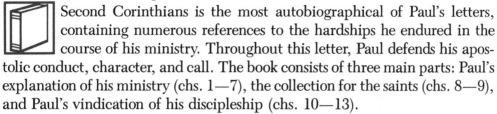

Second Corinthians is the most autobiographical of Paul's letters, containing numerous references to the hardships he endured in the course of his ministry. Throughout this letter, Paul defends his apostolic conduct, character, and call. The book consists of three main parts: Paul's explanation of his ministry (chs. 1—7), the collection for the saints (chs. 8—9), and Paul's vindication of his discipleship (chs. 10—13).

Paul's defense of his apostleship in chapters 10—13 is characterized by the masterful use of irony and sarcasm. Particularly in the so-called "Fool's Speech" (11:16—12:13), Paul mocks the vain preoccupation of some Corinthians with power and spectacular spiritual gifts by "boasting" of his weakness and the persecutions he had endured.

OUTLINE OF 2 CORINTHIANS

GALATIANS

alatians is a classic statement of the doctrine of justification by grace through faith. It was written to counter false teachers who believed a person must keep the Jewish law in order to be right with God. Like the epistle to the Romans, Galatians has played a strategic role in the history of the Christian church. Both Martin Luther and John Wesley recorded the crucial impact of this epistle on their lives.

Author

The Pauline authorship and the unity of this epistle are virtually unchallenged. In fact, the original manuscript of the letter was written by Paul himself (6:11), instead of being dictated to a secretary, as was Paul's usual practice.

Date

The date of the epistle is related to the question of to whom it was addressed. This uncertainty is due to the fact that the term "Galatia" was used in both a cultural/geographic sense and a political sense. The Roman political province of Galatia included some areas in southern Asia Minor (e.g., the cities of Pisidian Antioch, Iconium, Lystra, and Derbe) which were not part of the portion of central Asia Minor inhabited by Celtic tribes and known as "Galatia."

The "north Galatian theory" holds that Paul was speaking of Galatia in its earlier, more restricted sense. According to this theory, the churches of Galatia were located north of the cities Paul visited on his first missionary journey. Paul visited ethnic Galatia for the first time on his second missionary journey, probably while he was on his way to Troas (Acts 16:6). On his third missionary journey, Paul revisited the Galatian churches he had established (Acts 18:23) and wrote this epistle either from Ephesus (A.D. 53–56) or Macedonia (A.D. 56).

According to the "south Galatian theory," Paul was referring to "Galatia" in its wider political sense as a province of Rome. Accordingly, the churches ad-

Continued on page 401

Galatians at a Glance

FOCUS	GOSPEL OF GRACE DEFENDED		GOSPEL OF GRACE EXPLAINED		GOSPEL OF GRACE APPLIED	
REFERENCE	1:1 ———— 2:1	———— 3:1	———— 4:1	———— 5:1	———— 6:1	———— 6:18
DIVISION	PAUL'S APOSTLESHIP	PAUL'S AUTHORITY	BONDAGE OF LAW	FREEDOM OF GRACE	FRUIT OF THE SPIRIT	FRUITS OF THE SPIRIT
TOPIC	BIOGRAPHICAL EXPLANATION		DOCTRINAL EXPOSITION		PRACTICAL EXHORTATION	
TOPIC	AUTHENTICATION OF LIBERTY		ARGUMENTATION FOR LIBERTY		APPLICATION OF LIBERTY	
LOCATION	SOUTH GALATIAN THEORY: SYRIAN ANTIOCH NORTH GALATIAN THEORY: EPHESUS OR MACEDONIA					
TIME	SOUTH GALATIAN THEORY: A.D. 49 NORTH GALATIAN THEORY: A.D. 53–56					

Nelson's Complete Book of Bible Maps and Charts © 1993 by Thomas Nelson, Inc.

The Cities of Galatia

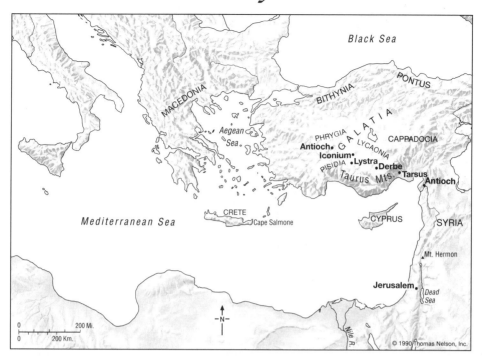

Continued from page 399

dressed were located in the cities he evangelized during his first missionary journey with Barnabas (Acts 13:13—14:23). This was just prior to the Jerusalem Council (Acts 15), so the Jerusalem visit described in 2:1–10 would have been the Acts 11:27–30 famine-relief visit, and the book of Galatians would have been written in A.D. 49.

Themes and Literary Structure

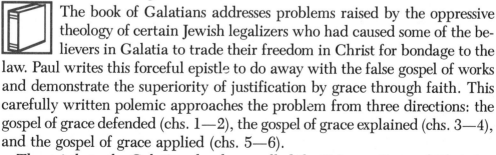

The book of Galatians addresses problems raised by the oppressive theology of certain Jewish legalizers who had caused some of the believers in Galatia to trade their freedom in Christ for bondage to the law. Paul writes this forceful epistle to do away with the false gospel of works and demonstrate the superiority of justification by grace through faith. This carefully written polemic approaches the problem from three directions: the gospel of grace defended (chs. 1—2), the gospel of grace explained (chs. 3—4), and the gospel of grace applied (chs. 5—6).

The epistle to the Galatians has been called the "Magna Carta of Christian liberty." Christ has freed believers from bondage to the law (legalism) and to sin (license) and has placed them in a position of liberty. The transforming

Cross of Christ provides for the believer's deliverance from the curse of sin, law, and self.

Galatians describes a dynamic faith-union with Christ (2:20), visibly portrayed in baptism (3:27), which relates all believers to each other as brothers and sisters (3:28).

Law and Grace Contrasted

Advocates of Judaistic legalism abrogated or set aside the grace of God, which left the atoning death of Christ with no more than exemplary significance. All modern attempts to set forth works, whether moral or religious, as the way of achieving salvation fall under the same Pauline condemnation as did the Judaizers opposed by this epistle.

See chart, "Law and Grace," on page 403.

Law and Grace

THE FUNCTION		THE EFFECT	
Of Law	*Of Grace*	*Of Law*	*Of Grace*
Based on works (3:10)	Based on faith (3:11, 12)	Works put us under a curse (3:10)	Justifies us by faith (3:3, 24)
Our guardian (3:23, 4:2)	Centered in Christ (3:24)	Keeps us for faith (3:23)	Christ lives in us (2:20)
Our tutor (3:24)	Our certificate of freedom (4:30, 31)	Brings us to Christ (3:24)	Adopts us as sons and heirs (4:7)
The law functions to (1) declare our guilt, (2) drive us to Christ, and (3) direct us in a life of obedience. However, the law is powerless to save.			

Nelson's Complete Book of Bible Maps and Charts © 1993 by Thomas Nelson, Inc.

Biblical Guidance for Families

TEXTS	ISSUE	SUMMARY
Rom. 9:6—11:36	Ethnic attitudes	Paul reviews some of the Jewish attitudes that had existed since the time of the patriarchs and appeals for humility and acceptance.
Rom. 14:1—15:6	Differences in spiritual maturity and convictions	Believers must practice grace and tolerance toward one another.
1 Cor. 5:1–13; 2 Cor. 2:1–11	Sexual immorality within families	Paul deals with a case of continuing incest within a believer's family.
1 Cor. 6:15–20; 1 Thess. 4:1–12	Temptation to sexual immorality	The body is God's temple; believers are to flee from sexual sins.
1 Cor. 7:1–7	Sexuality within marriage	Intimacy is crucial to the marriage relationship.
1 Cor. 7:8–20, 25–38	Singles and marriage	Paul expresses his own preference for singleness over marriage.
1 Cor. 7:39–40	Remarriage of widows	Remarriage to a believer is completely permissible.
Eph. 5:21–33; Col. 3:18–19; 1 Pet. 3:1–7	Spousal relationships	Paul and Peter challenge husbands and wives to mutual love and support.
Eph. 6:1–4; Col. 3:20–21	Child-parent relationships	The home should be characterized by obedient children and nurturing parents.
1 Tim. 3:1–13; Titus 1:5–16	Character	One of the major areas in which spiritual leaders should be evaluated is the home.
1 Tim. 5:3–16; James 1:27	Widows	Paul offers guidelines for the care of widows; James exhorts believers to meet the needs of widows and orphans.

EPHESIANS

Except for the book of Romans, the book of Ephesians is the most carefully written presentation of Christian theology in the New Testament. Paul wrote this epistle to make Christians more aware of the riches they have in Christ and to motivate them to draw upon these spiritual resources in daily living.

Author

The name Paul occurs at 1:1 and 3:1 as the author of this book, and the ancient tradition of the church supports this claim. Some have argued, however, that Ephesians differs in vocabulary and style, and that the view of the universal church as the body of Christ represents a later theological development. Arguments from vocabulary and style are notoriously subjective, however, and the richness of the theology in Ephesians is better attributed to Paul's own growth and meditation on the nature of the church.

Date

As one of Paul's "Prison Epistles" (the name given collectively to Ephesians, Philippians, Colossians, and Philemon), the letter would be dated to the period A.D. 60–63, corresponding to the time of Paul's first Roman imprisonment (cf. Acts 28:16–31). It was probably written at about the same time as Colossians.

The destination of the epistle is less certain. Because the phrase "in Ephesus" (1:1) was omitted in some early Greek manuscripts, some have suggested that the epistle was a circular letter addressed to the churches of Asia Minor as a whole and forwarded from church to church. Some scholars believe that this theory explains Paul's reference in Colossians 4:16, where he requested that the epistle to the Colossians be read along with the "epistle from Laodicea." This may refer to a copy of Ephesians with the name "Laodicea" inserted in a blank space so that the circular letter might also be read there.

Ephesians at a Glance

FOCUS	THE POSITION OF THE CHRISTIAN				THE PRACTICE OF THE CHRISTIAN			
REFERENCE	1:1 ——— 1:15 ——— 2:1 ——————— 3:14 ———				4:1 ——— 4:17 — 5:22 ——— 6:10 — 6:24			
DIVISION	PRAISE FOR REDEMPTION	PRAYER FOR REVELATION	POSITION OF THE CHRISTIAN	PRAYER FOR REALIZATION	UNITY IN THE CHURCH	HOLINESS IN LIFE	RESPONSIBIL-ITIES AT HOME AND WORK	CONDUCT IN THE CONFLICT
TOPIC	BELIEF				BEHAVIOR			
	PRIVILEGES OF THE CHRISTIAN				RESPONSIBILITIES OF THE CHRISTIAN			
LOCATION	ROME							
TIME	A.D. 60–61							

Themes and Literary Structure

The first half of Ephesians lists the believer's heavenly possessions in Christ Jesus: adoption, redemption, inheritance, power, life, grace, citizenship, and the love of Christ. There are no imperatives in chapters 1—3, which focus on the divine gifts to the believer. But chapters 4—6 include thirty-five directives that speak of believers' responsibility to conduct themselves according to their calling. Thus, the two main divisions of the book are: the position of the Christian (chs. 1—3), and the practice of the Christian (chs. 4—6).

The wonderful news of salvation in Ephesians is directed toward the goal of "the praise of His glory" (1:6, 12, 14). The word "glory" occurs eight times and refers to the exceeding excellence of God's love, His wisdom, and His power. God's glory is particularly revealed in His commitment to build a glorious, mature, and ministering church, "not having spot or wrinkle" (5:27).

The "heavenly" character of the believer's calling is stressed in Ephesians (1:3). Although previously dead in sin, the Christian has been raised with Christ and seated with Him in the "heavenly places" (2:6). This "heavenly" calling, in turn, provides the means and empowerment of the believer's life of obedience on earth (4:1, 7–10).

OUTLINE OF EPHESIANS

Part One: The Position of the Christian (1:1—3:21)

Part Two: The Practice of the Christian (4:1—6:24)

The City of Ephesus

At the end of his second missionary journey, Paul visited Ephesus where he left Priscilla and Aquila (Acts 18:18–21). Returning to the city on his third missionary journey, Paul spent nearly three years there (Acts 18:23—19:41). Paul's effective ministry began seriously to hurt the traffic in magic and images,

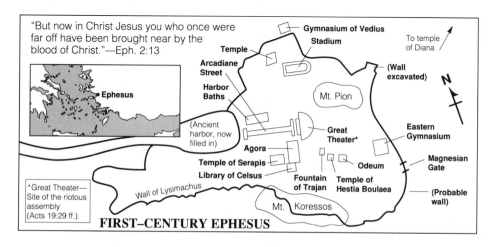

"But now in Christ Jesus you who once were far off have been brought near by the blood of Christ."—Eph. 2:13

Ephesus

Gymnasium of Vedius
Stadium
To temple of Diana
Temple
Arcadiane Street
(Wall excavated)
N
Harbor Baths
Mt. Pion
(Ancient harbor, now filled in)
Great Theater*
Eastern Gymnasium
Agora
Temple of Serapis
Library of Celsus
Odeum
Magnesian Gate
Fountain of Trajan
Temple of Hestia Boulaea
Wall of Lysimachus
(Probable wall)
*Great Theater—Site of the riotous assembly (Acts 19:29 ff.).
Mt. Koressos

FIRST–CENTURY EPHESUS

leading to an uproar in the huge Ephesian theater. Paul then left for Macedonia, but afterward he met with the Ephesian elders while on his way to Jerusalem (Acts 20:17–38).

Our Blessings in Christ

Paul's important phrase "in Christ" (or its equivalent) appears about thirty-five times, more than in any other New Testament book. Furthermore, the salvation of the believer is ensured by the work of all three Persons of the Trinity—the loving choice of the Father (1:3–6), the redeeming work of the Son (1:7–12), and the sealing of the Holy Spirit (1:13, 14).

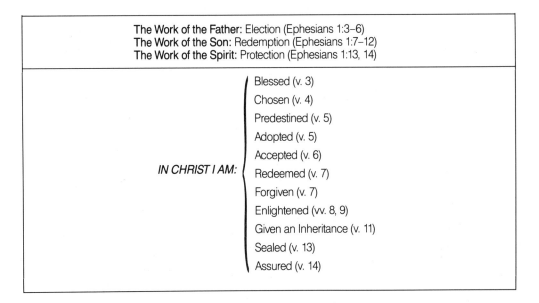

The Work of the Father: Election (Ephesians 1:3–6)
The Work of the Son: Redemption (Ephesians 1:7–12)
The Work of the Spirit: Protection (Ephesians 1:13, 14)

IN CHRIST I AM:

Blessed (v. 3)

Chosen (v. 4)

Predestined (v. 5)

Adopted (v. 5)

Accepted (v. 6)

Redeemed (v. 7)

Forgiven (v. 7)

Enlightened (vv. 8, 9)

Given an Inheritance (v. 11)

Sealed (v. 13)

Assured (v. 14)

Grace Abounding

Grace (Greek: *charis*) refers to the beneficial actions of God in which He reveals Himself, His gifts, and His life—all bestowals which grow out of His love rather than any sinful person's worth or merit.

Benefit:	Christ's spiritual blessings in heaven (v. 3); the forgiveness of sins (v. 7)
Origin:	Divine choice from eternity past (v. 4); the good pleasure of God's will (v. 5)
Purpose:	Love manifested in holiness and blamelessness (v. 4); to be joined with Christ (v. 10)
Privilege:	Adoption into God's family as beneficiaries of Christ (v. 5)
Cost:	The blood of Christ (v. 7)
Means:	Having heard the truth, trusting in Christ (vv. 12, 13)
Assurance:	The Holy Spirit as the down payment of our inheritance (vv. 13, 14)

The Work of Salvation

The work of salvation is essentially threefold: (1) justification, in which God declares the sinner righteous before Him, thus freeing the sinner forever from the legal penalty of sin; (2) sanctification, in which the sinner is progressively freed from the power of sin by the power of the Holy Spirit; and (3) glorification, which looks forward to the time when the believer will be completely freed from sin and conformed to the image of Christ.

Salvation: Man's Greatest Possession

Justification (Past Tense)	Sanctification (Present Tense)	Glorification (Future Tense)
Saved *immediately* from sin's penalty	Saved *progressively* from sin's power	Saved *ultimately* from sin's presence
"For by grace you have been saved through faith, and that not of yourselves; it is the gift of God." (Ephesians 2:8)		

Nelson's Complete Book of Bible Maps and Charts © 1993 by Thomas Nelson, Inc.

The Traits of New Creatures in Christ

1 Corinthians 13:3–8	Galatians 5:22–23	Philippians 4:8	Colossians 3:12–16
Love . . . • suffers long • is kind • does not envy • does not parade itself • is not puffed up • does not behave rudely • does not seek its own • is not provoked • thinks no evil • does not rejoice in iniquity • rejoices in the truth • bears all things • believes all things • hopes all things • endures all things	*The fruit of the Spirit is . . .* • love • joy • peace • longsuffering (patience) • kindness • goodness • faithfulness • gentleness • self-control	*Meditate on whatever things are . . .* • true • noble • just • pure • lovely • of good report • of any virtue • praiseworthy	*Put on these things . . .* • tender mercies • kindness • humility • meekness • longsuffering (patience) • Bear with one another. • Forgive one another. • Above all, put on love. • Let the peace of God rule in your hearts. • Be thankful. • Let the Word of Christ dwell in you richly. • Teach and admonish one another. • Sing with grace in your hearts.
"Now abide faith, hope, love, these three; but the greatest of these is love" (13:13).	"Against such there is no law . . . If we live in the Spirit, let us also walk in the Spirit" (5:23, 25).	"The things which you learned and received and heard and saw in me, these do, and the God of peace will be with you" (4:9).	"Whatever you do in word or deed, do all in the name of the Lord Jesus" (3:17).

PHILIPPIANS

hilippians is the epistle of joy and encouragement in the midst of adverse circumstances. Paul freely expresses his fond affection for the Philippian Christians, appreciates their consistent testimony and support, and lovingly urges them to center their actions and thoughts on the pursuit of the Person and power of Christ.

Author

 This letter is clearly identified as written by Paul (1:1), and Pauline authorship has never seriously been questioned. There has been frequent and vigorous debate, however, over the date and place of writing.

Date

The traditional view has been that Paul wrote Philippians between A.D. 61 and 63 from imprisonment in Rome. The references to the palace guard (1:13) and Caesar's household (4:22) fit with Paul's Roman imprisonment. In addition, Paul's statements in 1:12–20 and 4:22 strongly suggest that the imprisonment was fairly long. Thus, this letter appears to have been written sometime after the beginning of Paul's imprisonment recorded in Acts 28.

More recently, however, some scholars have suggested that Philippians was written about A.D. 55 during Paul's ministry in Ephesus (Acts 19; 20) or about A.D. 56–61 during his imprisonment at Caesarea (Acts 24—26). They point out that the terms "Caesar's household" and "palace guard" could instead refer to Roman authorities in provincial cities like Ephesus or Caesarea. Those who argue for Ephesus point out that the frequent travels between Paul's prison and Philippi implied by 1:26; 2:19, 23–26; 4:18 suggest that Paul was nearer to Philippi than a Roman imprisonment would allow.

It should be noted, however, that Acts does not mention an imprisonment in Ephesus, that Caesarea was much farther from Philippi than Rome was, and that reasonably swift travel was possible between Rome and Philippi, which

Continued on page 413

Philippians at a Glance

FOCUS	ACCOUNT OF CIRCUMSTANCES	THE MIND OF CHRIST	THE KNOWLEDGE OF CHRIST	THE PEACE OF CHRIST
REFERENCE	1:1 ———————— 2:1 ————————		3:1 ———————— 4:1 ———————— 4:23	
DIVISION	PARTAKE OF CHRIST	PEOPLE OF CHRIST	PURSUIT OF CHRIST	POWER OF CHRIST
TOPIC	SUFFERING	SUBMISSION	SALVATION	SANCTIFICATION
	EXPERIENCE	EXAMPLES	EXHORTATION	
LOCATION	ROME			
TIME	C. A.D. 62			

Nelson's Complete Book of Bible Maps and Charts © 1993 by Thomas Nelson, Inc.

Continued from page 411

was located on the main Roman road, the Via Egnatia. Therefore, the traditional view that this letter was written from Rome sometime between A.D. 61 and 63 is preferred.

Themes and Literary Structure

Philippians is one of Paul's most personal letters. In it he shares his own experience with Christ, and his struggle over whether to prefer dying to be with Christ or living to serve the Philippians (1:21–26). The Philippians were in his heart and they supported him in his imprisonment (1:7), a fact which explains the note of gratitude that Paul frequently sounds (1:3–11; 2:19–30; 4:10–20).

Philippians focuses on: Paul's account of his present circumstances (ch. 1), Paul's appeal to have the mind of Christ (ch. 2), his appeal to have the knowledge of Christ (ch. 3), and his appeal to have the peace of Christ (ch. 4).

Prominent in Philippians is the theme of joy. The word "joy" (Greek: *chara*) is found five times (1:4, 25; 2:2, 29; 4:1) and the verb "to rejoice" occurs eleven times (twice in 1:18; 2:17, 18; 4:4; and once in 2:28; 3:1; and 4:10). Despite his unpleasant circumstances in prison, Paul manifests a joyous confidence in God's provision for him personally and for the Philippian Christians.

Paul exhorts the Philippians to have a spirit of unity and mutual concern by embracing the attitude of humility (2:1–4), the greatest example of which is the incarnation and crucifixion of Christ (2:5–11). The *kenosis*, or "self-emptying" of Christ does not mean that He relinquished His essential deity, but that He withheld His preincarnate glory and voluntarily restricted His use of certain attributes (such as omnipresence).

OUTLINE OF PHILIPPIANS

Christ and Adam

Christians are exhorted to have the mind of Christ (2:5–11), the essence of which is humility and sacrificial love for others. Christ's example here contrasts with the very different mind of Adam, whose disobedience and pride are overturned by the obedience and humility of Christ.

See chart, "Adam and Christ: Comparison and Contrast," on page 415.

Seeking Christ

The book of Philippians teaches that the Christian life focuses on seeking Christ and the pursuit of intimacy with God. It is devoting oneself to knowing Jesus Christ, and one measure of spiritual maturity is the degree to which this pursuit becomes our consuming focus and desire.

SEEK...

• Christ above all (1:21; 3:7, 8) and FIND righteousness in Christ and the power of His resurrection (3:9–11)

• Christlike humility (2:5–7) and FIND God's will in the believer (2:12, 13)

• A divinely appointed goal (3:14) and FIND the prize of eternal salvation (3:14)

• All things that are true, noble, just, pure, lovely, virtuous, and praiseworthy (4:8) and FIND the presence of the God of peace (4:9)

Adam and Christ:
Comparison and Contrast

Adam	Christ
Made in the divine image.	Is the form and very essence of God.
Thought it a prize to be grasped at to be as God.	Thought it not a prize to be grasped at to be as God.
Aspired to a reputation.	Made himself of no reputation.
Spurned the role of God's servant.	Took upon Himself the form of a bondservant (slave).
Seeking to be like God,	Coming in the likeness of men,
And being made a man (of dust, now doomed),	And being found in appearance as a man (Rom. 8:3),
He exalted himself,	He humbled Himself,
And became disobedient unto death.	And became obedient to the point of death.
He was condemned and disgraced.	God highly exalted Him and gave Him the name and position of Lord.

Nelson's Complete Book of Bible Maps and Charts © 1993 by Thomas Nelson, Inc.

The Ten Favorite Myths

No.	Myth	See
1	Jesus Christ was only a great moral teacher.	Matt. 13:34–35
2	There is no evidence that Jesus rose from the dead.	Matt. 28:1–10
3	Science is in conflict with Christian faith.	John 4:48
4	It doesn't matter what you believe, all religions are basically the same.	Acts 4:12
5	Christianity is just a crutch for the weak.	1 Cor. 1:26
6	People become Christians through social conditioning.	1 Cor. 15:9–10
7	Christianity stifles personal freedom.	Gal 5:1–12
8	Christianity is other-worldly and irrelevant to modern life.	Heb. 12:1–2
9	The Bible is unreliable and not to be trusted.	2 Pet. 1:16
10	All the evil and suffering in the world proves there is no God.	Rev. 20:1–10

COLOSSIANS

olossians is perhaps the most Christ-centered book in the Bible. In it Paul stresses the preeminence of the Person of Christ and the completeness of the salvation He provides.

Author

The external testimony to the Pauline authorship of Colossians is ancient and consistent. The internal evidence is also very good; it not only claims to have been written by Paul (1:1, 23; 4:18), but the personal details and close parallels with Ephesians and Philemon strengthen the case.

Nevertheless, the authenticity of this letter has been challenged on the ground of vocabulary and thought. In its four chapters, Colossians uses fifty-five Greek words that do not appear in Paul's other epistles. The high Christology of Colossians has been compared to John's later concept of Christ as the Creator *Logos* (1:15–23; cf. John 1:1–18), with the conclusion that these concepts were too late for Paul's time. Also, it is sometimes argued that the Colossian heresy is a type of Gnosticism prevalent in the second-century A.D.

We must recognize, however, that Paul commanded a wide vocabulary, and the unique topics addressed in this letter, particularly the Colossian heresy, account for the vocabulary of the epistle. In addition, there is no reason to assume that Paul was unaware of Christ's work as Creator, especially in view of Philippians 2:5–11. Finally, the information regarding the Colossian heresy in chapter 2 points rather to what was probably an early form of Gnosticism, rather than full-fledged Gnosticism of the second-century variety.

Date

Paul wrote this epistle from prison, as he did Ephesians, Philippians, and Philemon. Although Caesarea and Ephesus have been suggested as possible locations of authorship, the bulk of evidence suggests that Paul wrote it in A.D. 60 or 61 during his first Roman imprisonment (Acts 28:16–31) and sent it with Tychicus and the converted slave Onesimus to Colosse (4:7–9; cf. Eph 6:21; Philem. 10–12).

Continued on page 418

Colossians at a Glance

FOCUS	SUPREMACY OF CHRIST			SUBMISSION TO CHRIST		
REFERENCE	1:1 ——————— 1:15 ——————— 2:4 ———			3:1 ——————— 3:5 ——————— 4:7 ——— 4:18		
DIVISION	INTRODUCTION	PREEMINENCE OF CHRIST	FREEDOM IN CHRIST	POSITION OF THE BELIEVER	PRACTICE OF THE BELIEVER	CONCLUSION
TOPIC	DOCTRINAL			PRACTICAL		
	WHAT CHRIST DID FOR US			WHAT CHRIST DOES THROUGH US		
LOCATION	ROME					
TIME	A.D. 60–61					

Nelson's Complete Book of Bible Maps and Charts © 1993 by Thomas Nelson, Inc.

Continued from page 416

Colosse was a minor city about one hundred miles east of Ephesus in the region of the seven Asian churches of Revelation 1—3. Located in the fertile Lycus Valley on the road from Ephesus to the east, Colosse had previously been a populous center of commerce, but by the time of Paul it had been eclipsed in importance by the neighboring cities of Laodicea and Hierapolis. Apart from this letter, Colosse exerted almost no influence on early church history.

The precise character of the Colossian heresy has been a matter of debate. The nature of this heresy can only be deduced from Paul's incidental references to it in his refutation in 2:8–23. It was apparently a religious system that combined elements from Hellenistic Greek speculation (2:4, 8–10), Jewish legalism (2:11–17), and Oriental mysticism (2:18–23). It involved a low view of the body (2:20–23) and probably of nature as a whole. With its stress upon the importance of circumcision, dietary regulations, and ritual observances, together with its worship of angels and preoccupation with mystical experiences, the Colossian heresy denied the sufficiency of Christ, and any attempt to fit Christ into such a system would undermine His Person and redemptive work.

Themes and Literary Structure

The resounding theme in Colossians is the preeminence and sufficiency of Christ in all things. The believer is complete in Him alone and lacks nothing because "in Him dwells all the fullness of the Godhead bodily" (2:9). The first part of the epistle is an exposition of Christ's supremacy (chs. 1—2); the second part explains the implications of Christ's supremacy in terms of the believer's submission to Christ the Lord (chs. 3—4).

Particularly in the second half of the epistle, Paul explores the implications of the believer's union with Christ. The believer's union with Christ in His death, resurrection and exaltation is the foundation upon which earthly life must be built (3:1-4). Because of their death with Christ, Christians must regard themselves as dead to the old way of sin (3:5–11); because of their resurrection with Christ, believers must regard themselves as alive to Him in righteousness and must put on the new qualities that are prompted by Christian love (3:12–17).

The new life in Christ is to be manifested in the personal relationships of the Christian. Paul provides specific instructions for husbands and wives, children, servants, and masters (3:18—4:1).

Ephesians and Colossians Compared

Though written at approximately the same time and reflecting similar themes, the books of Ephesians and Colossians have their own distinctive emphases. If the book of Ephesians can be labeled the epistle portraying the "Church of Christ," then the focus of Colossians must surely be the "Christ of the Church."

Ephesians	Colossians
Jesus Christ: Lord of the *church*	Jesus Christ: Lord of the *cosmos*
Emphasis on the *church* as the body of Christ but also affirms Christ as Head of the church.	Emphasis on *Christ* as the Head of the cosmos and the church.
Less personal and probably a *circular* epistle.	More personal and *local*-church-oriented.
Addresses the errors of false teaching less directly (heresy is not yet a major danger).	Speaks to the errors of false doctrine directly (heresy is more threatening).
Common themes treated extensively.	Common themes treated briefly.

Christ Above All

The apostle does not directly argue with the Colossians about their false doctrines. Rather, beginning in the first chapter, he builds a positive case for Christian truth by showing the preeminence of Christ in everything.

See chart, "The Preeminence of Christ," on page 421.

Focusing on Christ

The first two chapters of Colossians constitute one of the great Christological passages in Scripture. In stressing the role of the Son as Creator and Redeemer, and in his recognition that "in Him dwells all the fullness of the Godhead bodily" (2:9), Paul affirms the full deity of Christ.

See chart, "The Four Great Christological Passages," on page 422.

A Singing Faith

As is evident in the Old Testament, the Hebrew faith emphasized the joy of singing to the Lord, but Christianity is even more profoundly a singing faith. Singing can help to make teaching and preaching even more useful. The Colossians were to emphasize the ministry of teaching and admonition by the singing of psalms, hymns, and spiritual songs. See the following list.

Hymns and Songs

Personality	Description	Biblical Reference
Jesus and Disciples	A song in the Upper Room as they celebrated the Passover together just before the arrest of Jesus	Matt. 26:30
Mary	The Song of Mary, upon learning that she as a virgin would give birth to the Messiah	Luke 1:46–55
Zacharias	A song of joy at the circumcision of his son, who would serve as the Messiah's forerunner	Luke 1:68–79
Paul and Silas	A song of praise to God at midnight from their prison cell in Philippi	Acts 16:25
All Believers	The spiritual songs of thanksgiving and joy, which God wants all believers to sing	Eph. 5:19 Col. 3:16
144,000 Believers	A new song of the redeemed in heaven, sung to glorify God	Rev. 14:1–3

The Preeminence of Christ

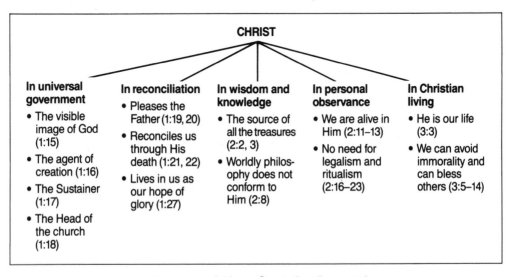

CHRIST

In universal government
- The visible image of God (1:15)
- The agent of creation (1:16)
- The Sustainer (1:17)
- The Head of the church (1:18)

In reconciliation
- Pleases the Father (1:19, 20)
- Reconciles us through His death (1:21, 22)
- Lives in us as our hope of glory (1:27)

In wisdom and knowledge
- The source of all the treasures (2:2, 3)
- Worldly philosophy does not conform to Him (2:8)

In personal observance
- We are alive in Him (2:11–13)
- No need for legalism and ritualism (2:16–23)

In Christian living
- He is our life (3:3)
- We can avoid immorality and can bless others (3:5–14)

The Four Great Christological Passages

	John 1; 14	Philippians 2	Colossians 1; 2	Hebrews 1; 2
(1) His Divine Relationship to the Father	The Word 1:1, 14	Form of God 2:6	The image of the invisible God 1:15, 19	The revelation of God 1:2
	Radiant glory 1:14; 14:7			
	Only begotten 1:14, 18	Equal with God 2:6	Firstborn 1:15, 18	Firstborn 1:6
	Son 3:16	Bondservant 2:7	The Son He (God) loves 1:13	Son 1:2a, 5, 8
(2) His Divine Work Creation of All	1:1–3		1:16–18	1:2, 3, 10
Salvation	1:12, 13	2:6–8	1:4, 5, 19–22; 2:6, 13–15	1:3; 2:10, 11
(3) His Divine Nature	*Theos* (God) 1:1, 18	*Theos* (God) 2:6	*Theotetos* (Godhead) 2:9	*Theos* (God) 1:8
Exclusively	1:18; 14:6	2:6	1:19; 2:9	1:3
In the Flesh	1:14	2:7, 8	2:9	1:6; 2:14–18

Nelson's Complete Book of Bible Maps and Charts © 1993 by Thomas Nelson, Inc.

The Definitive Christological Passages

The Christ	His Divine Relationship	His Divine Work	His Divine Name	His Divine Nature
The Gospel of John (John 1; 14)	The Word (John 1:1, 14) Radiant glory (John 1:14; 14:7) Only begotten (John 1:14, 18) Son (John 3:16)	Creation of all (John 1:1–3) Salvation (John 1:12, 13)	*Theos* (Gk., lit. God) (John 1:1, 18)	Fully God (John 1:18; 14:6) Fully man (John 1:14)
The Epistle to the Philippians (Phil. 2)	Form of God (Phil. 2:6) Equal with God (Phil. 2:6) Bondservant (Phil. 2:7)	Salvation (Phil. 2:6–8)	*Theos* (Gk., lit. God) (Phil. 2:6)	Fully God (Phil. 2:6) Fully man (Phil. 2:7, 8)
The Epistle to the Colossians (Col. 1; 2)	The image of the invisible God (Col. 1:15, 19) Firstborn (Col. 1:15, 18) The Son He [God] loves (Col. 1:13)	Creation of all (Col. 1:16–18) Salvation (Col. 1:4, 5, 19–22; 2:6, 13–15)	*Theotetos* (Gk., lit. Godhead) (Col. 2:9)	Fully God (Col. 1:19; 2:9) Fully man (Col. 2:9)
The Epistle to the Hebrews (Heb. 1; 2)	The revelation of God (Heb. 1:2) Firstborn (Heb. 1:6) Son (Heb. 1:2, 5, 8)	Creation of all (Heb. 1:2, 3, 10) Salvation (Heb. 1:3; 2:10, 11)	*Theos* (Gk., lit. God) (Heb. 1:8)	Fully God (Heb. 1:3) Fully man (Heb. 1:6; 2:14–18)

1 AND 2 THESSALONIANS

Writing with gratitude and affection to a church that he had visited only briefly, Paul's first and second epistles to the Thessalonians offer words of encouragement to a faithful but struggling church, and they focus particularly on the encouragement offered by the return of Christ.

Author

First Thessalonians went unchallenged as a Pauline epistle until the nineteenth century, when radical critics claimed that its dearth of doctrinal content made its authenticity suspect. But the proportion of doctrinal teaching in Paul's epistles varies widely, and 1 Thessalonians was written to deal with one particular doctrinal issue—the return of Christ.

The external attestation to the authenticity of 2 Thessalonians is even stronger than that for 1 Thessalonians. Internally, the vocabulary, style, and doctrinal content support the claims in 2 Thessalonians 1:1 and 3:7 that it was written by Paul.

Date

Both Thessalonian epistles were written during Paul's second missionary journey, thus making them among the earliest of the New Testament books. After a brief stay in Thessalonica, the capital city of Macedonia, Paul journeyed to the south through Berea and Athens to Corinth, where he spent eighteen months. During the early part of his stay in Corinth from A.D. 51 to 52, Paul wrote 1 Thessalonians.

See map, "Paul's First and Second Journeys," on page 370.

A few months later, while Paul was still in Corinth, he received word from Thessalonica that his teaching on the day of the Lord had been misunderstood by some in the Thessalonian church. Paul then wrote another epistle, 2 Thessalonians, to correct certain misunderstandings and further to encourage the church.

Continued on page 426

1 Thessalonians at a Glance

FOCUS	REFLECTIONS ON THE THESSALONIANS			INSTRUCTIONS TO THE THESSALONIANS			
REFERENCE	1:1 ——— 2:1 ———		2:17 ——— 4:1 ———		4:13 ——— 5:1 ———	5:12 — 5:28	
DIVISION	COMMENDATION FOR GROWTH	FOUNDING OF THE CHURCH	STRENGTHENING OF THE CHURCH	DIRECTION FOR GROWTH	THE DEAD IN CHRIST	THE DAY OF THE LORD	HOLY LIVING
TOPIC	PERSONAL EXPERIENCE			PRACTICAL EXHORTATION			
	LOOKING BACK			LOOKING FORWARD			
LOCATION	WRITTEN IN CORINTH						
TIME	C. A.D. 51						

Nelson's Complete Book of Bible Maps and Charts © 1993 by Thomas Nelson, Inc.

Continued from page 424

In Paul's time, Thessalonica was the prominent seaport and the capital of the Roman province of Macedonia. This prosperous city was located on the Via Egnatia, the main road from Rome to the east, and was within sight of Mount Olympus, legendary home of the Greek pantheon.

A city of perhaps 200,000 in the first century A.D., Thessalonica had a sizable Jewish population, and the ethical monotheism of the Jewish religion attracted many Gentiles who had become disenchanted with Greek paganism. According to 1 Thessalonians 1:9 and 2:14–16, most of the Thessalonian converts were Gentiles who came out of idolatry.

Themes and Literary Structure

After Paul's forced separation from the Thessalonians (Acts 17:1–9), he grew increasingly concerned about the progress of their faith. First Thessalonians was written to commend and encourage the Thessalonian believers, who were enduring persecution, and to offer consolation concerning their loved ones who had died in Christ. The theme of Christ's coming recurs throughout the epistle, and 1 Thessalonians 4:13—5:11 provides one of the fullest New Testament treatments of this crucial truth. The two major sections of 1 Thessalonians are: Paul's personal reflections of the Thessalonians (chs. 1—3), and Paul's instructions for the Thessalonians (chs. 4—5).

Regarding the doctrine of the Second Coming with which both Thessalonian epistles are concerned, 1 Thessalonians stresses the imminence of the Lord's coming, while 2 Thessalonians observes that certain events will precede the end. Thus, Scripture presents the Lord's return in terms of both signs and suddenness. Some Christians have concluded from this that 1 Thessalonians speaks of a "rapture" of the church which will precede the final day of the Lord while 2 Thessalonians speaks of the judgment of Christ upon evil. Other Christians, noting that Paul's primary intention in these epistles is to highlight the comfort which hope of the Lord's coming brings for Christians (as well as to point out the error of thinking that one need not work because of the imminence of Christ's appearing), have argued that Paul does not present a detailed chronology of the end times. Rather, they believe that Paul is highlighting both the need to be ready constantly for the Lord's return and yet, at the same time, to be diligent in doing God's work on earth.

A Comparison of Emphases in 1 and 2 Thessalonians

1 Thessalonians	2 Thessalonians
Addresses how the Thessalonians were evangelized as they received the Word of God	Addresses how the Thessalonians are being edified, noting their progress in faith, love, and patience
The imminency and importance of the Lord's return is emphasized	Misunderstandings about the Lord's return are corrected
The saints are comforted and encouraged	The saints are assured of God's judgment on His enemies

Second Thessalonians is the theological sequel to First Thessalonians. Not long after receiving 1 Thessalonians from Paul, some of the Thessalonian believers fell prey to false teaching, thinking the final day of the Lord had already begun. Paul wrote this brief letter to correct that error by pointing out that certain identifiable events will precede the final day of the Lord and to encourage the Thessalonian believers, whose faith was being tested by persecution. Addressing the problem of those who refused to work because they thought the end was near or already upon them, Paul encouraged all the Thessalonian Christians to attend to their labors and not to live off others. Second Thessalonians may be divided into three major sections: Paul's encouragement in persecution (ch. 1); Paul's explanation of the day of the Lord (ch. 2); and Paul's exhortation to the church (ch. 3).

OUTLINE OF 1 THESSALONIANS

2 Thessalonians at a Glance

FOCUS	ENCOURAGEMENT IN PERSECUTION			EXPLANATION OF THE DAY OF THE LORD		EXHORTATION TO THE CHURCH	
REFERENCE	1:1 ——— 1:5 ——————— 1:11 ———			2:1 ——— 2:13 ———————		3:1 ——— 3:6 —— 3:18	
DIVISION	THANKSGIVING FOR GROWTH	ENCOURAGEMENT IN PERSECUTION	PRAYER FOR BLESSING	EVENTS PRECEDING	COMFORT OF THE BELIEVER	WAIT PATIENTLY	WITHDRAW
TOPIC	DISCOURAGED BELIEVERS			DISTURBED BELIEVERS		DISOBEDIENT BELIEVERS	
	THANKSGIVING FOR THEIR LIFE			INSTRUCTION OF THEIR DOCTRINE		CORRECTION OF THEIR BEHAVIOR	
LOCATION	WRITTEN IN CORINTH						
TIME	C. A.D. 51						

Nelson's Complete Book of Bible Maps and Charts © 1993 by Thomas Nelson, Inc.

OUTLINE OF 2 THESSALONIANS

1 AND 2 TIMOTHY

In 1 and 2 Timothy, the aged and experienced apostle Paul writes to his much younger protégé Timothy, a young pastor facing heavy responsibility. Paul's letters provide Timothy with encouragement in ministry and with detailed instructions for church organization and life.

Author

Since the early nineteenth century, the Pastoral Epistles (1 Timothy, 2 Timothy, and Titus) have been attacked more than any other Pauline epistles on the issue of authorship. The similarity of these epistles requires that they be treated as a unit in terms of authorship.

External evidence supports Pauline authorship. Postapostolic church fathers such as Polycarp and Clement of Rome allude to them, and these epistles are identified as Pauline from the time of Irenaeus and Tertullian. Only Romans and 1 Corinthians have better attestation among the Pauline epistles.

Some scholars, however, view these letters as "pious forgeries" that appeared during the second century. Reasons cited for this view include certain differences in language, and the assumption that the church order reflected in the Pastorals reflects a period later than the lifetime of Paul. While there are differences between the Pastorals and the other Pauline epistles, these differences are adequately explained by the fact that the other epistles were written to churches, while the Pastorals were written to individuals. Some linguistic differences may be due to Paul's use of an amanuensis (secretary), possibly Luke, or merely due to the fact that diversity of subject produces diversity of vocabulary. Furthermore, the assumption that these books are forgeries implies that the alleged author/compiler was deliberately deceptive, and these volumes differ markedly from writings we know to be postapostolic and pseudepigraphic. Finally, these letters do not address common second-century problems such as Gnosticism.

1 Timothy at a Glance

FOCUS	DOCTRINE	PUBLIC WORSHIP	FALSE TEACHERS	CHURCH DISCIPLINE	PASTORAL MOTIVES
REFERENCE	1:1 ——————— 2:1	——————— 4:1	——————— 5:1	——————— 6:1	——————— 6:21
DIVISION	PROBLEM OF FALSE DOCTRINE	PUBLIC WORSHIP AND LEADERSHIP	PRESERVE TRUE DOCTRINE	PRESCRIPTIONS FOR WIDOWS AND ELDERS	PASTORAL MOTIVATIONS
TOPIC	WARNING	WORSHIP	WISDOM	WIDOWS	WEALTH
	DANGERS OF FALSE DOCTRINE	DIRECTIONS FOR WORSHIP	DEFENSE AGAINST FALSE TEACHERS	DUTIES TOWARD OTHERS	DEALINGS WITH RICHES
LOCATION	WRITTEN IN MACEDONIA				
TIME	c. A.D. 62–63				

Nelson's Complete Book of Bible Maps and Charts © 1993 by Thomas Nelson, Inc.

Date

In these epistles, Paul writes to Timothy, who had become his close associate on the second missionary journey (Acts 16:1–3). On the basis of the historical reconstruction below, 1 Timothy was written c. A.D. 63 and 2 Timothy c. A.D. 67.

Pauline authorship of the Pastoral Epistles requires Paul's release from his Roman imprisonment (Acts 28), the continuation of his missionary endeavors, and his imprisonment for a second time in Rome. Unfortunately, the order of events can only be reconstructed from hints, because there is no history such as the book of Acts covering the final years of the apostle. The following reconstruction is, therefore, only tentative.

As he anticipated (Phil. 1:19, 25, 26; 2:24), Paul was released from his first Roman imprisonment (c. A.D. 63). In fulfillment of his promise to the Philippians (Phil. 2:19–23), he sent Timothy to Philippi to relate the good news. Paul himself went to Ephesus (in spite of his earlier expectation in Acts 20:38) and to other Asian churches like Colosse (see Philem. 22). When Timothy rejoined him in Ephesus, Paul instructed his assistant to "remain in Ephesus" (1 Tim. 1:3) while he journeyed to Macedonia. When he saw that he might be delayed in Macedonia, Paul wrote 1 Timothy (c. A.D. 63), perhaps from Philippi (1 Tim. 3:14, 15). After he saw Timothy in Ephesus, the apostle journeyed to the island of Crete where, after a period of ministry, he left Titus to

Evidence of Following Jesus

- Displays the "beautiful attitudes" described by Jesus in His Sermon on the Mount (Matt. 5:3–16).

- Thinks with a transformed mind, expresses a spirit of genuine love, and shows respect for authority (Rom. 12:1–2; 13:1–7).

- Reflects the "lifestyle of love" (1 Cor. 13).

- Displays the fruits of the Spirit described by Paul (Gal. 5:22–26).

- Looks out for the interests of others in the humility of Christ (Phil. 2:1–4).

- Rejoices always, prays without ceasing, and in everything gives thanks (1 Thess. 5:16–18).

- Carries out works of faith and compassion (James 2:14–17), controls the tongue (3:1–11), and is known for wisdom (3:13).

- Holds to the truth about Jesus (2 John 4, 3 John 3–4) and defends it (Jude 3).

continue the work (Titus 1:5). From Corinth, Paul wrote his epistle to Titus (c. A.D. 63) because Zenas and Apollos were making a journey that would take them by way of Crete (Titus 3:13). He instructed Titus to join him in Nicopolis after the arrival of his replacement in Crete (Titus 3:12).

If he went to Spain as he had planned (Rom. 15:24, 28), Paul probably departed with Titus for that western province after his winter in Nicopolis. Early church tradition holds that Paul did indeed go to Spain, and he may have been there from A.D. 64 to 66. He returned to Greece and Asia—to Corinth, Miletus, and Troas (2 Tim. 4:13, 20)—and may have been arrested in Troas where he left his valuable books and parchments (2 Tim. 4:13, 15). After his arrest, Paul was imprisoned in Rome where he wrote 2 Timothy from his prison cell.

A Comparison of Paul's Two Roman Imprisonments

First Imprisonment	Second Imprisonment
Acts 28—Wrote the Prison Epistles	2 Timothy
Accused by Jews of heresy and sedition	Persecuted by Rome and arrested as a criminal against the Empire
Local sporadic persecutions (A.D. 60–63)	Neronian persecution (A.D. 64–68)
Decent living conditions in a rented house (Acts 28:30, 31)	Poor conditions, in a cold, dark dungeon
Many friends visited him	Virtually alone (only Luke with him)
Many opportunities for Christian witness were available	Opportunities for witness were restricted
Was optimistic for release and freedom (Phil. 1:24–26)	Anticipated his execution (2 Tim. 4:6)

Themes and Literary Structure

In his first letter to Timothy, Paul seeks to guide his younger and less experienced assistant Timothy in his weighty responsibility as the overseer of the work at Ephesus and other Asian cities. He writes, in effect, a challenge to Timothy to fulfill the task before him: combatting false teaching with sound doctrine, developing qualified leadership, teaching God's Word, and encouraging Christian conduct. Because of the personal and conversational character of this letter, it is loosely structured around five clear charges that end each section (1:18–20; 3:14–16; 4:11–20; 5:21–25; 6:20, 21). These sections deal with: doctrine (ch. 1), public worship (chs. 2—3), the danger of false teachers (ch. 4), church discipline (ch. 5), and pastoral motives (ch. 5).

OUTLINE OF 1 TIMOTHY

Continued on page 436

2 Timothy at a Glance

FOCUS	PERSEVERE IN PRESENT TESTINGS			ENDURE IN FUTURE TESTINGS		
REFERENCE	1:1 ——————— 1:6 ——————— 2:1		——————— 3:1 ——————— 4:1 ——————— 4:6 ——— 4:22			
DIVISION	THANKSGIVING FOR TIMOTHY'S FAITH	REMINDER OF TIMOTHY'S RESPONSIBILITY	CHARACTERISTICS OF A FAITHFUL MINISTER	APPROACHING DAY OF APOSTASY	CHARGE TO PREACH THE WORD	APPROACHING DEATH OF PAUL
TOPIC	POWER OF THE GOSPEL		PERSEVERANCE OF THE GOSPEL	PROTECTOR OF THE GOSPEL	PROCLAMATION OF THE GOSPEL	
	REMINDER		REQUIREMENTS	RESISTANCE	REQUESTS	
LOCATION	ROMAN PRISON					
TIME	C. A.D. 67					

Nelson's Complete Book of Bible Maps and Charts © 1993 by Thomas Nelson, Inc.

Continued from page 434

In 2 Timothy, Paul writes as one who knows his days on earth are quickly drawing to a close. About to relinquish his heavy burdens, the godly apostle seeks to challenge and strengthen his faithful but somewhat timid associate, Timothy, in his difficult ministry in Ephesus. Despite his bleak circumstances, this is a letter of encouragement that urges Timothy on to steadfastness in the fulfillment of his divinely appointed task. Central to everything in 2 Timothy is the sure foundation of the Word of God. Paul focuses on the need to persevere in present testings (chs. 1 and 2) and to endure in future testings (chs. 3 and 4).

OUTLINE OF 2 TIMOTHY

I. **Persevere in Present Testings**....................... 1:1—2:26

    A. Thanksgiving for Timothy's Faith.................... 1:1–5
    B. Reminder of Timothy's Responsibility 1:6–18
    C. Characteristics of a Faithful Minister............... 2:1–26

II. **Endure in Future Testings** .... 3:1—4:22

    A. Approaching Day of Apostasy..................... 3:1–17
    B. Charge to Preach the Word...................... 4:1–5
    C. Approaching Death of Paul...................... 4:6–22

Paul's charges to Timothy (particularly as summed up in 2 Tim. 4:1–5) provide an appropriate summary of the essential conduct of a minister of the gospel.

See chart, "Timothy's Ministry," on page 437.

Timothy's Ministry

Timothy must...	Because...
Share in suffering for the gospel (1:8; 2:3)	Through such sharing others will be saved (2:10)
Continue in sound doctrine (1:13; 2:15)	False doctrine spreads and leads to ungodliness (2:16, 17)
Flee youthful lusts (2:22)	He must be cleansed and set apart for the Master's use (2:21)
Avoid contentiousness (2:23–25)	He must gently lead others to the truth (2:24–26)
Militantly preach the gospel (4:2)	Great apostasy is coming (4:3, 4)

Nelson's Complete Book of Bible Maps and Charts © 1993 by Thomas Nelson, Inc.

TITUS

Like 1 Timothy, Titus was written by Paul to an associate who worked as Paul's apostolic representative. This brief letter focuses on Titus's role and responsibility in the organization and supervision of the churches on the island of Crete.

Author

The Pauline authorship of the Pastoral Epistles (1 and 2 Timothy and Titus) has been a subject of controversy in the modern period. The case for Pauline authorship of these epistles is substantial, however, and the alternative of viewing them as "pious forgeries" does not commend itself (see Author of 1 and 2 Timothy).

Date

Although a chronology must be reconstructed from incidental comments in the Pastoral Epistles, it appears that the book of Titus was written c. A.D. 63, after Paul's release from the Roman imprisonment described in Acts 28 and shortly after the composition of 1 Timothy. See Date of 1 and 2 Timothy for a more detailed chronology of Paul's life after the close of the book of Acts.

The Mediterranean island of Crete is 156 miles long and up to 30 miles wide. Its first-century inhabitants were notorious for untruthfulness and immorality (1:12, 13) and the expression "to act the Cretan" became an idiom meaning "to play the liar." A number of Jews from Crete were present in Jerusalem on the day of Pentecost (Acts 2:11) and some of them may have believed in Christ and introduced the gospel to their country. Although Paul was shipwrecked on Crete during his trip to Rome (Acts 27:7–13), he probably had little time for active ministry during that brief sojourn. The apostle spread the gospel in the cities of Crete after his release from Roman imprisonment and he left Titus there to finish organizing the churches (1:5).

Titus at a Glance

FOCUS	APPOINT ELDERS		SET THINGS IN ORDER	
REFERENCE	1:1 ——————— 1:10	——————— 2:1	——————— 3:1	——————— 3:15
DIVISION	ORDAIN QUALIFIED ELDERS	REBUKE FALSE TEACHERS	SPEAK SOUND DOCTRINE	MAINTAIN GOOD WORKS
TOPIC	PROTECTION OF SOUND DOCTRINE		PRACTICE OF SOUND DOCTRINE	
	ORGANIZATION	OFFENDERS	OPERATION	OBEDIENCE
LOCATION	PROBABLY WRITTEN IN CORINTH			
TIME	C. A.D. 63			

Nelson's Complete Book of Bible Maps and Charts © 1993 by Thomas Nelson, Inc.

Themes and Literary Structure

 Not long after Paul's departure from Crete, he wrote this letter to encourage and assist Titus in his task of organizing the churches. It stresses sound doctrine and warns against those who distort the truth, but it is also a conduct manual that emphasizes good deeds and the proper conduct of various groups within the churches. This epistle falls into two major sections: appoint elders (ch. 1), and set things in order (chs. 2, 3).

Underlying the instructions of Paul is the theme that Christ is building His church, carefully choosing the stones that make up this habitation for God. The deity and redemptive work of Christ are beautifully affirmed in 2:13, 14, and Paul presents Christ's Second Coming as an incentive to holy living (2:12, 13).

Men and women, young and old, each have their vital functions to fulfill in the church if they are to be living examples of the doctrine they profess. Throughout his letter to Titus, Paul stresses the necessary, practical working out of salvation in the daily lives of both the elders and the congregations.

See chart, "Paul's Word to Titus," on page 441.

OUTLINE OF TITUS

Paul's Word to Titus

To the Cretans:	Ignore fables and false commandments (1:14)
To the older men:	Be sober, reverent, temperate, trusting, loving, and patient (2:2)
To the older women:	Be reverent, teach good things, do not slander nor drink much wine (2:3)
To the younger women:	Be discreet, pure homemakers and love your husbands and children (2:4, 5)
To the young men:	Be sober-minded, do good works, and maintain right doctrine (2:6–8)
To servants:	Be obedient and respectful of masters (2:9, 10)

Nelson's Complete Book of Bible Maps and Charts © 1993 by Thomas Nelson, Inc.

PHILEMON

This briefest of Paul's epistles (only 334 words in the Greek text) is a model of courtesy, discretion, and loving concern for the forgiveness of one who would otherwise face severe consequences.

Author

The general consensus of scholarship recognizes Philemon as the work of Paul. There could have been no doctrinal motive for its forgery, and it is supported externally by consistent tradition and internally by no less than three references to Paul (vv. 1, 9, 19).

Date

Philemon is one of the four "Prison Epistles" (Ephesians, Philippians, and Colossians were the others). It was written in A.D. 60 or 61 and dispatched at the same time as Colossians during Paul's first Roman imprisonment. Philemon 22 reflects Paul's hope of release from captivity.

Reconstructing the background of this letter, it appears that a slave named Onesimus had wronged his master and escaped to Rome, where he found relative safety among the masses. Somehow, Onesimus came into contact with Paul, who led him to Christ. Knowing that Onesimus had a responsibility to return to Philemon, Paul sent him back with Tychicus to Colosse carrying the epistle to Philemon.

Philemon was a resident of Colosse and a convert of Paul (v. 19), perhaps through an encounter with Paul in Ephesus during Paul's third missionary journey. Philemon's house was large enough to serve as a meeting place for the church there (v. 2). He was benevolent to other believers (vv. 5–7), and his son Archippus evidently held a position of leadership in the church (Col. 4:17; Philem. 2). Philemon may have had other slaves besides Onesimus, and he was not alone as a slave owner among the Colossian believers (Col. 4:1). Thus, this letter provided guidelines for other master-slave relationships.

Philemon at a Glance

FOCUS	PRAYER OF THANKSGIVING	PETITION FOR ONESIMUS	PROMISE TO PHILEMON
REFERENCE	1 ——————————— 8	——————————— 17	——————————— 25
DIVISION	COMMENDATION OF PHILEMON'S LOVE	INTERCESSION FOR ONESIMUS	CONFIDENCE IN PHILEMON'S OBEDIENCE
TOPIC	PRAISE OF PHILEMON	PLEA OF PAUL	PLEDGE OF PAUL
	CHARACTER OF PHILEMON	CONVERSION OF ONESIMUS	CONFIDENCE OF PAUL
LOCATION	ROME		
TIME	c. A.D. 60–61		

Nelson's Complete Book of Bible Maps and Charts © 1993 by Thomas Nelson, Inc.

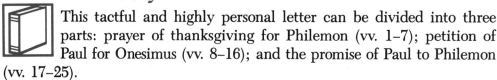

Themes and Literary Structure

This tactful and highly personal letter can be divided into three parts: prayer of thanksgiving for Philemon (vv. 1–7); petition of Paul for Onesimus (vv. 8–16); and the promise of Paul to Philemon (vv. 17–25).

Paul's epistle to Philemon is a testimony to the power of the grace of God in Christ Jesus and to the Christian love which unites believers. While he was formerly a thief and runaway slave, Philemon's slave Onesimus had been transformed by God's grace and was now a "beloved brother" of Philemon (v. 16).

See chart, "How Love Works," below.

OUTLINE OF PHILEMON

How Love Works

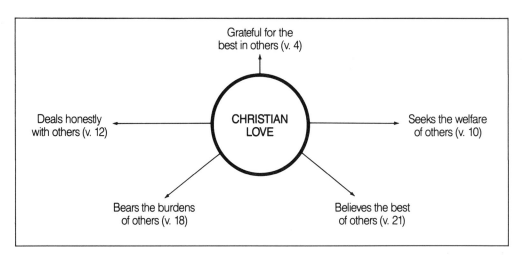

Nelson's Complete Book of Bible Maps and Charts © 1993 by Thomas Nelson, Inc.

HEBREWS

ebrews stands alone among the New Testament epistles in its style and approach, and it is the only New Testament book whose authorship remains a real mystery. This profound work builds a case for the superiority of Christ through a cumulative argument in which Christ is presented as "better" in every respect.

Author

Despite many suggestions, the author of Hebrews remains unknown. Clement of Alexandria (c. A.D. 150–215) named Paul as the author but argued that Luke translated the book into Greek. Origen (c. A.D. 185–253) concluded that the thoughts were those of Paul but that the phraseology and composition were those of someone who was recalling the apostle's teaching (e.g., Clement of Rome or Luke). Many others have been proposed as the possible author: Barnabas (suggested by Tertullian), Apollos (by Luther), Philip the evangelist (by William Ramsay), and Priscilla and Aquila (by Adolf von Harnack). Origen's famous remark still stands: "Who the author of the epistle is, God only knows."

Date

The place of writing is unknown, but a reasonable estimate of the date can be made. Hebrews was quoted c. A.D. 95 by Clement of Rome, but its failure to mention the cessation of the Old Testament sacrificial system with the destruction of Jerusalem in A.D. 70 indicates that it was written prior to that date. Timothy was still alive (12:23), persecution was mounting, and the old Jewish system was about to be removed (12:26, 27). All of this suggests a date between A.D. 64 and 68.

The recipients of this work were believers (3:1) who had come to faith through the testimony of eyewitnesses to Christ (2:3). They had endured hardships because of their stand for the gospel (10:32–34), but were in danger of drifting away. The repeated arguments regarding the superiority of Christ and His sacrifice over Moses and the Old Testament sacrificial system indicate that

Continued on page 447

Hebrews at a Glance

FOCUS	CHRIST'S PERSON						THE WALK OF FAITH		
				CHRIST'S WORK					
REFERENCE	1:1 ——— 1:4 ——— 3:1 ——— 4:14 — 8:1 ——— 9:1 ——— 10:19 ——— 12:1 ——— 13:1 — 13:25								
DIVISION	CHRIST OVER PROPHETS	CHRIST OVER ANGELS	CHRIST OVER MOSES	PRIEST-HOOD	COVENANT	SANCTUARY AND SACRIFICE	ASSURANCE OF FAITH	ENDURANCE OF FAITH	EXHORTATION TO LOVE
TOPIC	MAJESTY OF CHRIST			MINISTRY OF CHRIST			MINISTERS FOR CHRIST		
	DOCTRINE						DISCIPLINE		
LOCATION	PLACE OF WRITING UNKNOWN								
TIME	C. A.D. 64–68								

Nelson's Complete Book of Bible Maps and Charts © 1993 by Thomas Nelson, Inc.

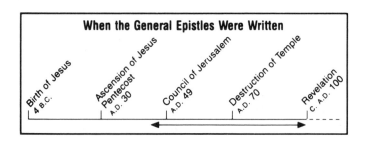

When the General Epistles Were Written

Birth of Jesus 4 B.C. — Ascension of Jesus Pentecost A.D. 30 — Council of Jerusalem A.D. 49 — Destruction of Temple A.D. 70 — Revelation C. A.D. 100

Continued from page 445
the recipients were probably Jewish Christians in danger of lapsing back into the Jewish religion.

Themes and Literary Structure

The author calls his book a "word of exhortation" (13:22), leading many to view it more as a written sermon than a letter. Hebrews is actually an extended exposition of numerous Old Testament passages, and the author relied upon the Septuagint (the Greek translation of the Old Testament) for his quotations. After using the Old Testament to demonstrate the superiority of Christ's Person (1:1—4:13) and the superiority of Christ's work (4:14—18:18), the writer applies these truths in a practical way to show the superiority of the Christian's walk of faith (10:19—13:25).

The basic theme of Hebrews is found in the word "better," describing the superiority of Christ in His Person and work (1:4; 6:9; 7:7, 19, 22; 8:6; 9:23; 10:34; 11:16, 35, 40; 12:24). The words "perfect" and "heavenly" are also prominent. He offers a better revelation, position, priesthood, covenant, sacrifice, and power.

Hebrews presents Christ as the divine-human Prophet, Priest, and King. His deity (1:3, 8) and humanity (2:9, 14, 17, 18) are asserted with equal force, and over twenty titles are used to describe His attributes and accomplishments (e.g., "heir of all things," "Apostle and High Priest," "Mediator," and "Author and Finisher of *our* faith").

OUTLINE OF HEBREWS

The Superiority of Christ

The first chapter of Hebrews is one of the most important Christological passages in Scripture (see also John 1:1; Phil. 2:6–11; and Col. 1:15–20). Christ's superiority over the Old Testament prophets and over the angels is portrayed through seven character affirmations and seven Scripture quotations.

See chart, "Christ's Superiority," on page 450.

The Works of Faith

The faith that the readers must maintain is defined in Hebrews 11:1–3 and illustrated in 11:4–40. The triumphs and accomplishments of faith in the lives of Old Testament believers should encourage Christians to look "unto Jesus, the author and finisher of *our* faith" (12:2).

See chart, "How Faith Works," on page 450.

The Hall of Fame of Faith

The hall of fame of the Scriptures is located in Hebrews 11 and records those who willingly took God at His word even when there was nothing to cling to but His promise.

Person	Scripture Reference
Abel	Genesis 4
Enoch	Genesis 5
Noah	Genesis 6
Abraham	Genesis 12
Jonah	Genesis 17
Isaac	Genesis 27
Jacob	Genesis 48
Joseph	Genesis 50
Moses' parents	Exodus 2
Moses	Exodus 2
Rahab	Joshua 2, 6
Gideon, Barak, Samson, Jephthah	Joshua 4, 6, 13, 11
David, Samuel, and the prophets	1 Samuel

Christ's Superiority

Jesus Is Greater Than the Prophets 1:1–3 Seven character affirmations:	Jesus Is Greater Than the Angels 1:4–14 Seven Scripture quotations:
Heir of all things (v. 2)	Psalm 2:7 (v. 5)
Creator (v. 2)	2 Samuel 7:14 (v. 3)
Manifestation of God's Being (v. 3)	Deuteronomy 32:43 or Psalm 97:7 (v. 6)
Perfect representation of God (v. 3)	Psalm 104:4 (v. 7)
Sustainer of all things (v. 3)	Psalm 45:6, 7 (vv. 8, 9)
Savior (v. 3)	Psalm 102:25–27 (vv. 10–12)
Exalted Lord (v. 3)	Psalm 110:1 (v. 13)

Nelson's Complete Book of Bible Maps and Charts © 1993 by Thomas Nelson, Inc.

How Faith Works

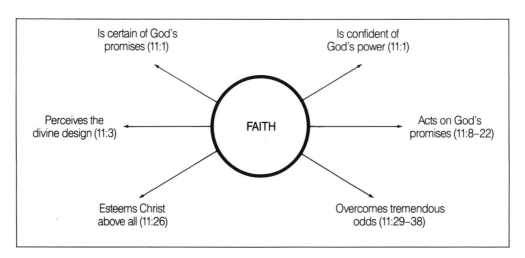

Nelson's Complete Book of Bible Maps and Charts © 1993 by Thomas Nelson, Inc.

THE GENERAL EPISTLES

The General Epistles, sometimes called the "Catholic Epistles" (the Greek term *katholikos* means "universal") include the epistles of James; 1 and 2 Peter; 1, 2, and 3 John; and Jude. In contrast to the Pauline epistles, which are named according to their recipients, the general epistles are designated by the name of their author. These letters, found near the end of the New Testament, are for the most part addressed to the church in general or to groups of churches (3 John is clearly addressed to an individual and 2 John may be)—hence the term "general."

Two Covenants Compared

THE OLD COVENANT (Heb. 9:1–10)	THE NEW COVENANT (Heb. 9:11–28)
Obsolete now that Christ has come (Heb. 8:13).	A better covenant brought about by Christ (Heb. 7:19; 8:6–7).
Originated at Mount Sinai (Gal. 4:24–25).	Originated from the Jerusalem above (Gal. 4:26–27).
Brought death and condemnation (2 Cor. 3:7–9).	Brings life (Eph. 2:1–13).
Impossible to obey perfectly because of human weakness and sin (Rom. 8:3).	Fulfilled perfectly by Christ (Luke 22:20; 1 Cor. 11:25).
Required annual atonement for sins (Heb. 9:7–8; 10:1–4).	Removes sin once for all and cleanses the conscience (Heb. 9:12; 10:2, 22).
Restricted access to God (Heb. 9:7–8).	Opened access to God for all (Heb. 9:15–16).

Like the Pauline epistles, the general epistles follow the customary form for Hellenistic Greek correspondence: an introduction listing the author and recipients with a greeting and thanksgiving, followed by the body or substance of the letter, and a conclusion.

The original destinations of the general epistles are often uncertain and the greetings are correspondingly general. James writes to Jewish Christians "scattered abroad," Peter to Christians throughout Asia Minor, and the Johannine letters were probably likewise written to churches and individuals in Asia Minor. Jude writes to an unnamed region troubled by false teachers.

JAMES

Faith without works cannot be called faith. Faith without works is dead, and a dead faith is worse than no faith at all. Faith must work; it must produce; mere mental assent is insufficient. Throughout his epistle to Jewish believers, James integrates true faith and everyday practical experience by stressing that true faith must manifest itself in works of faith.

Author

The author of this letter identifies himself simply as James, "a bond-servant of God and of the Lord Jesus Christ" (1:1). The name was quite common; and the New Testament lists at least five men named "James," two of whom were disciples of Jesus and one of whom was His brother. Tradition has ascribed the book to James, the brother of the Lord, and there is little reason to question this view, since the language of the epistle is somewhat similar to James' speech in Acts 15.

This James is mentioned twice in the Gospels (Matt. 13:55; Mark 6:3), both times as one of the brothers of Jesus. Although he is not called a follower of the Lord until after the resurrection, he was probably among the disciples who obeyed Jesus' command to wait in the Upper Room and who were there filled with the Holy Spirit (Acts 1:14; 2:4). When Peter left Palestine (Acts 12:17), James seems to have become the leader of the Jerusalem church.

It has been argued that the Greek of this epistle is too sophisticated for a Galilean such as James, but this assumes that he never had the opportunity or aptitude to develop a proficiency in *Koine* ("common") Greek. As a prominent church leader, it would have been to his advantage to become fluent in the universal language of the Roman Empire.

Date

According to the Jewish historian Josephus, James was martyred in A.D. 62. Those who accept him as the author of this epistle have proposed a date of writing ranging from A.D. 45 to the end of his life. However, several factors indicate that this may be the earliest New Testament

Continued on page 455

James at a Glance

FOCUS	TEST OF FAITH		CHARACTERISTICS OF FAITH	TRIUMPH OF FAITH		
REFERENCE	1:1 ——— 1:13 ———		1:19 ———————————— 5:7 ———	5:13 ———	5:19 ———	5:20
DIVISION	PURPOSE OF TESTS	SOURCE OF TEMPTATION	OUTWARD DEMONSTRATION OF INNER FAITH	ENDURES WAITING	PRAYS FOR AFFLICTED	CONFRONTS SIN
TOPIC	DEVELOPMENT OF FAITH		WORKS OF FAITH	POWER OF FAITH		
	RESPONSE OF FAITH		REALITY OF FAITH	REASSURANCE OF FAITH		
LOCATION	PROBABLY JERUSALEM					
TIME	C. A.D. 46–49					

Nelson's Complete Book of Bible Maps and Charts © 1993 by Thomas Nelson, Inc.

Continued from page 453

writing (c. A.D. 46–49): (1) there is no mention of Gentile believers or their relationship to Jewish Christians; (2) the allusions to the teaching of Christ bear so little verbal agreement with the Synoptic Gospels that James probably precedes the composition of the Gospels; (3) James uses the Greek term for "synagogue" in 2:2 (NKJV: "assembly") in addition to the term "church" (5:14), thus indicating a very simple church organization of elders and teachers (3:1; 5:14) which was patterned after the Jewish synagogue; and (4) James does not mention the issues involved in the Jerusalem Council of Acts 15 (A.D. 49).

Themes and Literary Structure

James is the Proverbs of the New Testament because it is written in the terse, moralistic style of wisdom literature. It is evident that James was profoundly influenced by the Old Testament as well as by the teaching of Jesus. Because of the many subjects in this epistle, it is difficult to outline. The outline used here is: the test of faith (1:1–18); the characteristics of faith (1:19—5:6); and the triumph of faith (5:7–20).

OUTLINE OF JAMES

Allusions to the Sermon on the Mount

The profound impact of the teaching of Jesus upon James is evident in the many allusions to His teaching, particularly the Sermon on the Mount. Sometimes called the "Amos of the New Testament" because of his concern for ethical integrity and justice, James peppers the 108 verses of his work with 54 imperatives in order to communicate the need for action on the part of his audience.

See chart, "James and the Sermon on the Mount," on page 457.

Paul and James Compared

Because of James's assertion in 2:24 that "a man is justified by works, and not by faith only," some church leaders (including Martin Luther) have felt that James contradicts the great Pauline teaching of justification by faith (cf. Rom. 3:28; Eph. 2:8). A careful reading of James and Paul reveals that the contradiction is only apparent. Paul, no less than James, realized that a genuine, living faith will issue in works of love and obedience (Gal. 5:6).

The difference between Paul and James lies in the fact that Paul attacks the problem of legalism, while James opposes libertines who felt that the quality of a Christian's conduct is irrelevant. For Paul, the question is how a genuine faith lays hold of the finished work of Jesus Christ—the contrast is between faith and works. For James, the question is how one demonstrates that one's faith is genuine—the contrast between a living and a dead faith.

See chart, "Paul and James Compared," on page 457.

Faith Alive

James wants his readers to demonstrate in their lives the qualities of a living faith. Such a living faith is more than mere knowledge and assent—it includes heartfelt trust that endures and obeys God.

Described as:	Results in:
Tested (1:2, 3)	Patience (1:3)
Without doubt (1:6–8)	Answered prayer (1:5)
Enduring temptation (1:12)	Eternal life (1:12)
More than belief (2:19, 20)	Faith perfected by works (2:22)
Believing God (2:23–25)	Righteousness before God (2:23)
James contrasts living faith to dead, or empty, faith. Dead faith does not result in the transformed life that is characteristic of living faith.	

James and the Sermon on the Mount

James	Sermon on the Mount	Subject
1:2	Matt. 5:10–12 (Luke 6:22, 23)	Joy in the midst of trials
1:4	Matt. 5:48	God's desire and work in us: perfection
1:5	Matt. 7:7	Asking God for good gifts
1:17	Matt. 7:11	God is the giver of good gifts
1:19, 20	Matt. 5:22	Command against anger
1:22, 23	Matt. 7:24–27	Contrast between hearers and doers (illustrated)
1:26, 27	Matt. 7:21–23	Religious person whose religion is worthless
2:5	Matt. 5:3	The poor as heirs of the kingdom
2:10	Matt. 5:19	The whole moral law to be kept
2:11	Matt. 5:21, 22	Command against murder
2:13	Matt. 5:7; 6:14, 15	The merciful blessed; the unmerciful condemned
2:14–26	Matt. 7:21–23	Dead, worthless (and deceiving) faith
3:12	Matt. 7:16 (Luke 6:44, 45)	Tree producing what is in keeping with its kind
3:18	Matt. 5:9	Blessing of those who make peace
4:2, 3	Matt. 7:7, 8	Importance of asking God
4:4	Matt. 6:24	Friendship with the world = hostility toward God
4:8	Matt. 5:8	Blessing on and call for the pure in heart
4:9	Matt. 5:4	Blessing and call for those who mourn
4:11, 12	Matt. 7:1–5	Command against wrongly judging others
4:13, 14	Matt. 6:34	Not focusing too much on tomorrow
5:1	(Luke 6:24, 25)	Woe to the rich
5:2	Matt. 6:19, 20	Moth and rust spoiling earthly riches
5:6	(Luke 6:37)	Against condemning the righteous man
5:9	Matt. 5:22; 7:1	Not judging—the Judge standing at the door
5:10	Matt. 5:12	The prophets as examples of wrongful suffering
5:12	Matt. 5:33–37	Not making hasty and irreverent oaths

Nelson's Complete Book of Bible Maps and Charts © 1993 by Thomas Nelson, Inc.

Paul and James Compared

	Paul	James
Concern	Legalists	Libertines
Emphasis	Justification with God by faith	Justification (vindication) before men by works
Perspective	Faith as a gift	Faith as genuine
Result	Justified as an eternal position by believing in Christ	Justified in daily proof by behaving like Christ

Nelson's Complete Book of Bible Maps and Charts © 1993 by Thomas Nelson, Inc.

1 PETER

P eter's first epistle addresses Christians facing persecution for their faith. As a comfort, Peter reminds them of their heavenly inheritance and he encourages them to live lives of submission to God's will.

Author

Some scholars have doubted that Peter wrote this letter. They claim that the good literary style and extensive vocabulary of the author could not have come from a Galilean fisherman. Nevertheless, there are strong reasons for believing that Peter is the author. The epistle contains references to Jesus' life and teaching. Scholars have also pointed out similarities between 1 Peter and Peter's speeches in Acts. First Peter also has similarities with Mark's Gospel, which may have been based upon Peter's preaching at Rome.

Peter's scribe, Silvanus (5:12), may have been responsible for much of the style and vocabulary. He probably applied his editorial skills to convey the message, personality, and apostolic authority of Peter the apostle.

Date

This epistle was written from "Babylon" (5:13), but scholars are divided as to whether this refers literally to Babylon in Mesopotamia or symbolically to Rome. There is no tradition that Peter went to Babylon, and in his day it was virtually deserted. On the other hand, tradition consistently indicates that Peter spent the last years of his life in Rome. As a center of idolatry, the term "Babylon" was an appropriate figurative designation for Rome (cf. Rev. 17; 18). Peter used other figurative expressions in this epistle, and it is not surprising that he would do the same with Rome. His mention of Mark (5:13) also fits this view because Mark was in Rome during Paul's first imprisonment (Col. 4:10). This epistle was probably written shortly before the outbreak of persecution under Nero in A.D. 64.

This letter is addressed "to the pilgrims of the Dispersion" (1:1), a term which could indicate that the recipients were Jewish Christians. On the other

Continued on page 460

1 Peter at a Glance

FOCUS	SALVATION OF THE BELIEVER		SUBMISSION OF THE BELIEVER	SUFFERING OF THE BELIEVER			
REFERENCE	1:1 ——— 1:13 ———		2:13 ———————	3:13 ———	3:18 ———	4:7 ———	5:1 — 5:14
DIVISION	SALVATION OF THE BELIEVER	SANCTIFICATION OF THE BELIEVER	GOVERNMENT, BUSINESS, MARRIAGE, AND ALL OF LIFE	CONDUCT IN SUFFERING	CHRIST'S EXAMPLE OF SUFFERING	COMMANDS IN SUFFERING	MINISTER IN SUFFERING
TOPIC	BELIEF OF CHRISTIANS		BEHAVIOR OF CHRISTIANS	BUFFETING OF CHRISTIANS			
	HOLINESS		HARMONY	HUMILITY			
LOCATION	EITHER ROME OR BABYLON						
TIME	C. A.D 63–64						

Nelson's Complete Book of Bible Maps and Charts © 1993 by Thomas Nelson, Inc.

Suffering in Divine Perspective

Human Suffering	Divine Perspective
Various trials (1 Pet. 1:6).	Rejoice; they are temporary (1 Pet. 1:6).
Unjust authority (1 Pet. 2:18).	Silence evil men by doing good. Follow the example of Christ (1 Pet. 2:21).
Suffering for doing what is right (1 Pet. 3:14).	Be ready to give testimony of your faith (1 Pet. 3:15).
Suffering because of a determination to resist carnal desires (1 Pet. 4:1).	Give up carnal pursuits (1 Pet. 4:2).
Religious persecution (1 Pet. 4:12–14).	Be partakers in Christ's sufferings (1 Pet. 4:13, 14).
Suffering as part of God's refining fire for spiritual growth (1 Pet. 4:19).	Commit your life to Him; He is faithful (1 Pet. 4:19).
Suffering from the attack of Satan (1 Pet. 5:8).	Resist Satan; be steadfast in faith (1 Pet. 5:9).

Continued from page 458

hand, the recipients are also described in terms more appropriate to Gentile converts (1:14, 18; 2:9, 10), and most scholars believe that they were predominantly Gentile Christians in churches throughout Asia Minor.

From the content of the letter, it is apparent that hostility and suspicion were mounting against Christians in the empire, and they were being reviled and abused for their lifestyles and talk about another kingdom. Christianity had not yet received the official Roman ban, but the stage was set for severe persecution and martyrdom in the near future.

Themes and Literary Structure

 The letter logically proceeds through the themes of the salvation of the believer (1:1—2:12); the submission of the believer (2:13—3:12); and the suffering of the believer (3:13—5:14).

The basic theme of 1 Peter is the proper response to Christian suffering. Knowing that his readers will be facing more persecution than ever before, Peter writes this letter to give them a divine perspective on these trials so they will endure without wavering in their faith.

This epistle presents Christ as the believer's example and hope in times of suffering. Christ's suffering is an example of what His followers may well face because they do what is right; personal suffering for the faith is also a means by which the Christian may share in the mind of Christ (4:1).

Peter discusses the believer's relationships in the world and appeals for an attitude of submission as the Christlike way to harmony and true freedom. Submission for the Lord's sake to those in governmental, social, and family authority will foster a good testimony to outsiders.

OUTLINE OF 1 PETER

Living Among Pagans

Peter addresses the important goal of believers pointing others to God by their godly lifestyles. Thus, they proclaim the praises of God (2:9), influence pagans to glorify God (2:12), win spouses to Christ by their examples (3:1), shame their ungodly critics (3:15, 16), and puzzle former companions (4:4). Christians are to be a redeeming force in the world, even though they suffer.

Christians are exhorted to be...	Because...
Good citizens (2:13, 14)	Foolish men will be silenced (2:15)
Obedient servants (2:18)	Christ is our example (2:21)
Submissive wives (3:1)	Some unbelieving husbands will be won by their example (3:1, 2)
Considerate husbands (3:7)	Their prayers will be heard (3:7)
Compassionate brothers and sisters (3:8)	They will inherit a blessing (3:9)

2 PETER

eter wrote his first epistle to encourage his readers to respond properly to external opposition. His second epistle focuses on internal opposition caused by false teachers whose "destructive heresies" (2:1) can seduce believers into error and immorality. While 1 Peter speaks of the new birth through the living Word, 2 Peter stresses the need for growth in the grace and knowledge of Christ. The best antidote for error is a mature understanding of the truth.

Author

Some scholars have doubted that Peter was the author of 2 Peter. They usually point to differences in style, vocabulary, and theology between 1 and 2 Peter. In addition, the external evidence for 2 Peter is weaker than that for any other New Testament book, and its canonicity was disputed until the fourth century A.D. Also, many argue that 2 Peter confronts the problem of Gnostic teachers in the church—a threat which dates to a period later than the lifetime of Peter. Finally, it is argued, because of the apparent literary relationship between 2 Peter and Jude, that 2 Peter was dependent upon Jude.

One cannot deny that the Greek of 1 Peter is much more polished than that of 2 Peter. But this difference can easily be accounted for if Peter used a different secretary to write the second epistle. Differences in vocabulary can also be explained in part by the differing subject matter of each letter.

The failure of 2 Peter to find quick acceptance was perhaps due to its brevity and apparent slow circulation among the churches. This delay in recognition meant that 2 Peter had to compete with several later heretical works that claimed to have been written by Peter (e.g., the Apocalypse of Peter)—though the contrast of 2 Peter with these later forgeries is striking.

The historical relationship between 2 Peter and Jude is by no means entirely clear. Although it is argued that 2 Peter quotes Jude and that Jude was written after Peter's death, it is possible that Jude quoted from 2 Peter or that both used a common source.

Continued on page 464

2 Peter at a Glance

FOCUS	CULTIVATION OF CHRISTIAN CHARACTER		CONDEMNATION OF FALSE TEACHERS			CONFIDENCE IN CHRIST'S RETURN	
REFERENCE	1:1 —— 1:15 —— 2:1 —— 2:4 —— 2:10 —— 3:1 —— 3:8 —— 3:18						
DIVISION	GROWTH IN CHRIST	GROUNDS OF BELIEF	DANGER	DESTRUCTION	DESCRIPTION	MOCKERY IN THE LAST DAYS	DAY OF THE LORD
TOPIC	TRUE PROPHECY		FALSE PROPHETS			PROPHECY: DAY OF THE LORD	
	HOLINESS		HERESY			HOPE	
LOCATION	PROBABLY ROME						
TIME	C. A.D 64–66						

Nelson's Complete Book of Bible Maps and Charts © 1993 by Thomas Nelson, Inc.

Continued from page 462

Finally, though some scholars maintain that the false teaching mentioned in 2 Peter was a form of Gnosticism that emerged after Peter's day, it is better to view the false teaching combatted here as an example of tendencies which later evolved into the full-fledged Gnosticism of the second century.

The alternative to Petrine authorship is a later forgery done in the name of Peter. Even the claim that 2 Peter was written by a disciple of Peter cannot overcome the problem of misrepresentation. In addition, while there are differences between 1 and 2 Peter, the differences are much more profound between the two Petrine epistles and the rest of the New Testament. Indeed, no other book is as much like 1 Peter as 2 Peter. In spite of the internal and external problems, the traditional position of Petrine authorship overcomes more difficulties than any other option.

Date

 This epistle was written just before the apostle's death (1:14), and probably originated from Rome. Peter's martyrdom took place between A.D. 64 and 66 (if Peter were alive in A.D. 67 when Paul wrote 2 Timothy during his second Roman imprisonment, it is likely that Paul would have mentioned him).

Themes and Literary Structure

Second Peter divides into three parts: the cultivation of Christian character (ch. 1); the condemnation of false teachers (ch. 2); the confidence of Christ's return (ch. 3).

As they cultivate Christian character, Peter urges his readers to grow in faith and in their knowledge of the truth found in the Word of God. In particular, the trustworthy character of Scripture is stressed, and 1:21 provides a striking description of the divine-human process of inspiration: "but holy men of God spoke *as they were* moved by the Holy Spirit." Also of relevance for our view of Scripture is the fact that Peter mentions the letters of "our beloved brother Paul" and places them on a level with the Old Testament Scriptures (3:15, 16).

Peter's condemnation of the false teachers describes their immoral lifestyles, the futility and destructiveness of their teachings, and the certainty of their destruction and judgment by God.

Peter's focus on the coming day of the Lord was apparently prompted by the false teacher's denial that divine judgment would ever come. In light of the coming day of the Lord, Peter exhorts his readers to live lives of holiness, steadfastness and growth.

First and Second Peter

A comparison of 1 and 2 Peter reveals a number of important differences—none of which are sufficient to disprove Petrine authorship. Differences in content are largely due to the different situations and problems addressed: 1 Peter deals primarily with the problem of external persecution while 2 Peter combats the threat of false teachers inside the church.

See chart, "A Comparison of 1 and 2 Peter," on page 466.

The Life of Peter

Peter's life was dramatically changed after the resurrection, and he occupied a central role in the early church and in the spread of the gospel to the Samaritans and Gentiles (Acts 2—10). After the Jerusalem Council in Acts 15, little is recorded of Peter's activities. He evidently traveled extensively with his wife (1 Cor. 9:5) and ministered in various Roman provinces. According to tradition, Peter was crucified upside down in Rome sometime prior to the death of Nero in A.D. 68.

See map, "The Life of Peter," on page 467.

A Comparison of 1 and 2 Peter

1 Peter	2 Peter
Theme: Hope in the midst of suffering	Theme: The danger of false teaching and practices
Christology: The sufferings of Christ for our salvation and example at His incarnation	Christology: The glory of Christ and the consummation of history at His return
The day of salvation when Christ suffered, died and rose from the dead	The day of the Lord when Christ returns in judgment
Redemptive title: Christ	Title of dominion: Lord
Be encouraged in your present trials	Be warned of eschatological judgment
We need hope to face our trials	We need full knowledge to face error
Numerous similarities to Paul (especially Ephesians and Colossians)	Almost identical similarities to Jude (compare 2 Peter 2 with Jude 4–18)

Nelson's Complete Book of Bible Maps and Charts © 1993 by Thomas Nelson, Inc.

The Life of Peter

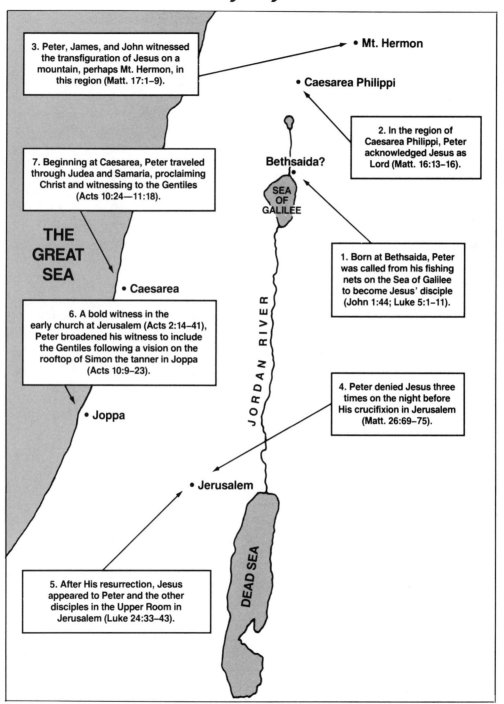

3. Peter, James, and John witnessed the transfiguration of Jesus on a mountain, perhaps Mt. Hermon, in this region (Matt. 17:1–9).

• Mt. Hermon

• Caesarea Philippi

2. In the region of Caesarea Philippi, Peter acknowledged Jesus as Lord (Matt. 16:13–16).

7. Beginning at Caesarea, Peter traveled through Judea and Samaria, proclaiming Christ and witnessing to the Gentiles (Acts 10:24—11:18).

Bethsaida?

SEA OF GALILEE

THE GREAT SEA

1. Born at Bethsaida, Peter was called from his fishing nets on the Sea of Galilee to become Jesus' disciple (John 1:44; Luke 5:1–11).

• Caesarea

6. A bold witness in the early church at Jerusalem (Acts 2:14–41), Peter broadened his witness to include the Gentiles following a vision on the rooftop of Simon the tanner in Joppa (Acts 10:9–23).

JORDAN RIVER

4. Peter denied Jesus three times on the night before His crucifixion in Jerusalem (Matt. 26:69–75).

• Joppa

• Jerusalem

DEAD SEA

5. After His resurrection, Jesus appeared to Peter and the other disciples in the Upper Room in Jerusalem (Luke 24:33–43).

Nelson's Complete Book of Bible Maps and Charts © 1993 by Thomas Nelson, Inc.

A Month-Long Journey with Jesus

	Day 1	Day 2	Day 3
To help you get acquainted with Jesus, here are 31 readings (one for each day of the month) listed in the order of their appearance in the New Testament.	**Matt. 1:18—2:23** Jesus is born, then becomes a refugee as an evil king seeks to destroy Him. Finally His family returns home.	**Matt. 4:1-11** Jesus confronts very real temptations.	**Matt. 13:54-58** Jesus faces rejection based on His family, their work, and the small size of His hometown.
Day 4	**Day 5**	**Day 6**	**Day 7**
Matt. 23:1-39 Jesus speaks out against deceit, pride, and hypocrisy.	**Matt. 25:31-46** Jesus judges according to mercy and compassion rather than outward displays of spirituality.	**Mark 4:1-41** Jesus begins to explain the kingdom of God, using stories and images from the workplace.	**Luke 2:1-52** Luke describes events connected with Jesus' birth—and tells of an incident during a boyhood trip to Jerusalem.
Day 8	**Day 9**	**Day 10**	**Day 11**
Luke 4:14-37 Jesus goes public with His purpose and immediately encounters opposition.	**Luke 6:17-49** Jesus teaches basic truths about attitudes, true charity, evaluating others, and making wise choices.	**Luke 9:18-36** Jesus talks with His followers about who He is.	**Luke 22:1—24:53** Jesus is betrayed, judged, executed, buried, resurrected, and reconnected with His followers.
Day 12	**Day 13**	**Day 14**	**Day 15**
John 1:1-18 John, one of Jesus' followers, describes how God became a man through Christ—full of grace and truth.	**John 5:19-47** Jesus explains His relationship with His Father and the implications for us.	**John 6:35-51** Jesus teaches that He is the bread of life, and tells how people can find Him.	**John 8:12-30** Jesus announces that He is the light of the world.

Day 16	**Day 17**	**Day 18**	**Day 19**
John 10:1-18 Jesus says that He is the good shepherd who seeks His Father's lost sheep.	**John 11:1—12:8** John describes Jesus' relationship with some of His friends, and their profound love and care for each other.	**John 14:1—15:8** Jesus explains that He is our source of spiritual life and productivity—the way to God.	**John 21:15-25** Jesus loved even the man who had denied Him and was jealous of another disciple.

Day 20	**Day 21**	**Day 22**	**Day 23**
Acts 2:22-42 Peter explains Christ to a massive crowd in Jerusalem, and welcomes 3,000 people into the faith.	**Rom. 5:1-21** Paul explains how Christ sets people free from sin and makes them acceptable to God.	**1 Cor. 15:1-28** Paul teaches about Christ's resurrection and the destruction of our enemy, death.	**Eph. 1:3-14** Paul describes Christ's work for us from three vantage points: before creation, in the present, and in eternity.

Day 24	**Day 25**	**Day 26**	**Day 27**
Phil. 2:5-16 Paul explains the choices Christ made in order to become a man, as well as the choices we should make in following Him.	**Col. 1:15-22** Paul states that Christ is Lord of all—yesterday, today, and tomorrow.	**1 Thess. 4:13—5:11** Paul explains that Jesus will return and bring history to its culmination.	**Heb. 1:1—2:18** The author of Hebrews describes Christ's complete and wonderful work on our behalf.

Day 28	**Day 29**	**Day 30**	**Day 31**
Heb. 4:14—5:10 Christ has experienced every kind of test or trial we will ever face.	**Heb. 9:23—10:18** Jesus takes away sin, once and for all. Forgiveness is ours in Him.	**1 Pet. 1:1-12** Peter tells us that our salvation in Christ is a reality that even the angels and Old Testament prophets did not understand.	**Rev. 5:1-14; 22:1-21** Christ will rule heaven and earth and will welcome believers to an eternity with Him.

1 JOHN

 Advanced in years, John wrote this fatherly epistle out of loving concern for his "children," whose steadfastness in the truth was being threatened by the lure of worldliness and the guile of false teachers.

Author

 Though this epistle does not state the name of its author, solid evidence suggests that it was written by John, the son of Zebedee and the brother of James (Mark 1:19, 20). Strong similarities between this letter and the Gospel of John substantiate the testimony of many early church fathers, including Papias, Polycarp, and Irenaeus, that both works are the products of John the apostle of Jesus. Both share many distinctively Johannine phrases, and the characteristics of limited vocabulary and frequent contrast of opposites are also common to both.

Date

 First John was probably written in Ephesus after the Gospel of John, but the date cannot be fixed with certainty. No persecution is mentioned, suggesting a date prior to A.D. 95 when persecution broke out near the end of the Roman emperor Domitian's reign (A.D. 81–96).

Themes and Literary Structure

 Like 2 Peter and Jude, 1 John has a negative and a positive thrust: it refutes erroneous doctrine and encourages its readership to walk in the knowledge of the truth. John lists the criteria and characteristics of fellowship with God and shows that those who abide in Christ can have confidence and assurance before Him. This simply written but profound work develops the basis of fellowship (1:1—2:27) and the behavior of fellowship (2:28—5:21).

A major theme of 1 John is fellowship with God (2:28). John wants his readers to have assurance of the indwelling God through their abiding relationship with Him. Phrases emphasizing Christian certainty occur five times in this brief epistle.

Against false teachers who denied the reality of the incarnation by saying that Jesus only appeared to have a human body, John strongly affirms that the

1 John at a Glance

FOCUS	BASIS OF FELLOWSHIP		BEHAVIOR OF FELLOWSHIP	
REFERENCE	1:1 —————— 2:15	————— 2:28	————— 5:4	———— 5:21
DIVISION	CONDITIONS FOR FELLOWSHIP	CAUTIONS TO FELLOWSHIP	CHARACTERISTICS OF FELLOWSHIP	CONSEQUENCES OF FELLOWSHIP
TOPIC	MEANING OF FELLOWSHIP		MANIFESTATIONS OF FELLOWSHIP	
	ABIDING IN GOD'S LIGHT		ABIDING IN GOD'S LOVE	
LOCATION	WRITTEN IN EPHESUS			
TIME	C. A.D. 90			

Nelson's Complete Book of Bible Maps and Charts © 1993 by Thomas Nelson, Inc.

Son of God took to Himself a complete and genuine human nature (4:2, 3). The heresy John confronts here was a forerunner of second-century Gnosticism, which taught that matter is essentially evil and spirit is essentially good. This dualistic error caused the false teachers to deny the incarnation of Christ. The true God, they taught, could never indwell a material body of flesh and blood, and therefore the human body that Jesus supposedly possessed was not real.

Another prominent theme in this epistle is love—the word appears more than thirty-five times in the epistle. The apostle uses the example of Cain to illustrate what love is not: hatred is murdering in spirit, and it arises from the worldly sphere of death. John then uses the example of Christ to illustrate what love is: love is practiced in self-sacrifice, not mere profession. This practical expression of love results in assurance before God and answered prayers because the believer is walking in obedience to God's commands to believe in Christ and love one another. See chart, "The Quality of Love," on page 472.

OUTLINE OF 1 JOHN

Part One: The Basis of Fellowship (1:1—2:27)

Part Two: The Behavior of Fellowship (2:28—5:21)

The Quality of Love

The Source of Love	The Effect of Love
God personifies love (4:8, 16)	We reflect God's love in the world (4:7)
God loved us (4:19)	We love God; our fear is gone; we keep His commands (4:18, 19; 5:3)
God gave His Son for us (4:9, 10)	We give our substance for others (3:17; 4:11)
Christ laid down His life for us (3:16)	We lay down our lives for others (3:16)

Nelson's Complete Book of Bible Maps and Charts © 1993 by Thomas Nelson, Inc.

2 AND 3 JOHN

Though among the briefest in Scripture, these two one-chapter books are of continuing relevance to the church. Second and Third John reflect similar circumstances and have similar contents: In each book the author warns against the divisiveness of false or self-serving teachers, and he offers encouragement to genuine believers. Particularly, 2 John cautions its readers about receiving heretics into their homes or churches, while 3 John encourages fellowship with Christian brothers.

Author

In both 2 and 3 John, the author identifies himself as "the Elder." This is not an argument against Johannine authorship of these epistles, since the content of these epistles reveals that his authority was far greater than that of an elder in a local church. The apostle Peter also referred to himself as an elder (1 Pet. 5:1).

The similarity of style, vocabulary, structure, and mood between 2 and 3 John makes it clear that these letters were written by the same author. In addition, both (especially 2 John) bear strong resemblances to 1 John and to the Fourth Gospel. Thus, the internal evidence lends clear support to the traditional view that these epistles were written by the apostle John.

Date

The parallels between 2 and 3 John suggest that these epistles were written about the same time (c. A.D. 90). Early Christian writers are unified in their testimony that the headquarters of John's later ministry was in the city of Ephesus, the principal city of the Roman province of Asia.

Second John is addressed to an "elect lady" and her children. Some scholars believe the address should be taken literally to refer to a specific woman and her children, while others prefer to take it as a figurative description of a local church.

Third John was occasioned by reports from an Asian church that a man

Continued on page 475

2 John at a Glance

FOCUS	ABIDE IN GOD'S COMMANDMENTS			ABIDE NOT WITH FALSE TEACHERS		
REFERENCE	1 ———— 4 ————— 5 ————— 7 ———— 10 ——— 12 — 13					
DIVISION	SALUTATION	WALK IN TRUTH	WALK IN LOVE	DOCTRINE OF FALSE TEACHERS	AVOID THE FALSE TEACHERS	BENEDICTION
TOPIC	WALK IN COMMANDMENTS			WATCH FOR COUNTERFEITS		
	PRACTICE THE TRUTH			PROTECT THE TRUTH		
LOCATION	WRITTEN IN EPHESUS					
TIME	C. A.D. 90					

Nelson's Complete Book of Bible Maps and Charts © 1993 by Thomas Nelson, Inc.

Continued from page 473

named Diotrephes had seized power, had rejected the teachers sent out by John, and was expelling those in his church who wanted to receive them.

Themes and Literary Structure

Second John has much in common with First John, including a warning about the danger of false teachers who deny the incarnation of Jesus Christ. John encourages the readers to continue walking in love but exhorts them to be discerning in their expression of love. The book may be divided into two parts: abide in God's commandments (vv. 1–6) and abide not with false teachers (vv. 7–13).

OUTLINE OF 2 JOHN

Third John stresses the theme of enjoying and continuing to have fellowship with fellow believers, especially full-time Christian workers. The truth and servanthood of Gaius, who had shown hospitality to John's teachers, is contrasted with the error and selfishness of Diotrephes, whose arrogance and lack of hospitality were evidence of blindness to God.

OUTLINE OF 3 JOHN

Continued on page 477

3 John at a Glance

FOCUS	COMMENDATION OF GAIUS			CONDEMNATION OF DIOTREPHES		
REFERENCE	1 ———— 2 ———— 5			———— 9 ———— 12	———— 13 ———— 14	
DIVISION	SALUTATION	GODLINESS OF GAIUS	GENEROSITY OF GAIUS	PRIDE OF DIOTREPHES	PRAISE FOR DEMETRIUS	BENEDICTION
TOPIC	SERVANTHOOD			SELFISHNESS		
	DUTY OF HOSPITALITY			DANGER OF HAUGHTINESS		
LOCATION	WRITTEN IN EPHESUS					
TIME	C. A.D. 90					

Nelson's Complete Book of Bible Maps and Charts © 1993 by Thomas Nelson, Inc.

Continued from page 475

The Life of John

In Acts 8:14, John is associated with "the apostles who were at Jerusalem," and Paul calls him one of the "pillars" of the Jerusalem church in Galatians 2:9. Apart from Revelation 1, the New Testament is silent about his later years, but early Christian tradition uniformly tells us that he left Jerusalem (probably not long before its destruction in A.D. 70) and that he ministered in and around Ephesus. The seven churches in the Roman province of Asia, mentioned in Revelation 2 and 3, were evidently part of his ministry.

John's effective testimony for Christ led the Roman authorities to exile him to the small, desolate island of Patmos in the Aegean Sea (Rev. 1:9). The date of his release from Patmos is unknown, but he was probably allowed to return to Ephesus after the reign of Domitian.

See map, "The Life of John," on page 478.

The Life of John

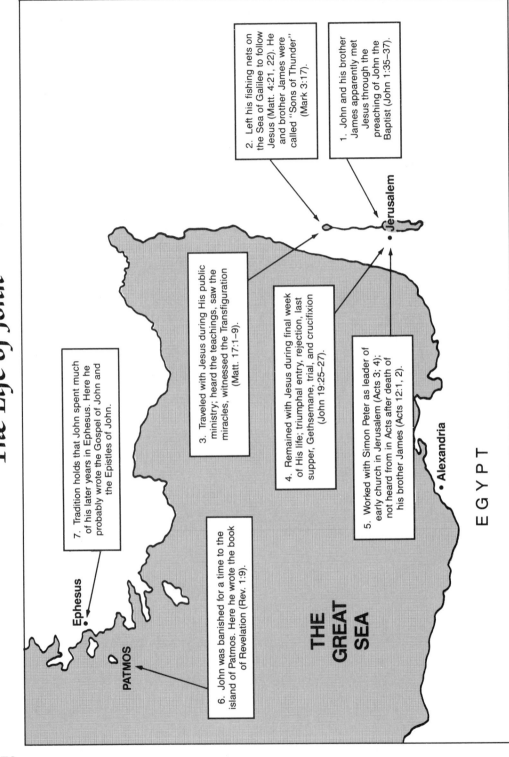

1. John and his brother James apparently met Jesus through the preaching of John the Baptist (John 1:35–37).

2. Left his fishing nets on the Sea of Galilee to follow Jesus (Matt. 4:21, 22). He and brother James were called "Sons of Thunder" (Mark 3:17).

3. Traveled with Jesus during His public ministry; heard the teachings, saw the miracles, witnessed the Transfiguration (Matt. 17:1–9).

4. Remained with Jesus during final week of His life; triumphal entry, rejection, last supper, Gethsemane, trial, and crucifixion (John 19:25–27).

5. Worked with Simon Peter as leader of early church in Jerusalem (Acts 3; 4); not heard from in Acts after death of his brother James (Acts 12:1, 2).

6. John was banished for a time to the island of Patmos. Here he wrote the book of Revelation (Rev. 1:9).

7. Tradition holds that John spent much of his later years in Ephesus. Here he probably wrote the Gospel of John and the Epistles of John.

Jerusalem

Ephesus

PATMOS

THE GREAT SEA

Alexandria

EGYPT

Nelson's Complete Book of Bible Maps and Charts © 1993 by Thomas Nelson, Inc.

JUDE

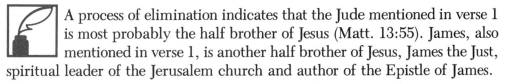
A surprisingly large number of the Pauline and non-Pauline epistles confront the problem of false teachers, and almost all of them allude to it. But Jude goes beyond all other New Testament epistles in its relentless and passionate denunciation of apostate teachers who had invaded the church.

Author

A process of elimination indicates that the Jude mentioned in verse 1 is most probably the half brother of Jesus (Matt. 13:55). James, also mentioned in verse 1, is another half brother of Jesus, James the Just, spiritual leader of the Jerusalem church and author of the Epistle of James.

Date

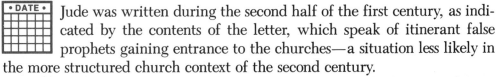
Jude was written during the second half of the first century, as indicated by the contents of the letter, which speak of itinerant false prophets gaining entrance to the churches—a situation less likely in the more structured church context of the second century.

Exactly when Jude is dated depends to some extent on the literary relationship with 2 Peter. There is marked similarity between Jude 4–19 and 2 Pet. 2:1—3:3, and because the wording is so similar, most scholars believe that Peter borrowed from Jude, or Jude used Peter's words, or both used ideas from a common source no longer extant. If Jude used 2 Peter, then it would be dated between the writing of 2 Peter (c. A.D. 64–66) and c. A.D. 80. If 2 Peter used Jude, then Jude could be dated between A.D. 60 and 65.

Themes and Literary Structure

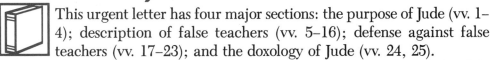
This urgent letter has four major sections: the purpose of Jude (vv. 1–4); description of false teachers (vv. 5–16); defense against false teachers (vv. 17–23); and the doxology of Jude (vv. 24, 25).

There is no obscurity in Jude's purpose. He had wished to discuss the doctrine of salvation, but the threat of subversive teachers compelled him to write and exhort his readers "to contend earnestly for the faith" (v. 3). Thus the

Continued on page 481

Jude at a Glance

FOCUS	PURPOSE	DESCRIPTION OF FALSE TEACHERS			DEFENSE AGAINST FALSE TEACHERS	DOXOLOGY
REFERENCE	1 —————— 5 ——————	8 ———————————— 14		———— 17 ——————	24 ———— 25	
DIVISION	INTRODUCTION	PAST JUDGMENT	PRESENT CHARACTERISTICS	FUTURE JUDGMENT	DUTY OF BELIEVERS	CONCLUSION
TOPIC	REASON TO CONTEND				HOW TO CONTEND	
	ANATOMY OF APOSTASY				ANTIDOTE FOR APOSTASY	
LOCATION	UNKNOWN					
TIME	C. A.D. 66–80					

Nelson's Complete Book of Bible Maps and Charts © 1993 by Thomas Nelson, Inc.

Continued from page 479

entire epistle is an assessment of false teachers, focusing particularly on the judgment to which they are doomed, and a strong warning to the recipients. The false teachers reject Christ's authority, but Jude stresses that Jesus is Lord, now and forever.

OUTLINE OF JUDE

REVELATION

J ust as Genesis is the book of beginnings, Revelation is the book of consummation. In it, the divine program of redemption is brought to fruition, and the holy name of God is vindicated before all creation.

The word "revelation" is a translation of the Greek word from which we derive the term "apocalypse" and refers to an unveiling of God's secret purposes. In the Revelation, this involved a command to the author to write about God's plans for his own day and for the future.

Author

The tradition that John the apostle wrote Revelation was widely held and almost unchallenged through the second century A.D. Five times the author identifies himself as John, and though the term "apostle" is never added, he appears to have been a man of stature in the churches (1:4, 9). Nevertheless, certain differences between Revelation and the other Johannine materials in the New Testament have led some scholars to question this tradition. There are significant differences between the Greek grammar and vocabulary of Revelation and that of the Gospel and epistles of John. Furthermore, there are theological differences in emphasis and the other Johannine writings avoid the use of the author's name.

It should be noted, however, that there are also a number of remarkable similarities between Revelation and the other books traditionally associated with the apostle John (e.g., the distinctive use of terms such as "word," "lamb," and "true," and the careful development of opposing themes such as light and darkness, love and hatred, good and evil). In addition, many of the differences can be explained by the unusual circumstances surrounding this book. Thus, the internal evidence, while problematic, need not overrule the early and strong external testimony to the apostolic origin of this important book.

Revelation at a Glance

FOCUS	"THINGS WHICH YOU HAVE SEEN"	"THINGS WHICH ARE"	"THINGS WHICH WILL TAKE PLACE"				
REFERENCE	1:1 ——————— 2:1 ———————	4:1 ———————	6:1 ——————— 19:7 ———	20:1 ———	21:1 — 22:21		
DIVISION	THE LORD JESUS CHRIST	SEVEN CHURCHES	THE JUDGE	TRIBULATION	SECOND COMING	MILLENNIUM	ETERNAL STATE
TOPIC	VISION OF CHRIST		VISION OF CONSUMMATION				
	THEOPHANY	TALKS	TRIBULATIONS		TRUMPETS		TOGETHER
LOCATION	WRITTEN ON THE ISLAND OF PATMOS						
TIME	C. A.D. 95–96						

Nelson's Complete Book of Bible Maps and Charts © 1993 by Thomas Nelson, Inc.

Date

Revelation was written at a time when Roman hostility to Christianity was erupting into overt persecution (1:9; 2:10, 13). Some scholars believe that the book should be given an early date during the persecution of Christians under Nero after the A.D. 64 burning of Rome. They point out that the numeric value of the Hebrew letters for "Nero Caesar" adds up to 666, the number of the beast (13:18). Evidence of this sort is weak, however, and a later date near the end of the reign of the emperor Domitian (A.D. 81–96) is preferable for several reasons. Second-century church tradition testifies to a later date during the reign of Domitian. Furthermore, it is thought that John moved from Jerusalem to Ephesus c. A.D. 67, but this would not allow John to establish an ongoing ministry in Asia during the reign of Nero. Finally, the contents of Revelation indicate that the Asian churches had been in existence for a number of years, long enough to have reached a point of complacency and decline (2:4; 3:1, 15–18).

Thus, it is likely that John wrote this book in A.D. 95 or 96. The date of his release from Patmos is unknown, but he was probably allowed to return to Ephesus after the reign of Domitian. Passages such as 1:11; 22:7, 9, 10, 18, 19 suggest that the book was completed on Patmos before John's release.

Themes and Literary Structure

Though the book includes portions which follow the epistolary form (1:4—3:22), much of Revelation is written in the form of apocalyptic literature (cf. Daniel and Zechariah) and it refers to itself as a prophetic book (1:3; 22:7, 10, 18, 19). The three major movements in this profound unveiling are captured in 1:19: "the things which you have seen" (ch. 1); "the things which are" (chs. 2 and 3); and "the things which will take place after this" (chs. 4—22).

The number "seven" assumes profound significance in Revelation (it occurs fifty-two times). Three cycles of seven judgments in chapters 6—16 consist of seven seals, seven trumpets, and seven bowls. Because of the rich symbolism of the book of Revelation, the interpretive approaches of the Christian community have differed radically. The major approaches to the book are discussed below.

OUTLINE OF REVELATION

Part One: "The Things Which You Have Seen" (1:1–20)

The Seven Churches

The book of Revelation contains special messages directed to churches in seven specific cities throughout the Roman province of Asia. These cities were important trade and communication centers, which were connected by major roads in New Testament times. Notice that John addressed the churches in exactly the order shown on the map on page 487—from Ephesus north to Pergamos, then south all the way to Laodicea. Some scholars believe Revelation was a circular letter that would have been read first by the Ephesian church, then passed on to the next church on the route.

See map, "The Seven Churches," on page 487.

The letters to the seven churches follow a similar pattern of commendation for faithfulness (except for Laodicea), criticism (except for Smyrna and Philadelphia), call to repentance, threat of judgment, and promise of reward to those who respond. The author is Christ; He speaks to those who have accepted His sacrifice and triumph, but who are failing in spiritual maturity or faithfulness.

See chart, "The Seven Churches of Revelation," on page 488.

Four Different Views on Revelation

The reader's approach to Revelation as a whole is conditioned by conclusions on two important interpretive questions—the historical referent of the visions in 6:1—18:24, and the character of the thousand-year period depicted in chapter 20.

The visions of 6:1—18:24 are usually viewed in one of four different ways. The "Preterist" (from the Latin term for "past") interpretation understands this passage to refer to events which occurred during the period of the Roman empire. The "Historical" interpretation understands Revelation to present a panoramic outline of church history from the apostolic era to the Second Coming of Christ. According to the "Idealist" approach, the book of Revelation depicts in symbolic fashion the great spiritual struggle between good and evil. Finally, the "Futurist" interpretation views Revelation as a description of future events which will accompany the end of the age.

See chart, "Summary of Four Views on Revelation," on page 488.

Whatever our view of the Millennium, we should focus on preparing for the Lord's Second Coming and His eternal reign (Heb. 10:13; 1 Cor. 15:25–27).

The Seven Churches

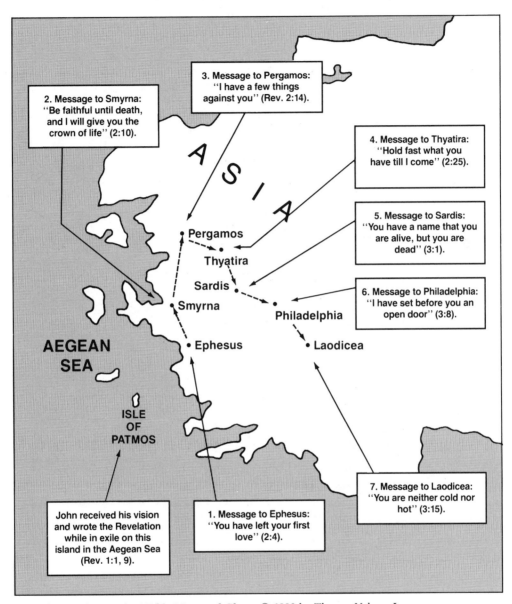

2. Message to Smyrna: "Be faithful until death, and I will give you the crown of life" (2:10).

3. Message to Pergamos: "I have a few things against you" (Rev. 2:14).

4. Message to Thyatira: "Hold fast what you have till I come" (2:25).

5. Message to Sardis: "You have a name that you are alive, but you are dead" (3:1).

6. Message to Philadelphia: "I have set before you an open door" (3:8).

7. Message to Laodicea: "You are neither cold nor hot" (3:15).

1. Message to Ephesus: "You have left your first love" (2:4).

John received his vision and wrote the Revelation while in exile on this island in the Aegean Sea (Rev. 1:1, 9).

ASIA

Pergamos

Thyatira

Sardis

Smyrna

Philadelphia

Ephesus

Laodicea

AEGEAN SEA

ISLE OF PATMOS

The Seven Churches of Revelation

	Commendation	Criticism	Instruction	Promise
Ephesus (2:1–7)	Rejects evil, perseveres, has patience	Love for Christ no longer fervent	Do the works you did at first	The tree of life
Smyrna (2:8–11)	Gracefully bears suffering	None	Be faithful until death	The crown of life
Pergamos (2:12–17)	Keeps the faith of Christ	Tolerates immorality, idolatry, and heresies	Repent	Hidden manna and a stone with a new name
Thyatira (2:18–29)	Love, service, faith, patience is greater than at first	Tolerates cult of idolatry and immorality	Judgment coming; keep the faith	Rule over nations and receive morning star
Sardis (3:1–6)	Some have kept the faith	A dead church	Repent; strengthen what remains	Faithful honored and clothed in white
Philadelphia (3:7–13)	Perseveres in the faith	None	Keep the faith	A place in God's presence, a new name, and the New Jerusalem
Laodicea (3:14–22)	None	Indifferent	Be zealous and repent	Share Christ's throne

Nelson's Complete Book of Bible Maps and Charts © 1993 by Thomas Nelson, Inc.

Summary of Four Views on Revelation

Interpretive Approach	**Basic Thesis**
Preterist	All the events of Revelation were fulfilled during the period of the Roman Empire.
Historical	Revelation is a panorama of church history from the apostolic era until the consummation.
Idealist	Revelation is not a representation of actual events, but is rather a symbolic depiction of the spiritual warfare between good and evil.
Futurist	Beginning with ch. 4, Revelation describes future events accompanying the end of the age.

Nelson's Complete Book of Bible Maps and Charts © 1993 by Thomas Nelson, Inc.

The Postmillennial View

The Millennium, a term meaning "thousand," refers to the thousand-year reign of Christ (20:1–6). Some Christians believe the Millennium will be an age of blessedness on the earth. Some believe the Millennium is the present church age—a period of indefinite length, or that the Millennium is a way of referring to the eternal state.

The Bible's only specific mention of the Millennium is in the book of Revelation (ch. 20). Interpreters differ greatly in their understanding of the Millennium and how it will occur. Postmillennialists expect Christ's visible return after the Millennium. They look for God to use the church's teaching and preaching to usher in a lengthy period (some interpret the thousand years literally, others symbolically) of peace and righteousness before Christ's return. Postmillennialists usually adopt either the "Historical" or "Preterist" view of Revelation as a whole.

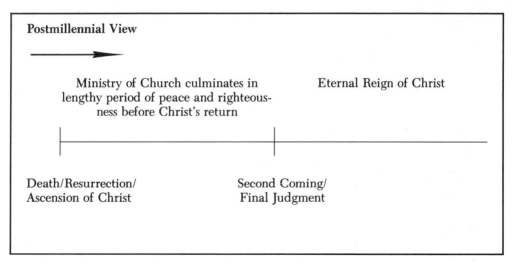

Postmillennial View

Ministry of Church culminates in lengthy period of peace and righteousness before Christ's return

Eternal Reign of Christ

Death/Resurrection/ Ascension of Christ

Second Coming/ Final Judgment

Nelson's Complete Book of Bible Maps and Charts © 1993 by Thomas Nelson, Inc.

The Premillennial View

Premillennialists believe that Christ will return before the Millennium. Interpreting Revelation 20 literally, they hold that Christ will reign on earth for a literal thousand years. Within this basic area of agreement, there are, nevertheless, a number of variant views—the most prevalent of which are the Premillennial-pretribulational and the Premillennial-posttribulational views. Premillennial-pretribulational scholars argue that there are two different peoples of God—Israel and the church—with two different prophetic programs. According to this view, the church will be "raptured" prior to a seven-year Great Tribulation. Following the tribulation, Christ will return to establish a thousand-year millennial kingdom centered in Jerusalem and involving the reinstitution of the Old Testament sacrificial system. The millennial kingdom will end with a futile rebellion by the forces of evil, after which will come the final judgment and beginning of the eternal reign.

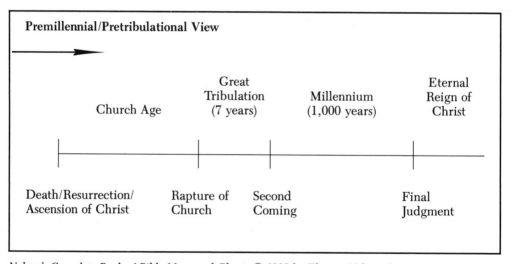

Nelson's Complete Book of Bible Maps and Charts © 1993 by Thomas Nelson, Inc.

The Premillennial/Posttribulational View

Premillennial/posttribulational scholars assert that Christ will return at the end of a seven-year Great Tribulation to establish a millennial kingdom. This kingdom will end with a rebellion by the forces of evil and the final judgment. This view often interprets prophecy in a non-literal way and does not usually view Israel and the church as the objects of completely different divine historical plans. Rather, Israel and the church ultimately form one people of God. Premillennialists of both types adopt the "Futurist" approach to the book of Revelation.

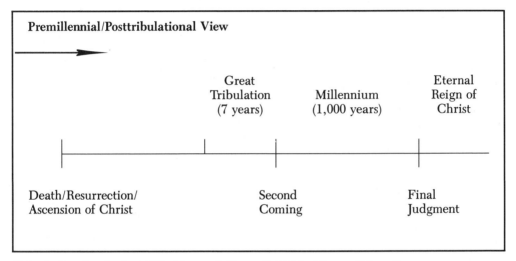

The Amillennial View

Amillennialists interpret Christ's millennial reign in an ideal or spiritual sense. While believing in the Second Coming, they reject the idea of a literal thousand-year reign on earth. Some see Christ's reign as having begun during His earthly ministry or at the time of His resurrection. They cite Peter's declaration that Christ now rules from the right hand of God (Acts 2:33–36). Israel and the church are viewed as forming one people of God, and the kingdom promises to Israel are seen as applying to the church age, or to the eternal existence in the new heavens and the new earth. The amillennial approach usually involves an "Idealist" view of Revelation as a whole.

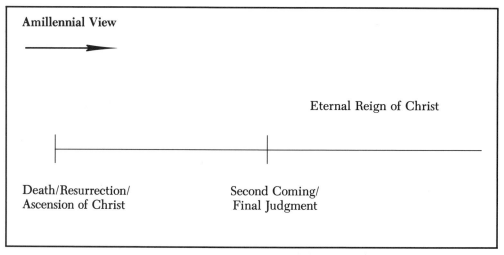

Nelson's Complete Book of Bible Maps and Charts © 1993 by Thomas Nelson, Inc.

Alphabetical Index of Full-Page Maps and Charts

Biblical Index of Full-Page Maps and Charts
The Old Testament

The New Testament